The Quick'n'Easy Cookbook

The Quick 'n' Easy Cookbook

Alison Burt

GALLEY PRESS

Photographic acknowledgments

Alcan Polyfoil 184 top.
Ambrosia 70, 71 top, 74 top, 81 top, 82 bottom.
American Rice Council 25 top, 37 top, 45 top, 57 bottom, 67 top, 113 bottom, 121 top, 127 top, 152 top, 213 top, 220 top.
Apple and Pear Development Council 123 bottom, 189 bottom, 250 top.
Australian Recipe Service 76 bottom, 192 top, 195 top.
Barry Bullough 7, 8 top, 9 top, 11 bottom, 12 top and bottom, 13 top and bottom, 14 top and bottom, 18 bottom, 19 bottom, 20 bottom, 23 bottom, 24 bottom, 25 bottom, 27 top, 29 bottom, 30 top, 32 bottom, 35 top, 36 bottom, 38 bottom, 39 top and bottom, 40 top and bottom, 41 bottom, 42 top and bottom, 43 bottom, 44 bottom, 45 bottom, 46 top, 49 bottom, 50 bottom, 51 top, 54 top and bottom, 55 bottom, 57 top, 60 bottom, 61 top, 63 top, 69 bottom, 71 bottom, 72 bottom, 73 top and bottom, 77 top, 78 bottom, 85 bottom, 86 bottom, 87 top and bottom, 89 bottom, 90 top, 91, 92 bottom, 94 top and bottom, 95 bottom, 96 top, 97 top, 99 bottom, 100 bottom, 101 bottom, 102 bottom, 103 top and bottom, 104 bottom, 105 top and bottom, 106 bottom, 107 top, 109 top and bottom, 111 bottom, 117 top and bottom, 118 bottom, 119 top, 121 bottom, 125 bottom, 128 top and bottom, 130 top, 131 top and bottom, 132 top, 133 top, 135 top and bottom, 136 top and bottom, 137 bottom, 138 bottom, 139 top, 141 top, 142 bottom, 143 top and bottom, 144 top, 145 top, 146 top, 147 top, 150 top and bottom, 154 bottom, 158 top, 164 bottom, 165 top and bottom, 166 top and bottom, 167 bottom, 168 top and bottom, 169 top, 171 bottom, 172 bottom, 173 bottom, 174 top, 177 top, 180 bottom, 181 top and bottom, 184 bottom, 186 top, 187 bottom, 191 bottom, 194 bottom, 198 top, 201 top and bottom, 204 top and bottom, 207 top, 209 top, 212 bottom, 215 top, 216 bottom, 217 bottom, 222 bottom, 223 top and bottom, 224 top, 227 bottom, 228 top, 229 bottom, 231 top, 234 top and bottom, 235 bottom, 236 top, 238 bottom, 241 top, 242 bottom, 243 top, 244 top, 245 bottom, 246 bottom, 248 top and bottom, 250 bottom, 252 top and bottom.
Be-Ro 251 top.
Birds Dessert Range 69 top, 76 top, 82 top, 83 bottom, 160 bottom, 231 bottom, 233 bottom, 240 bottom.
Bird's Eye Foods Ltd 185 top.
British Egg Information Service 15 top, 62 top and bottom, 64 bottom, 120 top, 139 bottom, 178 bottom, 180 top, 225 bottom, 246 top.
British Meat Service 46 bottom, 50 top, 116 top, 118 top, 125 top, 127 bottom, 133 bottom, 134 top, 144 bottom, 145 bottom, 193 bottom, 200 bottom, 204 bottom.
British Poultry Information Service 216 top.
British Sausage Bureau 126 top.
Cadbury Typhoo Ltd 20 top, 75 top, 84 top, 155 bottom, 156 top, 160 top, 161 top and bottom, 162 bottom, 163 bottom, 240 top, 242 top.
Carnation Milk Bureau 30 bottom, 32 top, 90 bottom, 115 bottom, 141 bottom, 178 top, 188 bottom.
Danish Food Centre 66 bottom, 104 top, 122 bottom, 200 top, 206 top, 208 bottom.

Dutch Dairy Bureau 53 bottom, 59 top, 100 top, 126 bottom, 208 top, 214 bottom, 227 top.
Eden Vale 22 top, 98 bottom, 112 bottom, 153 bottom, 157 top, 162 top, 203 top, 226 top and bottom.
Farmhouse English Cheese 68 top, 149 top.
Findus 35 top, 112 top.
Food from France (Sopexa) 225 top.
Fyffes Group Ltd 36 top, 56 bottom, 178 bottom.
Gales Honey 235 top.
Herring Industry Board 38 top, 190 top.
J. A. Sharwood Ltd 56 top, 65 bottom, 67 bottom, 78 top, 213 bottom.
John Lee 11 top, 16 top and bottom, 26 top, 48 top, 58 top, 79 top, 80 top, 81 bottom, 98 top, 99 top, 102 top, 130 bottom, 132 bottom, 154 top, 157 bottom, 175, 176 top, 179 top, 203 bottom, 205 bottom, 239 bottom, 247 top.
John West 218 top.
Kellogg's Kitchen 52 bottom, 137 top, 233 top.
Knorr 47 bottom, 134 bottom, 146 bottom, 197 top.
Lea & Perrins Worcestershire Sauce 211 bottom.
McDougalls 17 bottom, 28 top, 111 top, 170 bottom, 221 bottom.
McDougalls Pastry Mixes 171 top, 173 top, 238 top, 239 top, 249 top, 251 bottom
Milk Marketing Board 74 bottom, 80 bottom, 84 bottom, 86 top, 88 bottom, 232 bottom, 236 bottom.
Mushroom Growers Association 27 bottom, 41 top, 55 top, 115 top, 129 bottom.
National Dairy Council 108 top, 110 bottom.
New Zealand Lamb Information Bureau 119 bottom, 120 bottom, 192 bottom, 193 top, 194 top, 195 bottom, 196 top, 199 bottom.
Olives from Spain 177 bottom.
Pasta Information Centre 33 bottom, 34 bottom, 151 top, 202 top, 207 bottom.
Potato Marketing Board 28 bottom.
Princes 9 bottom, 83 top.
Pyrosil Cookware 138 bottom.
Swiss Cheese Union Inc 8 bottom, 183 top.
Tabasco Pepper Sauce 53 top, 140 bottom.
Tate & Lyle 21 top, 177 bottom.
Taunton Dry Blackthorn Cider 44 top, 151 bottom, 198 bottom, 219 bottom.
Tower 187 top.
Tupperware 72 top, 149 bottom, 182 bottom, 205 top, 218 bottom, 220 bottom, 232 top.
Walls Ice Cream 70 top, 75 bottom, 77 bottom, 89 top, 158 bottom, 159 bottom.
White Fish Kitchen 33 top, 34 top, 93 bottom, 114 top.

All other photographs by The Hamlyn Publishing Group Ltd.

Contents

Introduction	6
Useful Facts and Figures	6

10 Minute Dishes — 7

Starters — 7
Savouries — 7
Fish and shellfish — 15
Soups — 20

Main Courses — 33
Fish and shellfish — 33
Lamb — 39
Pork, bacon and ham — 43
Beef — 49
Poultry — 52
Liver and Kidneys — 57
Cheese dishes — 59
Egg dishes — 62
Vegetable dishes — 64
Salads — 67

Desserts — 69

20 Minute Dishes — 91

Starters — 91
Fish and shellfish — 91
Savouries — 97
Soups — 104

Main Courses — 109
Fish and shellfish — 109
Lamb — 116
Pork, bacon and ham — 121
Beef — 128
Veal — 135
Offal — 143
Egg dishes — 147
Cheese and vegetable dishes — 148

Desserts — 153

30 Minute Dishes — 175

Starters — 175

Main Courses — 189
Fish dishes — 189
Lamb — 192
Pork, bacon and ham — 200
Beef — 209
Veal — 215
Poultry and game — 216
Liver and kidneys — 224
Cheese and vegetable dishes — 225

Desserts — 229

Store-cupboard Standbys — 253

Index — 254

Introduction

As every busy person knows, it's not the cooking but the preparation of food that takes up valuable time in the kitchen. Once everything is prepared, other jobs can be tackled while the food is cooking, with just a quick dash back to the kitchen to take a look, give a stir or add an extra ingredient.

This book has been specially designed to help you plan your meals, whether for family or friends, according to the time you have available to prepare the ingredients. There are three main sections — each sub-divided into starters, main courses and desserts — the first giving recipes for 10-minutes preparation time, the second for 20-minutes preparation time and the third for 30-minutes. If, for example, you know you can spend 40 minutes in the kitchen preparing food, you might decide to serve two dishes only for a meal, choosing a 10-minute starter and a 30-minute main course. Alternatively, you could serve three dishes, two taking 10 minutes to prepare and the third 20 minutes. Or a 20-minute main course and a 20-minute dessert. The variety is endless and you will be sure to find exactly what you want for any occasion from this superb collection of recipes from around the world.

Useful Facts and Figures

Liquid measures

In this book decilitres (units of 100 ml) have been used for measuring liquids. The following table gives a few examples.

Imperial	Recommended dl	Equivalent ml
¼ pint	1.5 dl	150 ml
½ pint	3.0 dl	300 ml
¾ pint	4.5 dl	450 ml
1 pint	6.0 dl	600 ml
1½ pints	9.0 dl	900 ml
1¾ pints	10.0 dl (1 litre)	1000 ml (1 litre)

Solid measures

Exact conversion from Imperial to metric measures does not usually give very convenient working quantities and so the metric measures have been rounded off into units of 25 grams. The table below shows the recommended equivalents.

Ounces	Approx g to nearest whole figure	Recommended conversion to nearest unit of 25	Ounces	Approx g to nearest whole figure	Recommended conversion to nearest unit of 25
1	28	25	9	255	250
2	57	50	10	283	275
3	85	75	11	312	300
4	113	100	12	340	350
5	142	150	13	368	375
6	170	175	14	396	400
7	198	200	15	425	425
8	227	225	16 (1 lb)	454	450

Note When converting quantities over 20 oz first add the appropriate figures in the centre column, then adjust to the nearest unit of 25. As a general guide, 1 kg (1000 g) equals 2.2 lb or about 2 lb 3 oz. This method of conversion gives good results in nearly all cases, although in certain pastry and cake recipes a more accurate conversion is necessary to produce a balanced recipe.

Spoon measures

All spoon measures given in this book are level unless otherwise stated.

Notes for American and Australian users

In America the 8 oz measuring cup is used. In Australia the metric measures are now used in conjunction with the standard 250-ml measuring cup. The Imperial pint, used in Britain and Australia, is 20 fl oz, while the American pint is 16 fl oz. It is important to remember that the Australian tablespoon differs from both the British and American tablespoons. The British standard tablespoon, which has been used throughout this book, holds 17.7 ml, the American 14.2 ml and the Australian 20 ml. A teaspoon holds approximately 5 ml in all three countries.

British	American	Australian
1 teaspoon	1 teaspoon	1 teaspoon
1 tablespoon	1 tablespoon	1 tablespoon
2 tablespoons	3 tablespoons	2 tablespoons
3½ tablespoons	4 tablespoons	3 tablespoons
4 tablespoons	5 tablespoons	3½ tablespoons

An Imperial/American guide to solid and liquid measures

Imperial Solid measures	American	Imperial Liquid measures	American
1 lb butter or margarine	2 cups	¼ pint liquid	⅔ cup liquid
1 lb flour	4 cups	½ pint	1¼ cups
1 lb granulated or castor sugar	2 cups	¾ pint	2 cups
		1 pint	2½ cups
1 lb icing sugar	3 cups	1½ pints	3¾ cups
8 oz rice	1 cup	2 pints	5 cups (2½ pints)

American terms

The list below gives some American equivalents or substitutes for terms and ingredients used in this book.

British/American
Equipment and terms
deep cake tin/spring form pan
double saucepan/double boiler
flan tin/pie pan
frying pan/skillet
greaseproof paper/wax paper
grill/broil
loaf tin/loaf pan
piping bag/pastry bag
stoned/pitted
Swiss roll tin/jelly roll pan

British/American
Ingredients
aubergine/eggplant

bicarbonate of soda/baking soda
biscuits/crackers, cookies
cocoa powder/unsweetened cocoa
cornflour/cornstarch
courgettes/zucchini
cream, single/cream, light
cream, double/cream, heavy
essence/extract
flour, plain/flour, all-purpose
glacé cherries/candied cherries
icing/frosting
lard/shortening
shortcrust pastry/basic pie dough
spring onions/scallion
sultanas/seedless white raisins
yeast, fresh/yeast, compressed

Note When making any of the recipes in this book, only follow one set of measures as they are not interchangeable.

10 Minute Dishes

Time is short, but there's no need to worry. The secret is in the planning. Once you have decided what you are going to serve, the preparation will take very little time. Soups are a particularly good choice, either hot or cold according to the season. Thick Chicken Chowder makes use of left-overs; the ingredients for Chilled Cucumber and Tomato Soup are available all year round. Several of the starters are also excellent as luncheon or light supper dishes. For a main course there are lots of ways to serve both fish and meat with just one or two different ingredients to make old favourites taste extra special. Crispy Topped Fish Pie is sure to be a winner with younger members of the family. The desserts are incredibly simple to make from either store-cupboard standbys or fresh fruit. What could be more delicious than a made-in-a-moment Marsh-mallow Sundae or a Dreamy Raspberry Nest?

Quick Chicken Liver Pâté

Serves: 4–6 people
Preparation time:
10 minutes plus
chilling time
Cooking time:
5 minutes

This is a very quick pâté to make. It will store in the refrigerator for a few days when covered in butter. For speed, make this pâté in an electric blender.

12 oz/350 g chicken livers
4 oz/100 g butter or margarine
½ level teaspoon mixed dried herbs
salt and pepper
1 tablespoon sherry (optional)
extra butter, melted

Remove the sinews from the livers and cut each in half. Melt the butter or margarine in a frying pan, add the livers and cook gently until just tender (about 4–5 minutes). Mince the livers with a little of the butter or margarine. Put the minced livers and the rest of the cooking butter or margarine in a bowl with the herbs, salt and pepper, and sherry (if used). Beat them together until soft and smooth. Put the pâté into small individual serving pots and pour a little melted butter on top of each. Chill before using.

Chicken Liver Savouries

Serves: 4–6 people
Preparation time:
10 minutes plus
marinating time
Cooking time:
5–10 minutes

Prepare these savouries before-hand; they can be cooked and then served while the main course is being cooked. Use olive oil for preference.

2 oz/50 g button
  mushrooms
oil
1 level teaspoon
  dried thyme
salt and pepper
12 oz/350 g chicken
  livers
6 oz/175 g rashers
  streaky bacon

Wipe the mushrooms and cut off the stalks level with the caps. Put them into a shallow bowl, cover with oil and sprinkle with the thyme and salt and pepper. Leave for 1–2 hours. Meanwhile, wash and trim the chicken livers. Remove all the membranes. Remove the rind and bones from the bacon and then spread it with the back of a knife until it is twice the original length. Cut into pieces. Wrap a chicken liver in each piece of bacon and secure with a wooden cocktail stick. Drain the mushrooms and put a mushroom, or half a mush-room (if they are large), on the end of each stick. Grill over a hot fire until the bacon is crisp and the livers cooked. Serve immediately.

Fettucine all' Alfredo

Serves: 6 people
Preparation time:
5 minutes
Cooking time:
20–25 minutes

An Italian pasta dish which is particularly good made with genuine Swiss cheese. If you have difficulty buying Sbrinz, Parmesan can be used instead.

1 lb/½ kg fettucine
  (broad noodles)
salt and pepper
¼ pint/1.5 dl
  whipping cream
4 oz/100 g Gruyère
  cheese, freshly
  grated
2 oz/50 g butter
4 oz/100 g Sbrinz
  cheese, grated

Cook the noodles in a large sauce-pan with plenty of boiling salted water for about 10–15 minutes or until just cooked. Drain well in a colander. Put the cream into a saucepan with the Gruyère cheese. Heat very gently, without boiling, until melted and blended, stirring frequently. Gradually stir in the butter in small pieces. When this has melted, stir in the drained noodles and the Sbrinz cheese. Season with freshly ground black pepper and reheat gently without boiling. Serve as soon as possible.

Mushroom Risotto

Serves: 4–6 people
Preparation time:
10 minutes
Cooking time:
25 minutes

This tasty risotto makes a filling and inexpensive appetiser.

3 oz/75 g margarine
1 onion, sliced
8 oz/225 g
  mushrooms, sliced
8 oz/225 g long
  grain rice
¾ pint/4·5 dl chicken
  stock or water and
  chicken stock cube
salt and pepper
4 oz/100 g grated
  cheese

Melt the margarine in a saucepan and fry the onion until softened but not browned. Add the mushrooms and rice and cook gently, stirring, for 5 minutes. Add the stock and bring to the boil. Stir once and then reduce the heat; cover the pan tightly and cook for 15 minutes or until the rice is tender and all the liquid absorbed. Taste and adjust the seasoning. Serve on individual plates, sprinkled with the grated cheese.

Ham Rolls

Serves: 4 people
Preparation time:
10 minutes
Cooking time:
None

An exciting appetiser to serve when you entertain. Cook a ham collar joint for a family meal and use four slices of it for this recipe.

4 oz/100 g cooked
  long grain rice
  (about 1¼ oz/35 g
  uncooked)
1 dessert apple,
  peeled, cored and
  chopped
4 spring onions,
  chopped
1 pot turkey spread
2 level teaspoons
  curry powder or to
  taste
salt and pepper
4 thin slices boiled
  ham
green salad for
  serving

Put the rice into a bowl and mix in the apple, spring onions, turkey spread and curry powder. Add salt and pepper to taste. Divide the rice mixture equally into 4 and place on the slices of ham. Roll the ham around the stuffing. Arrange a green salad on a serving plate and place the ham rolls on top. Serve cold.

Tomato Topknots

Serves: 4 people
Preparation time:
10 minutes
Cooking time:
None

These little stuffed tomatoes are very quick to make and extremely good to eat. Reserve the tomato flesh for flavouring a casserole or stew.

4 large tomatoes
4 oz/100 g cottage cheese
1 level tablespoon finely grated onion
salt and pepper
2 tablespoons finely chopped pineapple
watercress for garnish

Slice the tops off the tomatoes about one-third of the way down. Carefully scoop out the tomato flesh with a teaspoon, without breaking the skin at all. Put the tomato shells, cut-side down, on a plate to drain. Mix the cottage cheese with the onion and season well with salt and pepper. Put a quarter of the pineapple in the base of each tomato, then pile the cottage cheese mixture on top. Serve as soon as possible, garnished with sprigs of watercress.

Leeks à la Grecque

Serves: 4 people
Preparation time:
10 minutes plus cooling and chilling time
Cooking time:
10 minutes

A nice fresh appetiser for winter. At other times of the year try using mushrooms instead. To skin tomatoes, dip them in boiling water for 1 minute; the skins will then slip off easily.

8 small or 4 large leeks
$\frac{1}{4}$ pint/1·5 dl water
2 tablespoons olive oil
1 tablespoon lemon juice
2 tomatoes, skinned and chopped
1 level teaspoon dried basil
$\frac{1}{4}$ level teaspoon dried thyme
1 bay leaf
1 clove garlic, crushed
salt and pepper
French bread or crispbread for serving (optional)

Wash the leeks thoroughly, cutting large leeks in half lengthwise. Put the leeks in a large saucepan with the water, oil, lemon juice, tomatoes, herbs, garlic and salt and pepper. Bring to the boil, cover the pan tightly and simmer gently for about 10 minutes or until the leeks are tender but still firm. Cool, then chill before serving. Serve French bread separately.

Celery with Cheese

Serves: 4 people
Preparation time:
5 minutes
Cooking time:
5 minutes

This is a good starter or light lunch or supper dish. It can be made entirely from food in your store cupboard.

1 (1 lb 3 oz/540 g) can celery hearts
salt and pepper
pinch of dried sage
4 oz/100 g Cheddar cheese
watercress for garnish

Drain the celery hearts thoroughly. Place them on 4 individual serving dishes and sprinkle with salt and pepper and a very little dried sage. Slice the cheese thinly and place the slices over the celery. Cook under a preheated very hot grill until the cheese is browned. Serve immediately, garnished with watercress.

Souper Soufflé

Serves 4 people
(2 people for a light meal)
Preparation time:
10 minutes
Cooking time:
35–40 minutes
Oven temperature:
375°F/190°C Mark 5

A delicious, quickly prepared soufflé which will serve two for lunch or supper. Use other soups if preferred.

1 (10½ oz/298 g) can condensed asparagus soup
4 eggs, separated

Lightly grease a 1½ pint/¾ litre capacity soufflé dish. Without diluting it, empty the soup into a saucepan and heat gently. Beat the egg yolks together and stir them into the soup. Cook very gently, stirring all the time, for 2–3 minutes. Do not allow the soup to boil. Whisk the egg whites together in a large bowl, until stiff. Fold the soup into the egg whites with a metal tablespoon. Pour the mixture into the soufflé dish and bake in a moderately hot oven (375°F/190°C Mark 5) for 35–40 minutes or until well risen and golden. Serve at once.

Eggs Mornay

Serves: 4 people
Preparation time:
10 minutes
Cooking time:
25 minutes

A store cupboard appetiser which is good for unexpected guests. It also makes a good lunch or supper dish.

6 oz/175 g small
    pasta (shells,
    elbow macaroni,
    or wagon wheels)
salt and pepper
2 oz/50 g margarine
1 oz/25 g plain flour
½ pint/3 dl milk
3 oz/75 g Cheddar
    cheese, grated
pinch of dry mustard
4 hard-boiled eggs
parsley for garnish

Cook the pasta in a large saucepan with plenty of boiling salted water for about 15 minutes or until just cooked. Meanwhile, heat half the margarine in a saucepan. Stir in the flour and cook, stirring, for 2–3 minutes. Blend in the milk and bring to the boil, stirring all the time. Boil for 2 minutes. Remove from the heat and stir in 2 oz/50 g of the cheese. Season with salt, pepper and mustard. Drain the pasta well in a colander. Melt the remaining margarine in the emptied saucepan and toss the pasta in it. Divide it equally between 4 individual heatproof serving dishes. Cut the hard-boiled eggs in half lengthwise and arrange 2 halves on each dish. Coat the eggs in the sauce and sprinkle the top with the remaining cheese. Cook the cheese under a hot grill until bubbling. Serve as soon as possible.

Eggs en Cocotte

Serves: 4 people
Preparation time:
10 minutes
Cooking time:
8–10 minutes
Oven temperature:
350°F/180°C Mark 4

Other cooked meat, fish or even vegetables could be cooked under the eggs. Serve as a meal starter or light supper dish.

2 oz/50 g margarine
1 small onion,
    chopped
1 oz/25 g
    mushrooms,
    sliced
2 oz/50 g cold
    cooked pork,
    minced
4–8 eggs
parsley for garnish

Heat half the margarine in a saucepan and fry the onion until softened. Add the mushrooms and pork. Cook, stirring, until hot and well mixed. Divide the pork mixture equally between 4 small, lightly greased individual heatproof dishes. Break 1 or 2 eggs into each dish, dot the tops with the remaining margarine. Put the dishes in a pan with hot water to come halfway up the sides. Bake in a moderate oven (350°F/180°C Mark 4) for 8–10 minutes or until the eggs are set but still creamy. Be careful not to overcook. Serve at once, in the hot dishes, garnished with a sprig of parsley.

Mushroom and Egg Appetiser

Serves: 2 people
Preparation time:
10 minutes
Cooking time:
5 minutes

This supper dish, very easy and quick to prepare, can also be served as a meal starter. It will then be enough for four people.

1 tablespoon oil
1 onion, chopped
4 tomatoes, skinned and sliced
4 hard-boiled eggs, sliced
1 (10½ oz/298 g) can condensed mushroom soup
2 tablespoons milk
3 oz/75 g cheese, grated
chopped parsley for garnish

Heat the oil in a frying pan and fry the onion until softened. Add the tomato and cook for 2–3 minutes. Put the onion and tomato in the base of a heatproof dish. Arrange the slices of hard-boiled egg on top. Heat the soup in a saucepan with the milk and 2 oz/50 g of the cheese. Stir until the cheese is melted; do not allow the soup to boil. Pour the soup over the egg and sprinkle with the remaining cheese. Cook under a hot grill until bubbling and golden. Serve garnished with chopped parsley.

Cheese and Pineapple Salad

Serves: 4 people
Preparation time:
10 minutes
Cooking time:
None

A refreshing appetiser. Use fresh pineapple if it is available and not too expensive.

6 oz/175 g Cheddar cheese
1 (12 oz/340 g) can pineapple cubes
2 level tablespoons chopped parsley
1 lettuce for serving
cucumber slices for garnish

Cut the cheese into ¼–½ inch/ 6–12 mm cubes. Drain the pineapple and put it, with the cheese, into a mixing bowl. Stir in the parsley. Arrange the lettuce on 4 individual serving plates and spoon the cheese mixture into the middle. Arrange thin slices of cucumber on top.

Lychee and Sesame Salad

Serves: 4–6 people
Preparation time:
10 minutes
Cooking time:
None

If you live near a shop which specialises in Chinese food you will be able to buy Chinese cabbage. Use it instead of lettuce. The sesame seeds are available in larger super-markets or health food shops. Fry the sesame seeds lightly in a dry frying pan to toast them.

5–6 lettuce leaves
5 tablespoons oil
3 tablespoons vinegar
3 level tablespoons sesame seeds, toasted
1 level teaspoon brown sugar
1 teaspoon soy sauce
$\frac{1}{4}$ level teaspoon dry mustard
salt and pepper
1 (5 oz/142 g) can water chestnuts, sliced
$\frac{1}{2}$ (9$\frac{1}{2}$ oz/269 g) can bean sprouts, drained and rinsed
4 spring onions, sliced
1 (11 oz/311 g) can lychees

Wash the lettuce leaves and place in the refrigerator to crisp. Combine the oil, vinegar, sesame seeds, sugar, soy sauce, mustard and salt and pepper to taste in a large serving bowl. Add the water chestnuts, bean sprouts, spring onions and lychees. Shred the lettuce into the bowl and toss together lightly. Serve at once.

Liptauer Cheese

Serves: 6–8 people
Preparation time:
5 minutes plus resting time
Cooking time:
None

This Hungarian dish makes a good meal starter, can be used as a dip or as a cheese spread.

4 oz/125 g curd cheese
2 oz/50 g margarine or butter, softened
1 teaspoon French or German mustard
2 teaspoons chopped capers
2 teaspoons chopped chives
1 teaspoon anchovy essence or 1 anchovy, finely chopped
1 teaspoon paprika pepper
salt and pepper
lettuce and bread for serving

Beat all the ingredients together until very thoroughly mixed. Taste and adjust the seasoning. Cover and put aside in a cool place for at least 2 hours before using.

Place in a pretty dish, garnish with young lettuce leaves and serve with sesame bread or crusty French bread.

Prawn and Potato Appetiser

Serves: 4 people
Preparation time:
10 minutes plus
cooling and chilling
time
Cooking time:
20 minutes

Just a few prawns
give this dish a hint
of luxury. Chopped
ham or luncheon
meat may be used for
a more economical
meal.

12 oz/350 g potatoes
salt and pepper
2 tablespoons lemon
  juice
4 tablespoons olive
  oil
1 clove garlic, crushed
  (optional)
$\frac{1}{4}$ level teaspoon
  French mustard
large pinch each of
  paprika pepper and
  castor sugar
4 oz/100 g prawns
4 hard-boiled eggs
1 small green pepper
  or 2 sticks celery,
  chopped

Peel the potatoes and cook in boiling salted water until tender. Drain. Put the lemon juice, olive oil, garlic, mustard, paprika pepper, castor sugar and salt and pepper into a screw-top jar. Shake the dressing until creamy. Slice the potatoes while still warm and put them in a bowl. Pour over the dressing and toss lightly. Put aside until cold, then stir in the prawns. Slice the eggs and arrange round 4 individual serving plates. Pile the potato and prawns in the middle and decorate with the chopped pepper or celery. Serve chilled.

Tuna and Tomato Toasts

Serves: 4 people
Preparation time:
5 minutes
Cooking time:
About 15 minutes

These toasted
appetisers are an ideal
starter to a meal or
they can be served as
a light lunch or
supper dish. Divide
the toast into fingers,
squares or rounds
for variation.

4 small slices bread
2 oz/50 g butter
1 (7 oz/198 g) can
  tuna
1 tablespoon lemon
  juice
1 tablespoon tomato
  ketchup
salt and pepper
lemon slices and
  watercress for
  garnish

Toast the bread and spread with half the butter. Flake the tuna into a bowl. Mix in the lemon juice, tomato ketchup and the remaining butter. Season well and heap it onto the hot toast. Heat for a few minutes under the grill. Garnish with lemon slices and watercress and serve hot.

Mussels with Parsley Butter

Serves: 4 people
Preparation time:
10 minutes
Cooking time:
5–10 minutes

A speedy way to serve mussels, which make a very good first course. Mussels are at their best in late spring and summer.

50 mussels
4 oz/100 g butter
2 level tablespoons chopped parsley
1 clove garlic, crushed (optional)
salt and pepper
2 teaspoons lemon juice
1 oz/25 g fine dry breadcrumbs

Wash the mussels, then scrub them very well and remove any beard. Discard any that are opened. Put the mussels in a large saucepan with $\frac{1}{4}$ pint/1·5 dl water. Cover the pan then cook quickly, shaking the pan gently until all the mussels have opened. Discard any that remain closed. With the mussels still in their shells, arrange them in a serving dish with any remaining cooking liquid. Melt the butter in a saucepan and add the parsley, garlic, salt and pepper and lemon juice. Heat until beginning to brown. Pour the butter over the mussels and sprinkle with the breadcrumbs. Cook under a hot grill until the breadcrumbs begin to brown. Serve immediately.

Mussels Aurora

Serves: 4 people
Preparation time:
10 minutes
Cooking time:
10 minutes

An easy way to prepare mussels which appeals to everyone. If fresh mussels are not available, buy a jar of bottled mussels; 12 oz/350 g would be enough when served as a meal starter. Mussels are at their best in the spring.

about 50 mussels
salt
1 oz/25 g margarine
1 onion, finely chopped
1 clove garlic, crushed (optional)
1 (6 oz/170 g) can tomatoes
freshly ground black pepper
chopped parsley for garnish

Wash the mussels in several changes of water and remove any beard. Discard any mussels which are open. Put the mussels in a large saucepan with $\frac{1}{2}$ pint/3 dl salted water. Heat rapidly, shaking the pan occasionally until all the shells have opened. Keep warm. Melt the margarine in a saucepan and fry the onion and garlic until softened. Add the tomatoes, bring to the boil. Season to taste. Put the mussels into a serving dish, spoon the sauce over the top and serve sprinkled with chopped parsley.

Fish Fritters

Serves: 4 people
Preparation time:
10 minutes
Cooking time:
10 minutes

A very tasty dish
for lunch, supper
or to start a meal.

4 oz/100 g cold
  cooked white fish
2 oz/50 g plain flour
salt and pepper
2 eggs, separated
3 tablespoons milk
1 level teaspoon
  chopped parsley
1 small onion, grated
oil for frying
slices of lemon for
  serving

Flake the fish, removing all the bones and skin. Sift the flour into a mixing bowl and stir in the fish with salt and pepper, the egg yolks, milk, parsley and onion. Whisk the egg whites until stiff and fold into the fish mixture.

Heat about ¼ inch/6 mm oil in a large frying pan and fry tablespoons of the mixture until golden, turning once. Drain on absorbent kitchen paper, then serve with slices of lemon.

Fish in Sweet and Sour Sauce

Serves: 4–6 people
Preparation time:
10 minutes
Cooking time:
15 minutes

Ask your fishmonger to skin the fish when you buy it. If you have trouble in buying fresh ginger use ½ level teaspoon ground ginger instead. To skin tomatoes, dip them in boiling water for 1 minute; the skins will then slip off easily.

1 lb/500 g white fish
  fillets
2 carrots, sliced
  lengthways
3 sticks celery, cut
  diagonally
3 tablespoons oil
4 tablespoons
  vinegar
4 level tablespoons
  sugar
1 level teaspoon
  finely chopped
  fresh ginger
½ level teaspoon salt
½ level tablespoon
  cornflour
3 tomatoes, skinned
  and coarsely
  chopped

Cut the fish into 1 inch/25 mm pieces. Place the carrots and celery in boiling salted water for 5 minutes, then drain. Heat the oil in a saucepan, add the fish pieces and fry gently for 5–7 minutes or until cooked. Remove the fish and drain.

Pour off the excess oil from the saucepan. Stir in the vinegar, sugar, ginger, salt, cornflour, tomatoes, carrots, celery and ¼ pint/1·5 dl water. Bring to the boil, stirring continuously, add the fish and reheat. Serve in a warm dish.

Quick Vichyssoise

Serves: 6–8 people
Preparation time:
10 minutes plus
chilling time
Cooking time:
None

This is a store cupboard version of a classic cold soup. Fresh milk can be used if you have plenty available.

1 oz/25 g margarine
2 onions, grated or finely chopped
2 pints/1 litre white veal stock or water and chicken stock cubes
1 (4–6 servings) packet instant potato
4 oz/100 g skimmed milk powder
1 tablespoon single cream
salt and pepper
paprika pepper, chopped chives and extra cream for garnish

Melt the margarine in a large saucepan and fry the onion until soft, without browning. Add the stock and bring to the boil. Stir in the instant potato. Put the skimmed milk powder in a measuring jug and make up to 2 pints/1 litre with cold water. Add to the saucepan, then allow the soup to cool. Stir in the cream, taste and adjust the seasoning. Chill until needed. To serve, pour the soup into individual soup bowls and place a swirl of cream in the centre of each one. Sprinkle with paprika pepper and chives.

Consommé Brunois

Serves: 4 people
Preparation time:
5 minutes
Cooking time:
5 minutes
Oven temperature:
450°F/230°C Mark 8

Canned consommé is impressive served in this way. Make your own Melba toast from fresh or leftover bread, as given in the recipe.

2 slices of white bread for Melba toast
1 (15 oz/428 g) can beef consommé
2 tablespoons sherry (optional)
4 tablespoons cooked diced carrot, turnip, celery, leek, peas (as available)

To make the Melba toast, toast the slices of bread lightly on both sides. While still warm, cut off the crusts and carefully divide the bread through the middle to make each piece into 2 very thin slices. Put these slices into a very hot oven (450°F/230°C Mark 8) for 1–2 minutes or until curled and golden. Cool on a rack. Put the consommé into a saucepan and heat until boiling, stir in the sherry. Put a tablespoon of mixed vegetables in each of the 4 individual soup cups. Pour in the soup and serve immediately with the Melba toast.

Chilled Cucumber and Tomato Soup

Serves: 4 people
Preparation time:
10 minutes plus
chilling time
Cooking time:
15 minutes
Calories: about 25
calories per serving

This is a good soup
for summer when
cucumbers are at
their best and
cheapest. If you have
not got a blender,
press the cucumber
through a sieve with
the other ingredients.

1 small cucumber
½ pint/3 dl chicken
    stock or water and
    chicken stock cube
½ dessert apple,
    peeled and cored
1 (8 oz/226 g) can
    tomatoes
salt and pepper

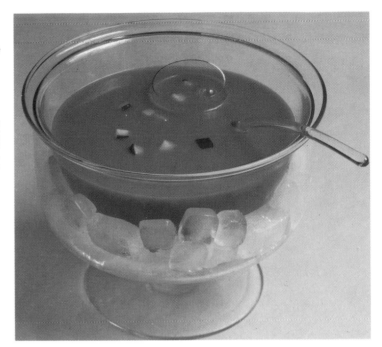

Cut 1 inch/25 mm off the cucumber and reserve for the garnish. Peel the rest of the cucumber, chop, and place in a saucepan with the stock. Bring to the boil then simmer until the cucumber is tender (about 15 minutes). Cool slightly then pour into an electric blender. Add the remaining ingredients and blend at high speed until smooth. Taste and adjust seasoning. Cool then chill. Serve garnished with diced cucumber.

Iced Tomato Orange Soup

Serves: 4 people
Preparation time:
5 minutes plus
chilling time
Cooking time:
None

A very speedy chilled
soup, ideal for
summer entertaining.

1 pint/6 dl tomato
    juice
2 level teaspoons
    castor sugar
grated rind and
    juice of ½ lemon
1 level teaspoon
    grated onion
1 teaspoon
    Worcestershire
    sauce
1 small can
    evaporated milk
1 small can tuna,
    drained
salt and pepper
slices of cucumber
    and sprigs of mint
    for garnish

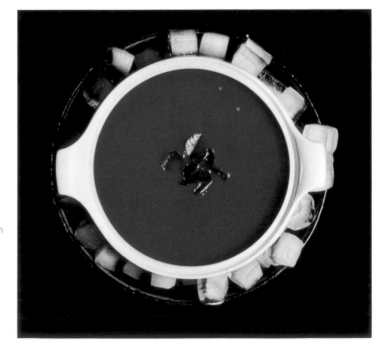

Chill all the ingredients. Put them all in a bowl except the garnish and mix together well. Pour into chilled soup bowls or a tureen and garnish with the cucumber and mint.

21

Cucumber, Tomato and Yoghourt Soup

Serves: 6 people
Preparation time:
10 minutes
Cooking time:
None

A refreshing and healthy soup, ideal for a summer meal starter.

4 (5 fl oz/142 ml) cartons natural yoghourt
1 (19 fl oz/540 ml) can tomato juice
rind and juice of 1 lemon
½ cucumber
salt and pepper
extra cucumber and lemon slices for garnish

Place the yoghourt and tomato juice in a bowl and whisk together. Stir in the lemon rind and juice. Peel the cucumber and cut it into ¼ inch/6 mm cubes, stir it into the bowl with salt and pepper to taste. Chill in the refrigerator, then pour into serving bowls. Garnish with slices of cucumber and lemon.

Iced Cucumber and Yoghourt Soup

Serves: 4–6 people
Preparation time:
10 minutes
plus chilling time
Cooking time:
None

This soup is very good served before a curry. Cucumbers are available all the year.

1 cucumber
1 pint/6 dl yoghourt
1 tablespoon vinegar
2 teaspoons olive oil
1 level teaspoon castor sugar
salt and pepper
¼ level teaspoon dry mustard
1 level tablespoon chopped mint
sprigs of mint for garnish

Slice some of the cucumber thinly and reserve for garnish. Peel and grate the rest coarsely or cut into dice. Combine the yoghourt, vinegar olive oil, sugar, salt and pepper and mustard. Mix them all together well. Stir in the cucumber and mint. Chill until needed. Serve garnished with the reserved cucumber slices and sprigs of mint.

Chilled Spanish Vegetable Soup

Serves: 6 people
Preparation time:
10 minutes plus
soaking and chilling
times
Cooking time:
None

This delicious soup is an ideal starter to a summer meal, when the vegetables are in season. Serve with fried bread croûtons.

2 tomatoes, skinned
1 red or green
  pepper
½ cucumber, peeled
2 spring onions
6 tablespoons olive
  oil
3 tablespoons
  vinegar
salt and pepper
2 pints/1 litre brown
  beef stock or
  water and beef
  stock cubes
½ pint/3 dl tomato
  juice

Remove the seeds from the tomatoes and pepper and cut them into ¼ inch/6 mm dice. Dice the cucumber. Slice the spring onions thinly. Mix all the vegetables together in a bowl. Sprinkle in the oil, vinegar and salt and pepper. Toss lightly then leave for 1 hour. Drain the vegetables and stir them into the beef stock with the tomato juice. Taste and adjust the seasoning. Chill well before serving.

Quick Curried Celery Soup

Serves: 4 people
Preparation time:
5 minutes plus
chilling time
Cooking time:
None

A delicious and quickly prepared soup, ideal for unexpected guests.

1 (10½ oz/298 g)
  can condensed
  cream of celery
  soup
1 dessert apple,
  peeled and cored
1 (5 fl oz/142 ml)
  carton soured
  cream
1 level tablespoon
  curry powder
  or to taste
2 level teaspoons
  chopped parsley

Put the soup in a bowl, fill the empty soup can with water and add this to the soup. Grate the apple coarsely into it. Add the soured cream, curry powder and parsley. Whisk all the ingredients together very thoroughly until well blended. Chill before serving.

Chilled Cauliflower and Spring Onion Soup

Serves: 4 people
Preparation time.
10 minutes plus
chilling time
Cooking time:
30 minutes

A delicious and
refreshing soup. It
can also be served
hot. Cauliflowers are
at their best in the
summer.

8 spring onions
1 lb/½ kg
    cauliflower
    flowerets
2 sticks celery,
    chopped
½ pint/3 dl chicken
    stock or water
    and chicken stock
    cube
½ pint/3 dl milk
salt and pepper
thin cream for
    serving (optional)

Slice the white part of the onions. Reserve the green tops for garnish. Put the cauliflower into a saucepan with the celery, onion and stock. Bring to the boil, cover the pan and simmer very gently for about 30 minutes. Reserve some of the cauliflower flowerets for garnish. Press the soup through a sieve with a wooden spoon or purée it in an electric blender. Put aside until cool. Stir in the milk then chill until needed. Taste and adjust the seasoning. Cut the reserved cauliflower into smaller pieces. Chop the green spring onion tops for garnish. Add the cauliflower flowerets to the soup and sprinkle with the chopped spring onion. Add a teaspoon of cream to each serving, if liked.

Reggello Soup

Serves: 4 people
Preparation time:
10 minutes
Cooking time:
10 minutes

A substantial and
delicious soup. It is
very inexpensive to
make. Use any small
pasta — stars, shells,
alphabets, small
macaroni —
whichever is
available. Use olive
oil for preference.

2 tablespoons oil
2 rashers streaky
    bacon, chopped
1 onion, finely
    chopped
1 clove garlic,
    crushed
1 tomato, skinned
    and sliced
1½ pints/9 dl
    chicken stock (or
    water and chicken
    stock cubes)
2 level teaspoons
    dried basil
8 oz/225 g small
    pasta
2 oz/50 g grated
    Parmesan cheese
    for serving

Heat the oil in a large saucepan and fry the bacon, onion and garlic, stirring until softened but not browned. Add the tomato, chicken stock and basil. Bring to the boil, then add the pasta and simmer until the pasta is cooked (about 10 minutes). Serve a bowl of Parmesan cheese separately.

Chinese Rice Soup

Serves: 6–8 people
Preparation time:
10 minutes
Cooking time:
35 minutes

A quickly prepared
and economical
soup. Serve it on
cold evenings.

1 tablespoon oil
4 oz/100 g long
  grain rice
3 pints/1½ litres
  chicken stock or
  water and chicken
  stock cubes
1 carrot, finely
  grated
2 sticks celery, finely
  grated
salt and pepper
chopped parsley for
  garnish

Heat the oil in a large saucepan and fry the rice, stirring, for 2–3 minutes. Add the stock, bring to the boil, then simmer for 30 minutes. Just before serving, stir in the grated vegetables. Taste and adjust the seasoning. Serve piping hot, sprinkled with chopped parsley.

Scotch Broth

Serves: 4–6 people
Preparation time:
10 minutes
Cooking time:
1 hour 50 minutes

Scotch broth is a
meal in itself. If it is
to be served as a
soup, remove the
cooked lamb from
the bones and dice it.

1 lb/½ kg middle
  neck of lamb
2 oz/50 g pearl
  barley
salt and pepper
2 carrots, diced
1 turnip, diced
1 leek, sliced
chopped parsley for
  garnish

Wash the lamb, trimming off excess fat and gristle. Put the meat in a saucepan with the pearl barley, salt and 1½ pints/9 dl water. Bring to the boil, cover the pan and simmer gently for 1½ hours. Add the prepared vegetables and cook for a further 20 minutes. Taste and season. Pour into individual soup plates and serve garnished with parsley.

Tomato Soup

Serves: 4–6 people
Preparation time:
5 minutes
Cooking time:
50 minutes

This soup is made with canned tomatoes so it is an economical recipe which can be made at any time of the year.

1 onion, chopped
1 carrot, chopped
1 stick celery, chopped
½ oz/15 g margarine
1 rasher streaky bacon, chopped
1 level tablespoon plain flour
1 (20 oz/569 g) can tomatoes
¾ pint/4·5 dl chicken stock or water and chicken stock cube
1 level tablespoon tomato purée
salt and pepper
½ level teaspoon sugar
½ level teaspoon dried basil
1 bay leaf
chopped parsley and fried bread croûtons for garnish

Prepare the fresh vegetables. Melt the margarine in a saucepan and fry the bacon until softened. Add the vegetables and cook, stirring, for a further 5 minutes. Stir in the flour then all the remaining ingredients, including a little salt and pepper. Bring to the boil and simmer gently for 45 minutes. Press the soup through a sieve with a wooden spoon or remove the bay leaf and purée in an electric blender. Return to the saucepan, taste and adjust the seasoning. Reheat, garnish with chopped parsley and croûtons and serve.

Cream of Cucumber Soup

Serves: 4–6 people
Preparation time:
10 minutes
Cooking time:
20 minutes.

Serve this soup piping hot in the winter, chilled in the summer.

1 large cucumber
salt and pepper
1 pint/6 dl white veal stock or water and chicken stock cube
¾ oz/20 g margarine
¾ oz/20 g plain flour
6 tablespoons milk

Slice some of the cucumber thinly and reserve for garnish. Remove about three-quarters of the skin from the remaining cucumber and chop the vegetable coarsely. Cook the cucumber for 1 minute in a saucepan with boiling salted water to cover, then drain. Return the cucumber to the pan, add the stock. Bring to the boil, then cover the pan and simmer gently until the cucumber is very tender. Press through a sieve with a wooden spoon or purée in an electric blender. Melt the margarine in a clean saucepan, add the flour and cook, stirring, for 2–3 minutes. Blend in the cucumber purée and bring to the boil, stirring constantly. Simmer for 2–3 minutes. Stir in the milk. Taste and adjust the seasoning. Serve garnished with the reserved cucumber slices.

German Beer Soup

Serves: 4 people
Preparation time:
10 minutes
Cooking time:
About 10–15 minutes

A quick to make and deliciously different soup. Any light beer can be used in this recipe.

2 (12 fl oz/340 ml) bottles or cans of lager
2 oz/50 g sugar
3 egg yolks
4 tablespoons soured cream
½ level teaspoon ground cinnamon
¼ level teaspoon salt
¼ level teaspoon pepper

Heat the beer and sugar together in a large saucepan, stir until the sugar has dissolved and remove from the heat. Place the egg yolks in a large bowl, slowly whisk in the soured cream, then the hot beer, cinnamon, salt and pepper. Return the mixture to the saucepan and stir over a low heat until slightly thickened. Do not boil. Serve immediately.

Country-Style Mushroom Soup

Serves: 6 people
Preparation time:
10 minutes
Cooking time:
25 minutes

A low-calorie soup — ideal if you are slimming and need a light and easily made lunch or supper. Use organically grown vegetables, if liked.

8 oz/225 g carrots, diced
12 oz/350 g onions, chopped
½ head celery, sliced
4 oz/100 g sliced green beans
8 oz/225 g mushrooms, sliced
1 pint/6 dl tomato juice
1½ pints/9 dl water
2 tablespoons Worcestershire sauce
bouquet garni (1 bay leaf, 1 sprig of thyme, 3 parsley stalks tied together)
salt and pepper

Place the carrots, onions, celery, green beans and mushrooms (reserving a few slices for garnish) in a saucepan. Add the tomato juice, water, Worcestershire sauce, bouquet garni, and salt and pepper to taste. Cover the pan, place it over the heat and simmer for 25 minutes. Remove 3 tablespoons of vegetables from the pan and put aside. Blend the soup until smooth in an electric blender or rub it through a sieve with a wooden spoon. Return it to the pan with the reserved vegetables, heat through, remove the bouquet garni. Serve the soup with the reserved mushrooms as a garnish.

Cream of Leek Soup

Serves: 4–6 people
Preparation time:
10 minutes
Cooking time:
35 minutes

This soup is good served with crunchy fried bread croûtons. Cut bread into dice and fry in hot shallow oil until crisp and golden. Drain well on absorbent kitchen paper. Sprinkle with salt before serving.

1 lb/½ kg leeks
1 oz/25 g margarine
1 oz/25 g plain flour
1½ pints/9 dl chicken stock or water and chicken stock cubes
1 egg yolk
¼ pint/1·5 dl milk
salt and pepper

Cut the dark green tops off the leeks and discard. Slice the leeks in half lengthwise and wash well. Chop. Melt the margarine in a large saucepan and cook the leeks gently, stirring all the time, for 5 minutes. Sprinkle in the flour and cook for 1 minute. Blend in the stock, bring to the boil, stirring all the time, then simmer gently for about 30 minutes or until the leeks are very tender. Press through a sieve with a wooden spoon or purée in an electric blender. Return the soup to the saucepan. Whisk the egg yolk and milk together until mixed. Stir into the soup and reheat gently, without boiling. Taste and adjust the seasoning before serving.

Quick Potato Soup

Serves: 4 people
Preparation time:
10 minutes
Cooking time:
15 minutes

It is always nice to know soup recipes that are quick, economical and delicious, like this one.

1 lb/½ kg potatoes
1 large onion
2 oz/50 g margarine
1½ pints/9 dl white veal stock or water and chicken stock cubes
salt and pepper
¼ pint/1·5 dl milk
grated cheese or chopped parsley for garnish

Peel and grate the potatoes and onion. Put them in a saucepan with the margarine, stock and salt and pepper. Bring to the boil, then simmer gently for about 15 minutes or until the vegetables are tender. Stir in the milk and reheat. Taste and adjust the seasoning. Serve piping hot, sprinkled with grated cheese or chopped parsley.

Mushroom Soup

Serves: 4 people
Preparation time:
10 minutes
Cooking time:
15 minutes

This soup is best made with large flat mushrooms, as they have most flavour. Mushroom stalks are also good, and are inexpensive. Serve hot or chilled.

1 oz/25 g margarine
1 small onion, chopped
4 oz/100 g mushrooms
1½ pints/9 dl chicken stock or water and chicken stock cubes
¼ pint/1·5 dl thin cream
salt and pepper
chopped parsley for garnish

Melt the margarine in a large saucepan and fry the onion until softened but not browned. Reserve 1 mushroom for garnish, then chop the rest coarsely. Add the mushrooms to the saucepan and fry quickly, stirring until softened. Add the stock, bring to the boil and simmer for 10 minutes. Press through a sieve with a wooden spoon or purée in an electric blender. Stir in the cream. Taste and adjust the seasoning. Either chill for serving cold, or reheat without boiling, for serving hot. Serve garnished with slices of the reserved mushroom and sprinkled with chopped parsley.

Golden Lentil Soup

Serves: 6–8 people
Preparation time:
10 minutes
Cooking time:
1 hour 50 minutes

Almost a meal in itself, this soup makes an ideal light lunch or supper, served with crusty or wholemeal bread.

8 oz/225 g lentils
2 tablespoons oil
1 leek, finely chopped
1 onion, grated
1 carrot, grated
2 sticks celery, finely chopped
1 level teaspoon tomato purée
1½ oz/40 g margarine
1½ oz/40 g plain flour
¾ pint/4·5 dl brown beef stock or water and beef stock cube
salt and pepper
2 oz/50 g cheese, grated

Put the lentils in a saucepan with 1½ pints/9 dl water. Bring to the boil, cover the pan and simmer for 1 hour. Heat the oil in a saucepan and fry the leek, onion, carrot and celery gently for 5–10 minutes, stirring occasionally. Add the vegetables and tomato purée to the cooked lentils. Melt the margarine in the same saucepan, add the flour and cook, stirring, for 2–3 minutes. Blend in the stock and bring to the boil, stirring until smooth. Add to the lentil mixture and bring to the boil, stirring. Simmer very gently for 30 minutes. Taste and adjust the seasoning. Pour the soup into a heatproof serving dish, sprinkle the cheese on top and cook under a hot grill until golden. Serve as soon as possible.

Egg Soup

Serves: 4 people
Preparation time:
5 minutes
Cooking time:
5 minutes

This recipe really requires the use of home-made chicken stock. Stock cubes should only be used as a last resort.

1½ pints/9 dl chicken stock
2 eggs
1 oz/25 g Parmesan cheese, grated
1 level tablespoon chopped parsley

Put the stock into a saucepan and bring slowly to the boil. Beat the eggs, cheese and parsley together in a small bowl. Add the egg mixture to the stock, stirring all the time. Cook for 2—3 seconds then serve immediately.

Creamy Corn Soup

Serves: 4 people
Preparation time:
5 minutes
Cooking time:
25 minutes

A quickly prepared soup that is popular with children.

1½ oz/40 g margarine
1 (12 oz/340 g) can sweetcorn, drained
1 tablespoon finely chopped green pepper
1½ pints/9 dl chicken stock or water and chicken stock cubes
1 teaspoon Worcestershire sauce
1½ oz/40 g plain flour
1 small can evaporated milk
salt and pepper
2 oz/50 g cheese, grated

Melt the margarine in a saucepan, add the sweetcorn and green pepper. Fry gently, stirring frequently, for 5 minutes. Stir in the stock and Worcestershire sauce. Bring to the boil, then cover the pan and simmer for 10—15 minutes or until the vegetables are very tender. Whisk the flour into the evaporated milk, then gradually stir the mixture into the soup. Bring to the boil, stirring all the time, then simmer for 5 minutes. Taste and adjust the seasoning. Serve sprinkled with grated cheese.

Cheddar Cheese Soup

Serves: 4 people
Preparation time:
5 minutes
Cooking time:
15 minutes

A warming soup which is good for entertaining as well as for family meals.

1½ oz/40 g margarine
1 large onion, sliced
2 sticks celery, chopped
1 oz/25 g plain flour
1 pint/5 dl milk
½ pint/3 dl white veal stock or water and chicken stock cube
pinch of ground nutmeg
5 oz/150 g Cheddar cheese, grated
salt and pepper

Melt the margarine in a saucepan and fry the onion and celery until softened. Add the flour and cook, stirring, for 2 minutes. Blend in the milk, stock and nutmeg and bring to the boil, stirring all the time. Simmer for 5 minutes. Remove the pan from the heat and stir in 4 oz/100 g of the cheese. Taste and adjust the seasoning. Serve in individual soup bowls sprinkled with the remaining cheese

Thick Chicken Chowder

Serves: 4 people
Preparation time:
5 minutes
Cooking time:
15–20 minutes

This thick soup makes good use of leftover chicken and vegetables. If cooked vegetables are not available, use raw and cook in the chowder until tender.

4 oz/100 g cooked chicken
1 tablespoon oil
2 rashers streaky bacon, diced
1 onion, chopped
2 level tablespoons plain flour
3 cooked carrots, diced
3 cooked potatoes, diced
4 oz/100 g cooked sweetcorn or peas
1 pint/6 dl chicken stock or water and chicken stock cube
½ pint/3 dl milk
salt and pepper
chopped parsley for garnish

Cut the chicken into pieces. Heat the oil in a saucepan and fry the bacon until softened. Add the onion and cook until beginning to brown. Sprinkle with flour, then stir in the chicken, carrots, potato, sweetcorn, chicken stock and milk. Bring to the boil, then simmer for 10–15 minutes. Taste and adjust the seasoning. Serve sprinkled with chopped parsley.

Cream of Pea and Ham Soup

Serves: 6–8 people
Preparation time:
5 minutes plus
soaking time
Cooking time:
2 hours 25 minutes

A delicious home-made family soup. Serve for lunch or supper with cheese and crusty bread.

8 oz/225 g split peas
2 oz/50 g margarine
1 onion, finely chopped
1 stick celery, finely chopped
1 medium-sized potato, grated
2 oz/50 g lean cooked ham, diced
1½ pints/9 dl white veal stock or water and chicken stock cubes
1 large (13 fl oz/ 368 ml) can evaporated milk
salt and pepper

Put the split peas in a bowl, cover with cold water and leave to soak for up to 6 hours. Melt the margarine in a saucepan, add the onion and cook gently, covered, for 10 minutes. Add the celery and potato and fry for a further 10 minutes, stirring occasionally. Drain the soaked split peas and add them to the vegetables with the ham and stock. Bring to the boil, then cover the pan and simmer gently for 2 hours. Stir in the evaporated milk. Reheat gently, taste and adjust the seasoning. Serve piping hot.

Beetroot Soup

Serves: 4 people
Preparation time:
5 minutes
Cooking time:
20 minutes

Beetroot is available all the year round. This soup is an economical and delicious starter for any occasion, at any time. Make your own stock, or in an emergency use canned beef consommé.

1 pint/6 dl clear beef stock
1 large beetroot, uncooked
salt and pepper
1 (5 fl oz/142 ml) carton natural yoghourt
chopped chives for garnish

Pour the stock into a saucepan and heat gently until boiling. Peel the beetroot and grate it coarsely into the stock. Simmer the soup for 15 minutes. Taste and adjust seasoning. Pour the soup into 4 individual serving bowls and spoon some of the yoghourt on top of each. Garnish with chopped chives.

Main Courses

Cheese and Onion Topped Cutlets

Serves: 4 people
Preparation time:
10 minutes
Cooking time:
7–10 minutes

This stuffing not only makes the fish tastier but it also helps to make a more substantial meal. Use any inexpensive white fish.

4 (4 oz/100 g) fish cutlets
2 oz/50 g cheese, grated
½ level teaspoon mixed dried herbs
1 small onion, finely chopped
1 egg, beaten
salt and pepper
½ level teaspoon dry mustard
1 oz/25 g margarine
4 tomatoes for serving
parsley and lemon wedges for garnish

Wash and dry the fish, remove the bone and skin if necessary. Put the cheese into a bowl with the herbs and onion. Add enough beaten egg to make a soft mixture. Season with salt, pepper and mustard. Put the margarine in a grill pan and heat under a very hot grill until sizzling.

Put the cutlets in the pan, then spread the stuffing on top and cook under the hot grill for 7–10 minutes or until the fish is cooked. Cut the tomatoes in half and cook beside the fish. Serve the fish with the grilled tomatoes. Garnish with parsley and lemon wedges.

Baked Fish with Pasta Shells

Serves: 4 people
Preparation time:
10 minutes
Cooking time:
50 minutes
Oven temperature:
400°F/200°C Mark 6

Lemon and parsley flavoured pasta is a good accompaniment to fish. Use any inexpensive white fish – haddock, cod, coley, snapper and so on.

4 white fish cutlets or steaks
salt and pepper
2 oz/50 g cheese, grated
3 oz/75 g margarine or butter
¼ pint/1·5 dl cider or fish stock
2 tomatoes
6 oz/175 g pasta shells
2 level teaspoons grated lemon rind
2–3 level teaspoons chopped parsley
parsley for garnish

Place the fish in a lightly greased ovenproof dish. Sprinkle with salt and pepper. Cover the fish with grated cheese and dot with 1 oz/25 g of the margarine or butter. Pour in the cider or fish stock. Cover the dish with greaseproof paper and bake the fish in a hot oven (400°F/200°C Mark 6) for 20 minutes. Cut the tomatoes in half and put them beside the fish in the dish. Dot with margarine and sprinkle with salt and pepper. Continue cooking,

uncovered, for 15 minutes or until the fish is golden. Meanwhile, cook the pasta in a large saucepan with 3 pints/1½ litres boiling salted water for 12 minutes, or until just tender. Drain well, in a colander. Melt the remaining margarine or butter in the saucepan. Add the shells, lemon rind, parsley, salt and pepper. Just before serving, spoon the pasta round the cooked fish. Serve garnished with a sprig of parsley.

33

Fish with Egg and Herb Sauce

Serves: 4 people
Preparation time:
10 minutes
Cooking time:
20 minutes

Use white fish such as haddock, whiting, cod or snapper as available. The herbs too can be used according to which are in season and can be obtained fresh.

4 fish steaks
½ pint/3 dl milk
1 bay leaf
salt and pepper
1 oz/25 g margarine
1 oz/25 g plain flour
1 level tablespoon chopped fresh herbs (e.g. parsley, dill or tarragon)
1 egg yolk
1 teaspoon lemon juice
1 hard-boiled egg and parsley for garnish

Wash the fish steaks and put them in a shallow saucepan with the milk and the bay leaf. Season with salt and pepper, then bring to the boil and simmer for about 15 minutes or until the fish is cooked and will flake easily. Drain the fish and keep hot. Measure the cooking liquid (remove the bay leaf) and make up to ½ pint/3 dl again with water if necessary. Melt the margarine in a saucepan, stir in the flour and cook stirring constantly, for 2–3 minutes. Blend in the cooking liquid and bring to the boil, stirring. Cook for 2 minutes. Remove from the heat, season to taste and stir in the herbs, egg yolk and lemon juice. Arrange the fish on a serving dish and pour over the sauce. Garnish with chopped hard-boiled egg and parsley. Serve with green vegetables in season.

Pasta Brunch

Serves: 4–6 people
Preparation time:
10 minutes
Cooking time:
30 minutes

Serve this unusual dish for a quick supper or a delicious brunch. Use smoked haddock, cod or other fish which is inexpensive at the time. The spaghetti and fish must be piping hot when the eggs are added.

8 oz/225 g spaghetti
salt
2 oz/50 g butter
1 level tablespoon chopped parsley
freshly ground black pepper
12 oz/350 g smoked fish
lemon juice
3 eggs

Put 4 pints/2 litres of salted water in a large pan, bring to the boil. Add the spaghetti and cook for about 10–15 minutes or until just tender. Drain well in a colander, then return to the saucepan and add the butter and parsley and season with black pepper. Keep hot. Meanwhile, put the fish in a shallow pan with enough water to almost cover it. Bring to the boil then poach the fish until it flakes easily (about 15 minutes). Drain, flake and mix into the spaghetti. Season to taste with lemon juice. Have ready a hot serving bowl and put the fish and spaghetti into it. Beat the eggs and stir into the bowl. Mix thoroughly with wooden pasta forks or salad servers.

Crispy Topped Fish Pie

Serves: 4–5 people
Preparation time:
10 minutes
Cooking time:
55 minutes
Oven temperature:
375°F/190°C Mark 5

A simple and convenient recipe for making a little fish serve a number of people. Use frozen fish for convenience.

12 oz/350 g haddock
  fillets
salt and pepper
1 small onion,
  thinly sliced
¼ pint/1·5 dl milk
¾ oz/20 g margarine
  or butter
¾ oz/20 g plain flour
3 oz/75 g cheese,
  grated
3 large tomatoes,
  skinned and sliced
1 small packet of
  potato crisps

Cut the fish into ½–1 inch/12–25 mm strips and place in a lightly greased 2 pint/1 litre capacity ovenproof dish. Season, arrange the onion on top, pour over the milk and cover the dish. Bake in a moderately hot oven (375°F/190°C Mark 5) for 30 minutes. Melt the margarine in a saucepan, stir in the flour and cook, stirring, for 2 minutes. Pour off the liquor from the cooked fish. Keep the fish hot. Blend the liquor into the saucepan, bring to the boil, stirring constantly, cook for 2 minutes. Remove the pan from the heat and stir in 2 oz/50 g of the cheese. Taste and adjust seasoning. Place the tomato slices over the fish and pour the sauce on top. Crush the crisps lightly and sprinkle them and the remaining cheese on top. Return the casserole to the oven for about 20 minutes or until lightly browned. Serve very hot.

Whiting Meunière

Serves: 4 people
Preparation time:
10 minutes
Cooking time:
5 minutes

A very quick, easy and delicious way of cooking fish. Whiting is particularly inexpensive; other fish such as flounder, plaice and flathead, can be served in the same way.

4 (6 oz/175 g)
  whiting fillets
plain flour
salt and pepper
1 egg
4 oz/100 g butter
  or margarine
1 level tablespoon
  chopped parsley
1 tablespoon lemon
  juice

Wash and dry the fish fillets. Mix the flour with salt and pepper. Beat the egg lightly, on a plate. Dip the fish into the seasoned flour then in beaten egg. Heat the butter or margarine in a large frying pan. Fry the fillets until golden brown on both sides, turning once. Put the fish on a heated serving dish. Add the parsley and the lemon juice to the frying pan, heat until beginning to brown. Pour the butter over the fillets. Serve as soon as possible.

35

Fish with Bananas

Serves: 2 people
Preparation time:
5 minutes
Cooking time:
10–15 minutes

Use plaice, flounder
or flathead fillets,
whichever is good
value at the time.

2 rashers streaky
  bacon
1 oz/25 g margarine
2 fish fillets
2 bananas

Remove the rinds from the bacon. Spread each rasher to twice its length. Cut each rasher in half and roll up. Cook the bacon rolls in the grill pan under a hot grill, until cooked and golden. Remove from the pan and keep hot. Melt half the margarine in the grill pan and put in the fish, skin-side down. Cook under a hot grill, basting occasionally with the margarine. Melt the remaining margarine in a frying pan. Slice the bananas in half lengthwise and fry them in the margarine, turning once. Put the fish on a serving plate and top with the bananas and bacon rolls.

Herbed Fish Parcels

Serves: 4–6 people
Preparation time:
10 minutes
Cooking time:
30 minutes
Oven temperature:
400°F/200°C Mark 6

Serve as a starter or
as a main course.
Serve the fish in the
foil at a barbecue.
Use cod, coley or
snapper. Other herbs
can be used instead
of parsley if liked.

1 lb/$\frac{1}{2}$ kg white fish
1 small onion, finely
  chopped
4 tablespoons oil
4 teaspoons lemon
  juice
4 teaspoons chopped
  parsley
salt and pepper

Skin the fish and cut into 4 or 6 portions. Place each piece of fish on a lightly oiled square of foil. Sprinkle with onion, oil, lemon juice, parsley, salt and pepper. Fold up the foil to make 4 or 6 parcels. Fold the edges together. Cook over a hot fire or in a hot oven (400°F/200°C Mark 6) for 30 minutes or until the fish is cooked. Serve very hot.

Fish Kebabs on Curry Rice

Serves: 4 people
Preparation time:
10 minutes plus
marinating time
Cooking time:
20–25 minutes

Use any white fish
which is an
economical buy at
the time, whiting,
haddock, coley,
snapper, jewfish and
so on.

1 lb/½ kg white fish
vinegar
celery salt
Worcestershire sauce
2 level teaspoons
 chopped parsley
1 oz/25 g margarine
8 oz/225 g long
 grain rice
1–2 level teaspoons
 curry powder or to
 taste
1 level teaspoon salt
½ cucumber
1 onion
8 oz/225 g tomatoes
4 oz/100 g button
 mushrooms
salt and pepper
oil for brushing

Wash the fish, dry and place in a shallow dish. Sprinkle with a little vinegar, celery salt, Worcestershire sauce and the parsley. Put aside for 1–2 hours. Heat the margarine in a saucepan and fry the rice, stirring, for 2 minutes. Stir in the curry powder then add the salt and ¾ pint/4.5 dl water. Bring to the boil, then stir once; cover the pan tightly and simmer for 15 minutes or until the rice is tender and all the liquid absorbed. Put the rice in a serving dish and keep hot. Cut the fish into large cubes. Wipe the cucumber and cut into ¼ inch/6 mm slices. Cut the onion and tomatoes into quarters. Thread the fish cubes, onion, cucumber, tomatoes and button mushrooms onto 4 skewers. Season with salt and pepper. Brush the kebabs with oil and cook them over a hot fire (or under a hot grill) until browned all over. Serve the kebabs on the rice.

Prawn Risotto

Serves: 4 people
Preparation time:
10 minutes
Cooking time:
25 minutes

Prawns are a luxury
which go a long way
in a risotto. If the
budget is really tight
use mussels or
cockles instead.

1 oz/25 g margarine
1 small onion,
 chopped
2 oz/50 g
 mushrooms, sliced
8 oz/225 g long
 grain rice
¾ pint/4.5 dl chicken
 stock or water and
 chicken stock cube
1 small packet
 frozen peas
1 small red pepper,
 diced
4 oz/100 g peeled
 prawns
chopped parsley
 for garnish
lemon wedges for
 serving

Melt the margarine in a large saucepan and fry the onion until softened. Add the mushrooms and cook, stirring, for 1–2 minutes more. Add the rice and the stock. Bring to the boil, cover the pan, and cook for 10 minutes. Stir in the peas, pepper and prawns, bring to the boil again. Cover the pan and continue cooking for a further 10 minutes or until the rice is tender and the liquid absorbed. Garnish with chopped parsley and serve with lemon wedges.

Herrings with Tomato Sauce

Serves: 4 people
Preparation time:
10 minutes
Cooking time:
25 minutes

Herrings are an oily fish and are unlikely to need extra fat while being grilled. The tomato sauce is also good with grilled mackerel.

1 tablespoon oil
1 large onion, sliced
1 (14 oz/396 g) can tomatoes, roughly chopped
1 clove garlic, crushed
1 level teaspoon dried marjoram
1 level teaspoon sugar
salt and pepper
4 herrings

Make the sauce: Heat the oil in a saucepan and fry the onion gently for 5 minutes, until transparent but not brown. Add the can of tomatoes, garlic, marjoram, sugar, salt and pepper. Bring to the boil, then cover the pan and simmer for 20 minutes.

Meanwhile clean and bone the fish or ask your fishmonger to do this for you. Make three cuts in the flesh at the thickest part on each side. This allows the heat to penetrate the flesh more evenly and prevents the fish splitting. Place under a hot grill for about 10–15 minutes, or until the fish is cooked.

Place the fish on a heated serving dish and pour over the sauce. The sauce may be sieved if a smooth texture is preferred.

Fish Curry

Serves: 4 people
Preparation time:
10 minutes
Cooking time:
25 minutes

An extremely economical meal at any time. Even if you are not slimming, try serving this curry with cauliflower instead of rice. Cauliflowers are most plentiful in the late summer and autumn.

1½ lb/¾ kg coley, cod or other white fish
1 tablespoon lemon juice
2 onions
1 bay leaf
6 peppercorns
1 small apple
1 oz/25 g margarine
1 oz/25 g plain flour
1 level tablespoon curry powder or to taste
salt
1 cauliflower for serving

Place the fish in a saucepan with water to cover, add the lemon juice, one of the onions peeled and sliced, the bay leaf and peppercorns. Bring to the boil, then cover the pan and simmer gently for 15 minutes or until the fish is cooked. Cool, strain the liquid and reserve. Remove the skin and bones from the fish and flake. Peel and chop the remaining onion; peel, core and chop the apple. Melt the margarine gently in a clean pan. Fry the onion and apple in the margarine until softened but not browned. Stir in the flour and curry powder and cook, stirring, for 2–3 minutes. Measure ½ pint/3 dl of the reserved fish stock and add it slowly to the pan, stirring, until boiling, thickened and smooth. Cook for 2–3 minutes. Add the cooked fish. Adjust the seasoning. Meanwhile wash the cauliflower and cook in boiling salted water. Drain and arrange it round a serving dish. Pour the fish into the middle and serve.

Lamb with Yoghourt

Serves: 4 people
Preparation time:
5 minutes plus
marinating time
Cooking time:
10 minutes

Use middle neck chops or, for a really economical meal, breast of lamb cut into thick slices. Serve with freshly boiled rice.

1½ lb/¾ kg lamb
1 (5 fl oz/142 ml) carton yoghourt
1 small onion, grated
1 level tablespoon curry powder or to taste
¼ level teaspoon each ground ginger, cinnamon and cloves
1 tablespoon oil
1 tablespoon lemon juice
salt and pepper

Trim the lamb and put into a shallow dish. Mix all the remaining ingredients together and pour over the lamb. Marinate the meat for 3–4 hours, turning occasionally.

Cook the lamb over a hot fire (or under a hot grill) until tender. Baste frequently with the marinade. Heat any remaining marinade gently and serve as a sauce.

Lamb Florentine

Serves: 4 people
Preparation time:
10 minutes
Cooking time:
20 minutes

Fresh spinach is available all the year. You could, however, use frozen spinach for speed. For a real budget meal, use nettles instead; they are a good substitute for spinach. This dish is a meal on its own.

4 or 8 lamb chops
1 oz/25 g margarine
4 tomatoes
1 small onion, chopped
2 lb/1 kg fresh spinach
1 teaspoon salt
¼ level teaspoon grated nutmeg
3 tablespoons top-of-the-milk

Trim the chops of excess fat and put on a rack in the grill pan. Dot with half the margarine. Grill the chops for 10 minutes, turning occasionally. Cut the tomatoes in half and grill them alongside the chops. Melt the remaining margarine in a large saucepan. Fry the onion until softened. Wash the spinach thoroughly and put it in the pan with the onion and the salt.

Cover the pan and cook very gently for 7–10 minutes until the spinach is cooked. Press the spinach and onion through a sieve or purée in an electric blender. Return the purée to the pan and stir in the nutmeg and the top-of-the-milk. Reheat. Arrange the spinach in a serving dish and arrange the chops and tomatoes on top.

Turmeric Lamb Chops

Serves: 4 people
Preparation time:
5 minutes
Cooking time:
15–20 minutes

An excellent way to
serve lamb chops for
a special occasion.

¼ level teaspoon
  turmeric
2 teaspoons hot
  water
1 (¼ pint/142 ml)
  carton soured
  cream
1 small onion
1 clove garlic,
  crushed
salt and pepper
4 lamb chump chops

Place the turmeric in a small bowl and mix with the hot water. Cool, then stir in the soured cream. Grate the onion into the bowl and add the crushed garlic and salt and pepper. Stir well together. Place the chops under a hot grill and cook for about 7–10 minutes on each side, depending on the thickness. Leave the chops on the grill rack and spread them with the turmeric mixture. Return under the grill for a further 5 minutes. Serve.

Lamb Chops Rosemary

Serves: 4 people
Preparation time:
5 minutes
Cooking time:
About 10 minutes

A quick and delicious
way of cooking lamb
chops. If you are
doubtful as to how
tender the chops are,
marinate them in oil.

4 lamb chops
1 tablespoon oil
1 level teaspoon
  chopped dried
  rosemary
1 clove garlic,
  crushed (optional)
salt and pepper
parsley for garnish

Trim the chops, if necessary, and wipe with a damp cloth. Put the oil in a small bowl with the rosemary, garlic, salt and pepper. Mix well. Rub the oil mixture all over the chops. If time allows, marinate the chops in the oil for 30 minutes. Cook under a hot grill for about 10 minutes or until cooked. Serve garnished with parsley.

Lamb Paprika-Style

Serves: 4–8 people
Preparation time:
10 minutes
Cooking time:
25 minutes

The mushrooms in this dish make it suitable to serve when entertaining. Only one other vegetable need be served; a salad or green vegetable in season would be ideal. Mushrooms are good value at all times of the year. Use breast of lamb, cut into ribs, for family meals.

1 oz/25 g butter or margarine
8 oz/225 g button mushrooms
salt and pepper
½ pint/3 dl tomato juice
2 level teaspoons paprika pepper
1 teaspoon Worcestershire sauce
4–8 lamb cutlets
watercress for garnish

Melt the butter or margarine in a large frying pan. Add the mushrooms and sprinkle with salt and pepper. Cook, stirring frequently, for 3 minutes. Pour in the tomato juice, paprika pepper and Worcestershire sauce. Bring to the boil and simmer for 10 minutes. Mean-while, put the lamb cutlets in a grill pan, season with salt and pepper and grill for about 10 minutes or until tender, turning once. Place the meat on a serving dish and pour over the mushrooms and sauce. Serve garnished with watercress.

Braised Lamb Shanks

Serves: 4 people
Preparation time:
10 minutes
Cooking time:
About 2 hours

If lamb shanks are unobtainable, use middle neck chops instead. If you own a freezer, cut the shanks off the lamb shoulders before roasting and save them for this recipe.

2 tablespoons oil
4 lamb shanks
1 onion, chopped
1 clove garlic, crushed
1 carrot, sliced
1 stick celery, sliced
1 (14 oz/398 g) can tomatoes
1 level teaspoon salt
½ level teaspoon pepper
½ level teaspoon sugar
5 tablespoons stock or water
1 teaspoon Worcestershire sauce
parsley for garnish

Heat the oil in a large heavy-based saucepan. Add the lamb shanks and fry until browned all over. Remove the shanks and drain off most of the fat. Return to the heat, add the onion, garlic, carrot and celery, and cook for about 5 minutes or until the onion is soft, stirring frequently. Stir in the can of tomatoes, salt, pepper, sugar, stock or water and Worcestershire sauce. Return the shanks to the pan, cover and simmer for 1½–2 hours or until the meat is tender. Add more liquid if necessary. Serve garnished with parsley.

Lamb and Peach Bake

Serves: 4 people
Preparation time:
10 minutes
Cooking time:
25 minutes
Oven temperature:
375°F/190°C Mark 5

A very quick and special way of using up leftover cooked lamb.

8 oz/225 g cooked
   lamb
2 small packets
   potato crisps
1 small packet frozen
   peas
2 oz/50 g cheese,
   grated
1 (10 oz/284 g) can
   cream of celery
   soup
1 (15 oz/426 g) can
   peach slices

Cut the lamb into ½ inch/1 cm cubes. Arrange three-quarters of the crisps in a casserole dish. Then add the lamb, peas and three-quarters of the grated cheese in layers. Pour the soup over the top. Cover and bake in a moderately hot oven (375°F/190°C Mark 5) for 20 minutes. Drain the peach slices and arrange them on top of the casserole. Sprinkle with the remaining cheese and brown under a hot grill for a few minutes. Sprinkle on the rest of the crisps and serve.

Barbecued Chops with Curry Sauce

Serves: 4 people
Preparation time:
10 minutes
Cooking time:
25 minutes

Lamb chops are good barbecue fare; they are easy to eat out-of-doors.

4 lamb chops
ground ginger
salt
1 tablespoon oil
1 onion, chopped
1 clove garlic,
   crushed
1 level tablespoon
   curry powder or to
   taste
1 teaspoon tabasco
   sauce
1 (8 oz/226 g) can
   tomatoes
4 tablespoons water

Trim the chops and rub a little ground ginger and salt into each one. Grill the chops over a hot fire (or under a hot grill) for about 15–20 minutes or until tender. Meanwhile, heat the oil in a saucepan and fry the onion until softened. Stir in the garlic and curry powder. Cook for 2 minutes. Add all the remaining ingredients and bring to the boil. Cover the pan and simmer for 5 minutes. Serve some sauce over each chop.

Chinese Roast Pork

Serves: 4–6 people
Preparation time:
10 minutes plus
marinating time
Cooking time:
40–45 minutes
Oven temperature:
425°F/220°C Mark 7
then 350°F/180°C
Mark 4

For special occasions use pork fillet, but a piece of boned belly of pork, rolled and tied if necessary, is more economical for everyday meals. If a larger joint is to be cooked, allow 35 minutes per lb/ 500 g roasting time. Serve with rice and a salad.

1 lb/500 g boneless
  pork joint
1 level tablespoon
  tomato purée
1 level teaspoon
  ground fennel
1 tablespoon soy
  sauce
½ level tablespoon
  soft brown sugar
1 clove garlic,
  crushed
1 level teaspoon
  finely chopped
  fresh ginger
oil for brushing

Trim the pork and remove the skin, but keep it in one piece. Mix together the remaining ingredients, except the oil, in a small bowl. Place the meat in a dish, brush with oil and coat with the sauce. Leave to marinate for 1–2 hours. Place the pork on a rack in a roasting pan and brush it lightly with oil. Roast in a hot oven (425°F/220°C Mark 7) for 10 minutes. Reduce the oven to moderate (350°F/180°C Mark 4) and roast for a further 30–35 minutes. Serve hot or cold.

Grilled Pork Susanna

Serves: 4 people
Preparation time:
5 minutes
Cooking time:
20 minutes

Use up scraps of cheese to make this delicious topping.

4 rashers belly pork
6 oz/175 g cheese,
  grated
½ level tablespoon
  prepared mustard
4 tablespoons cider
  or beer
1 tomato, sliced, for
  garnish

Grill the pork rashers for 5–7 minutes on each side. Mix the cheese, mustard and cider or beer together, in a bowl. Spread the topping equally over the pork rashers. Grill until brown. Garnish with a slice of tomato.

Somerset Pork with Cider Sauce

Serves: 4 people
Preparation time:
10 minutes
Cooking time:
15 minutes

A good dish for entertaining. For family meals use belly pork rashers or spare rib chops with this delicious sauce.

8 thin slices fillet end leg of pork
2 level tablespoons plain flour
salt and pepper
2 oz/50 g butter or margarine
1 large onion, finely chopped
6 oz/175 g mushrooms, sliced
½ pint/3 dl dry cider
4 tablespoons cream or top-of-the-milk
chopped parsley for garnish

Place each piece of pork between 2 sheets of polythene and beat with a meat mallet or wooden rolling pin until ¼ inch/6 mm thick. Season the flour with salt and pepper and coat the pork. Heat the butter in a large frying pan and cook the pork for about 3 minutes on each side (longer if thicker cuts of pork are used). Drain well and keep hot. Add the onion and mushrooms to the frying pan and cook gently, stirring, until they are tender but not browned. Stir in any remaining flour and cook, stirring, for 2 minutes. Remove the pan from the heat and blend in the cider. Return to the heat and bring to the boil, stirring all the time. Boil for 2 minutes. Add the cooked pork and seasoning and stir in the cream. Reheat, if necessary, but do not allow to boil. Serve garnished with chopped parsley.

Gingered Pork Chops with Pineapple

Serves: 2 people
Preparation time:
10 minutes
Cooking time:
45 minutes
Oven temperature:
375°F/190°C Mark 5

You could use loin chops for this recipe but they are more expensive. Belly pork rashers are also good, and inexpensive.

2 spare rib pork chops
1 level tablespoon brown sugar
1 tablespoon vinegar
1 level teaspoon ground ginger
2 teaspoons Worcestershire sauce
salt and pepper
1 (8 oz/226 g) can pineapple pieces
watercress for garnish

Put the chops in a shallow oven-proof dish. Mix together in a small bowl the sugar, vinegar, ground ginger. Worcestershire sauce, salt and pepper and 2 tablespoons syrup from the canned pineapple. Pour over the chops, and cook, un-covered, in a moderately hot oven (375°F/190°C Mark 5) for 30 minutes or until the chops are almost cooked. Baste once with the sauce. Drain the pineapple and scatter it over the chops. Continue cooking for 10–15 minutes. Serve garnished with watercress.

Pork Chops with Creamy Curry Sauce

Serves: 4 people
Preparation time:
10 minutes
Cooking time:
30 minutes

Curried pork makes a deliciously different meal. Use spare rib chops or, for a really economical meal, belly pork rashers. Serve with small bowls of raisins, mango chutney, desiccated coconut and other curry accompaniments.

4 pork chops
4 tomatoes, skinned
4 pineapple rings
4 bananas, peeled
8 oz/225 g long
  grain rice
¾ pint/4·5 dl water
salt and pepper
1½ oz/40 g margarine
1½ oz/40 g plain
  flour
1 level tablespoon
  curry powder or
  to taste
1 pint/6 dl milk
extra curry powder
  (optional)
lettuce and parsley
  for garnish

Cook the chops under a hot grill for about 20 minutes or until tender, turning occasionally. Add the tomatoes to the grill pan after 10 minutes. Add the pineapple rings and bananas after 15 minutes so that they are heated through. Keep the chops and fruit hot. Meanwhile put the rice in a saucepan with the water and 2 level teaspoons salt. Bring to the boil, stir, then cover the pan tightly. Simmer for 15 minutes or until the rice is cooked and the liquid absorbed. Make the sauce: Melt the margarine in a saucepan and stir in the flour and curry powder. Cook, stirring, for 2–3 minutes. Blend in the milk, then bring to the boil, stirring constantly. Cook, stirring, for 2–3 minutes. Taste and adjust the seasoning. Put the rice on a serving plate and sprinkle with a little curry powder if liked. Arrange the chops on top and decorate with the fruit and tomatoes. Garnish with lettuce and parsley. Serve the curry sauce separately.

Slow Roast Spare Ribs

Serves: 4 people
Preparation time:
5 minutes
Cooking time:
1½–2 hours
Oven temperature:
300°F/150°C Mark 2

Ask your butcher for Chinese-style spare ribs in one piece. This inexpensive roast is best eaten with your fingers. Serve with potato crisps and a barbecue sauce if liked.

3–4 lb/1½–2 kg pork
  spare ribs
salt and pepper
1 level teaspoon
  dried rosemary

Wipe the pork and put it in a roasting pan. Sprinkle liberally with salt, a little pepper and the rosemary. Roast in a slow oven (300°F/150°C Mark 2) for 1½–2 hours. Cut the pork into individual ribs and serve hot.

45

Pineapple Pork Rashers

Serves: 4 people
Preparation time:
10 minutes
Cooking time:
15–20 minutes

This recipe can be used with other cuts of pork but it will then be more expensive.

1 lb/½ kg belly pork
2 tablespoons vinegar
1 (15½ oz/440 g) can pineapple pieces
2 level tablespoons tomato purée
1 level tablespoon brown sugar
1 small onion, finely chopped
1 teaspoon Worcestershire sauce
salt and pepper
½ level teaspoon mixed dried herbs
few drops chilli sauce

Slice the pork into rashers or ask your butcher to do this for you. Mix all the remaining ingredients together in a saucepan and bring to the boil, stirring. Simmer for 5 minutes. Cook the pork over a hot fire or under a hot grill for 15–20 minutes until cooked and golden. Brush the meat occasionally with the sauce. Serve the remaining sauce poured over the cooked pork.

Devilled Spare Rib Pork Chops

Serves: 4 people
Preparation time:
10 minutes
Cooking time:
20–25 minutes

The nuts on these inexpensive chops give them a lovely crunchy texture.

1 level tablespoon prepared mustard
1 level tablespoon brown sugar
1 tablespoon melted butter or margarine
salt and pepper
4 spare rib pork chops
2 oz/50 g cashew nuts or peanuts, chopped
chutney
potato crisps

Combine the mustard, sugar, butter and salt and pepper to taste in a small bowl. Spread the mixture equally over each chop. Grill under a medium hot grill until tender. Sprinkle the nuts over the chops and return to the grill until the nuts have browned. Serve the chops immediately, accompanied by chutney and potato crisps.

Baked Apricot Bacon

Serves: 8 people
Preparation time:
10 minutes
Cooking time:
1 hour 50 minutes
Oven temperature:
350°F/180°C Mark 4
then 425°F/220°C
Mark 7

Choose an inexpensive joint of bacon such as collar or forehock. Remove any bones and roll if necessary.

4 lb/2 kg bacon joint
1 bay leaf
1 small can apricot halves
1 tablespoon vinegar
watercress and cherries for garnish

Put the joint in a large saucepan and cover with cold water. Bring to the boil, then drain and replace with fresh cold water. Bring to the boil again, add the bay leaf, then simmer gently for 1 hour. Drain and wrap in foil. Bake in a moderate oven (350°F/180°C Mark 4) for 30 minutes. Remove from the oven, peel off the skin. Mix 3 tablespoons of the syrup from the can of apricot halves with the vinegar. Spoon the mixture over the bacon. Cook in a hot oven (425°F/220°C Mark 7) for 10 minutes. Baste 2 or 3 times. The joint should be browned. Heat the apricot halves in the remaining syrup. Serve the bacon garnished with the apricot halves, cherries and watercress.

Country Risotto

Serves: 4 people
Preparation time:
10 minutes
Cooking time:
25 minutes

Use up the remains of a bacon joint this way. Cooked beef or pork could be used instead of bacon.

2 tablespoons oil
8 oz/225 g long grain rice
1 (1½ pint/852 ml) packet Florida (or spring vegetable) soup
1 pint/6 dl water
1 (7½ oz/213 g) can button mushrooms
6 oz/175 g cooked ham or bacon, chopped
salt and pepper
Parmesan cheese for serving

Heat the oil in a large saucepan and fry the rice, stirring continuously, for 2–3 minutes without browning. Add the contents of the packet of soup and the water. Bring to the boil, then cover the pan and simmer gently for 10 minutes. Drain the mushrooms and add them to the saucepan with the ham. Bring to the boil again, then simmer as before for a further 10–15 minutes or until all the water is absorbed. Taste and adjust the seasoning. Serve piping hot, sprinkled with grated Parmesan cheese.

Ham and Cottage Cheese Salad

Serves: 4 people
Preparation time:
10 minutes
Cooking time:
None

Serve this salad as a supper dish or light summer lunch with slices of fresh French bread.

8 oz/225 g cottage cheese
salt and pepper
1 inch/25 mm cucumber, chopped
pinch of curry powder
4 slices ham
few strips red or green pepper and cress for garnish

Combine the cottage cheese, seasoning, cucumber and curry powder. Divide between the slices of ham and roll up. Arrange strips of red or green pepper across each ham roll and garnish with cress.

Ham and Tomato Pancakes

Serves: 2 people
Preparation time:
10 minutes
Cooking time:
20 minutes

A quickly prepared supper for two. Use leftover cold meat instead of bacon, if available.

2 oz/50 g plain flour
salt and pepper
1 egg
¼ pint/1·5 dl milk
lard
4 rashers streaky bacon, chopped
1 (8 oz/226 g) can tomatoes
1 small packet frozen mixed vegetables
Worcestershire sauce
pinch of sugar

Sift the flour with a pinch of salt into a mixing bowl. Make a well in the centre and add the egg. Mix the egg into the flour, then gradually add the milk, beating well all the time. Heat a little lard in a 7 inch/18 cm frying pan and add a quarter of the batter. Cook until golden brown underneath, then turn over and cook on the other side until golden. Fry 3 more pancakes in the same way. Place the pancakes on a plate over a pan of hot water until needed. Fry the bacon until beginning to brown. Add the tomatoes and mixed vegetables. Bring to the boil, stirring, then boil rapidly until beginning to thicken. Season and add a dash of Worcestershire sauce and the sugar. Place a quarter of the mixture on each pancake and roll up tightly. Serve piping hot.

48

Steak and Bean Hot Pot

Serves: 4–6 people
Preparation time:
10 minutes plus
soaking time for
the beans
Cooking time:
2–2½ hours
Oven temperature:
325°F/170°C Mark 3

A very substantial
'meal-in-a-dish'.
Choose an
inexpensive cut of
beef such as blade,
chuck steak or skirt.
For a variation, use
stewing lamb.

8 oz/225 g haricot
  beans
1 lb/½ kg stewing
  steak
1 oz/25 g plain flour
salt and pepper
8 oz/225 g parsnips,
  sliced
8 oz/225 g carrots,
  sliced
2 level teaspoons
  dried thyme

Soak the beans in cold water to cover, overnight. Trim excess fat off the meat and cut into 1 inch/25 mm cubes. Mix the flour with salt and pepper. Coat the meat in the seasoned flour. Mix the meat, drained beans, parsnips, carrots and thyme in a casserole. Season to taste. Add enough water to cover. Cover the casserole and cook in a moderately slow oven (325°F/170°C Mark 3) for 2–2½ hours or until the meat is tender.

Corned Beef and Onion Hash

Serves: 4 people
Preparation time:
10 minutes
Cooking time:
10 minutes

If you have cold
mashed potatoes left
over use them instead
of the instant potato.

1 tablespoon oil
2 onions, sliced
1 (7 oz/199 g) can
  corned beef,
  chopped
1 (7½ oz/213 g) can
  baked beans
3 level tablespoons
  tomato ketchup
pinch of mixed dried
  herbs
1 (2½ oz/71 g) packet
  instant potato
salt and pepper
chopped parsley

Heat the oil in a large frying pan, add the onion and fry until tender. Chop the corned beef finely and add it to the onions with the baked beans, tomato ketchup and herbs. Make up the potato as directed on the side of the packet and stir it into the ingredients in the frying pan. Add salt and pepper according to taste. Serve garnished with chopped parsley.

Boiled Salt (Corned) Beef

Serves: 6–8 people
Preparation time:
10 minutes plus
soaking time for
the meat
Cooking time:
40 minutes per lb/
½ kg plus 40 minutes
over

This is a satisfying
and inexpensive
meal. Choose salt
(corned) silverside or
brisket. Serve with a
parsley sauce if liked,
using half milk and
half the cooking
liquor.

2–3 lb/1–1½ kg
 salt beef
3 onions, peeled
1 bay leaf
12 peppercorns
1 beef stock cube
8 oz/225 g small
 carrots
Dumplings:
4 oz/100 g self
 raising flour
½ level teaspoon
 baking powder
2 oz/50 g shredded
 suet
cold water to mix

Tie the meat securely in shape with
string. Put it in a deep bowl and
cover with cold water. Soak for
3 hours or more, overnight if the
beef is very salty. Put in a large
saucepan with fresh cold water to
cover and bring to the boil. Boil for
5 minutes then skim. Add the
onions, bay leaf, peppercorns and
crumbled stock cube. Cover the
pan and simmer gently for 40
minutes per lb/½ kg plus 40 minutes
over. Add the carrots 1 hour before
cooking time is completed.

Meanwhile, make the dumplings:
Sift the flour and baking powder
into a bowl, stir in the suet and
enough water to make a dough.
Shape the dough into small balls,
about 1 inch/25 mm across. Put
the dumplings into the cooking
liquid 20 minutes before cooking
time is completed. Serve the drained
meat on a hot serving plate surrounded by the vegetables and
dumplings.

Sesame Steak

Serves: 4 people
Preparation time:
5 minutes plus
marinating time
Cooking time:
8–10 minutes

Sesame seeds are
available from health
food shops or
Oriental grocery
stores. Their flavour
is very distinctive.
Use skirt steak for a
very inexpensive
meal. Otherwise
choose top rump or
oyster blade steak.

1½ lb/¾ kg frying
 steak
¼ pint/1·5 dl oil
1 tablespoon vinegar
1 tablespoon soy
 sauce
1 level tablespoon
 sugar
1 small onion, finely
 chopped
1 clove garlic,
 crushed
salt and pepper
2 level tablespoons
 sesame seeds

Cut the steak into 1–1½ inch/
2–3 cm slices and put in a shallow
bowl. Mix all the remaining ingredients together and pour over the
steak. Cover the dish and put aside
for 8 hours or overnight. Drain the

steak and cook over a hot fire (or
under a hot grill) until tender (about
8–10 minutes). Turn occasionally
and baste frequently with the
marinade. Serve hot.

Mince Hot Pot

Serves: 6 people
Preparation time:
10 minutes
Cooking time:
45 minutes
Oven temperature:
375°F/190°C Mark 5

A complete meal in one dish. It can be made in advance if liked, but melt the margarine and brush the potato well to stop it discolouring.

1 tablespoon oil
1 onion, chopped
1 lb/½ kg minced beef
1 (8 oz/226 g) can tomatoes
1 (7¾oz/220 g) can baked beans
½ level tablespoon plain flour
½ level teaspoon meat extract
1 level teaspoon salt
½ level teaspoon pepper
1 lb/½ kg potatoes, thinly sliced
1 oz/25 g margarine
3 oz/75 g cheese, grated

Heat the oil in a frying pan and fry the onion and minced beef for 5 minutes, stirring occasionally. Stir in the can of tomatoes, baked beans, flour, meat extract, salt and pepper. Pour the mixture into a 1½ pint/ 9 dl ovenproof dish. Arrange the potato slices on top of the meat, dot with the margarine and bake in a moderately hot oven (375°F/ 190°C Mark 5) for 30 minutes. Sprinkle with the cheese and return to the oven for 10 minutes. Serve.

Chilli Con Carne

Serves: 4 people
Preparation time:
10 minutes plus soaking time for the beans
Cooking time:
30 minutes

Chilli con carne is a very hot, peppery dish. Reduce the amount of chilli powder slightly when you first make it for the family.

8 oz/225 g haricot beans
2 tablespoons oil
1 onion, chopped
1 small green pepper, chopped (optional)
2 sticks celery, chopped
½–1 level tablespoon chilli powder
1 lb/½ kg minced beef
1 (8 oz/226 g) can tomatoes
¼ pint/1·5 dl beef stock or water and beef stock cube

Place the haricot beans in a bowl, cover with cold water and soak for up to 6 hours. Heat the oil in a saucepan and fry the onion, pepper and celery very gently, stirring oc- casionally, until softened. Drain the beans, then add to the pan with all the other ingredients. Bring to the boil and simmer gently for about 30 minutes, stirring occasionally.

51

Cheesy Oven-Fried Chicken

Serves: 4 people
Preparation time:
10 minutes
Cooking time:
About 40 minutes
Oven temperature:
400°F/200°C Mark 6

This dish can be served hot or cold. It is ideal picnic fare. At home, serve with fried potatoes and a salad.

1 (2½ lb/1 kg) chicken
1 level tablespoon plain flour
salt and pepper
½ level teaspoon dry mustard
1 egg, beaten
2 oz/50 g soft white breadcrumbs
2 oz/50 g Cheddar cheese, grated
2 oz/50 g margarine

Cut the chicken into 4 portions and wipe with a damp cloth. Season the flour with salt, pepper and mustard. Coat the chicken in the flour then in beaten egg and finally in the breadcrumbs and cheese, mixed together.

Place in a roasting pan and dot with small pieces of margarine. Cook in a hot oven (400°F/200°C Mark 6) for about 40 minutes or until golden and tender.

Summer Chicken

Serves: 4 people
Preparation time:
10 minutes
Cooking time:
1½ hours
Oven temperature:
350°F/180°C Mark 4

This delicious casserole actually improves in flavour when kept overnight. Ideal for a special summer lunch.

1 (3 lb/1½ kg) chicken
2 oz/50 g plain flour
salt and pepper
1 tablespoon oil
¾ pint/4 dl chicken stock or water and chicken stock cube
bouquet garni (sprig of thyme, 1 bay leaf and 2 parsley stalks)
salt and pepper
1 oz/25 g margarine
¼ pint/1.5 dl grapefruit drink
parsley for garnish

Cut the chicken into 4 pieces. Season half the flour with salt and pepper. Coat the chicken with the seasoned flour. Heat the oil in a large frying pan, add the chicken pieces and fry until golden brown all over. Transfer the chicken to a casserole. Pour in the stock, add the bouquet garni and salt and pepper to taste. Cover the casserole and cook in a moderate oven (350°F/180°C Mark 4) for 1 hour. Meanwhile, melt the margarine in a saucepan, stir in the remaining flour and cook gently for 2–3 minutes. Remove from the heat and slowly stir in the grapefruit drink. Remove the chicken joints from the casserole and put them onto a plate. Remove and discard the bouquet garni. Pour the stock into a saucepan and bring to the boil. Boil rapidly, stirring occasionally, until reduced by half. Stir in the grapefruit mixture, return to the boil, stirring continuously, until thickened; cook for 2–3 minutes. Return the chicken to the casserole and pour over the sauce. Cool and leave in the refrigerator or cool place overnight. Reheat the next day in a moderate oven (350°F/180°C Mark 4) for 30 minutes. Serve garnished with parsley.

Devilled Chicken

Serves: 4 people
Preparation time:
10 minutes
Cooking time:
45 minutes
Oven temperature:
400°F/200°C Mark 6

This recipe is also suitable for slimmers. Use chicken joints for convenience but a whole chicken is cheaper to buy.

1 (3 lb/1½ kg) chicken
3–4 tablespoons chutney, chopped
1 level tablespoon tomato purée
¼ level teaspoon made mustard
salt and cayenne pepper
¼ level teaspoon tabasco pepper sauce

Chop the chicken into joints, wipe them and make 2 or 3 deep cuts in each. Mix all the remaining ingredients together in a bowl and stuff the cuts in the chicken.

Place the chicken in a roasting pan, cover the pan with foil and bake in a hot oven (400°F/200°C Mark 6) for 45 minutes or until the chicken is tender.

Spicy Chicken

Serves: 4 people
Preparation time:
10 minutes
Cooking time:
1 hour
Oven temperature:
400°F/200°C Mark 6

A high-protein dish which could be served with wholemeal pasta or brown rice. Use organically grown vegetables and a free-range chicken for the best flavour.

1 (3 lb/1½ kg) chicken
salt and pepper
1 tablespoon oil
2 onions, sliced
2 sticks celery, sliced
1 small green pepper, sliced (optional)
1 (14 oz/396 g) can tomatoes
3 level teaspoons horseradish sauce
3 oz/75 g Edam cheese, grated

Chop the chicken into 4 portions and place in a roasting pan. Season with salt and pepper. Roast in a hot oven (400°F/200°C Mark 6) for 30–40 minutes or until cooked. Heat the oil in a large frying pan, add the onions, celery, and pepper if liked; fry gently for about 10 minutes or until softened. Add the

tomatoes, horseradish sauce and salt and pepper to taste, fry for a further 5 minutes. Place the chicken portions in a warmed serving dish, pour over the sauce, sprinkle with the grated cheese and place under a hot grill for a few minutes to brown. Serve.

Fried Chicken Drumsticks

Serves: 4—8 people
Preparation time:
10 minutes
Cooking time:
15—20 minutes

Drumsticks can be bought individually and make ideal single portions for buffet parties or picnics. The crisp breadcrumb coating makes them more substantial.

8 chicken drumsticks
plain flour
salt and pepper
1 egg, beaten
fine dry breadcrumbs
oil for deep-frying

Dip the drumsticks in seasoned flour then in beaten egg. Finally, coat them in the breadcrumbs. Heat the oil until hot (a $\frac{1}{2}$ inch/12 mm cube of bread will brown in less than 1 minute) then fry the chicken until golden and tender, about 15—20 minutes. Drain well on absorbent kitchen paper. Serve hot or cold.

Chicken Surprise Parcels

Serves: 4 people
Preparation time:
10 minutes
Cooking time:
40 minutes
Oven temperature:
400°F/200°C Mark 6

This dish can be served hot or cold and is ideally suited for outdoor entertaining. Serve for picnics or barbecues, when the parcels can be cooked over an open fire if necessary.

4 chicken joints
salt and pepper
Worcestershire sauce
1 onion, peeled and sliced
2 oz/50 g mushrooms, sliced
1 tablespoon lemon juice
2 oz/50 g margarine

Wipe the chicken and season with salt and pepper. Place each joint in the centre of a square of foil and sprinkle with Worcestershire sauce. Put the onion and mushrooms on top, sprinkle with lemon juice then dot with margarine. Close the foil parcels, using double folds. Place on a baking tray and cook in a hot oven (400°F/200°C Mark 6) for about 40 minutes or until the chicken is tender. Fold back the foil for the last 10 minutes to allow the chicken to brown. Serve in the foil.

Chicken Rosemary

Serves: 4 people
Preparation time:
10 minutes
Cooking time:
1 hour
Oven temperature:
350°F/180°C Mark 4

An ideal dish for those on low-calorie diets. Use a free-range chicken for the best flavour.

8 oz/225 g button mushrooms
1 onion, sliced
½ level teaspoon salt
paprika pepper
1 (3 lb/1½ kg) chicken
1 (14 oz/396 g) can tomatoes
½ pint/3 dl tomato juice
2 teaspoons Worcestershire sauce
1 level teaspoon chopped rosemary
sprigs of rosemary for garnish

Place the mushrooms and onion in a shallow, ovenproof dish, sprinkle with the salt and a little paprika pepper. Chop the chicken into 4 portions and arrange them in the dish. Drain the juice from the canned tomatoes and mix it with the tomato juice and Worcestershire sauce; pour onto the chicken. Roughly slice the tomatoes and add to the dish. Sprinkle with the rosemary and salt and paprika pepper to taste. Bake in a moderate oven (350°F/180°C Mark 4) for 1 hour, basting occasionally with the juice. Serve each portion of chicken surrounded by the vegetables from the base of the casserole and a sprig of rosemary.

Chicken à la King

Serves: 4 people
Preparation time:
10 minutes
Cooking time:
40—45 minutes

An ideal way of using up leftover chicken. Very good for special occasions.

8 oz/225 g cold cooked chicken
3 oz/75 g margarine
1 onion, finely chopped
4 oz/100 g mushrooms, chopped
1 green pepper, chopped
1 (10½ oz/298 g) can condensed chicken or mushroom soup
8 oz/225 g long grain rice
salt
1 level tablespoon chopped parsley, and extra for garnish

Cut the chicken into bite-sized pieces. Melt 2 oz/50 g of the margarine in a frying pan and fry the onion until softened. Add the mushrooms and the pepper and cook, stirring, for a further 2—3 minutes. Stir in the soup and the chicken. Bring to the boil and simmer very gently for 10—15 minutes. Meanwhile, cook the rice in a large saucepan with plenty of boiling salted water for 10—15 minutes. Drain well, then stir in the parsley and the remaining margarine. Arrange the rice on a serving plate and pile the chicken mixture on top. Garnish with chopped parsley.

Hasty Sweet and Sour Chicken

Serves: 4 people
Preparation time:
10 minutes
Cooking time:
About 15 minutes

This is a quick dish to make because it uses ready-prepared sweet and sour sauce. Keep a can in your store cupboard for emergencies.

1 lb/500 g cooked chicken, diced
2 (7½ oz/213 g) cans sweet and sour sauce
6 sticks celery, sliced
4 oz/100 g mushrooms, sliced
salt and pepper
12 oz/350 g egg noodles

Place the chicken, sweet and sour sauce, celery and mushrooms in a saucepan. Heat thoroughly, stirring continuously. Taste and add salt and pepper. Meanwhile cook the egg noodles in boiling salted water as directed on the packet. Serve the noodles on a large plate and pour on the chicken mixture or serve them separately.

Chicken with Bananas

Serves: 2 people
Preparation time:
10 minutes
Cooking time:
30 minutes

Cook this dish for a quick meal at home or for a special dinner for two.

2 chicken portions
2 oz/50 g plain flour
1 level teaspoon salt
1 level teaspoon curry powder
oil for frying
2 bananas
freshly boiled rice for serving
lemon wedges for garnish

Wipe the chicken portions with a damp cloth. Toss them lightly in flour seasoned with salt and curry powder. Heat a little oil in a frying pan and fry the chicken until browned all over. Reduce the heat and cover the pan. Cook the chicken for a further 15 minutes or until tender. Slice the bananas in half and add them to the pan. Cook uncovered for a further 5 minutes. Pile the hot rice onto a serving dish. Arrange the chicken and bananas on top. Serve garnished with lemon wedges.

Chicken Livers with Peanuts

Serves: 4 people
Preparation time:
10 minutes
Cooking time:
15 minutes

This is a really quick and easy dish to prepare. You can use sliced water chestnuts instead of bamboo shoots if preferred and lamb's liver (cut into thin slices) instead of chicken livers.

2 tablespoons oil
1 (5 oz/142 g) can bamboo shoots, drained and sliced
2 oz/50 g peanuts
8 oz/225 g chicken livers
2 spring onions, finely chopped
2 tablespoons soy sauce
1 clove garlic, crushed
$\frac{1}{2}$ teaspoon root ginger, finely chopped
$\frac{1}{2}$ level teaspoon salt
1 level tablespoon brown sugar
$\frac{1}{4}$ pint/1·5 dl chicken stock or water and chicken stock cube
1 level tablespoon cornflour

Heat the oil in a large frying pan and fry the bamboo shoots and peanuts, stirring frequently, for about 5 minutes. Remove and drain on absorbent kitchen paper. Add the chicken livers to the pan and fry gently until golden brown all over. Remove from the pan and drain. Place the spring onions, soy sauce, garlic, ginger, salt, sugar and stock in the frying pan. Blend the cornflour with a little liquid in a small bowl and stir it into the frying pan. Bring to the boil, stirring, and simmer for 2–3 minutes. Return the livers to the pan and reheat. Serve in a heated dish, sprinkled with the peanuts and bamboo shoots.

Chicken Livers with Apple on Rice

Serves: 3–4 people
Preparation time:
10 minutes
Cooking time:
20 minutes

Serve this dish as a meal starter or for a light lunch or supper. Add a tablespoon of port or red wine to the gravy for special occasions.

salt
6 oz/175 g long grain rice
2 oz/50 g margarine or butter
12 oz/350 g chicken livers
1 apple, peeled, cored and sliced
1 oz/25 g plain flour
$\frac{1}{2}$ pint/3 dl chicken stock or water and chicken stock cube

Put 2 pints/1 litre salted water in a saucepan. Bring to the boil, then sprinkle in the rice. Cook, uncovered, for 12–15 minutes or until the rice is tender. Drain well in a sieve. Meanwhile, heat the margarine in a saucepan and fry the chicken livers and apple for about 5 minutes or until the livers are tender. Remove the livers and apple and keep hot. Stir in the flour and cook, stirring, for 2–3 minutes or until the flour is lightly browned. Stir in the stock, bring to the boil, stirring constantly until thickened and smooth. Cook for 2 minutes. Put the rice on a serving plate, arrange the chicken livers and apple on top and pour the gravy over. Serve as soon as possible.

Liver with Parsley and Orange

Serves: 4 people
Preparation time:
5–10 minutes
Cooking time:
7 minutes

Liver is an almost essential meat for dieters. It contains a lot of minerals and vitamins necessary for good health and is low in fat.

1 lb/½ kg lambs' or calves' liver
salt and pepper
1 tablespoon oil
1 orange
2 tablespoons chopped parsley
extra orange slices for garnish

Slice the liver into ½ inch/12 mm slices or ask your butcher to do this for you. Sprinkle with salt and pepper. Heat the oil in a frying pan and fry the liver on both sides until cooked (about 5 minutes). Remove the liver from the pan and keep hot. Pour off any oil left in the pan. Put the orange juice and finely grated rind in the pan with the parsley. Heat gently then pour over the liver. Serve garnished with orange slices.

Kidneys Sauté Turbigo

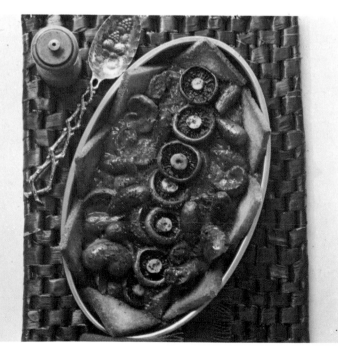

Serves: 4 people
Preparation time:
10 minutes
Cooking time:
30 minutes

An inexpensive dish which is good enough for the most special occasion.

1 oz/25 g margarine
1 carrot, sliced
1 onion, sliced
1 oz/25 g plain flour
½ pint/3 dl stock or water and beef stock cube.
salt and pepper
4 lambs' kidneys
1 tablespoon oil
4 thin sausages, halved
4 oz/100 g button mushrooms
4 slices of bread, toasted
parsley for garnish

Melt the margarine in a heavy-based saucepan. Add the carrot and onion and fry gently until beginning to brown. Stir in the flour and cook until the mixture is a good brown colour. Stir frequently and take care not to burn the mixture. Remove from the heat and gradually blend in the stock. Return to the heat and bring to the boil, stirring continuously. Cover the pan and simmer the sauce for 15 minutes. Strain the sauce through a sieve into a second saucepan. Taste for seasoning.
Prepare the kidneys: Remove the skins, cut in half and cut out the cores. Heat the oil in a frying pan and fry the kidneys for 4–5 minutes. Drain. Add the sausages to the pan and fry for about 10 minutes or until cooked. Drain. Finally fry the mushrooms, adding a little more oil if necessary. Put the kidneys into the sauce and heat through. Pour the kidney mixture into an ovenproof dish with the sausages and mushrooms on top. Cut the toast into triangles and arrange them round the dish. Sprinkle with parsley.

Dutch Cheese and Tomato Medley

Serves: 4 people
Preparation time:
5 minutes
Cooking time:
20 minutes

A very quickly prepared supper dish which is good value at any time of the year.

1 oz/25 g butter or margarine
1 clove garlic, crushed
2 large onions, chopped
8 oz/225 g bacon, chopped
4 oz/100 g mushrooms, sliced
1 (14 oz/396 g) can tomatoes
1 (14 oz/396 g) can potatoes, drained and sliced
salt and pepper
6 oz/175 g Gouda cheese, grated

Heat the butter in a large frying pan and fry the garlic for a few minutes. Add the onion, bacon and mushrooms and fry, stirring occasionally, for 5–10 minutes. Add the tomatoes, with the juice, potatoes and salt and pepper. Stir well, cook until the potatoes are hot. Remove from the heat and stir in most of the cheese, reserving just a little for garnish. Serve the medley, sprinkled with the reserved cheese.

Cheese Pudding

Serves: 4 people
Preparation time:
10 minutes plus soaking time
Cooking time:
40 minutes
Oven temperature:
400°F/200°C Mark 6

A very economical lunch or supper dish. Serve with tomato sauce.

4 oz/100 g fresh white breadcrumbs
1 pint/6 dl milk
4 oz/100 g Cheddar cheese, grated
½ small onion, finely chopped
4 eggs, separated
pinch of dry mustard

Put the breadcrumbs into a heatproof bowl. Heat the milk until almost boiling then pour it onto the breadcrumbs. Soak for 30 minutes. Stir in 3½ oz/85 g of the cheese, the onion, egg yolks and mustard. Whisk the egg whites until stiff and fold into the cheese mixture. Pour into a lightly greased 2 pint/1 litre pie dish and sprinkle the remaining cheese on top. Bake in a hot oven (400°F/200°C Mark 6) for 40 minutes or until well risen and golden. Serve hot.

Macaroni Cheese Special

Serves: 4 people
Preparation time:
10 minutes
Cooking time:
10 minutes

A meal in a dish which is exceptionally quick to make. Serve for a supper or light lunch. Make your own macaroni cheese if you have the time.

1 oz/25 g margarine
1 onion, chopped
4 rashers streaky bacon, chopped
2 (15 oz/426 g) cans macaroni cheese
1 small packet frozen mixed vegetables, cooked
1 oz/25 g cheese, grated
8 bacon rolls for garnish

Heat the margarine in a saucepan, add the onion and fry gently for 3 minutes. Stir in the bacon and fry for another 3 minutes. Add the cans of macaroni cheese and heat through, stirring. Spread the mixed vegetables in a heatproof dish, put the macaroni cheese on top and sprinkle with the cheese. Place under a hot grill until the cheese has melted and is beginning to brown. Grill the bacon rolls alongside the macaroni until cooked. Place them on top and serve.

Sweet and Sour Cheese

Serves: 4 people
Preparation time:
5 minutes
Cooking time:
10 minutes

A very quickly prepared, inexpensive and tasty meal. Serve with hot, freshly cooked rice.

1 carrot, sliced
2 sticks celery, sliced
¼ pint/1·5 dl chicken stock or water and chicken stock cube
1 (12 oz/340 g) can pineapple pieces
1 clove garlic, crushed (optional)
1 level tablespoon tomato purée
1 level teaspoon sugar
2 tablespoons vinegar
1 level tablespoon cornflour
6 oz/175 g Cheddar cheese, diced
salt and pepper

Put the carrot and celery into a saucepan with the stock. Bring to the boil, then simmer for 5 minutes. Add the pineapple, including the syrup, the garlic, tomato purée and sugar. Blend the vinegar with the cornflour and stir into the mixture. Bring to the boil, stirring all the time. Simmer for 2–3 minutes. Remove from the heat and stir in the cheese. Taste and adjust the seasoning. Serve as soon as possible.

Cheese and Cucumber Salad

Serves: 4 people
Preparation time:
10 minutes
Cooking time:
None

A quick to prepare and interesting salad which is a meal in itself. Use a firm cheese such as Edam or Cheddar.

8 oz/225 g cheese
1 small cucumber
1 lb/½ kg potatoes, peeled and cooked
4 tomatoes, skinned
Dressing:
6 tablespoons oil
2 tablespoons vinegar
1 level teaspoon tomato paste
1 level teaspoon made mustard
few drops tabasco sauce
pinch of sugar
salt and pepper to taste

Cut the cheese into ½ inch/12 mm cubes. Peel and dice the cucumber. Dice the potatoes. Slice the tomatoes. Put all the dressing ingredients into a screw-top jar. Mix the cheese, cucumber and potatoes in a bowl.

Shake all the dressing ingredients together until creamy, then pour over the salad. Toss lightly and put into a serving bowl. Arrange the tomato slices on top.

Cheesy Potato Casserole

Serves: 4 people
Preparation time:
10 minutes
Cooking time:
1 hour
Oven temperature:
325°F/170°C Mark 3

A recipe for potatoes which are cooked in the oven is always useful. Cook a casserole and a baked pudding in the same oven to save fuel.

1 lb/½ kg old potatoes
salt and pepper
2 oz/50 g Cheddar cheese, grated
½ pint/3 dl milk
2 oz/50 g margarine

Peel the potatoes and cut into ¼ inch/6 mm slices. Arrange the potatoes in layers in an ovenproof dish. Season each layer with salt and pepper and sprinkle with grated cheese. Reserve a little cheese for the top. Pour the milk

into the dish. dot the top with margarine and sprinkle the remaining cheese on top. Bake in a moderately slow oven (325°F/ 170°C Mark 3) for 1 hour or until the potatoes are tender and the top browned.

Macaroni and Eggs Lyonnaise

Serves: 4 people
Preparation time:
10 minutes
Cooking time:
20 minutes

This is an ideal lunch or supper dish for colder days. It is inexpensive and satisfying, besides being quick to prepare. Serve with a green salad or peas.

3 oz/75 g butter or margarine
8 oz/225 g onions, sliced
1½ oz/40 g plain flour
¾ pint/4 dl milk
salt and pepper
6 oz/175 g short cut macaroni
4 hard-boiled eggs
3 oz/75 g cheese, grated

Melt 2 oz/50 g of the butter or margarine in a saucepan. Add the onion and fry gently, stirring constantly, until softened and beginning to brown. Add the flour and cook, stirring, for 1–2 minutes. Blend in the milk and bring to the boil, stirring constantly. Season to taste with salt and pepper, then simmer very gently for 20 minutes. Meanwhile, put 4 pints/2 litres salted water in a large saucepan. Bring to the boil, then add the macaroni and cook for 10–12 minutes or until just tender. Drain well in a colander and stir into the sauce. Taste and adjust the seasoning. Put a layer of macaroni and sauce in the bottom of a shallow, lightly greased ovenproof dish. Cut the eggs in half lengthways and place them, cut-side down, on the macaroni. Cover the eggs with the remaining macaroni and sauce. Sprinkle with the cheese and dot with the remaining butter. Cook under a hot grill until golden and bubbling. Serve immediately.

Egg and Onion Pie

Serves: 4 people
Preparation time:
10 minutes
Cooking time:
15 minutes
Oven temperature:
450°F/230°C Mark 8

An extremely good dish for a cold evening. Add chopped bacon to the onion, for extra flavour.

3 oz/75 g margarine
3 onions, sliced
6 hard-boiled eggs
2 oz/50 g plain flour
¾ pint/4 dl milk
2 oz/50 g Cheddar cheese, grated
salt and pepper

Melt 1 oz/25 g of the margarine in a frying pan and fry the onions slowly until softened but not browned. Put the onions in the bottom of an ovenproof dish. Slice the eggs and put on top of the onions. Melt the remaining margarine in a saucepan, stir in the flour and cook for 2 minutes. Blend in the milk and bring to the boil stirring continuously. Cook for 2–3 minutes. Remove the pan from the heat and stir in 1½ oz/40 g of the cheese. Season to taste. Pour the sauce over the eggs. Sprinkle with the remaining cheese. Cook in a very hot oven (450°F/230°C Mark 8) until browned. Serve as soon as possible.

Curried Eggs

Serves: 4 people
Preparation time:
5 minutes
Cooking time:
15 minutes

Leftover cooked fish,
meat or vegetables
can be used instead
of eggs.

8 oz/225 g long grain
  rice
salt
4 eggs
1 (1½ oz/42 g) packet
  curry sauce

Cook the rice in boiling salted water for 15 minutes or until cooked; drain well. Meanwhile boil the eggs for 10 minutes, then shell them. Make the curry sauce as directed on the side of the packet. Arrange a bed of hot rice on a serving plate, cut the hot eggs in half lengthways and place on the rice. Pour over the sauce. Serve as soon as possible.

Coconut Spiced Eggs

Serves: 4 people
Preparation time:
10 minutes
Cooking time:
35 minutes

This Malayan curry
is usually served
with a tomato and
onion salad. If fresh
tomatoes are cheap,
use them in
preference to the
canned variety. Cook
8 oz/225 g long
grain rice to serve
with this dish.

2 onions, sliced
½ level teaspoon
  . chilli powder
½ inch/12 mm slice
  root ginger, finely
  chopped
1 clove garlic,
  crushed
1 (8 oz/226 g) can
  tomatoes
1 tablespoon tomato
  purée
pinch of fenugreek
pinch of ground
  turmeric
1 tablespoon lemon
  juice
1 oz/25 g desiccated
  coconut
¼ pint/1·5 dl milk
4 eggs
lemon butterflies for
  garnish

Place the onions, chilli, ginger, garlic, tomatoes, tomato purée, fenugreek, turmeric, lemon juice and coconut in a saucepan. Cook gently, stirring frequently, until the sauce is well mixed and nearly dry (about 30 minutes). Cook rapidly for 2 minutes, stirring constantly, until soft and pulpy. Stir in the milk and reheat without boiling. Hard- boil the eggs. Remove the shells, and cut the eggs in half lengthways. Place a bed of rice on a serving plate and arrange the hot hard- boiled egg halves on top. Spoon the spicy sauce over the eggs. Serve as soon as possible, gar- nished with lemon butterflies.

Country Omelette

Serves: 4 people
Preparation time:
10 minutes
Cooking time:
10 minutes

A filling and substantial omelette. You can use any vegetables you may have left over.

4 eggs
salt and pepper
2 oz/50 g margarine
2 rashers streaky
   bacon, chopped
1 onion, sliced
1 large cooked
   potato, diced
½ red pepper or
   cooked carrot,
   chopped
½ green pepper or 1
   stick celery,
   chopped

Beat the eggs together, beat in 2 tablespoons water and salt and pepper. Heat the margarine in a large frying pan and fry the bacon and onion until the onion is softened. Add the remaining vegetables and fry for a further 2–3 minutes, stirring with a fork. Pour in the beaten egg and cook quickly, stirring, until the egg is cooked underneath. Reduce the heat and continue cooking until the egg is set. Serve immediately.

Celery Custard

Serves: 4 people
Preparation time:
10 minutes
Cooking time:
35 minutes
Oven temperature:
375°F/190°C Mark 5

Serve this dish for supper or lunch. It is very light but satisfying—very good for invalids, slimmers and small children.

1 (1 lb 3 oz/540 g)
   can celery hearts
1 pint/6 dl milk
5 eggs
2 oz/50 g Cheddar
   cheese, grated
salt and pepper

Drain the celery hearts, then chop them and drain again in a sieve. Put the milk into a bowl, add the eggs and beat just until mixed. Strain the custard, then mix in the cheese and salt and pepper. Put the celery in an ovenproof dish and pour the egg mixture on top. Put the dish in a roasting pan, add enough water to come halfway up the sides of the dish. Cover the dish and the pan completely with foil. Cook in a moderately hot oven (375°F/190°C Mark 5) for 35 minutes. Serve as soon as possible.

Braised Celery with Mushrooms

Serves: 4 people
Preparation time:
10 minutes
Cooking time:
35 minutes

A delicious dish for autumn or winter, when celery and mushrooms are both readily available.

1 head celery
1 pint/6 dl chicken stock or water and chicken stock cubes
4 oz/100 g mushrooms
2 oz/50 g margarine
1 oz/25 g plain flour
¼ pint/1·5 dl milk
1 oz/25 g Cheddar cheese, grated

Scrub the celery until very clean. Put the stock in a saucepan, bring to the boil. Add the celery and cook for 20—25 minutes or until very tender. Drain the celery and put in a heatproof dish. Reserve the stock. Slice the mushrooms, fry in half the margarine. Drain well. Scatter the mushrooms over the celery. Melt the remaining margarine in a saucepan, stir in the flour and cook gently for 2—3 minutes. Add the milk and ¼ pint/1 dl of the reserved stock. Bring to the boil, stirring, then simmer for 2—3 minutes. Pour the sauce over the vegetables and sprinkle with the cheese. Cook under a hot grill until bubbling. Serve hot.

Gobi Dahl Curry

Serves: 4 people
Preparation time:
10 minutes
Cooking time:
55 minutes

An extremely inexpensive dish which is ideal for vegetarians. Lentils are cheap and good for you. Serve this curry with a selection of side salads — tomato and onion, sliced banana, or cubed melon.

4 oz/100 g lentils
1 tablespoon oil
2 onions, chopped
1—2 level tablespoons curry powder
1 level tablespoon plain flour
2 oz/50 g salted peanuts
1 oz/25 g desiccated coconut
2 tablespoons mango chutney
1 pint/6 dl white stock or water and chicken stock cube
1 medium-sized cauliflower, cut into flowerets
juice of ½ lemon
salt

Place the lentils in a saucepan and cover with cold water. Bring to the boil, cover, and simmer for 5 minutes, then drain. Heat the oil in a large saucepan and fry the onions gently, stirring occasionally, for 5 minutes or until they are soft. Stir in the curry powder and flour and cook, stirring, for 2 minutes. Add the lentils, peanuts, coconut, chutney and stock. Bring to the boil, stirring continuously, then simmer for 30 minutes. Add the cauliflower, lemon juice and salt to taste. Cover and simmer for 15 minutes. Serve hot.

Aubergine (Eggplant) Casserole

Serves: 4 people
Preparation time:
10 minutes plus
salting time
Cooking time:
35–40 minutes
Oven temperature:
350°F/180°C Mark 4

A good vegetarian
casserole. Aubergines
are at their best and
cheapest in the
summer.

3 aubergines
salt and pepper
2 tablespoons oil
3 level tablespoons
tomato ketchup or
fresh tomato sauce
2 (5 fl oz/142 ml)
cartons natural
yoghourt

Cut the aubergines into ¼ inch/ 6 mm slices. Layer the slices in a colander and sprinkle each layer with salt. Leave for 30 minutes, then rinse off any excess salt, drain well and pat dry with absorbent kitchen paper. Heat the oil in a frying pan and fry the aubergine slices until they are browned on both sides. Layer the aubergine slices in an ovenproof dish with the tomato sauce and yoghourt; sprinkle each layer with a little pepper. Cover and bake in a moderate oven (350°F/180°C Mark 4) for 35–40 minutes.

Danish Blue Cauliflower Cheese

Serves: 3–4 people
Preparation time:
10 minutes
Cooking time:
30 minutes

A tasty variation of
an old favourite.

1 medium-sized
cauliflower
salt and pepper
4 oz/100 g Danish
blue cheese
2 oz/50 g butter or
margarine
1 onion, finely
chopped
1½ oz/40 g plain
flour
½ pint/3 dl milk
3 rashers streaky
bacon

Trim the cauliflower, removing any coarse outer leaves and hollowing out the stalk slightly to help the cooking. Wash the cauliflower well in cold salted water and cook in fresh boiling salted water for 15–20 minutes or until tender. Drain well, reserving ¼ pint/1 dl of the liquid. Put the cauliflower in a heatproof dish and keep hot. Grate half the cheese and cut the remainder into small cubes. Melt the butter in a saucepan and fry the onion for 5 minutes, without browning. Add the flour and cook, stirring, for 2–3 minutes. Blend in the milk and reserved cauliflower water and bring to the boil, stirring constantly. Simmer for 2 minutes. Remove the saucepan from the heat and stir in the grated cheese; taste and season. Pour the sauce over the cauliflower and keep hot. Grill the bacon until crisp and cut into strips. Sprinkle the cheese cubes and bacon onto the cauliflower and grill under a hot grill for 2 minutes. Serve immediately.

66

Spanish Rice Salad

Serves: 6 people
Preparation time:
10 minutes
Cooking time:
12–15 minutes

Cook the rice in advance if liked, even the day before. Double the quantities for a good buffet party salad.

8 oz/225 g long grain rice
½ green pepper
½ red pepper
3 sticks celery, chopped
1 onion, finely chopped
Dressing:
6 tablespoons oil
2 tablespoons vinegar
½ level teaspoon salt
¼ level teaspoon pepper
¼ level teaspoon French mustard
pinch of sugar

Cook the rice in boiling salted water for 12–15 minutes or until tender. Drain, rinse under cold running water. Remove the seeds from the peppers and chop finely. Combine the rice, peppers, celery and onion in a bowl. Leave in the refrigerator until ready to use. Place all the dressing ingredients in a screw-top jar. Shake the jar vigorously until the dressing is thick and creamy. Add to the salad and toss well together. Pile the salad onto a serving plate, garnish with the tomato wedges.

Malayan Rice Salad

Serves: 4 people
Preparation time:
10 minutes
Cooking time:
20 minutes

A rice salad with a difference. If your budget won't stretch to shrimps, use a small can of tuna fish. Drain and flake it well.

6 oz/175 g long grain rice
1 (4 oz/113 g) packet frozen mixed vegetables
1 small can shrimps, drained
2 tablespoons mayonnaise
2 tablespoons mango chutney
2–3 level teaspoons curry powder
salt and pepper
6 oz/175 g white cabbage, shredded

Cook the rice in a large saucepan of fast-boiling salted water for 12–15 minutes or until tender. Drain well and rinse through with cold water to cool. Cook the mixed vegetables according to the instructions on the side of the packet. Rinse with cold water. In a large bowl combine the shrimps, mayonnaise, chutney, curry powder, rice and vegetables. Toss together gently, taste and adjust the seasoning. Arrange the shredded cabbage in a serving dish and top with the rice mixture.

Special Day Potato Salad

Serves: 6 people
Preparation time:
10 minutes plus
cooling time
Cooking time:
20 minutes

A summer salad
which is a delicious
meal in itself.

2 lb/1 kg potatoes
salt and pepper
8 oz/225 g Cheshire
 cheese, diced
½ head celery,
 chopped
6 spring onions,
 coarsely chopped
6 radishes, thinly
 sliced
½ pint/3 dl
 mayonnaise
2 teaspoons
 horseradish sauce
2 level tablespoons
 chopped parsley

Peel and cook the potatoes in boiling salted water for 20 minutes or until tender. Drain, cool and dice the potato; put in a mixing bowl with the cheese, celery, spring onions and radishes. Mix altogether. Blend the mayonnaise with the horseradish sauce and salt and pepper to taste. Fold the mayonnaise gently into the potato mixture. Spoon into a serving bowl and serve garnished with the chopped parsley.

Macaroni Salad

Serves: 4 people
Preparation time:
10 minutes plus
chilling time
Cooking time:
10–12 minutes

A quick to prepare
and substantial salad
which uses leftover
meat.

8 oz/225 g short cut
 macaroni
salt
¼ pint/1·5 dl
 mayonnaise
8 oz/225 g cooked
 meat
1 level tablespoon
 chopped parsley
1 lettuce for serving
1 small cooked
 beetroot

Cook the macaroni in a large saucepan with plenty of boiling salted water for 10–12 minutes. Drain well in a colander. Rinse in cold water until cool. Put the mayonnaise in a bowl and mix in the macaroni. Chill. Cut the meat into pieces and add to the macaroni with the parsley. Toss lightly. Line a serving dish with lettuce leaves and pile the macaroni salad in the middle. Slice the beetroot and put some at each end of the dish. Serve as soon as possible.

Desserts

Dreamy Raspberry Nests

Serves: 6 people
Preparation time:
10 minutes
Cooking time:
None

An impressive store cupboard dessert for entertaining in a hurry. Use fresh raspberries if available or other fruit if preferred. Meringues store very well for months in an airtight container.

1 (15 oz/426 g) can
  raspberries
1 sachet dessert
  topping mix
$\frac{1}{4}$ pint/1.5 dl milk
1 packet (6)
  meringue nests

Drain the raspberries well. Make up the dessert topping mix with the milk, as directed on the side of the packet. Place a layer of the dessert topping on the base of each meringue nest. Divide the raspberries between the nests and top with a swirl of the dessert topping.

Raspberry Glasses

Serves: 4 people
Preparation time:
10 minutes
Cooking time:
None

A quickly prepared dessert which helps to 'stretch' the fruit in order to serve more people. Use other soft fruit if liked.

8 oz/225 g
  raspberries
icing sugar
4 macaroon biscuits
$\frac{1}{2}$ pint /3 dl natural
  yoghourt

Hull the raspberries and inspect them for dirt and insects. Dredge them well with sifted icing sugar. Crush the biscuits and put one into each of 4 tall serving glasses. Divide the raspberries equally between the glasses. Pour yoghourt over the raspberries just before serving.

Iced Brandy Snaps

Serves: 4 people
Preparation time:
10 minutes
Cooking time:
None

Buy ready-made
brandy snaps and leave
out the fresh cream if
your budget is limited.

1 family-sized block
 (17 fl oz/$\frac{1}{2}$ litre)
 vanilla ice cream
12 brandy snaps
8 teaspoons ginger
 marmalade
$\frac{1}{4}$ pint/1·5 dl
 whipped cream

Have 4 serving plates ready and place 2 scoops of ice cream on each one, with a brandy snap on either side. Put a teaspoonful of ginger marmalade on each scoop of ice cream and a brandy snap across the centre. Pipe some whipped cream along the side of each brandy snap.

Pear and Strawberry Fluff

Serves: 4–6 people
Preparation time:
10 minutes plus
chilling time
Cooking time:
None

A quick and easy
dessert which is
ideal for the summer
when strawberries
are in season. Use
frozen or canned
fruit at other times
of the year.

1 (1 pint/569 ml)
 packet fruit
 cocktail jelly
1 (15$\frac{1}{2}$ oz/440 g)
 can creamed rice
1 ripe pear, peeled,
 cored and diced
4 oz/100 g
 strawberries,
 quartered

Place the jelly in a measuring jug and make up to $\frac{1}{2}$ pint/3 dl with boiling water. Stir until the jelly is dissolved and put in a cool place until syrupy and beginning to set. Pour the jelly into a bowl and whisk well until light and fluffy. Fold in the creamed rice, pear and strawberries. Spoon the dessert into 4–6 individual serving glasses. Chill before serving.

Raspberry Rice Sundae

Serves: 4 people
Preparation time:
10 minutes plus
setting time
Cooking time:
None

Canned or frozen fruit
could be used instead
of fresh raspberries
when they are not in
season.

1 (1 pint/569 ml)
raspberry jelly
8 oz/225 g
raspberries
1 (15½ oz/440 g) can
creamed rice
¼ pint/1.5 dl
whipping cream for
decoration
(optional)

Dissolve the jelly in ½ pint/3 dl boiling water. Leave to cool. Press the raspberries through a sieve or blend until puréed in an electric blender, reserving a few for decoration. Stir the purée into the cooled jelly. When the mixture has just reached setting point, stir in the rice. Divide the mixture between 4 serving dishes and leave to set. Whip the cream until stiff enough to leave a trail. Decorate each sundae with cream and top with a raspberry.

Cottage Cheese Ice Cream

Serves: 6 people
Preparation time:
10 minutes plus
freezing time
Cooking time:
None

An inexpensive
home-made ice
cream. Delicious
served with seasonal
fresh fruit.

4 oz/100 g cottage
cheese
4 oz/100 g castor
sugar
½ teaspoon vanilla
essence
1 large (13 fl oz/
368 ml) can
evaporated milk,
chilled
2 level teaspoons
gelatine
2 tablespoons hot
water

Sieve the cottage cheese into a bowl. Add the sugar and vanilla essence and beat until fluffy. Whisk the evaporated milk until thick. Sprinkle the gelatine into the hot water. Stir until dissolved. Pour in the gelatine and mix well. Add the cheese mixture and whisk together lightly. Pour into ice cube trays and freeze until firm.

Cottage Strawberries

Serves: 4 people
Preparation time:
10 minutes
Cooking time:
None

Strawberries are the ideal choice for a summer picnic, when they are in season. Use other fresh, canned or frozen fruit at other times of the year.

4 oz/100 g strawberries
8 oz/225 g cottage cheese
grated rind of 1 orange
2 level tablespoons castor sugar, or to taste

Chop the strawberries coarsely and put them in a bowl. Add the cottage cheese, orange rind and sugar and fold together with a spoon until all the ingredients are thoroughly mixed. Spoon the mixture into 4 individual airtight containers and leave in the refrigerator until ready to take on the picnic.

Frozen Pineapple and Banana Snow

Serves: 6 people
Preparation time:
10 minutes plus freezing time
Cooking time:
10 minutes

An ice cream to make at home. You will find that the pineapple and banana flavours go together well. It is a firm favourite with children.

2 level teaspoons gelatine
½ pint/3 dl water
8 oz/225 g granulated sugar
1 level teaspoon grated lemon rind
2 ripe bananas
4 tablespoons lemon juice
½ pint/3 dl pineapple juice
1 small can evaporated milk
2 egg whites
crushed pineapple for serving (optional)

Turn the refrigerator to its coldest setting. Dissolve the gelatine in a little of the water in a bowl over hot water. Place the remaining water in a saucepan with the sugar and lemon rind. Stir over a low heat until the sugar has dissolved, then boil gently for 5 minutes. Cool slightly, then stir in the dissolved gelatine. Mash the bananas with the lemon juice, then add to the gelatine mixture with the pineapple juice and evaporated milk. Stir together well. Pour into the refrigerator ice cube trays (the dividers removed) and freeze until nearly firm. Spoon it into a bowl and beat well. Whisk the egg whites until stiff, then fold them into the banana mixture and return to the freezer trays. Freeze until firm. Serve topped with a little crushed pineapple.

Orange Water Ice

Serves: 4–6 people
Preparation time:
5 minutes plus
cooling and freezing
times
Cooking time:
10 minutes

A refreshing home-
made ice well worth
making for summer
entertaining and
inexpensive enough
for family meals.
Try serving it in
hollowed out oranges
decorated with mint
leaves for a special
occasion.

rind and juice of 3
    oranges
6 oz/175 g sugar
1 pint/6 dl water
1 tablespoon lemon
    juice

Turn the refrigerator to its coldest setting. Place the thinly peeled rind of the oranges (no pith), sugar and water in a saucepan. Heat gently, stirring all the time to dissolve the sugar, then boil rapidly without stirring for 8 minutes. Remove from the heat, stir in the orange and lemon juices and leave it to become cold. Remove the orange rind. Pour into the refrigerator ice cube trays (without the dividers) and freeze until firm round the edges. Pour into a bowl, beat until smooth, then freeze until firm.

Granita di Limone

Serves: 6 people
Preparation time:
10 minutes plus
cooling and freezing
time
Cooking time:
None

Italy has a reputation
for delicious ices.
A very refreshing
and inexpensive end
to a meal.

1 pint/6 dl water
4 oz/100 g sugar
½ pint/3 dl lemon
    juice

Turn the refrigerator to its coldest setting. Bring the water and sugar to the boil in a saucepan and continue boiling for 5 minutes. Remove from the heat, cool slightly, then stir in the lemon juice. Pour the liquid into the ice cube trays from the refrigerator (dividers removed). Place in the freezing compartment of the refrigerator until frozen (about 3 hours). Stir twice during this time to prevent ice crystals forming.

Pineapple Poll

Serves: 4 people
Preparation time:
10 minutes plus
setting time
Cooking time:
About 5 minutes

A quick and easy
dessert to make but
leave time for it to set.
Use other flavours of
fruit and jelly for
variation.

1 (15 oz/426 g) can
pineapple slices
1 (1 pint/569 ml)
packet pineapple
jelly
1 (15½ oz/440 g) can
semolina
whipped cream for
decoration
angelica

Drain the juice from the canned
pineapple rings and chop the fruit.
Break the jelly into pieces and put
it in the juice in a saucepan, heat
gently to dissolve it, stirring. Stir in
the semolina and chopped pineapple. Remove from the heat and
leave to cool slightly. Spoon it into
4 individual serving dishes and leave
in a cool place to set. Decorate the
top with a slice of pineapple, whipped cream and angelica.

Butterscotch Creams

Serves: 4 people
Preparation time:
5 minutes
Cooking time:
10 minutes

This cream can also
be used as a filling
for a pastry or
biscuit-crust case.
Stir in nuts or glacé
fruits for special
occasions.

1 oz/25 g butter
1 level tablespoon
golden syrup
1 oz/25 g soft
brown sugar
¾ pint/4·5 dl milk
1½ oz/40 g cornflour
¼ pint/1 dl thin
cream
whipped cream for
decoration
(optional)
chopped nuts and
angelica for
decoration

Put the butter, golden syrup and
sugar in a saucepan and heat gently,
stirring, until melted. Mix 2 tablespoons of the milk with the cornflour. Put the remaining milk in the
pan with the syrup mixture, heat
until nearly boiling. Pour the hot
milk onto the cornflour, stirring
constantly. Return it all to the pan
and bring to the boil, stirring. Cook
for 2–3 minutes. Remove from the
heat, cool, then stir in the cream.
Serve hot or cold in individual
dishes, decorated with cream (if
liked) and nuts and angelica.

Coffee Cloud Dessert

Serves: 4 people
Preparation time:
10 minutes plus
setting time
Cooking time:
None

This is a dessert for special occasions. Use imitation or canned cream for family meals.

1 maple and walnut
  jelly cream dessert
  milk
2 eggs, separated
¼ pint/1·5 dl
  whipping cream
2 teaspoons rum or
  brandy (optional)
grated chocolate
  for decoration

Make up the jelly cream with milk, as instructed on the side of the packet. Add the egg yolks and beat well. Put aside in a cool place until almost set. Fold in 1 tablespoon of the cream, lightly whipped, and the rum or brandy, if used. Whisk the egg whites until stiff and fold into the jelly cream mixture. Divide the dessert between 4 serving glasses and put in a cool place until set. Decorate with the remaining cream, whipped until stiff. Sprinkle with grated chocolate.

Rich Chocolate Delight

Serves: 4–6 people
Preparation time:
10 minutes
Cooking time:
None

This is a very quick dessert to prepare. If preferred you can use hazel nuts instead of walnuts.

1 family-sized block
  (17 fl oz/½ litre)
  chocolate ice
  cream
4 oz/100 g walnuts,
  roughly chopped
4 tablespoons
  whipped cream

Place the ice cream in serving glasses in alternate layers with the walnuts. Top with a rose of whipped cream and serve immediately.

75

Marshmallow Sundae

Serves: 4 people
Preparation time:
5 minutes
Cooking time:
None

A quick and easy dessert. You could keep all the ingredients in your store cupboard for emergencies.

1 (16 oz/454 g) can fruit cocktail
6 marshmallows
1 sachet dessert topping mix
milk to mix
glacé cherries for decoration

Drain the fruit cocktail. Cut the marshmallows into pieces. Mix the fruit and marshmallows together in a bowl. Make up the topping mix with the milk, then fold half into the fruit and marshmallow mixture. Put into 4 sundae dishes and decorate with the remaining topping and glacé cherries.

Honey Fruit Fanfare

Serves: 6 people
Preparation time:
10 minutes plus freezing time
Cooking time:
5 minutes

A speedy home-made ice cream, ideal for special occasions. Serve with crisp biscuits.

½ pint/3 dl whipped cream
3 tablespoons honey
2 tablespoons lemon juice
½ oz/15 g gelatine
2 tablespoons water
1 orange, peeled and chopped
1 (1 lb 13 oz/825 g) can peach slices, chopped (reserve a few for decoration)
2 oz/50 g glacé cherries, halved
1 oz/25 g angelica, chopped
1 oz/25 g hazelnuts or walnuts, chopped

Beat together the whipped cream, honey and lemon juice. Put the gelatine and water into a bowl and stand the bowl in a saucepan of hot water. Heat gently, stirring until the gelatine is dissolved. Allow to cool, then add to the cream mixture. Stir in the fruit and nuts. Pour the mixture into a shallow cake tin or refrigerator ice cube tray (without dividers). Freeze until firm then cut into squares, decorate with the reserved peach slices and serve immediately.

Pineapples in Caramel

Serves: 4 people
Preparation time:
5 minutes plus
overnight chilling
Cooking time:
5 minutes

The fruit improves in flavour when soaked overnight. Orange segments and cherries are also good served this way.

1 (14 oz/396 g) can pineapple slices
3 oz/75 g castor sugar
2 tablespoons boiling water
few drops brandy or rum essence

Drain the pineapple slices, reserving the juice. Measure $\frac{1}{4}$ pint/1.5 dl of the juice, adding a little water if necessary. Put the liquid in a saucepan with the castor sugar, bring to the boil, stirring until the sugar has dissolved. Boil until the syrup has turned golden brown. Stir in the boiling water. Pour the caramel into a bowl and leave to cool. Add a few drops of brandy or rum essence, or to taste. Add the pineapple slices, cover the bowl and chill in the refrigerator or cool place overnight. Serve 2 pineapple slices per person and pour the syrup over them.

Crunchy Ice Cream Mincemeat Tarts

Serves: 6 people
Preparation time:
10 minutes plus
chilling time
Cooking time:
5 minutes

These make a change from the more usual mincemeat tarts. The ice cream makes a delicious topping. The mincemeat can be heated first, if liked, to cook the suet. Allow to become cold before using.

2 oz/50 g margarine
1½ oz/40 g castor sugar
2 tablespoons golden syrup
8 oz/225 g digestive biscuits, crushed
4 heaped tablespoons mincemeat
1 family-sized block (17 fl oz/½ litre) vanilla ice cream

Melt the margarine in a saucepan, stir in the sugar until dissolved. Mix in the syrup. Add the biscuit crumbs and stir until they are evenly coated. Press the mixture into individual flan rings or patty tins. Chill in the refrigerator. When firm, remove the tart shells from the tins. Fill each one with mincemeat and top with a scoop of ice cream.

Eastern Fruit Salad

Serves: 4 people
Preparation time:
5 minutes plus
chilling time
Cooking time:
None

This is an ideal light dessert to serve after a hot curry. Serve it accompanied by crisp, sweet biscuits.

1 (11 oz/311 g) can lychees
1 (11 oz/311 g) can mandarin orange segments
½ honeydew melon, cubed
4 pieces bottled stem ginger, sliced

Mix together the lychees and orange segments with both syrups and the melon in a large bowl. Leave in the refrigerator to chill.

Add the sliced ginger and a little of the ginger syrup. Mix thoroughly and serve.

Banana and Lemon Delight

Serves: 4 people
Preparation time:
10 minutes plus
setting time
Cooking time:
None

A good dessert for children. Use evaporated milk instead of fresh milk for special occasions.

½ oz/15 g gelatine
3 tablespoons hot water
¾ pint/4·5 dl lemon squash (undiluted)
5 bananas
¼ pint/1·5 dl milk lemon juice

Dissolve the gelatine in the water then add it to the lemon squash. Mash 4 of the bananas well in a large bowl then gradually mix in the milk. Whisk in the lemon squash mixture. Pour into a large serving bowl and chill until set. Slice the remaining banana thinly then dip the slices in lemon juice to prevent them discolouring. Decorate the top of the dessert with the slices.

Italian Pears

Serves: 4 people
Preparation time:
10 minutes plus
cooling and chilling
time
Cooking time:
5 minutes

Pears are in the
shops all the year
round but home-
grown pears are most
plentiful and
cheapest in the
autumn.

4 dessert pears
1 lemon
1 orange
2 oz/50 g honey
4 cloves

Peel and core the pears carefully.
Dip in lemon juice to prevent them
becoming discoloured. Peel the
rinds of the orange and lemon very
thinly and put them in a saucepan

with the honey, cloves and orange
juice. Bring to the boil then simmer
for 5 minutes. Strain, then pour
over the pears; cool and chill before
serving.

Autumn Apple Mould

Serves: 4 people
Preparation time:
10 minutes plus
setting time
Cooking time:
20 minutes

If you have
windfalls in the
autumn, mix them
with blackberries
for this delicious
dessert.

1 lb/½ kg apples
8 oz/225 g
  blackberries
1 orange
sugar to taste
pinch of ground
  cinnamon
1½ level tablespoons
  gelatine
extra blackberries
  for decoration

Peel and core the apples, slice and
put into a saucepan with the
blackberries. Add the grated orange
rind. Squeeze and measure the
orange juice, make up to ½ pint/3 dl
with water. Add the liquid to the
saucepan, cover and cook the
apples and blackberries until very
tender. Rub the fruit through a
sieve to make a smooth soft purée.

Stir in sugar to taste, with the
cinnamon. Put ¼ pint/1 dl water in
a small saucepan, heat gently then
sprinkle in the gelatine. Stir until
dissolved. Mix the gelatine with
the purée. Pour into a 1½ pint/8 5 dl
capacity mould and chill until set.
Unmould and serve decorated with
extra blackberries.

Rhubarb Jelly

Serves: 4 people
Preparation time:
5 minutes plus
setting time
Cooking time:
5–10 minutes

Rhubarb is cheapest in the spring and early summer. When it is not available, try using apples instead. This recipe is a good one for slimmers if it is made with low calorie squash and liquid artificial sweetener

1 lb/½ kg rhubarb
¼ pint/1·5 dl lemon squash undiluted
finely grated rind of ½ lemon
scant ½ oz/15 g gelatine
brown sugar to taste

Wipe the rhubarb, cut it into 1 inch/25 mm pieces and put into a saucepan with the lemon squash and the lemon rind. Bring to the boil and simmer gently until cooked. Dissolve the gelatine in 3 tablespoons of the hot liquid and pour back into the pan. Taste and add sufficient brown sugar, allowing it to dissolve in the hot cooking juice. Pour into a mould or individual dishes and leave to set.

Orange Condé

Serves: 4 people
Preparation time:
10 minutes plus
setting time
Cooking time:
2 hours

This recipe makes a delicious cold dessert – good enough for special occasions, economical enough for family meals.

2 oz/50 g short grain rice
1 pint/6 dl milk
1 small orange
1½ oz/40 g castor sugar
1 (1 pint/569 ml) packet orange jelly
2 glacé cherries

Put the rice and milk into the top of a double saucepan with a thin strip of orange peel. Place over simmering water, cover and cook for about 2 hours or until the rice is cooked. Stir in the sugar then allow to cool. Remove the orange rind. Pour into 4 serving glasses and leave until cold and set. Make the jelly with 1 pint/5·5 dl water. Pour a little on top of the rice in each glass. Place thin slices of orange in the jelly with half a glacé cherry for decoration. Chill until set before serving.

Chocolate and Pear Coronet

Serves: 6 people
Preparation time:
10 minutes plus
setting time
Cooking time:
5 minutes

A speedy dessert
especially popular
with children. Don't
forget to allow time
for it to set.

2 level tablespoons
  cornflour
2 level tablespoons
  cocoa
¼ pint/1.5 dl milk
1 (1 lb 13 oz/865 g)
  can creamed rice
1 (15½ oz/440 g) can
  pear halves
little whipped cream
chocolate buttons

Place the cornflour and cocoa in a small bowl and blend in 4 tablespoons of the milk. Place the remaining milk and rice in a saucepan, bring to boiling point, stir a little into the cocoa mixture, then return to the milk and rice in the pan, stirring. Rinse an 8 inch/20 cm shallow round cake tin in cold water, pour the mixture into it. Cool, then leave to set in the refrigerator. Turn out onto a plate. Drain the pears and arrange the halves on the chocolate rice mould. Decorate with whipped cream and chocolate buttons.

Summer Pudding

Serves: 4–6 people
Preparation time:
10 minutes plus
chilling time
Cooking time:
None

Stale leftover bread
can be used for this
recipe. Use fresh soft
fruit when available
in the summer. Cook
with a very little
water and sugar to
taste just until the
juice runs.
Gooseberries and
rhubarb are also
good alternatives.
Frozen fruit needs no
cooking but it will
require the addition
of sugar.

5–6 large thin slices
  white bread
1–1¾ lb/½–¾ kg
  mixed fruits, e.g.
  raspberries,
  blackberries,
  blackcurrants,
  redcurrants etc.
  (fresh or frozen)
whipped cream for
  decoration
  (optional)

Remove the crusts from the slices of bread and line the sides and base of a 5 inch/13 cm diameter pudding basin. Fill the lined basin with the fruit, then cover with the remaining bread. Place a tightly fitting plate or saucer on top, put a heavy weight on the plate and leave in a cool place overnight. Unmould onto a plate just before serving. Decorate with whipped cream if liked.

Rum and Ginger Dessert

Serves: 4–6 people
Preparation time:
10 minutes
Cooking time:
None

A very good recipe for transforming ginger cake into a luxury dessert. Leftover sponge cake could also be used. Use orange juice instead of rum if liked.

8 slices ginger cake
2½ tablespoons rum
2 sachets powdered topping mix
milk
glacé cherries and angelica for decoration

Put the slices of cake into a shallow dish. Sprinkle them with 2 tablespoons of the rum. Make up the topping mix with milk as directed on the side of the packet. Add the remaining ½ tablespoon rum and mix well. Sandwich together 4 of the slices of cake with one-quarter of the topping mix.

Sandwich the other 4 slices together with another quarter of the topping mix. Stand the 2 sandwiches end to end on a plate, with the slices vertical. Cover the cake completely with the remaining topping mix. Decorate with cherries and angelica. Chill well before serving.

Creamed Gooseberry Mould

Serves: 4–6 people
Preparation time:
10 minutes plus setting time
Cooking time:
None

Use ½ pint/3 dl gooseberry purée made with cooked fresh gooseberries when they are in season in the summer.

1 (10½ oz/298 g) can gooseberries
1 (2½ oz/70 g) packet lemon flavour jelly cream dessert
1 (15½ oz/440 g) can creamed rice
whipped cream and strawberries for decoration (optional)

Press the gooseberries through a sieve with a wooden spoon, to make a purée, or blend the gooseberries until puréed in an electric blender. Put the gooseberry purée in a small saucepan and bring it gently to the boil. Sprinkle the jelly cream dessert into a bowl.

Stir in the hot gooseberry purée and stir until the jelly cream is dissolved. Stir in the creamed rice and pour into a 1 pint/6 dl capacity soufflé dish or mould. Chill until set. Unmould onto a plate and decorate with stiffly whipped cream and strawberries, if liked.

Cherry and Pineapple Mould

Serves: 6–8 people
Preparation time:
10 minutes plus
setting time
Cooking time:
None

This versatile dessert
is ideal for
entertaining,
especially when
there is a crowd to
feed. It is also very
low in calories.

2 (1 pint/569 ml)
packets strawberry
jelly
1 (16 oz/456 g) can
pineapple rings
¾ pint/4·5 dl milk
1 (6 oz/170 g) can
cherries

Put the jellies in a measuring jug. Drain the pineapple and heat the syrup until boiling. Pour the syrup onto the jellies and stir until dissolved. Make up the jelly to 1 pint/ 5.5 dl with water. Chop all the pineapple rings except one. Mix the chopped pineapple with a little of the jelly and put it into a very lightly oiled mould. Put in a cool place until set. Add the milk to the remaining liquid jelly (warm gently if set) and pour it on the set jelly in the mould. Chill until set. Just before serving, unmould the jelly onto a plate and decorate with the remaining pineapple ring and the drained cherries.

Pear Lime Cream

Serves: 4 people
Preparation time:
10 minutes plus
setting time
Cooking time:
None

A delicious creamy
dessert. Keep all the
ingredients in your
store cupboard ready
for unexpected
guests.

1 (15 oz/428 g) can
pears
1 (1 pint/569 ml)
packet lime jelly
1 sachet powdered
topping mix
milk
pear halves for
decoration
(optional)

Drain the can of pears, reserving the syrup. Put the jelly in a measuring jug, heat the pear syrup until boiling, then pour onto the jelly. Stir until the jelly is dissolved. Add enough cold water to make up to 1 pint/5·5 dl. Put the jelly in a cool place until almost set. Make up the powdered topping mix with milk as instructed on the side of the packet. Whisk the jelly and topping mix together. Chop the pears and stir into the mixture. Pour into a serving dish or mould. Put into a cool place until set. Serve, unmoulded if necessary, decorated with pear halves if liked.

Dreamy Chocolate Mallow

Serves: 6 people
Preparation time:
10 minutes plus
chilling time
Cooking time:
10 minutes

An ideal party
dessert. Use canned
cream for economy.

2 oz/50 g
marshmallows
2 oz/50 g plain
chocolate
1 level tablespoon
cocoa
2 tablespoons milk
few drops vanilla
essence
¼ pint/1.5 dl whipped
cream
1 (8 inch/20 cm)
sponge flan case
chocolate buttons
and angelica for
decoration
(optional)

Place the marshmallows, chocolate, cocoa, milk and vanilla essence in a heatproof bowl. Place the bowl over a saucepan of simmering water. Heat gently, stirring, until the mixture has melted and combined.

Put aside to cool. Fold in half the whipped cream and pour into the flan case. Just before serving, decorate the top with the remaining cream. Decorate with chocolate buttons and angelica.

Mandarin Cream Trifle

Serves: 6–8 people
Preparation time:
10 minutes plus
chilling time
Cooking time:
None

This trifle makes a
very quickly
prepared and
deliciously different
dessert. Add 2
tablespoons sherry
to the orange juice
when entertaining.

1 chocolate Swiss
roll
1 (11 oz/311 g) can
mandarin oranges
1 (1 pint/569 ml)
packet orange
instant dessert
1 pint/5·5 dl milk
whipped cream for
decoration

Slice the Swiss roll and place it on the base of a serving dish. Drain the mandarin oranges and sprinkle some of the juice over the Swiss roll. Make up the instant dessert with the milk, as directed on the

side of the packet. Stir in the mandarin oranges. Pour the orange mixture over the Swiss roll. Cool. Decorate the top with whipped cream. Chill before serving.

Crusted Pineapple Slices

Serves: 6 people
Preparation time:
10 minutes
Cooking time:
7 minutes

A quick to make dessert which is popular with all ages but especially liked by children. Try this recipe with canned or fresh peach or apricot halves for variation.

2 egg whites
2 teaspoons lemon juice
6 oz/175 g castor sugar
½ level teaspoon lemon rind
1 oz/25 g desiccated coconut
6 canned pineapple rings

Place the egg whites in a heatproof bowl and whisk them until just stiff. Whisk in the lemon juice, sugar and lemon rind. Place the bowl over a saucepan of boiling water and continue whisking for 5 minutes. Remove from the heat and fold in the coconut. Leave to cool slightly. Place the pineapple rings on a heatproof plate. Pile the egg white mixture on top of each pineapple ring. Brown the tops under a moderately hot grill and serve warm or cold.

Bermuda Peaches

Serves: 4 people
Preparation time:
5 minutes
Cooking time:
10–15 minutes
Oven temperature:
350°F/180°C Mark 4

A very easy to prepare and delicious dessert. Serve these peaches for any occasion.

1 (15 oz/426 g) can peach slices
juice of 1 lemon
pinch of ground nutmeg
½ level teaspoon ground cinnamon
¼ teaspoon rum essence
4 oz/100 g ginger biscuits, crushed

Drain the peach slices and arrange them in a shallow ovenproof dish. Mix the syrup with the lemon juice, nutmeg, cinnamon and rum essence. Pour the syrup over the peach slices. Put the dish in a moderate oven (350°F/180°C Mark 4) for 10–15 minutes or until hot. Sprinkle the crushed ginger biscuits over the top and serve as soon as possible.

Hasty Pudding

Serves: 4–6 people
Preparation time:
10 minutes
Cooking time:
10 minutes

This is a good pudding for emergencies. All the ingredients will probably be in your store cupboard.

Biscuit base:
3 oz/75 g butter or margarine
2 oz/50 g castor sugar
6 oz/150 g digestive biscuits, crushed
Filling:
3 oz/75 g butter or margarine
2 oz/50 g plain flour
¾ pint/4 dl milk
pinch of ground nutmeg
1 bay leaf
grated rind of ½ lemon
2 oz/50 g castor sugar
1 level teaspoon ground cinnamon
lemon slices for decoration

Make the biscuit base: Melt the butter in a saucepan, stir in the sugar and biscuit crumbs. Press the mixture over the base and sides of a deep 8 inch/20 cm pie plate.
Make the filling: Melt 2 oz/50 g butter or margarine in a saucepan, stir in the flour, and cook, stirring, for 2 minutes. Add the milk, the nutmeg, bay leaf and lemon rind. Bring to the boil, stirring, then simmer for 2–3 minutes. Pour the mixture into the biscuit base, remove the bay leaf. Dot the top with the remaining butter and sprinkle with the castor sugar and cinnamon. Cook under a hot grill until browned. Decorate with lemon slices and serve hot.

Indian Banana Fritters

Serves: 4 people
Preparation time:
10 minutes
Cooking time:
10 minutes

Bananas are a popular food in India and banana fritters make a delicious dessert. Buy loose bananas; they are often sold cheaper and bruised bananas can be used in this recipe.

4 large ripe bananas
4 oz/100 g plain flour
2 eggs
2 tablespoons milk
oil for deep-frying
1 oz/25 g castor sugar

Place the bananas in a bowl and mash well with a fork. Sieve the flour into a large bowl, then beat in the eggs one at a time, then the milk. Mix in the mashed banana well. Fill a deep frying pan one-third to half full of oil and heat it to 375°F/190°C (½ inch/12 mm cube of bread will brown in 30 seconds). Drop heaped teaspoonfuls of the banana mixture into the oil and fry for 10 minutes or until golden. Drain well on absorbent kitchen paper. Serve on a warm dish, sprinkled with castor sugar.

Spiced Gooseberry Charlotte

Serves: 2 people
Preparation time:
10 minutes
Cooking time:
30 minutes
Oven temperature:
350°F/180°C Mark 4

Use fresh goose-
berries when in
season. Currants,
rhubarb or other
soft berries are
also good. Sweeten
to taste.

1 (15 oz/428 g) can
  gooseberries
juice of ½ lemon
1 oz/25 g fresh
  breadcrumbs
¼–½ level teaspoon
  ground cinnamon
½ oz/15 g margarine

Drain the can of gooseberries and put into an ovenproof dish. Sprinkle with the lemon juice. Mix the breadcrumbs with the cinnamon and press over the fruit. Dot the top with small pieces of margarine and bake in a moderate oven (350°F/180°C Mark 4) for 25–30 minutes. Serve hot.

Marmalade Peach Casserole

Serves: 4 people
Preparation time:
10 minutes
Cooking time:
15–20 minutes
Oven temperature:
350°F/180°C Mark 4

If fresh peaches are
available and not
too highly priced,
use them in
preference to canned
ones. Look out for
fresh peaches all
summer. Poach
halves in a syrup until
tender (about 15
minutes).

1 (1 lb 3 oz/540 g)
  can peach halves
orange marmalade
1 tablespoon lemon
  juice
finely grated rind
  of 1 orange

Drain the peaches, reserve the syrup. Arrange the peach halves, hollow-side upwards, in a shallow ovenproof dish. Fill the hollows with orange marmalade. Measure ¼ pint/1·5 dl of the peach syrup and stir in the lemon juice and orange rind. Pour over the peaches. Cover the dish and bake in a moderate oven (350°F/180°C Mark 4) for 15–20 minutes. Serve hot.

Raisin and Lemon Pudding

Serves: 6 people
Preparation time:
10 minutes
Cooking time:
1½ hours

A quick-mix pudding with a really tangy lemon sauce.

3 oz/75 g soft margarine
3 oz/75 g castor sugar
grated rind of 1 lemon
5 oz/150 g self raising flour
pinch of salt
2 eggs, beaten
1 tablespoon milk
4 oz/100 g raisins
Sauce:
1 level tablespoon arrowroot
½ pint/3 dl water
grated rind of 1 lemon
juice of 2 lemons
4 oz/100 g castor sugar

Lightly grease a 1½ pint/8 dl pudding basin. Place the soft margarine, sugar, lemon rind, flour, salt, eggs, milk and raisins into a mixing bowl. Stir together, then beat for 2 minutes. Spoon the mixture into the prepared pudding basin. Cover with a double layer of greased greaseproof paper. Secure it with string tied under the rim of the basin. Steam the pudding in a steamer over boiling water, or in a large saucepan with water to come halfway up the sides of the basin, for 1½ hours.

Meanwhile, make the sauce: Blend the arrowroot in a saucepan with a little of the water, stir in the rest of the ingredients. Heat the sauce and boil for 2–3 minutes or until thickened, stirring constantly. Turn the pudding out of the basin onto a serving plate. Pour a little of the sauce over the top and serve the rest in a small jug. Serve hot.

Baked Lemon Egg Custard

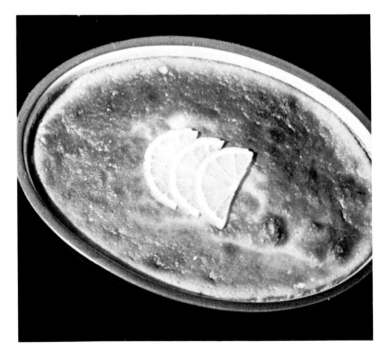

Serves: 4 people
Preparation time:
10 minutes
Cooking time:
50–60 minutes
Oven temperature:
325°F/170°C Mark 3

Egg custard makes a delicious dessert. It is especially good for children and people on diets. Add other flavourings to your taste.

4 eggs
1 pint/6 dl milk
1 oz/25 g castor sugar
grated rind of 1 lemon
lemon slices for decoration

Beat the eggs and milk together in a bowl. Strain the custard into a lightly greased 1½ pint/9 dl capacity ovenproof dish and stir in the sugar and lemon rind. Stand the dish in a larger pan with enough water to come halfway up the sides of the dish. Bake in a moderately slow oven (325°F/170°C Mark 3) for 50 minutes to 1 hour or until firm and set. Serve decorated with lemon slices.

Christmas Puffs

Makes: 8 Christmas puffs
Preparation time: 10 minutes
Cooking time: 20 minutes
Oven temperature: 400°F/200°C Mark 6 then 325°F/170°C, Mark 3

These make an excellent economical dessert at any time, but especially at Christmas. If you have time, make your own vol-au-vent cases from home-made flaky or rough puff pastry, using 8 oz/200 g flour, 6 oz/150 g fat, pinch of salt, ½ teaspoon lemon juice, and ¼ pint/1·25 dl cold water.

1 (13 oz/368 g) packet frozen puff pastry
little milk
4 tablespoons mincemeat
1 family-sized (17½ fl oz/½ litre) block vanilla ice cream

Roll out the pastry on a lightly floured surface to a square 10 × 10 inches/25 × 25 cm. Cut out sixteen 2½ inch/6 cm circles. From 8 of the circles cut out an inner circle of 1 inch/25 mm diameter (these make the lids). Place the 8 complete circles on a baking tray and brush with milk, taking care not to let any milk spill over the edges. Lay the circles with the centres cut out on top of those on the baking tray. Place the pastry lids on the baking tray, separately.

Brush with milk and bake in a hot oven (400°F/200°C Mark 6) for 10 minutes; remove the lids. Reduce the oven temperature to moderately slow (325°F/170°C Mark 3) and cook for a further 10 minutes. Remove the vol-au-vent cases from the baking tray and cool on a wire rack. Cook the mincemeat in a saucepan, then cool. Place ½ tablespoon mincemeat in each vol-au-vent and divide the ice cream between them. Top each with a pastry lid and serve.

Apricot Orange Casserole

Serves: 4 people
Preparation time: 10 minutes
Cooking time: 20 minutes
Oven temperature: 350°F/180°C Mark 4

If another casserole is to be served on the same menu, put the apricot and orange casserole under it in the oven and extend the cooking time a little.

1 large orange
1 (1 lb 3 oz/540 g) can apricot halves
pinch of ground nutmeg
1 tablespoon sherry (optional)

Grate the orange rind finely. Peel the orange, removing all the skin and pith. Slice thinly. Arrange the orange slices in the bottom of a casserole. Drain the apricots and arrange the halves on top of the oranges. Mix the apricot syrup with the orange rind, nutmeg, and sherry if used. Pour the syrup into the casserole. Cover and cook in a moderate oven (350°F/180°C Mark 4) for about 20 minutes. Serve warm.

Fruit in Syrup

Serves: 4 people
Preparation time:
5 minutes
Cooking time:
5–20 minutes

Use any fruit which is in season and inexpensive. Stoned fruit such as plums and cherries are good, as are apples, pears, gooseberries, rhubarb and many more.

2 lb/1 kg prepared fruit
1 pint/6 dl water
8 oz/225 g sugar
1 lemon or orange

Remove the stones from the fruit if necessary. Peel, core and thinly slice apples and pears. Top-and-tail gooseberries. Cut rhubarb into 1 inch/25 mm lengths. Put the water in a saucepan, add the sugar, grated rind and juice of an orange or lemon. Heat, stirring, until the sugar is dissolved. Boil for 2–3 minutes. Add the prepared fruit and simmer gently until it is tender but still keeps its shape. This will take from 2–20 minutes according to the variety of fruit, how ripe it is and how thinly you slice it. Serve warm.

Fruity Rice Pudding

Serves: 4 people
Preparation time:
10 minutes
Cooking time:
About 2 hours

The most delicious way of serving rice pudding we know. Even the children will ask for more. Milk could be used to make the syrup up to ¾ pint/4 dl instead of water, if preferred.

2 oz/50 g short grain rice
1 oz/25 g castor sugar
¼ pint/1·5 dl evaporated milk
1 (8 oz/226 g) can fruit cocktail

Put the rice in a sieve and wash well in cold running water. Put the rice and sugar into the top of a double saucepan with the evaporated milk and the syrup from the can of fruit cocktail, made up to ¾ pint/4 dl with water. Cook the rice over simmering water, stirring occasionally, for about 2 hours or until tender and the liquid absorbed. Stir in the fruit cocktail, reserving some for decoration. Pour the rice into a heated serving dish and decorate with the reserved fruit.

20 Minute Dishes

Dishes that take only 15 minutes to prepare have also been included in this section, giving you a little extra time for any other dish you may be preparing. There are lots of ideas for serving vegetables as a starter. Bhugias, savoury doughnuts from India, are an exotic beginning to any meal, or you could serve a simple fresh Tomato and Cucumber Salad flavoured with dill. For a hearty main course Smoked Haddock Cobbler or Lancashire Hot Pot will prove very popular, and for those hot summer days a Waldorf Chicken Salad or a Cold Spiced Meat Loaf will be very refreshing. With pastry mixes and packets of frozen pastry readily available, there are some delicious desserts to prepare which formerly would have taken too much time. Take advantage of them to make a mouth-watering Belgian Gozette or a Quick Cherry Strudel. When fruit is out of season, use canned or dried to make unusual and tempting desserts such as Gooseberry Mist or Yoghourt Fruit Jellies. And for a dessert with a difference, why not surprise your friends with a Frozen Christmas Pudding!

Fish in Mustard Mayonnaise

Serves: 4–6 people
Preparation time: 15 minutes
Cooking time: 15–20 minutes

A very tasty meal starter which everyone enjoys. Use whichever white fish is best value at the time.

1 lb/½ kg white fish (cod, coley or snapper)
salt and pepper
1 bay leaf
½ pint/3 dl milk
2 egg yolks
½ pint/3 dl oil
vinegar
2 level teaspoons prepared mustard
1 tablespoon chopped chives
scallop shells, if available
radishes and sprigs of parsley for garnish

Put the fish into a saucepan, sprinkle with salt and pepper. Add the bay leaf and milk and bring to the boil. Cook for 15–20 minutes or until the fish flakes easily. Drain and flake the fish into a bowl, removing any skin and bones. Allow to cool. Put the egg yolks into a bowl. Add the oil, drop by drop, beating well all the time until the mayonnaise is thick and creamy. Add vinegar to taste, then stir in the mustard and chives. Add the sauce to the fish and mix lightly. Taste and adjust the seasoning. Divide the mixture between 4–6 small dishes (or scallop shells, as in the picture, if available). Serve cold, garnished with radishes and sprigs of parsley.

Kipper Pâté

Serves: 4–6 people
Preparation time:
15 minutes
Cooking time:
None

An inexpensive pâté which is very quickly prepared. Serve with toast.

12 oz/350 g kipper fillets
2 oz/50 g margarine or butter
1 (5 fl oz/142 ml) carton soured cream
pinch of ground nutmeg

Put the kipper fillets into a bowl, cover with boiling water and put aside for 5 minutes. Drain, then remove the skin and any bones. Put the fish into an electric blender with the margarine or butter and blend until smooth (or beat the kipper and butter together with a wooden spoon until smooth). Spoon the kipper mixture into a bowl and beat in the soured cream and nutmeg. Press the pâté into a suitable dish and put in a cool place until firm.

Limed Fish

Serves: 4 people
Preparation time:
20 minutes plus overnight soaking
Cooking time:
None

A Polynesian dish. Serve with crusty bread. Good for a light lunch or meal starter. Any other fine-fleshed fish can be used, such as plaice, flounder and flathead.

1 lb/½ kg whiting
juice of 2 lemons
¼ pint/1.5 dl milk
3 oz/75 g desiccated coconut
1 clove garlic, crushed
Garnish:
slices of hard-boiled egg
onion rings
diced cucumber
tomato slices

Fillet the fish and remove the skin or ask your fishmonger to do this for you. Put the fish in a glass bowl and pour over the lemon juice. Cover the bowl and leave in the refrigerator or cold place overnight. Stir it occasionally with a wooden spoon. The next day, remove the fish from the bowl and drain off the lemon juice. Place the milk and coconut in a saucepan, bring to the boil, remove from the heat and leave to cool. Blend the mixture in an electric blender or strain through a sieve. Add the garlic to the coconut milk. Divide the fish into 6–8 portions and place it in 6 or 8 individual serving dishes. Pour the coconut milk mixture over the fish and garnish with the slices of egg onion rings, diced cucumber and tomato.

Smoked Haddock Mousse

Serves: 6 people
Preparation time:
20 minutes plus
cooling and setting
time
Cooking time:
15 minutes

Serve as a meal
starter or for a light
lunch or supper.
Other fish (fresh or
smoked) can be used
instead of smoked
haddock if it is a
better buy. This
recipe makes
comparatively little
fish give ample
servings.

1 lb/½ kg smoked
haddock
¾ pint/4·5 dl milk
peppercorns
1 small onion, sliced
1 bay leaf
scant ½ oz/15 g
gelatine
2 eggs, separated
1 lemon
Worcestershire sauce
cucumber, tomato
and watercress for
garnish

Put the smoked haddock into a
saucepan with the milk, peppercorns, onion and bay leaf. Bring to
the boil then cover the pan and
simmer gently for about 15 minutes
or until the fish will flake easily.
Drain the fish and flake the flesh
into small pieces. Strain the cooking
milk into a measuring jug and make
up to ¾ pint/4·5 dl again with more
milk if necessary. Dissolve the
gelatine in the milk, heat it in a
bowl over a saucepan of hot water
if necessary. Put the egg yolks into
a large bowl and add the milk and
the gelatine, whisking well all the
time. Add the finely grated lemon
rind, the lemon juice and Worcestershire sauce to taste. Cool until it is
syrupy and beginning to set. Stir in
the flaked fish. Whisk the egg
whites until stiff then fold them
into the gelatine mixture. Pour the
mousse into a 7 inch/18 cm
diameter mould and chill until set.
Unmould just before needed and
serve garnished with cucumber and
tomato slices and sprigs of watercress.

Spinach Ring with Fish Sauce

Serves: 4–6 people
Preparation time:
15 minutes
Cooking time:
1 hour
Oven temperature:
350°F/180°C Mark 4

A good way of
cooking fresh
spinach. Spinach is
an excellent
vegetable to grow
in a small garden. It
has no specific
season and is
available at most
times of the year.
Team this ring with
other creamy fillings.

2 lb/1 kg fresh
spinach
2 oz/50 g margarine
2 oz/50 g plain flour
1 pint/5 dl milk
salt and pepper
3 egg yolks
pinch of ground
nutmeg
1 lb/½ kg snapper,
whiting or coley
4 oz/100 g cheese,
grated
tomatoes for garnish

Wash the spinach well, then cook in
a very little boiling salted water until
tender. Drain well and chop. Melt
the margarine in a saucepan, stir in
the flour and cook, stirring constantly, for 2–3 minutes. Add the
milk, bring to the boil, stirring,
and simmer for 2 minutes. Season.
Put half the sauce into another
saucepan. Beat the egg yolks and
nutmeg into one half of the sauce,
with the chopped spinach. Pour the
spinach mixture into a lightly
greased mould and bake in a
moderate oven (350°F/180°C Mark
4) for 30–40 minutes. Meanwhile,
poach the fish in a saucepan, with
water to cover, for 15 minutes or
until it will flake easily. Flake the
fish and stir it into the remaining
sauce with 3 oz/75 g of the grated
cheese. Reheat if necessary. Unmould the cooked spinach ring
onto a serving plate. Fill the centre
with the fish sauce. Sprinkle with
the remaining cheese and garnish
with slices of tomato.

Seafood Cocktail

Serves: 4 people
Preparation time:
20 minutes plus
cooling and chilling
time
Cooking time:
15–20 minutes

Add prawns, shrimps
or other shellfish to
the white fish mixture
if the budget will
allow.

12 oz/350 g white
    fish
milk
salt and pepper
1 bay leaf
2–3 tablespoons
    tomato juice or
    tomato ketchup
1 tablespoon lemon
    juice
1 level teaspoon
    prepared horse-
    radish sauce
1 level teaspoon
    grated onion
few drops
    Worcestershire
    sauce
pinch of sugar
1 stick celery, finely
    chopped
5 tablespoons
    mayonnaise
lettuce for serving
lemon slices for
    garnish

Put the fish into a saucepan with milk to cover. Sprinkle with salt and pepper and add the bay leaf. Cook the fish for 15–20 minutes or until it flakes easily. Drain the fish, remove any skin and bones. Flake into chunks and put aside until cold. Mix together the tomato juice, lemon juice, horseradish sauce, onion, Worcestershire sauce, sugar, celery and mayonnaise.

Chill. Shred the lettuce very finely and divide equally between 4 glasses. Put the fish on top and coat with the sauce. Serve garnished with lemon slices.

Fish Curls

Serves: 4–6 people
Preparation time:
15 minutes plus
marinating time
Cooking time:
5 minutes

An excellent way of
serving fine-fleshed
fish such as sole,
plaice or flounder.
The crisp batter
complements the fish
and makes it serve
more people. Serve it
with tartare or tomato
sauce.

1 lb/½ kg fish fillets
2 tablespoons oil
2 teaspoons vinegar
1 teaspoon lemon
    juice
1 level teaspoon
    chopped parsley
½ small onion,
    chopped
salt
pinch of cayenne
    pepper
2 oz/50 g plain
    flour
1 egg
2 tablespoons milk
oil for deep-frying

Cut the fillets into ½ inch/12 mm wide strips. Mix together 1 tablespoon of the oil, the vinegar, lemon juice, parsley, onion, salt and cayenne pepper in a bowl. Add the fish strips and leave for 30 minutes. Drain and dry the fillets thoroughly on absorbent kitchen paper. Sift the flour and a pinch of salt into a mixing bowl. Beat in the egg, milk

and the remaining 1 tablespoon oil. Coat the fish in the batter. Fill a deep frying pan one-third to half full of oil and heat it to 350°F/ 180°C (a ½ inch/12 mm cube of bread will brown in 1 minute). Fry the pieces of fish until golden, placing them in the pan one by one to prevent them sticking together. Drain well before serving.

Taramasalata

Serves: 4 people
Preparation time:
20 minutes
Cooking time:
None

An inexpensive and always popular starter to a meal.

4 oz/100 g smoked
  cod's roe
1–2 cloves garlic,
  crushed
1 tablespoon lemon
  juice
4 tablespoons olive
  oil
4 tablespoons water
2 slices white bread
black olives
hot toast for serving

Remove any skin from the cod's roe. Place it in a bowl and pound well with a wooden spoon. Mix in the garlic, lemon juice, olive oil and water. Remove the crusts from the white bread. Soak the bread in water, squeeze out as much as possible, then beat it into the cod's roe mixture. Continue beating until the mixture is a thick, smooth purée. Put it into a serving dish and garnish with black olives. Serve the pâté with fingers of hot toast.

Whitebait Fritters

Serves: 3–4 people
Preparation time:
15 minutes
Cooking time:
5–7 minutes

Whitebait are small fish which are eaten whole. They are usually very inexpensive, especially in the spring. These fritters can be served as a lunch or supper dish or as a meal starter.

4 oz/100 g plain
  flour
1 level teaspoon salt
1 egg
¼ pint/1·5 dl milk
½ pint/3 dl whitebait
oil for frying
lemon wedges for
  serving

Sift the flour and salt into a mixing bowl. Make a 'well' in the centre and add the egg. Mix the egg into the flour, gradually adding the milk. Beat well. Prepare the whitebait. Wash thoroughly in cold running water. Drain very well on absorbent kitchen paper. When ready to fry the fritters, stir the whitebait into the batter. Heat ¼ inch/6 mm of oil in a frying pan until very hot. Fry tablespoonfuls of the mixture until golden, turning once. Drain well on absorbent kitchen paper. Serve with lemon wedges.

95

Kromeskies

Serves: 4 people
Preparation time:
20 minutes
Cooking time:
About 10 minutes

Use any leftover cold meat available for this recipe. Serve for lunch or supper or even as a meal starter, with a well-flavoured tomato sauce.

4 oz/100 g cold cooked meat
1 oz/25 g margarine
1 onion, chopped
5 oz/125 g plain flour
$\frac{1}{4}$ pint/1 dl milk
1 level teaspoon chopped parsley
1 teaspoon lemon juice
salt and pepper
1 egg, separated
$\frac{1}{4}$ pint/1 dl water
2 rashers streaky bacon
oil for deep-frying

Chop the meat finely. Melt the margarine in a saucepan and fry the onion until softened. Add 1 oz/ 25 g flour and cook, stirring, for 2–3 minutes. Add the milk and bring to the boil, stirring constantly, then boil for 2 minutes. Stir in the parsley, lemon juice, salt and pepper and then the meat. Leave until cold. Sift the remaining flour, with a pinch of salt, into a mixing bowl. Add the egg yolk then, gradually, the water. Beat until smooth. Remove the rind and any bones from the bacon and 'spread' each rasher, with the back of a knife, until twice its original length. Cut the bacon into 3 inch/7 cm strips, dip into boiling water and leave for 1 minute. Put a tablespoon of the meat mixture onto each piece of bacon and roll into cork shapes. Whisk the egg white until stiff and fold it into the batter. Fill a deep frying pan one-third to half full of oil and heat it to 350°F/180°C (a $\frac{1}{2}$ inch/12 mm cube of bread will brown in 1 minute). Dip the cork shapes into the batter, then deep-fry until golden. Drain on absorbent kitchen paper and serve hot.

Family Pâté

Serves: 4–6 people
Preparation time:
15 minutes plus cooling time
Cooking time:
2 hours
Oven temperature:
350°F/180°C Mark 4

An easily made and inexpensive pâté which all the family will enjoy.

8 rashers streaky bacon
8 oz/225 g pigs' liver
1 onion
8 oz/225 g pork sausagemeat
1 level teaspoon salt
$\frac{1}{4}$ level teaspoon black pepper
1 level teaspoon mixed dried herbs
1 egg
3 small bay leaves
parsley for garnish

Remove the rinds and any bones from the bacon. Spread the rashers with the back of a knife until they are doubled in length. Line a 1 pint/ 6 dl capacity dish with the bacon, reserving some rashers for the top. Remove any sinews from the liver then mince it coarsely with the onion. Mix in the sausagemeat, salt, pepper, herbs and egg. Spoon the mixture into the prepared dish and lay the reserved bacon rashers on top. Put the bay leaves on the bacon. Cover with a piece of greased greaseproof paper then a piece of foil. Put the dish in a roasting pan with cold water to come halfway up the sides. Cook in a moderate oven (350°F/180°C Mark 4) for 2 hours. Uncover the pâté and cover with fresh greaseproof paper. Place a heavy weight on top and leave in a cool place overnight or until firm. Serve garnished with parsley.

Bhugias

Serves: 6 people
Preparation time:
15 minutes
Cooking time:
5–10 minutes

Bhugias are a sort of savoury doughnut. Serve them at a buffet party or as a starter to a meal with boiled rice. A good way of using up leftover vegetables but a packet of frozen vegetables can also be used if none are available.

4 oz/100 g plain flour
1 level teaspoon ground turmeric
$\frac{1}{4}$ level teaspoon chilli powder
1 level tablespoon finely sliced spring onions
1 clove garlic, crushed
2 green chillies, finely chopped
2 eggs, beaten
milk
4 tablespoons cooked mixed vegetables
salt and pepper
oil for deep-frying

Sieve together the flour, turmeric, and chilli powder into a large bowl. Add the spring onions, garlic, chillies, and eggs. Mix into a thick batter; add a little milk if necessary. Gently stir in the vegetables and salt and pepper, taking care not to break up the vegetables. Fill a deep frying pan one-third to half full of oil and heat to 375°F/190°C (a $\frac{1}{2}$ inch/12 mm cube of bread will brown in 30 seconds). Drop heaped teaspoonfuls of the mixture into the oil and fry for about 5–10 minutes or until golden brown. Drain on absorbent kitchen paper and serve.

Carrot and Dill Ring

Serves: 4 people
Preparation time:
20 minutes plus setting time
Cooking time:
None

This is a delicious, herby vegetable mould.

1 lb/$\frac{1}{2}$ kg carrots
1 onion
1 green pepper, chopped
2 level teaspoons dill
1 level tablespoon chopped basil
1 level tablespoon soft brown sugar
1 tablespoon white vinegar
salt and pepper
2 level tablespoons gelatine
4 tablespoons water
fresh herbs for garnish

Grate the carrots and onion into a bowl. Add the green pepper, dill, basil, sugar, vinegar and salt and pepper to taste. Dissolve the gelatine in the water in a small bowl over hot water and stir it into the carrot mixture. Rinse an 8 inch/ 20 cm ring mould in cold water, then pour the mixture into it. Chill in the refrigerator until set. Unmould onto a serving plate and garnish with fresh herbs.

Cucumber Cheese Barrels

Serves: 4 people
Preparation time:
20 minutes
Cooking time:
None

Cucumbers are cheapest in the summer and autumn.

1 cucumber
8 oz/225 g cream cheese
1–2 teaspoons curry powder
2 tablespoons mayonnaise
salt and pepper
radishes for garnish

Wipe the cucumber with a damp cloth and divide into 8 pieces. Make a slight indentation in the top of each piece, using a teaspoon to remove some of the flesh. Mix the cream cheese, curry powder, mayonnaise and seasoning. Place in a piping bag, fitted with a large star tube, and pipe cheese filling on top of each cucumber barrel. Slice the radishes and garnish.

Cottage Cheese Stuffed Tomatoes

Serves: 4 people
Preparation time:
15 minutes
Cooking time:
None

These should be eaten with a fork. Keep the insides of the tomatoes for flavouring stews and casseroles.

4 large tomatoes
8 oz/225 g cottage cheese
1 spring onion, chopped
1 stick celery, chopped
1 dessert apple, chopped
salt and pepper
few lettuce leaves for garnish

Slice the tops off the tomatoes, then scoop out the insides with a teaspoon, being careful not to break the skin. Turn the tomatoes upside down on a wire rack over a tray, to drain. Mix the remaining ingredients together in a bowl with salt and pepper to taste. Divide the mixture between the tomato cups, piling it in generously. Serve on a bed of lettuce.

Courgette (Zucchini) and Tomato Special

Serves: 4–6 people
Preparation time:
20 minutes plus
salting time
Cooking time:
35–40 minutes
Oven temperature:
350°F/180°C Mark 4

Courgettes and tomatoes are cheapest in the summer. To skin the tomatoes, dip them in boiling water for 1 minute; the skins will then slip off easily.

1 aubergine
salt and pepper
1½ oz/40 g butter
1 onion, sliced
2 cloves garlic,
  crushed
1 red or green
  pepper, sliced
3 courgettes, sliced
8 oz/225 g tomatoes,
  skinned and sliced
4 oz/100 g
  mushrooms, sliced
pinch of basil
chopped parsley for
  garnish

Slice the aubergine into rounds. Sprinkle with salt and leave for 30 minutes, then rinse and dry. Melt the butter and fry the onion and garlic for 5 minutes. Add the red or green pepper, courgettes and aubergine. Sauté for a further 5 minutes. Place in a casserole dish, season and sprinkle with basil. Arrange sliced tomatoes and mushrooms on top. Add 2 tablespoons water, cover and bake in a moderate oven (350°F/180°C Mark 4) for 35–40 minutes. Garnish with chopped parsley.

French Beans Vinaigrette

Serves: 4 people
Preparation time:
15 minutes plus
cooling and chilling
time
Cooking time:
10 minutes

French beans are a summer vegetable. This makes a good salad to serve with a main course or as an appetiser.

1 lb/½ kg French
  beans
salt
Dressing:
4 tablespoons olive
  oil
1 tablespoon vinegar
¼ level teaspoon
  French mustard
¼ level teaspoon
  castor sugar
salt and pepper
1–2 cloves garlic,
  crushed (optional)
2 level teaspoons
  chopped parsley

Wash the beans then cook them in boiling salted water for about 10 minutes or until just tender. Meanwhile put all the dressing ingredients in a screw-top jar and shake until well combined. Drain the beans and put into a bowl with the dressing. Put in a cool place until cold. Chill before serving.

Cheese Croquettes

Makes: 12 savouries
Preparation time:
20 minutes plus
cooling time
Cooking time:
10–15 minutes

A very inexpensive
savoury which
should be served
piping hot, on
cocktail sticks.

4 oz/100 g margarine
4 oz/100 g plain
    flour
½ pint/3 dl milk
8 oz/225 g Gouda
    cheese, grated
2 eggs, separated
2 level tablespoons
    chopped chives
salt and pepper
1 teaspoon
    Worcestershire
    sauce
about 4 oz/100 g
    browned
    breadcrumbs
oil for deep-frying

Melt the margarine in a saucepan, stir in the flour and cook for 2–3 minutes. Remove from the heat, gradually blend in the milk and beat well until smooth. Return to the heat and stir until very thick. Remove from the heat. Stir in the cheese, egg yolks, chives, salt and pepper to taste, and Worcestershire sauce. Leave the mixture in a cool place for as long as possible, preferably overnight. Shape the mixture into 12 croquettes. Place the egg whites in a bowl and the breadcrumbs on a plate. Coat the croquettes in egg white, then breadcrumbs. Fill a deep frying pan one-third to half full of oil and heat it to 350°F/180°C (a 1 inch/ 25 mm cube of bread will brown in 1 minute). Add the croquettes and fry for 10–15 minutes or until golden brown. Drain on absorbent kitchen paper and serve.

Potted Cheese

Makes: 8 oz/225 g
potted cheese
Preparation time:
15 minutes
Cooking time:
None

This is a good way of
using up stale cheese.
Serve with toast or
crackers, as a spread.
Caraway seeds could
be used instead of
herbs, as a variation.
Leave for 1 week
before using.

8 oz/225 g cheese,
    grated
3 tablespoons beer
½ level tablespoon
    each chopped
    parsley and chives
pinch of dried thyme
2 oz/50 g margarine
salt and pepper to
    taste
pinch of dry mustard
melted butter

Put all the ingredients except the melted butter into a heatproof bowl. Stand the bowl over a saucepan of simmering water. Heat the cheese, stirring frequently, until the mixture is thoroughly combined and creamy. Allow to cool, beat well and spoon while still warm into one serving pot or several small ones. Pour melted butter on top to seal. Cover the pots with greaseproof paper and chill. Before serving, remove the melted butter and allow the cheese to stand for 1 hour at room temperature.

Stuffed Eggs

Serves: 4 people
Preparation time:
20—25 minutes
Cooking time:
None

Serve for special occasions. These eggs can be accompanied by a salad for a light lunch or supper. They can also be an appetiser before the main course or with drinks.

4 eggs
½ level teaspoon dried parsley or ½ level tablespoon fresh parsley
salt and pepper
4 level tablespoons mayonnaise

Hard-boil the eggs in boiling water to cover for 10—15 minutes. Stir the cooking eggs for the first 2 minutes to help keep the yolks in the middle. Drain and cool the eggs in cold water. Shell and cut each egg in half lengthwise. Scoop out the yolks into a bowl, add the parsley, salt and pepper and mayonnaise. Beat until smooth. Pile the yolks back into the whites or pipe them with a large star pipe.

Baked Mushrooms in Cheese Sauce

Serves: 4 people
Preparation time:
20 minutes
Cooking time:
20 minutes
Oven temperature:
350°F/180°C Mark 4

A tasty and economical appetiser that is quick to prepare.

8 large mushrooms
6 rashers streaky bacon, chopped
1 onion, chopped
1 oz/25 g margarine
1 oz/25 g plain flour
½ pint/3 dl milk
4 oz/100 g well flavoured cheese
1 teaspoon lemon juice
salt and pepper
pinch of dry mustard
1 oz/25 g dry breadcrumbs

Wash the mushrooms and remove the stalks. Chop the stalks. Fry the bacon in a saucepan until softened, add the onion and continue frying until cooked but not browned. Stir in the chopped mushroom stalks and cook for a further 2 minutes. Heat the margarine in another saucepan, add the flour and cook, stirring, for 2 minutes. Blend in the milk and bring to the boil, stirring all the time. Boil for 2—3 minutes. Remove the sauce from the heat and stir in 3 oz/75 g of the cheese, the lemon juice and the fried mixture. Season to taste and add dry mustard. Place the mushroom caps in an ovenproof dish and pour over the sauce. Mix the bread-crumbs with the remaining cheese and sprinkle on top. Cook in a moderate oven (350°F/180°C Mark 4) for 20 minutes or until browned on top.

Savoury Filled Tomatoes

Serves: one person
Preparation time:
15 minutes
Cooking time:
None

Serve the tomatoes on a bed of lettuce leaves and accompany with 2 low-calorie crispbreads.

2 large tomatoes
Cottage cheese filling:
1 oz/25 g cottage cheese
½ stick celery, chopped
few chopped chives
pinch of curry powder
salt and pepper
Tuna filling:
½ (3½ oz/98 g) can tuna, flaked
1 oz/25 g mushrooms, chopped
1 tablespoon chopped parsley
pinch of thyme
salt and pepper
Grapefruit and orange cocktail:
1 small grapefruit
1 small orange
little orange juice

Cut the tops off the tomatoes and scoop out the insides with a teaspoon. Invert over a plate to drain. Mix the ingredients for each filling together and pile each into the tomato shells.

Make the grapefruit and orange cocktail. Peel and segment the fruits, removing all the pith. Serve in a glass, with a little juice poured over.

Tomato and Cucumber Salad

Serves: 4 people
Preparation time:
15 minutes
Cooking time:
None

A fresh and crisp salad which is ideal to serve with barbecued meat. It can also be a delicious starter.

4 large tomatoes, skinned
¼ cucumber
1 small onion
1 tablespoon vinegar
2 tablespoons oil
salt and pepper
pinch of sugar
1 level teaspoon dried dill weed

Slice the tomatoes, cucumber and onion as thinly as possible. Place the tomato in a shallow serving dish, divide the onion into rings and scatter half over the tomatoes. Top with the cucumber then the re-maining onion rings. Put the vinegar, oil, salt, pepper, sugar and dried dill weed in a screw-top jar. Shake until well combined. Pour the dressing over the salad and chill before serving.

Cheese Walnut Balls

Makes: about 12
savouries
Preparation time:
15 minutes plus
chilling time
Cooking time:
None

Very rich and
delicious savouries
which are quick and
easy to make.

4 oz/100 g blue
  vein cheese
4 oz/100 g cream
  cheese
pinch of cayenne
  pepper
1 tablespoon milk
2 oz/50 g broken
  walnuts

Finely grate the blue cheese into a bowl, add the cream cheese and cayenne pepper. Beat well together with a wooden spoon until smooth, stir in the milk. Finely chop the walnuts and place them on a plate

Roll the mixture into small balls about 1 inch/25 mm in diameter, then coat them with the chopped walnuts. Chill, then serve on cock-tail sticks.

Peanut and Tomato Salad

Serves: 4 people
Preparation time:
20 minutes
Cooking time:
None

A vegetarian meal
starter or light
lunch or supper.
It is very low in
calories.

2 crisp dessert apples
2 teaspoons lemon
  juice
2 oz/50 g salted
  peanuts
4 tomatoes, skinned
few lettuce leaves
  for serving
Dressing:
1 tablespoon white
  vinegar
2 tablespoons oil
1 clove garlic,
  crushed
pinch of dry mustard
$\frac{1}{4}$ level teaspoon
  sugar
$\frac{1}{4}$ level teaspoon
  pepper
lettuce for serving

Peel, core and roughly chop the apples. Put them into a bowl and stir in the lemon juice. Chop the peanuts and slice the tomatoes and add them to the apple.
Make the dressing: Place all the

ingredients in a screw-top jar and shake well. Add the dressing to the tomato mixture and toss gently together to coat all the ingredients. Serve the salad in a bowl lined with lettuce leaves.

Danish Blue Savoury

Serves: 4–6 people
Preparation time:
20 minutes plus
setting time
Cooking time:
None

Use imitation or
canned cream if the
budget is very tight.
Serve this savoury as
an appetiser or as
part of a buffet table.

½ oz/15 g gelatine
4 tablespoons hot
    water
4 oz/100 g Danish
    blue cheese
¼ pint/1·5 dl
    whipping cream
2 oz/50 g walnuts,
    chopped
2 eggs, separated
2 tablespoons
    tomato ketchup
lettuce for serving
black grapes and
    walnut halves for
    garnish (optional)

Dissolve the gelatine and the hot water in a small bowl, put it over a saucepan of boiling water and stir until the gelatine is dissolved. Cool. Put the cheese into a mixing bowl and mash it until soft. Beat the cream until fairly stiff. Add the chopped walnuts to the cheese with the egg yolks and tomato ketchup and mix well. Whisk the egg whites until stiff. Mix the cooled gelatine into the cheese, then fold in first the cream then the egg whites. Pour into a well greased mould and put into a cool place until set. Unmould onto a plate just before serving. Arrange lettuce round the mould and garnish with grapes and walnuts, if liked.

French Onion Soup

Serves: 6 people
Preparation time:
20 minutes
Cooking time:
1 hour

Use a good brown
stock for a deep
colour. It is best to
use a tasty cheese —
Gruyère or Parmesan
would be ideal.

1 lb/½ kg onions
2 oz/50 g margarine
1 level teaspoon salt
½ level teaspoon
    pepper
½ level teaspoon dry
    mustard
2 level teaspoons
    plain flour
1¾ pints/1 litre beef
    stock or water and
    beef stock cubes
4–6 slices French
    bread, lightly
    toasted
2 oz/50 g cheese,
    grated

Slice the onions thinly. Heat the margarine in a large saucepan, add the onion rings, salt, pepper and mustard. Cook, stirring occasionally, over a very gentle heat until the onion is browned (about 20–30 minutes). Stir in the flour, then blend in the stock. Bring to the boil and simmer for 30 minutes. Place the slices of toasted bread in a soup tureen or put one into each soup bowl. Sprinkle the bread with the grated cheese and carefully pour over the hot soup. The toast and cheese will float to the surface. Place under a hot grill until the cheese is beginning to brown. Serve straightaway.

Philippine Islands Fish Soup

Serves: 6 people
Preparation time:
20 minutes
Cooking time:
55 minutes

You can use other flat fish besides plaice or flathead; ask your fishmonger which is good value at the time. He will also fillet the fish for you. Keep the head and bones for making the fish stock. Watercress may be used instead of spinach. To skin tomatoes, dip them in boiling water for 1 minute; the skins will then slip off easily.

1½ lb/750 g fillets of
    plaice or flathead
2 pints/1 litre cold
    water
2 bay leaves
1 level teaspoon salt
1 lb/500 g tomatoes,
    skinned and sliced
2 onions, sliced
¼ level teaspoon chilli
    powder
1 lb/500 g spinach,
    shredded
salt and pepper

Place the fish heads and bones in a saucepan, add the water, bay leaves and salt. Cover, bring to the boil, then simmer for 20–30 minutes. Strain the stock and discard the bones. Place the tomatoes, onions and chilli powder in a saucepan, add the fish stock. Cover the pan and bring to the boil, then simmer for 10 minutes. Cut the fish fillets into 1 inch/25 mm pieces, add to the pan and simmer for a further 12–15 minutes or until the fish is cooked. The fish will turn clear white when it is done. Add the spinach, cook for 2–3 minutes. Taste the soup and adjust the seasoning. Serve immediately.

Royal Soup

Serves: 4 people
Preparation time:
15 minutes
Cooking time:
15 minutes

A delicious soup for any occasion. Make sure that you use a good, well flavoured chicken stock.

2 hard-boiled eggs
2 oz/50 g cooked
    chicken
2 oz/50 g cooked
    ham
1½ pints/9 dl chicken
    stock
2 tablespoons
    sherry (optional)
salt and pepper
chopped parsley
    for garnish

Chop the eggs, chicken and ham coarsely and divide them between 4 warmed soup bowls. Put the stock into a saucepan, adding the sherry if used. Bring to the boil, then taste and adjust the seasoning. Divide equally between the soup bowls and sprinkle with chopped parsley. Serve as soon as possible.

Cider Apple Soup

Serves: 4–6 people
Preparation time:
15 minutes plus
chilling time.
Cooking time:
10 minutes

An inexpensive soup
but one which
invariably impresses.
Apples are available
all the year.

1 lb/$\frac{1}{2}$ kg dessert
    apples
$\frac{3}{4}$ pint/4·5 dl chicken
    stock or water
    and chicken stock
    cube
$\frac{1}{2}$ level teaspoon
    ground cinnamon
$\frac{3}{4}$ level teaspoon
    ground ginger
2 level tablespoons
    fresh white
    breadcrumbs
1 lemon
2 level tablespoons
    sugar
$\frac{1}{4}$ pint/1·5 dl cider
$\frac{1}{4}$ pint/1·5 dl milk
soured cream and
    extra ground
    cinnamon for
    garnish

Peel, core and slice the apples thinly. Put them in a saucepan with the chicken stock, cinnamon, ginger, breadcrumbs, lemon juice and finely grated lemon rind. Bring to the boil, then simmer gently for 10 minutes or until the apple is soft. Reserve some slices for garnish.

Stir in the sugar. Using a wooden spoon, press the apples through a sieve, or purée in an electric blender. Stir in the cider and milk. Chill until needed. Serve in individual dishes, garnished with the reserved apple slices, soured cream, and a little ground cinnamon.

Potato and Onion Soup

Serves: 6 people
Preparation time:
15 minutes
Cooking time:
30 minutes

A very cheap to
make soup. Good
for chilly days,
served piping hot.
Take on picnics in a
vacuum flask.

12 oz/350 g
    potatoes
2 onions
2 carrots
1 small can tomatoes
1 pint/6 dl chicken
    stock or water and
    chicken stock
    cubes
1 oz/25 g margarine
$1\frac{1}{2}$ level teaspoons
    salt
1 level teaspoon
    sugar
$\frac{1}{2}$ pint/3 dl milk

Coarsely chop the potatoes, onions and carrots and place them in a large saucepan. Add the can of tomatoes, stock, margarine, salt and sugar. Bring to the boil, stirring occasionally, and simmer for 30 minutes or until the vegetables

are well-cooked. Press the soup through a sieve to make a purée, or put into an electric blender and blend at high speed for 10 seconds. Return the soup to the rinsed saucepan, add the milk and reheat, stirring frequently.

Supper Vegetable Broth

Serves: 4–6 people
Preparation time:
15 minutes
Cooking time:
50 minutes

A warming and satisfying soup to serve on cold days. It is filling enough to be a supper on its own or served with crusty bread.

1 lb/½ kg potatoes
12 oz/350 g carrots
8 oz/225 g leeks
1½ oz/40 g margarine
1¾ pints/1 litre chicken stock or water and chicken stock cubes
¼ pint/1·5 dl milk
salt and pepper
chopped parsley for garnish

Peel the potatoes and carrots. Cut them into small dice. Prepare the leeks, leaving most of the green on. Slice thinly then wash carefully. Melt the margarine in a large saucepan, add the prepared vegetables and cover the pan. Cook very gently for 10–15 minutes, shaking the pan very gently occasionally. The vegetables should be softened but not browned. Add the stock. Bring to the boil, cover and simmer for 30–35 minutes or until the vegetables are tender and the soup thickening. Add the milk, reheat. Taste and adjust seasoning. Serve garnished with chopped parsley.

Minestrone

Serves: 6 people
Preparation time:
20 minutes plus chilling time
Cooking time:
3¼–3¾ hours

A filling and substantial Italian soup which makes an economical lunch or supper. Serve with crusty bread if liked. The beef bones and haricot beans can be cooked in a pressure cooker.

1 lb/½ kg beef bones
2 oz/50 g haricot beans
salt and pepper
2 tablespoons olive oil
2 onions, chopped
1 clove garlic, crushed (optional)
4 oz/100 g minced beef
1 stick celery, chopped
4 oz/100 g cabbage, shredded
2 carrots, finely chopped
1 (14 oz/396 g) can tomatoes
2 oz/50 g spaghetti, broken
2 level tablespoons chopped parsley
Parmesan cheese for serving

The day before the soup is to be served, put the beef bones in a large saucepan with the haricot beans, salt and pepper and cold water to cover. Bring to the boil, skim, then cover the pan and simmer gently for 2½–3 hours. Pour into a bowl, cover and cool. Chill overnight. Next day, remove any fat from the surface. Remove the bones, cut off any meat and return it to the stock. Heat the oil in a clean saucepan and fry the onions, garlic, and minced beef until the onion is softened and the meat browned. Pour off the excess oil. Add the stock and beans and the celery, cabbage, carrots and tomatoes. Bring to the boil, then cover the pan and simmer for 15 minutes. Add the broken spaghetti and parsley and continue cooking for 15 minutes more. Taste and adjust the seasoning. Serve very hot with grated Parmesan cheese if liked.

Vichyssoise

Serves: 6 people
Preparation time:
15 minutes plus
chilling time
Cooking time:
25 minutes

A refreshing and
nutritious cold
vegetable soup, ideal
for summer meals.
Health food addicts
will want to use
organically grown
vegetables.

2 leeks
1 onion
1 oz/25 g butter
12 oz/350 g
  potatoes
½ pint/3 dl chicken
  stock or water
  and chicken stock
  cube
salt and pepper
½ pint/3 dl milk
little whipped cream
  and chopped
  chives for garnish

Chop the leeks and onion. Heat the butter in a large saucepan, add the leeks and onion and fry gently for 5 minutes; do not brown. Thinly slice the potatoes, add them to the saucepan with the stock and salt and pepper to taste. Bring to the boil, then cover the pan and simmer for about 20 minutes or until the vegetables are very tender. Stir in the milk. Blend the soup until smooth in an electric blender or rub it through a sieve with a wooden spoon to make a purée. Cool, then chill before serving. Place a little whipped cream in the centre of each serving and sprinkle with a few chopped chives.

Butterbean and Bacon Soup

Serves: 4–6 people
Preparation time:
15 minutes plus
soaking time
Cooking time:
2–2½ hours

An inexpensive,
filling and tasty soup.

6 oz/175 g butterbeans
½ oz/15 g
  margarine
1 onion, chopped
6 rashers streaky
  bacon
2 pints/1 litre
  chicken stock or
  water and chicken
  stock cubes
bouquet garni (sprig
  of thyme,
  1 bay leaf, 3
  parsley stalks,
  tied together)
1 oz/25 g cornflour

Put the beans in a bowl, cover with cold water and leave to soak overnight. Next day, melt the margarine in a saucepan and add the onion and 4 of the bacon rashers, chopped. Fry gently for 5–10 minutes, stirring frequently. Add the stock, the drained beans and the bouquet garni. Bring to the boil, cover the pan and simmer for 1½–2 hours. Reserve some beans for garnish. Press the soup through a sieve with a wooden spoon or remove the bouquet garni and purée the soup in an electric blender. Return the soup to the saucepan and add the remaining 2 rashers of bacon, cut into strips, and the cornflour, blended with a little water. Bring to the boil, stirring, then simmer for 15 minutes. Return the beans for the garnish to the soup and reheat if necessary.

Main Courses

Mackerel in Foil

Serves: 4 people
Preparation time:
15 minutes
Cooking time:
30–35 minutes
Oven temperature:
350°F/180°C Mark 4

Mackerel are available most of the year but are at their best and cheapest in the spring. Other fish, fillets or cutlets, can be cooked in the same way.

4 mackerel
salt and pepper
1 lemon
1 teaspoon made mustard
parsley and lemon wedges for garnish

Gut the fish, cut off the heads and fins. Season the mackerel inside with salt and pepper, lemon juice and a little mustard. Enclose each fish in foil and bake them in a moderate oven (350°F/180°C Mark 4) for 30–35 minutes. Unwrap the mackerel but serve still in the foil, garnished with lemon wedges and parsley.

Tuna Shell Pie

Serves: 4 people
Preparation time:
15 minutes
Cooking time:
15–20 minutes

An ideal supper dish. It is a complete meal on its own and very quick to prepare.

4 oz/100 g pasta shells
2 oz/50 g margarine
1 onion, chopped
1 (10 oz/284 g) can cream of mushroom soup
1 (7½ oz/213 g) can tuna
1 small packet frozen mixed vegetables
¼ level teaspoon mixed dried herbs
salt and pepper
1 oz/25 g soft white breadcrumbs

Cook the shells in a saucepan of boiling salted water until tender (about 10 minutes). Drain. Heat 1 oz/25 g margarine in a large saucepan and fry the onion until softened. Stir in the shells, soup, flaked tuna, mixed vegetables and herbs. Season to taste. Heat thoroughly then pour into a heatproof dish. Sprinkle the breadcrumbs on top, dot with 1 oz/25 g margarine and put under a hot grill until browned.

German Herring Salad

Serves: 4—6 people
Preparation time:
15 minutes
Cooking time:
None

An inexpensive and piquant salad. Toss the apple in a little lemon juice to prevent it discolouring and assemble the salad just before serving.

4 rollmops
¼ pint/1·5 dl mayonnaise
1 level teaspoon castor sugar
½ level teaspoon dry mustard
1 tablespoon vinegar
salt and pepper
2 large cooked potatoes, diced
1 small cooked beetroot, diced
1 lettuce
1 red-skinned apple, cored and diced
2 large gherkins or pickled cucumber, sliced
4 spring onions, sliced

Cut the rollmops into strips. Put the mayonnaise in a bowl and mix in the sugar, mustard, vinegar and salt and pepper. Add the potato and beetroot and gently fold into the mayonnaise. Arrange a bed of lettuce on a serving plate and put the potato mixture on it. Arrange the rollmops on top with the apple, gherkins and spring onion round the sides. Serve as soon as possible.

Fisherman's Supper

Serves: 4—6 people
Preparation time:
20 minutes
Cooking time:
About 1 hour
Oven temperature:
400°F/200°C Mark 6

Use haddock, cod, snapper, or any white fish which is good value at the time. The cheese can be omitted for variation; add 1 level tablespoon chopped parsley instead. Mash the potato with a little margarine and milk.

1 lb/½ kg white fish
salt and pepper
1 pint/6 dl milk
2 oz/50 g margarine
2 oz/50 g plain flour
4 oz/100 g cheese, grated
½ level teaspoon made mustard
¼ level teaspoon ground nutmeg
8 oz/225 g tomatoes, skinned
2 lb/1 kg potatoes, cooked and mashed

Place the fish in a saucepan, season, then pour in ½ pint/3 dl of the milk. Bring to the boil, then simmer for 15—20 minutes or until the fish is cooked. Meanwhile, heat the margarine in another saucepan, stir in the flour and cook, stirring, for 2—3 minutes. Remove from the heat and gradually blend in the rest of the milk. Drain the fish and stir the cooking liquid into the sauce. Return to the heat, bring to the boil, stirring, and cook for 2—3 minutes. Remove from the heat, stir in the cheese, mustard and nutmeg. Flake the fish and put it into a 2 pint/1.2 litre ovenproof dish. Pour over the sauce. Slice the tomatoes, reserve some for garnish and spread the rest over the sauce. Pipe or spread the mashed potato over the top. Cover and leave in the refrigerator or cool place overnight. Before serving, bake in a hot oven (400°F/200°C Mark 6) for 30 minutes until heated through and the potato golden brown. Garnish with the reserved tomato slices.

Salmon Loaf

Makes: one 1 lb/½ kg loaf
Preparation time:
15 minutes plus chilling time
Cooking time:
None

A speedy dish for summer entertaining. Use tuna or cooked smoked haddock for family meals.

1 (7½ oz/213 g) can salmon
1 (7½ oz/213 g) can potato salad
2 hard-boiled eggs, chopped
4 oz/100 g cucumber, chopped
1 level tablespoon chopped parsley
1 oz/25 g fresh white breadcrumbs
salt and pepper
Garnish:
sprigs of parsley
salad vegetables
slices of lemon and green pepper (optional)

Lightly grease a 1 lb/½ kg loaf tin. Drain the salmon and remove any skin and bones. Flake it into a mixing bowl. Add the remaining ingredients except the garnish. Beat well to blend all the ingredients. Press the mixture into the prepared loaf tin, smooth the top and chill in the refrigerator for at least 2 hours. Turn out onto a serving dish and garnish with the parsley, salad vegetables, and slices of lemon and pepper if liked.

Smoked Haddock Cobbler

Serves: 4 people
Preparation time:
20 minutes
Cooking time:
About 25 minutes
Oven temperature:
425°F/220°C Mark 7

The filling and topping for this pie cook very quickly at the same time.

1 lb/½ kg smoked haddock fillets
1 (1⅛ oz/31 g) packet cheese sauce
½ pint/3 dl milk
4 oz/100 g frozen peas
Scones:
8 oz/225 g self raising flour
1 level teaspoon baking powder
½ level teaspoon salt
¼ level teaspoon pepper
¼ level teaspoon mixed dried herbs
2 oz/50 g soft margarine
7 tablespoons milk
milk for glazing

Skin the smoked haddock, cut it into 1 inch/2 cm pieces and put in an ovenproof dish. Make up the packet of cheese sauce with the milk, stir in the peas and pour the sauce over the fish.
Make the scones: Sift the flour, baking powder, salt and pepper into a bowl. Stir in the herbs, margarine and milk until thoroughly mixed. Knead the dough lightly on a floured surface. Roll it out to ½ inch/1 cm thick, cut out rounds using a 1½ inch/4 cm pastry cutter. Arrange the scones over the top of the fish and sauce. Brush the scones with milk and bake in a hot oven (425°F/220°C Mark 7) for 25 minutes or until golden. Serve hot.

Prawn Curry

Serves: 4 people
Preparation time:
15 minutes
Cooking time:
15–20 minutes

Thaw the prawns before adding them to the curry. If you like a really hot curry, add more curry powder. Cook 8 oz/225 g long grain rice to serve with this dish.

1 tablespoon oil
1 onion, chopped
1–2 level tablespoons curry powder
2 level teaspoons plain flour
¼ pint/1·5 dl white stock or water and chicken stock cube
2 teaspoons lemon juice
1 teaspoon brown sugar
2 level tablespoons chutney
1 (8 oz/226 g) can tomatoes
8 oz/225 g frozen mixed vegetables
4 oz/100 g frozen prawns

Heat the oil in a large saucepan and fry the onion gently for 5 minutes, stirring occasionally. Stir in the curry powder and flour and cook, stirring, for 2–3 minutes. Blend in the stock and lemon juice, bring to the boil, stirring continuously. Add the remaining ingredients, mix well, cover the pan and simmer for 15–20 minutes. Serve with boiled rice.

Cod in Yoghourt Tartare Sauce

Serves: one person
Preparation time:
15 minutes
Cooking time:
50 minutes
Oven temperature:
375°F/190°C Mark 5
then 350°F/180°C
Mark 4

A low-calorie dish – ideal for slimmers who eat alone.

1 cod steak
salt and pepper
1 bay leaf
⅛ oz/4 g margarine
Sauce:
1 (5 fl oz/142 ml) carton natural yoghourt
1 egg
½ level teaspoon capers
1 small gherkin, chopped
grated rind of ½ lemon
1 level tablespoon chopped parsley
4 level teaspoons fresh breadcrumbs

Place the fish in a small ovenproof dish. Season with salt and pepper, add the bay leaf and dot with the margarine. Cover with foil and bake in a moderately hot oven (375°F/190°C Mark 5) for 30 minutes. Remove the foil, drain the fish and remove any skin and bones. Return it to the cooking dish.
Make the sauce: Beat together the yoghourt, egg, capers, gherkin, lemon rind, parsley and salt and pepper to taste. Pour the sauce over and around the fish. Sprinkle with the breadcrumbs. Place the dish in a roasting pan with water to come halfway up the sides. Bake in a moderate oven (350°F/180°C Mark 4) for 20 minutes or until the top is golden brown.

Fish Casserole with Onions

Serves: 4 people
Preparation time:
20 minutes
Cooking time:
45 minutes
Oven temperature:
350°F/180°C Mark 4

Serve this for a family lunch. Any smoked fish such as cod or haddock, or white fish such as coley, haddock, cod, snapper or jewfish can be used.

1 lb/½ kg fish
milk
1 bay leaf
4 peppercorns
1 oz/25 g margarine
4 onions, sliced
½ oz/15 g plain flour
2 oz/50 g grated
   cheese
salt and pepper
chopped parsley for
   garnish

Wash the fish and put into a shallow pan with enough milk to cover. Add the bay leaf and peppercorns and bring to the boil. Simmer gently for 15 minutes or until the fish will flake easily. Drain the fish, reserve the liquid. Flake the fish into an ovenproof casserole, removing all bones and skin. Melt the margarine in a saucepan and add the onions. Fry gently, stirring frequently, until the onion is softened. Sprinkle in the flour and cook, stirring, for 2–3 minutes.

Strain and measure the reserved liquid and make up to ½ pint/3 dl with more milk if necessary. Add the liquid to the saucepan and bring to the boil, stirring, simmer for 2–3 minutes. Remove from the heat and stir in the cheese. Taste and season. Pour the sauce over the fish. Put the casserole in a moderate oven (350°F/180°C Mark 4) until it starts to brown (about 20 minutes). Serve garnished with chopped parsley.

Fish Goulash with Herbed Rice

Serves: 4–6 people
Preparation time:
15 minutes
Cooking time:
45 minutes

Any white fish is good for this recipe. Ask the fishmonger to remove the skin.

1½ lb/¾ kg fish fillets
lemon juice
celery salt
pepper
1 green pepper or
   2 sticks celery
1 (14 oz/396 g) can
   tomatoes
2 level tablespoons
   chopped chives
3 oz/75 g butter or
   margarine
8 oz/225 g long
   grain rice
1 teaspoon salt
1 level tablespoon
   chopped parsley
1 level tablespoon
   chopped mint

Wash the fish, dry and sprinkle with lemon juice, celery salt and pepper. Cut the green pepper into 1 inch/25 mm squares and put in a saucepan with the tomatoes, 1 level tablespoon chopped chives, 2 oz/50 g margarine and ¼ pint/1·5 dl water. Bring to the boil, stirring, then simmer gently for 10 minutes. Add the fish, cover the pan and cook gently for a further 15–20 minutes or until the fish flakes easily. Mean-

while put the rice and salt in a saucepan with ¾ pint/4·5 dl water. Bring to the boil, stir once, then cover the pan tightly. Simmer for 15 minutes or until the rice is tender and the liquid absorbed. Mix in the remaining chives, parsley and mint. Arrange the herbed rice in a ring on a serving plate, put the fish goulash in the centre. Serve as soon as possible.

Mackerel with Mustard Sauce

Serves: 2 people
Preparation time:
15 minutes
Cooking time:
20 minutes

If mackerel are not
available, use
herrings or mullet.

2 (12 oz/350 g)
  mackerel
1½ oz/40 g margarine
1 oz/25 g plain flour
½ pint/3 dl milk
1 level tablespoon
  dry mustard
1 tablespoon lemon
  juice
1 level teaspoon
  sugar
salt and pepper
parsley and chopped
  chives for garnish

Clean and bone the fish or ask your fishmonger to do this for you. Make three cuts in the flesh at the thickest part on each side. Dot with ½ oz/15 g of the margarine and cook under a hot grill for about 10 minutes, or until the fish is cooked. Meanwhile, melt the remaining margarine in a saucepan and stir in the flour. Cook, stirring, for 2–3 minutes. Add the milk and bring to the boil, stirring constantly; simmer for 2–3 minutes. Blend the mustard with the lemon juice and sugar and stir into the sauce. Reheat, taste and season. Put the fish on a serving plate, pour over a little sauce and serve the remainder separately. Garnish with chives and parsley.

Paprika Fish Turbans

Serves: 2–4 people
Preparation time:
20 minutes
Cooking time:
45–50 minutes
Oven temperature:
350°F/180°C Mark 4

Ask your fishmonger
to fillet the fish
or do this yourself.
Use flathead or
flounder if plaice is
not available.

4 small fillets plaice
paprika pepper
¼ pint/1·5 dl milk
1 bay leaf
8 oz/225 g long
  grain rice
pinch of ground
  turmeric
salt and pepper
1 oz/25 g margarine
1 oz/25 g plain flour
1 tablespoon lemon
  juice
pinch of sugar

Prepare the fillets, wash and dry thoroughly. Sprinkle each with a little paprika pepper and roll up. Place in a lightly greased ovenproof dish with the milk, ¼ pint/1·5 dl water and the bay leaf. Cover the dish with greased greaseproof paper and bake the fish in a moderate oven (350°F/180°C Mark 4) for about 30 minutes or until cooked. Meanwhile cook the rice in boiling salted water, with the turmeric added, for 10–15 minutes or until tender. Drain and keep hot. Make the sauce: Melt the margarine in a saucepan and stir in the flour. Cook, stirring, for 2 minutes. Drain the fish and keep warm. Measure the cooking liquid, remove the bay leaf and make up to ½ pint/3 dl with water if necessary. Blend the liquid into the roux, bring to the boil, stirring all the time. Boil for 2 minutes. Stir in the lemon juice, salt and pepper and sugar. Arrange the rice on a serving dish and put the fish turbans on top. Pour over the sauce and garnish with some more paprika pepper.

Cod Peppers

Serves: 4 people
Preparation time:
15 minutes
Cooking time:
35 minutes
Oven temperature:
400°F/200°C Mark 6

A high-protein/
low-calorie dish.
Peppers are at their
cheapest in the
summer. Other
vegetables such as
tomatoes or onions
can be used. For
real economy, wrap
the cod stuffing in
cabbage leaves.

4 small red or green
  peppers
8 oz/225 g cod fillet
1 small onion,
  chopped
8 oz/225 g
  mushrooms
salt and pepper
3 teaspoons anchovy
  essence

Place the whole peppers in a large saucepan of boiling water for 2–3 minutes. Drain and leave them to cool. Cut the peppers in half, lengthways, scoop out the pith and seeds. Place the cod fillet in a saucepan. Cover it with water and add the onion, half the mushrooms and salt and pepper to taste. Bring to the boil, cover and simmer for 15 minutes or until cooked. Drain the fish and flake it into a bowl, add the drained vegetables, anchovy essence, 2 tablespoons of the fish stock and salt and pepper to taste. Fill the pepper halves with the mixture, place them in an ovenproof dish, cover with foil and bake in a hot oven (400°F/200°C Mark 6) for 20 minutes. Open the foil, sprinkle with the remaining mushrooms. Cover again and bake for a further 15 minutes. Serve hot.

Corn and Haddock Supper

Serves: 4 people
Preparation time:
20 minutes
Cooking time:
25 minutes

A delicious creamy
supper dish which
is ideal for
entertaining. It
'stretches' a little
fish into ample
servings for 4 people.
Use 1 pint/6 dl milk
in place of
evaporated milk and
sweetcorn liquid, if
preferred.

12 oz/350 g smoked
  haddock
8 fl oz/2·25 dl
  evaporated milk
1 (7 oz/199 g) can
  sweetcorn
1½ oz/40 g plain
  flour
1 level teaspoon
  made mustard
1½ oz/40 g margarine
4 oz/100 g Cheddar
  cheese, grated
3 large tomatoes,
  sliced
1 oz/25 g soft white
  breadcrumbs
parsley for garnish

Place the haddock in a saucepan with just enough water to cover. Bring to the boil then simmer gently until the fish flakes easily (about 15 minutes). Drain the fish and flake it coarsely, removing any skin and bones. Reserve the fish stock. Measure the evaporated milk. Open the sweetcorn and drain, make the evaporated milk up to 1 pint/6 dl with the sweetcorn liquid. Whisk the flour, mustard and liquid together in a saucepan. Add the margarine then bring to the boil, stirring constantly, until thickened and boiling. Cook for 2–3 minutes. Remove from the heat and stir in 3 oz/75 g of the cheese. Beat until the cheese is melted. Stir the fish and corn into the sauce. Pour into a 2½ pint/1¼ litre capacity pie dish. Arrange the tomatoes on top and sprinkle with the remaining cheese and breadcrumbs. Cook under a hot grill until the top is golden. Serve garnished with parsley.

Lamb and Bean Casserole

Serves: 4–6 people
Preparation time:
20 minutes plus
soaking time for the
beans
Cooking time:
2 hours
Oven temperature:
325°F/170°C Mark 3

If it is not to be eaten straightaway, cool then store in a cool place for up to 24 hours. It keeps well and the flavours mellow. Reheat when needed.

8 oz/225 g red kidney
  beans
1½ lb/¾ kg boneless
  lamb
1 oz/25 g plain flour
salt and pepper
2 tablespoons oil
2 onions, sliced
1 lb/½ kg carrots
1 green pepper, sliced
  (optional)
¾ pint/4 dl beef stock
  or water and beef
  stock cube

Soak the beans in cold water to cover for up to 6 hours. Cut the lamb into 1 inch/25 mm pieces. Season the flour. Coat the lamb in the seasoned flour. Heat the oil in a saucepan and fry the lamb until lightly browned all over. Put the lamb into an ovenproof dish with the onions, carrots, green pepper, beans and stock. Cover the dish and cook in a moderately slow oven (325°F/170°C Mark 3) for 2 hours. Serve.

Lamb and Vegetable Pie

Serves: 4–6 people
Preparation time:
20 minutes
Cooking time:
45 minutes
Oven temperature:
400°F/200°C Mark 6

This useful recipe turns leftover lamb or other cold cooked meat and vegetables into a tasty pie.

Pastry:
6 oz/170 g plain
  flour
pinch of salt
1½ oz/40 g lard
1½ oz/40 g margarine
Filling:
2 oz/50 g margarine
2 oz/50 g plain flour
½ pint/3 dl milk
¼ level teaspoon
  cayenne pepper
2 oz/50 g cheese
8 oz/225 g cooked
  mixed vegetables,
  diced
6 oz/175 g cooked
  lamb, cubed
1 onion, finely
  chopped
1 level tablespoon
  chopped parsley
½ oz/15 g fine dry
  breadcrumbs

Make the pastry: Sift the flour and salt into a bowl, add the fat and rub in with your fingertips until the mixture resembles fine breadcrumbs. Add sufficient cold water to make a firm dough. Knead lightly, then roll out on a lightly floured surface. Line a 9 inch/23 cm flan ring standing on a baking tray. Prick the base with a fork, line with greaseproof paper and baking beans. Bake in a hot oven (400°F/200°C Mark 6) for 10 minutes, remove the paper and beans and continue cooking for a further 10 minutes.
Make the filling: Melt the margarine in a pan and stir in the flour. Cook, stirring, for 2–3 minutes. Blend in the milk and boil, stirring, for 2 minutes. Remove from the heat and season with salt and cayenne pepper. Grate the cheese and stir in half with the vegetables, lamb, onion and parsley; reheat gently. Pour the filling into the pastry case. Mix the remaining cheese with the breadcrumbs and sprinkle on top. Return the pie to the oven for a further 20 minutes or until lightly browned.

Irish Stew

Serves: 4 people
Preparation time:
15 minutes
Cooking time:
2 hours
Oven temperature:
325°F/170°C Mark 3

Serve this stew with fresh vegetables. The potatoes can be brushed with a little oil or butter to help them brown.

2 oz/50 g plain flour
1½ level teaspoons salt
½ level teaspoon pepper
2 lb/1 kg middle neck or scrag end of lamb
2 onions
1½ lb/¾ kg potatoes
1 level tablespoon chopped parsley for garnish

Sift the flour, salt and pepper into a bowl. Trim the chops and coat them with the seasoned flour. Slice the onions and put one-third of them in a casserole, cover with half the chops. Make a layer with the second third of the onions, then add the rest of the chops and top with the remaining onion slices. Add enough cold water to cover the onions. Cover the casserole and bake in a moderately slow oven (325°F/170°C Mark 3) for 1¼ hours. Remove from the oven. Cover the stew with the potatoes, cut into thin slices. Cook, uncovered, for a further 45 minutes. Serve hot, garnished with chopped parsley.

Saté Kambing

Serves: 4–6 people
Preparation time:
20 minutes plus marinating time
Cooking time:
10–15 minutes

Marinating the lamb not only gives it a delicious flavour but also helps to tenderise the meat and offset the fattiness. Serve on a bed of rice, accompanied by a tomato and onion salad.

2 lb/1 kg boned breast of lamb
¼ pint/1·5 dl cider vinegar
1 onion, grated
2 cloves garlic, crushed
2 level teaspoons salt
½ level teaspoon chilli powder
2 level teaspoons ground coriander
1 level teaspoon ground cumin
½ level teaspoon ground turmeric
1 level teaspoon ground ginger

Cut the lamb into ½ inch/12 mm cubes and put into a bowl. Stir in the vinegar, put aside for 30 minutes. Drain. Mix together the onion, garlic, salt, chilli powder, coriander, cumin, turmeric and ground ginger in a large bowl. Add to the lamb, coat well and leave for a further 30 minutes. Thread the pieces of meat on 4–6 skewers. Place under a hot grill for 10–15 minutes or until cooked through, turning frequently.

Lamb in the Round

Serves: 4–6 people
Preparation time:
20 minutes
Cooking time:
25 minutes per lb/
½ kg plus 25 minutes
over
Oven temperature:
350°F/180°C Mark 4

A tasty and
economical joint –
good enough for
entertaining. Serve
with roast potatoes
and gravy.

6 onions
1 level teaspoon
   chopped dried
   rosemary
1 level teaspoon
   chopped parsley
salt and pepper
1 boned shoulder of
   lamb
2 oz/50 g margarine

Finely chop 3 of the onions and
mix them with the rosemary, parsley
and salt and pepper to taste. Use
this mixture to stuff the boned
shoulder of lamb. Hold the meat
together with a skewer then tie it
into a round shape with string.
Weigh the lamb, then place it in a

roasting pan. Slice the remaining
onions and arrange them round the
meat. Melt the margarine and brush
it over the meat. Roast in a moderate oven (350°F/180°C Mark 4)
for 25 minutes per lb/½ kg plus
25 minutes over. Remove any
skewers and string, and serve.

Boiled Lamb and Caper Sauce

Serves: 6–8 people
(or according to the
size of the joint)
Preparation time:
20 minutes
Cooking time:
25 minutes per lb/
½ kg plus 25 minutes
over

The meat can be
stuffed if liked. This
makes a very
inexpensive and tasty
meal.

1 rolled breast of
   lamb or shoulder
   of mutton
1 swede or turnip,
   chopped
1 stick celery
1 carrot
6 cloves
1 onion
1 level tablespoon
   salt
Sauce:
1 oz/25 g margarine
1 oz/25 g plain flour
1 level tablespoon
   capers, chopped
1 teaspoon caper
   vinegar
salt and pepper

Weigh the meat. Put it in a large
saucepan, cover it with water and
add the prepared vegetables; stick
the cloves into the onion. Bring the
water to the boil, skim the surface
and simmer, covered, for 25 minutes per lb/½ kg plus 25 minutes
over. Skim frequently. Drain the
meat and vegetables, reserving the
liquid. Make the sauce: Heat the
margarine in a saucepan, stir in the
flour and cook for 2 minutes, stir-

ring. Remove from the heat. Gradually stir in ½ pint/3 dl of reserved
lamb stock. Return to the heat and
bring to the boil, stirring constantly
until the sauce thickens (about 3
minutes). Remove from the heat,
stir in the chopped capers and
caper vinegar (from the bottle) and
salt and pepper to taste. Serve the
lamb surrounded by the vegetables
Serve the sauce separately

Lamb Cutlets in Pastry

Serves: 4 people
Preparation time:
20 minutes plus
marinating time
Cooking time:
30–35 minutes
Oven temperature:
450°F/230°C Mark 8
then 350°F/180°C
Mark 4

Make these rather
small cutlets into a
more substantial
meal. Top the cutlets
with pâté or stuffing
if liked before
wrapping in pastry.

4 lamb cutlets
4 tablespoons oil
3 tablespoons
vinegar
1 level tablespoon
chopped mint
1 onion, finely
chopped
½ level teaspoon dry
mustard
1 level teaspoon
sugar
salt and pepper
1 (13 oz/368 g)
packet frozen puff
pastry
milk for glazing
mint for garnish

Prepare the cutlets and place them in a large bowl. Whisk together the oil, vinegar, mint, onion, mustard, sugar, salt and pepper, pour them over the lamb. Leave to marinate for at least 4 hours, turning occasionally. Cut the pastry into 4 equal portions. On a lightly floured surface, roll out each portion large enough to wrap round a lamb cutlet. Drain the cutlets, place each on a piece of pastry. Damp the edges with water, fold the pastry over and pinch the edges together to seal them. Brush with milk. Place them on a baking tray and bake in a hot oven (450°F/230°C Mark 8) for 15 minutes. Reduce the oven temperature to moderate (350°F/180°C Mark 4) and bake for a further 15–20 minutes. Serve garnished with sprigs of mint.

Lancashire Hot Pot

Serves: 4 people
Preparation time:
20 minutes
Cooking time:
2½ hours
Oven temperature:
350°F/180°C Mark 4

A complete meal in a
casserole. This is
tasty and
economical, an ideal
family dish.

1 oz/25 g plain
flour
salt and pepper
1 lb/½ kg middle
neck of lamb
2 lambs' kidneys
4 onions
8 oz/225 g carrots
1½ lb/¾ kg potatoes
¾ pint/4·5 dl stock or
water and beef
stock cube

Place the flour on a plate and season with salt and pepper. Trim the lamb cutlets and coat them with the seasoned flour. Skin and core the kidneys. Slice the kidneys, onions, carrots and potatoes. Place the cutlets, onions, kidneys, carrots and potatoes in layers in a large casserole, finishing with a layer of potatoes. Pour in the stock. Cover the casserole and bake in a moderate oven (350°F/180°C Mark 4) for 2 hours. Remove the lid and bake for a further 30 minutes to brown the potatoes.

Creamy Lamb and Mushrooms

Serves: 4 people
Preparation time:
15 minutes
Cooking time:
25 minutes
Oven temperature:
375°F/190°C Mark 5

An exciting lunch or supper dish made from cold cooked lamb.

4 eggs
¼ pint/1·5 dl single cream or top-of-the-milk
salt and pepper
8 oz/225 g cooked lamb
¼ pint/1·5 dl stock or water and a beef stock cube or gravy
1 oz/25 g margarine
4 oz/100 g medium-sized mushrooms

Lightly grease a 1 pint/6 dl casserole dish. Whisk the eggs together in a bowl. Whisk in the cream, or top-of-the-milk, and salt and pepper to taste. Mince or finely chop the lamb and mix it with the stock or gravy. Pile it into the greased casserole dish. Heat the margarine in a frying pan and gently fry the mushrooms keeping them whole. Place the mushrooms, stalks uppermost, on top of the meat. Pour over the egg mixture. Bake in a moderately hot oven (375°F/190°C Mark 5) for 25 minutes or until the egg mixture is set. Serve immediately.

Creamed Lamb with Cucumber

Serves: 6 people
Preparation time:
20 minutes
Cooking time:
25 minutes

An interesting way of using up leftover cooked lamb.

½ cucumber
½ oz/15 g margarine
¼ level teaspoon ground nutmeg
¼ level teaspoon basil
1 level teaspoon chopped mint
1 level teaspoon salt
½ level teaspoon pepper
2 tablespoons vinegar
1 lb/½ kg cooked lamb
3 spring onions
Sauce:
1 oz/25 g margarine
1 oz/25 g plain flour
½ pint/3 dl milk
½ teaspoon lemon juice
1 hard-boiled egg chopped
Garnish:
parsley sprigs
grilled bacon rolls (optional)

Halve the cucumber lengthwise and remove the seeds, scraping them out with a teaspoon. Cut the cucumber into 1 inch/25 mm slices. Heat the margarine in a saucepan and stir in the cucumber, nutmeg, basil, mint, salt and pepper and vinegar, cover and simmer gently for 10 minutes. Remove the lid and boil rapidly to reduce the liquid a little. Cut the lamb into ¼ inch/6 mm dice. Thinly slice the spring onions. Stir the lamb and onions into the cucumber mixture and gently heat through.
Make the sauce: Heat the margarine in a saucepan, stir in the flour and cook, stirring, for 2–3 minutes. Remove from the heat and slowly blend in the milk. Stir in the lemon juice, hard-boiled egg and the cucumber and lamb mixture. Cook gently for 5–10 minutes. Place on a serving dish and garnish with parsley and bacon rolls, if used.

Pork with Orange Sauce

Serves: 4 people
Preparation time:
15 minutes
Cooking time:
1 hour

Orange and pork go very well together. Use spare rib chops or belly pork rashers if the budget is very tight.

4 pork chops
2 level tablespoons plain flour
salt and pepper
2 oz/50 g lard or dripping
2 level tablespoons brown sugar
½ level tablespoon ground ginger
juice and grated rind of 2 oranges
½ pint/3 dl chicken stock or water and chicken stock cube
8 oz/225 g long grain rice
¾ pint/4·5 dl water
orange segments and parsley for garnish

Trim the chops, remove the rind with any excess fat. Season the flour with salt and pepper and coat the chops with it. Heat the lard in a large saucepan and fry the chops until browned on both sides (about 10 minutes). Remove the chops from the pan and keep warm. Stir any remaining flour into the saucepan with the sugar, ginger, orange rind, juice and stock. Bring to the boil, stirring. Return the chops to the pan, reduce the heat, cover and cook very gently for 45–50 minutes. Put the rice into a saucepan with the water and 2 level teaspoons salt. Bring to the boil, stir, then cover the pan tightly. Cook the rice gently for 15 minutes or until the liquid is absorbed and the rice is tender. Put the rice on a serving plate and arrange the chops on top. Pour the sauce over the top and serve garnished with orange segments and sprigs of parsley.

Spare Ribs in Honey Sauce

Serves: 4–6 people
Preparation time:
15 minutes
Cooking time:
1½ hours
Oven temperature:
325°F/170°C Mark 3

Use thin slices of belly pork if Chinese-style spare ribs are not available.

3 lb/1½ kg pork spare ribs
3 tablespoons oil
1 large onion, chopped
1 clove garlic, crushed
2 tablespoons lemon juice
4 tablespoons orange juice
2 tablespoons honey
salt and pepper
1 level tablespoon prepared mustard
4 tablespoons soy sauce
½ pint/3 dl white stock or water and chicken stock cube

Cut the spare ribs into individual ribs or ask your butcher to do this for you. Place the ribs in a roasting pan. Heat the oil in a saucepan and fry the onion and garlic until softened but not browned. Stir in all the remaining ingredients and bring to the boil. Pour the sauce over the ribs and cook in a moderately slow oven (325°F/170°C Mark 3) for 1½ hours, basting frequently. Drain off the sauce and serve hot.

Pork Casserole with Herb Scone Topping

Serves: 4 people
Preparation time:
20 minutes
Cooking time:
1 hour 45 minutes
Oven temperature:
325°F/170°C Mark 3
then 400°F/200°C
Mark 6

A 'whole food' casserole. Use plenty of chopped parsley for flavour.

1½ lb/750 g leg of pork
4 level tablespoons wholewheat plain flour
salt and pepper
1 onion, chopped
2 cloves garlic, crushed
1 level teaspoon ground ginger
6 prunes, stoned
1 bay leaf
1 level tablespoon chopped parsley
½ pint/3 dl chicken stock or water and chicken stock cube
Topping:
6 oz/175 g wholewheat self raising flour
pinch of salt
3 oz/75 g margarine
2 level tablespoons chopped parsley
cold water to mix

Cut the pork into 1 inch/25 mm cubes. Mix the flour with salt and pepper to taste in a bowl. Coat the pieces of pork with the seasoned flour, then place them in an ovenproof dish with the onion, garlic, ginger, prunes, bay leaf, parsley and stock. Cover and put into a moderately slow oven (325°F/170°C Mark 3) for 1½ hours. Remove the bay leaf.
Make the topping: Place the flour and salt in a bowl, add the margarine and rub in with your fingertips until the mixture resembles fine breadcrumbs. Stir in the chopped parsley and sufficient cold water to make a firm dough. Roll out on a lightly floured surface to the size of the casserole dish. Carefully place the dough over the filling and score the surface with a knife into squares. Place in a hot oven (400°F/200°C Mark 6) for 10–15 minutes or until cooked and browned on top. Serve hot.

Bacon Olives

Serves: 4 people
Preparation time:
20 minutes
Cooking time:
1 hour 25 minutes

Back bacon rashers are ideal for this interesting dish. For everyday family meals however, try using a cheaper cut such as collar.

1 large onion, sliced
3 oz/75 g fresh white breadcrumbs
1 level teaspoon dried sage
½ level teaspoon salt
¼ level teaspoon pepper
2 oz/50 g margarine
8 back bacon rashers
4 oz/100 g mushrooms, sliced
¼ pint/1·5 dl water
2 level teaspoons cornflour
2 tomatoes for serving

Make the stuffing: Put the onion into a saucepan with boiling water to cover. Cook until tender (about 10–15 minutes). Drain the onion and chop. Put into a mixing bowl with the breadcrumbs, sage, salt and pepper. Melt half the margarine and add to the bowl. Combine the stuffing ingredients thoroughly. Spread some of the stuffing on each rasher of bacon. Roll up the rashers and tie with fine string. Melt the remaining margarine in a large saucepan. Fry the bacon rolls until beginning to brown. Add the mushrooms and cook for a further 2–3 minutes. Pour in the water, cover the pan and bring to the boil. Simmer gently for 1 hour. Remove the bacon rolls and cut off the string, put them on a serving dish and keep hot. Mix the cornflour with a little cold water in a bowl, then stir it into the hot cooking liquid. Bring to the boil again, stirring. Simmer for 2 minutes. Pour the sauce over the bacon olives. Serve with fried tomatoes.

Wholewheat Cider Pancakes

Serves: 4 people
Preparation time:
20 minutes
Cooking time:
15 minutes

Use all white flour if wholewheat is not readily available. 2 sticks of celery could be used instead of the pepper for family meals.

Batter:
2 oz/50 g plain flour
2 oz/50 g whole-
 wheat plain flour
½ level teaspoon salt
1 egg, beaten
½ pint/3 dl dry cider
lard for frying
Filling:
3 rashers bacon
1 large onion
1 green pepper
4 oz/100 g
 mushrooms
1½ oz/40 g butter or
 margarine
salt and pepper
3 oz/75 g grated
 cheese
parsley for garnish

Mix the flours and salt together in a mixing bowl. Make a well in the centre and add the egg. Beat in the egg, then half the cider until a smooth batter is formed. Stir in the remaining cider. Heat a little lard in a 7 inch/18 cm frying pan. Pour in enough batter to just cover the base of the pan. Cook quickly until brown underneath, then turn the pancake over and cook the other side. Make 7 more pancakes in the same way. Keep the pancakes hot by stacking them on a plate over a saucepan of simmering water.

Make the filling: Chop the bacon, onion, pepper and mushrooms. Heat the butter or margarine in a large saucepan and add all the filling ingredients, reserving a little of the cheese for garnish. When hot and softened, divide the filling equally between the pancakes. Roll up the pancakes and serve sprinkled with the reserved cheese and garnished with parsley.

West Country Baked Pork Chops

Serves: 4 people
Preparation time:
20 minutes
Cooking time:
45 minutes
Oven temperature:
400°F/200°C Mark 6

For a cheaper meal use spare rib chops or even belly pork rashers. Use chicken stock for family meals, cider when entertaining.

1 lb/450 g cooking
 apples
1 onion, chopped
1 level tablespoon
 castor sugar
1 level tablespoon
 dried rosemary
4 pork chops
¼ pint/1·5 dl cider
salt and pepper
4 level tablespoons
 toasted
 breadcrumbs
3 oz/75 g cheese,
 grated
1 oz/25 g butter
1 red-skinned dessert
 apple

Lightly grease a shallow ovenproof dish. Peel, core and slice the cooking apples and arrange the slices over the base of the dish. Sprinkle with the chopped onion, sugar and rosemary. Trim the chops, removing the rind and surplus fat and arrange them on top of the apples. Pour in the cider and sprinkle with salt and pepper to taste. Mix together the bread-crumbs and grated cheese. Cover each chop with the mixture and a sliver of butter. Bake in a hot oven (400°F/200°C Mark 6) for 45 minutes or until the chops are tender, with a crispy golden crust on top. Core and slice the dessert apple. Fry the apple rings in a little butter in a frying pan, then arrange them on top of the cooked pork.

Savoury Luncheon Mousse

Serves: 4–6 people
Preparation time:
20 minutes plus
setting time
Cooking time:
None

This recipe can also be made with other cold meat such as luncheon meat or tongue. It uses up leftover egg whites as well.

6 oz/175 g cooked ham
1 oz/25 g margarine
1 oz/25 g plain flour
½ pint/3 dl milk
¼ pint/1·5 dl chicken stock or water and chicken stock cube
1 level tablespoon gelatine
1 level teaspoon tomato purée
salt and cayenne pepper
2 egg whites
cold cooked mixed vegetables for serving

Mince the ham finely. Melt the margarine in a saucepan, stir in the flour and cook, stirring, for 2–3 minutes. Blend in the milk and bring slowly to the boil, stirring constantly. Simmer for 2–3 minutes. Put the stock into a saucepan and heat gently, sprinkle in the gelatine and stir until dissolved. Mix the sauce with the stock, ham, tomato purée and salt and cayenne pepper to taste. Cool until beginning to set. Whisk the egg whites until stiff. Fold into the ham mixture. Pour into a 1½ pint/¾ litre capacity ring mould. Chill until set. Unmould and serve garnished with cooked mixed vegetables.

Jellied Pork Brawn

Serves: 4 people
Preparation time:
20 minutes plus
setting time
Cooking time:
2½ hours

An inexpensive and traditional dish that is ideal with salad. For extra flavour crumble a beef stock cube into the stock after cooking.

½ pig's head (including the tongue)
1 onion
1 carrot
1 stick celery
12 peppercorns
1 bouquet garni (1 bay leaf, sprig of thyme, and 3 parsley stalks)
salt and pepper
ground cloves

Wash the pig's head and remove the brains. Peel the onion and carrot, scrub the celery. Put the pig's head, vegetables, peppercorns, bouquet garni and ½ level tablespoon salt in a large saucepan. Cover with cold water, bring to the boil, then simmer for 2½ hours. Remove the head and strain the stock. Cut the meat off the head and dice. Skin and dice the tongue. Mix the meat and season well with salt and pepper. Add a good pinch of ground cloves. Put the meat in a 1½ pint/9 dl capacity pudding basin and stir in ¾ pint/4·5 dl of the well strained stock. Put in a cool place, preferably the refrigerator, until set. Serve sliced.

Pork Fricassee

Serves: 4 people
Preparation time:
15 minutes
Cooking time:
20–25 minutes

For special occasions
use white wine
instead of stock.
Serve with savoury
rice.

1½ lb/¾ kg hand or
  shoulder pork
1 tablespoon oil
2 onions, chopped
1 oz/25 g plain flour
¼ pint/1.5 dl. chicken
  stock or water and
  chicken stock cube
¼ pint/1.5 dl. milk
½ level teaspoon dried
  thyme
1 level teaspoon salt
½ level teaspoon
  pepper
4 oz/100 g button
  mushrooms

Cut the pork into ½ inch/1 cm cubes. Heat the oil in a heavy-based saucepan, add the pork and fry until well browned all over, stirring frequently. Add the onion and continue frying gently for 5 minutes. Stir in the flour. Remove the pan from the heat, blend in the stock, milk, thyme, salt and pepper. Return to the heat and cook until thickened, stirring continuously. Stir in the mushrooms. Cover the pan and simmer for 15 minutes. Serve at once.

Paprika Pork Casserole

Serves: 4 people
Preparation time:
15 minutes
Cooking time:
1½ hours
Oven temperature:
350°F/180°C Mark 4

Use spare rib pork
chops for this
recipe; they are
much cheaper than
loin chops.
Alternatively, use
boneless pork and
cut into 1 inch/
25 mm cubes.

4 spare rib pork
  chops
2 onions, sliced
2 oz/50 g
  mushrooms, sliced
2 sticks celery,
  chopped
2 level tablespoons
  paprika pepper
salt and pepper
¾ pint/4 dl beef
  stock or water and
  beef stock cube
1 level tablespoon
  cornflour
chopped parsley for
  garnish

Trim the chops and remove excess fat. Mix the onions, mushrooms and celery together and put into a heatproof casserole. Arrange the chops on the vegetables. Stir the paprika pepper and salt and pepper to taste into the stock and pour over the chops. Cover the casserole and cook in a moderate oven (350°F/180°C Mark 4) for 1½ hours. Remove the chops and put on a serving plate. Mix the cornflour with a little cold water, then stir it into the cooking liquor. Bring to the boil and simmer, stirring, for 2–3 minutes. Pour the sauce over the chops and serve garnished with chopped parsley.

Wellington Sausage Roll

Serves: 4–6 people
Preparation time:
15 minutes plus
cooling time
Cooking time:
55 minutes
Oven temperature:
425°F/220°C Mark 7
then 400°F/200°C
Mark 6

This is quick to
prepare if you use
frozen puff pastry,
but more economical
if you make your own
flaky pastry, using
8 oz/200 g flour.

1 lb/½ kg skinless
  sausages
1 oz/25 g lard
4 oz/100 g
  mushrooms, sliced
1 small onion, finely
  chopped
1 oz/25 g margarine
1 oz/25 g plain flour
¼ pint/1.25 dl milk
1 (13 oz/368 g)
  packet frozen puff
  pastry
little milk for glazing

Fry the sausages in the lard, turning occasionally, until brown all over. Drain on absorbent kitchen paper and leave to cool. Fry the mushrooms for 3–5 minutes. Drain on absorbent kitchen paper. Fry the onion in the margarine until transparent but not brown. Stir in the flour and cook for 2–3 minutes, stirring constantly. Remove the pan from the heat and blend in the milk. Return to the heat and cook for 2 minutes, stirring constantly. Stir in the mushrooms. Leave to cool. Roll out the pastry on a lightly floured board to a rectangle 13×10 inches/ 32×25 cm. Spread one-quarter of the sauce down the centre and arrange 4 sausages in pairs lengthwise on top. Spread over another quarter of the sauce. Press the remaining sausages on top and spread the remaining sauce over the top and sides. Fold the pastry to make a parcel and seal the edges with a little milk. Place on a baking tray with the pastry join underneath. Decorate the roll with the pastry trimmings. Brush all over with milk. Make 3–4 small slits in the top of the pastry to allow steam to escape during cooking. Bake in a hot oven (425°F/220°C Mark 7) for 20 minutes or until well risen and coloured. Reduce the oven temperature to moderately hot (400°F/200°C Mark 6) for a further 15 minutes until crisp and golden.

Nasi Goreng

Serves: 6 people
Preparation time:
20 minutes
Cooking time:
40–45 minutes

This is a typically
Indonesian dish but
the recipe has been
slightly adapted to
suit Western tastes.
Make the omelette
for garnish very
thin, like a pancake.
Serve accompanied
by peanuts, crisps
and a green salad.

8 oz/225 g long
  grain rice
12 oz/350 g
  shoulder of pork
4 oz/100 g butter
8 oz/225 g onions,
  sliced
12 oz/350 g cooked
  mixed vegetables
salt and pepper
3 level teaspoons
  curry powder or to
  taste
2 tablespoons soy
  sauce
1 egg
extra butter
2 tomatoes

Cook the rice in a large saucepan of boiling salted water for 12–15 minutes or until tender. Drain and rinse in hot running water. Meanwhile, cut the pork into 1 inch/ 25 mm cubes. Melt half the butter in a large saucepan. Add the onions and pork and fry, stirring occasionally, for about 20 minutes or until the pork is browned and cooked through. Add the remaining butter, cooked rice, vegetables, salt and pepper, curry powder and soy sauce. Gently heat through until piping hot, stirring occasionally. Beat the egg lightly in a small bowl with 2 teaspoons water. Heat a small piece of butter in an omelette pan and add the egg. Cook quickly, stirring with a fork until the omelette has set. Continue cooking until the top is nearly dry. Remove from the pan and cut into strips. Put the pork and rice mixture into a heatproof serving dish, garnish with strips of omelette and small wedges of tomato. Place under a hot grill for a few moments then serve immediately.

Chinese Pork

Serves: 4 people
Preparation time:
15 minutes
Cooking time:
About 10 minutes

Chinese cooking is always quick and easy. This recipe is ideal for special occasions. Serve with rice.

12 oz/350 g shoulder pork
1 (16 oz/454 g) can bean sprouts
2 oz/50 g blanched almonds or walnuts
1 tablespoon soy sauce
2 tablespoons chicken stock or water and chicken stock cube
1 level teaspoon sugar
2 tablespoons oil
2 spring onions, thinly sliced
1 pineapple ring, chopped
salt and pepper

Cut the pork into ½ inch/1 cm cubes. Drain the bean sprouts, rinse with cold running water and drain again. Split the almonds in half. Mix together the soy sauce, stock and sugar in a small bowl. Heat the oil in a frying pan, add the pork and fry, stirring, until browned all over. Stir in the almonds and spring onions, fry for 3–5 minutes. Drain off any oil. Add the remaining ingredients, including the bean sprouts, combine thoroughly, cover the pan and cook for 2 minutes. Serve.

Pork Charlotte

Serves: 4 people
Preparation time:
15 minutes
Cooking time:
30 minutes

This is a complete meal. For special occasions use cider instead of stock.

1½ lb/¾ kg belly pork
salt and pepper
1 oz/25 g lard
1 lb/½ kg potatoes, sliced
8 oz/225 g leeks, sliced
½ pint/3 dl chicken stock or water and chicken stock cube
2 oz/50 g cornflour
Topping:
3 oz/75 g breadcrumbs
1 level teaspoon mixed dried herbs
1 tablespoon oil

Cut the pork into ½ inch/1 cm cubes and place in a mixing bowl. Sprinkle with salt and pepper. Heat the lard in a heatproof casserole, add the pork and fry until browned all over, stirring frequently. Add the potatoes, leeks and stock blended with the cornflour. Bring to the boil, stirring occasionally, and simmer for 20 minutes.
Make the topping: Mix together the breadcrumbs, herbs and oil in a bowl and sprinkle it onto the meat mixture. Place the casserole under a hot grill until golden.

Cold Spiced Meat Loaf

Serves: 4 people
Preparation time:
15 minutes plus
setting time
Cooking time:
None

Serve this meat loaf
with a salad. An ideal
supper for slimmers.
Use cold leftover
roast meat as
available.

½ pint/2·5 dl stock or
    water and beef
    stock cube
¾ oz/20 g gelatine
2 hard-boiled eggs
¼ pint/1·5 dl tomato
    juice
1 small onion, grated
¼ teaspoon each
    ground cinnamon
    and nutmeg
salt and pepper
1 tablespoon lemon
    juice
1 level teaspoon
    sugar
2 sticks celery,
    chopped
12 oz/350 g cold
    roast lamb or beef,
    diced
lettuce and
    watercress for
    serving

Heat the stock in a saucepan until
hot but not boiling. Sprinkle in the
gelatine and stir until dissolved (do
not boil). Pour a very thin layer of
stock on the base of a lightly oiled
loaf tin. Allow to set. Slice the
hard-boiled eggs and arrange the
slices on the jellied stock. Put the
remaining stock in a bowl and stir
in the tomato juice, onion, spices,
salt and pepper, lemon juice, sugar,
celery and diced meat. Mix thoroughly. Put into the loaf tin. Chill
until set. Serve unmoulded on a
bed of lettuce and watercress.

Meatballs with Barbecue Sauce

Serves: 4 people
Preparation time:
15 minutes
Cooking time:
35 minutes

Serve these
meatballs for a meal
starter or for the
main course. They
are very economical
to make.

Meatballs:
12 oz/350 g
    minced beef
1 oz/25 g
    breadcrumbs
1 onion, grated
1 egg
1 tablespoon
    tomato purée
salt and pepper
oil for frying
Sauce:
4 oz/100 g tomato
    chutney
1 onion, very finely
    chopped
1 level tablespoon
    French mustard
2 tablespoons
    Worcestershire
    sauce
¼ pint/1·5 dl water
salt and pepper

Make the meatballs by mixing all
the ingredients together thoroughly,
and shaping into 1½ inch/3 cm balls.
Make the sauce: Put all the ingredients in a small saucepan and
bring to the boil, stirring. Boil for
2–3 minutes. Place the meatballs
in a frying pan with a little oil over
a hot fire, and fry for 20–30 minutes
or until they are browned and
cooked. Serve the meatballs with
the sauce poured over the top.

Steak and Vegetable Pie

Serves: 4 people
Preparation time:
20 minutes
Cooking time:
2 hours 20 minutes
Oven temperature:
400°F/200°C Mark 6

Vegetables help to make the meal go further. Add a crisp pastry top to make a more substantial dish.

1 lb/½ kg chuck or blade steak
1 oz/25 g plain flour
salt and pepper
1 tablespoon oil
1 onion, chopped
1 large carrot, sliced
1 turnip, sliced
Pastry:
8 oz/200 g plain flour
pinch of salt
2 oz/50 g margarine
2 oz/50 g lard
milk to glaze

Cut the steak into 1 inch/25 mm cubes. Coat with 1 oz/25 g plain flour seasoned with salt and pepper. Heat the oil in a saucepan and fry the vegetables and meat until the meat is browned all over. Add ¼ pint/1·5 dl water and bring to the boil, stirring. Cover and simmer gently for 1½ hours, stirring occasionally. Pour into a 2 pint/1 litre capacity pie dish and leave until cold.
Meanwhile make the pastry: Sift the plain flour into a mixing bowl with a pinch of salt. Rub the margarine and lard into the mixture until it resembles fine breadcrumbs. Stir in enough cold water to make a firm dough. Roll out the pastry on a lightly floured surface, until 1 inch/25 mm larger than the pie dish all round. Cut off a ½ inch/12 mm strip of pastry and place it on the edge of the dish. Moisten and cover with the pastry lid. Brush with milk. Bake the pie in a hot oven (400°F/200°C Mark 6) for about 40 minutes or until golden. Serve hot.

Beef, Bacon and Mushroom Casserole

Serves: 4–6 people
Preparation time:
15 minutes
Cooking time:
2½ hours
Oven temperature:
325°F/170°C Mark 3

A quick to prepare casserole which is good enough to serve when entertaining. Use chuck steak, or shin for real economy.

1 lb/½ kg stewing steak
8 oz/225 g bacon
plain flour
salt and pepper
2 sticks celery, chopped
3 onions, sliced
8 oz/225 g button mushrooms
bouquet garni
   (1 sprig of thyme, 1 sprig of parsley and 1 bay leaf)

Cut the steak and bacon into 1 inch/25 mm cubes. Season some flour with salt and pepper. Coat the meat in the seasoned flour and put it into a casserole with all the remaining ingredients. Pour in enough water to almost cover the ingredients. Cover the casserole and cook in a moderately slow oven (325°F/170°C Mark 3) for 2½ hours or until the meat is tender. Remove the bouquet garni and serve.

Curried Beef Salad

Serves: 4 people
Preparation time:
15 minutes
Cooking time:
None

A delicious and quickly prepared salad which is good for any time of the year. Use other cold meat if liked or as available.

½ pint/¼ litre mayonnaise
2 level teaspoons curry powder
½ level teaspoon sugar
salt and pepper
6 oz/175 g cold roast beef
8 oz/225 g cold boiled potatoes
2 sticks celery, sliced
¼ cucumber, diced
1 small apple, cored and grated
1 tablespoon lemon juice
1 onion, grated
½ (8 oz/225 g) can pineapple pieces
lettuce for serving

Put the mayonnaise in a large bowl and stir in the curry powder, sugar and salt and pepper. Cut the beef and potatoes into ½ inch 12 mm cubes and add them to the mayonnaise with the celery, cucumber, apple, lemon juice, onion and the drained pineapple pieces. Toss all the ingredients together lightly and chill. Serve on a bed of lettuce.

Russian Cotletti with Mushroom Sauce

Serves: 4 people
Preparation time:
20 minutes
Cooking time:
20–30 minutes

A very inexpensive dish which could be served for a special occasion.

1 lb/500 g minced beef
2 oz/50 g fresh breadcrumbs
1 egg
salt and pepper
extra breadcrumbs
oil for frying
Mushroom sauce:
4 oz/100 g mushrooms, chopped
1 onion, finely chopped
1 oz/25 g butter
salt and pepper
2 teaspoons plain flour
¼ pt/1·5 dl soured cream
tomatoes and parsley for garnish

Mix the minced beef, breadcrumbs, egg, and salt and pepper together thoroughly. Divide into 4 equal portions and form each one into a cutlet shape. Press some extra breadcrumbs all over each cutlet.

Heat ¼ inch/7 mm oil in a frying pan and fry the cutlets for about 15–20 minutes until well browned and cooked.

Meanwhile make the mushroom sauce. Fry the mushrooms and onion in the butter gently for 5–10 minutes or until softened. Season well and sprinkle in the flour. Cook for another 1–2 minutes. Stir in the soured cream. Simmer for 2 minutes.

Drain the cutlets on absorbent kitchen paper, then serve hot with the sour cream mushroom sauce. Garnish with tomato wedges and parsley.

Braised Oxtail

Serves: 4 people
Preparation time:
15 minutes
Cooking time:
About 3 hours

A very tasty and
filling dish, ideal for
cold evenings.

1 oxtail
1 oz/25 g plain flour
salt and pepper
1 oz/25 g dripping
   or lard
2 onions, sliced
1 clove garlic,
   crushed (optional)
2 carrots, chopped
1 turnip, chopped
2 sticks celery,
   chopped
1 (14 oz/396 g) can
   tomatoes
1 bay leaf
chopped parsley
   for garnish

Ask your butcher to chop the oxtail into 1½–2 inch/3–5 cm pieces. Put the flour on a plate and season with salt and pepper. Wipe the oxtail pieces with a clean damp cloth, then coat in the seasoned flour. Heat the dripping or lard in a heavy-based saucepan. Fry the oxtail until browned all over. Remove the oxtail from the pan and add the onions and garlic. Fry until softened. Add the other vegetables and cook for a further 5 minutes. Return the oxtail to the pan and add the bay leaf. Reduce the heat and cover the pan tightly. Cook very gently for 2–3 hours. Serve garnished with chopped parsley.

Poor Man's Beef Stroganoff

Serves: 4 people
Preparation time:
15 minutes
Cooking time:
1 hour 10 minutes

Try this stroganoff
next time you
entertain. It is
especially good for
a buffet party. Use
top rump (round),
topside or skirt steak.
Serve with rice or
noodles.

1 lb/½ kg frying
   steak
3 oz/75 g margarine
¼ pint/1·5 dl beef
   stock or water and
   beef stock cube
2 onions, thinly
   sliced
4 oz/100 g
   mushrooms, sliced
1 level tablespoon
   tomato purée
salt and pepper
¼ level teaspoon
   ground nutmeg
2 level teaspoons
   cornflour
1 (5 fl oz/142 ml)
   carton soured
   cream

Cut the beef into thin strips about 2 inches/5 cm long and ¼ inch/6 mm wide. Heat 2 oz/50 g of the margarine in a large saucepan and fry the steak until browned. Add the stock and bring to the boil. Cover the pan tightly. Simmer gently for 30 minutes. Meanwhile, fry the onions and mushrooms in the remaining margarine, until softened. Add them to the beef with the tomato purée, salt and pepper, and nutmeg. Cover the pan again and continue cooking for 30 minutes or until the beef is tender. Mix the cornflour with a little water in a small bowl then stir it into the saucepan. Boil for 2–3 minutes. Remove from the heat and stir in the soured cream.

Beef Roll

Serves: 4 people
Preparation time:
20 minutes
Cooking time:
1 hour
Oven temperature:
350°F/180°C Mark 4

A delicious and very inexpensive dish. The children love it.

1 lb/½ kg minced beef
salt and pepper
½ level teaspoon mixed dried herbs
2 oz/50 g soft breadcrumbs
1 large onion, grated
¼ pint/1·5 dl milk or beef stock
1 small packet frozen mixed vegetables
4 tablespoons tomato ketchup
parsley for garnish

Put the minced beef into a mixing bowl with salt and pepper, herbs, breadcrumbs, onion and milk or stock. Mix very thoroughly. Put the meat mixture onto a piece of foil and pat out gently to a 9 inch/ 23 cm square. Spread the mixed vegetables on the meat and roll up like a Swiss roll. Fold the foil around the roll securely, seal the ends together. Put on a baking tray and cook in a moderate oven (350°F/ 180°C Mark 4) for 30 minutes. Unwrap the foil and spread on the tomato ketchup. Continue cooking for a further 30 minutes. Serve garnished with parsley.

Braised Steak Roll

Serves: 3–4 people
Preparation time:
15 minutes
Cooking time:
2 hours
Oven temperature:
325°F/170°C Mark 3

Skirt is a cheaper cut of beef which makes delicious stews at any time but lends itself particularly to this dish as it comes in a flat piece.

1 lb/½ kg skirt steak
1 onion, chopped
1 small can tomatoes
1 clove garlic, crushed
1 level teaspoon mixed dried herbs
salt and pepper

Wipe the meat with a clean damp cloth and place it between two pieces of polythene. Beat it with a rolling pin until ¼–½ inch/6–12 mm thick. Put all the remaining ingredients into a saucepan, bring to the boil and boil rapidly, stirring occasionally, until thick. Spread the tomato mixture over the steak and roll up like a Swiss roll. Wrap the roll in foil and cook in a moderately slow oven (325°F/170°C Mark 3) for 1½ hours. Remove the foil and cook for a further 30 minutes. Serve cut into slices.

Karti Kebabs

Serves: 6 people
Preparation time:
15 minutes plus
marinating time
Cooking time:
10–15 minutes

This recipe can also
be cooked slowly in
the oven (300°F/
150°C Mark 2) for
about 2–3 hours.
Place the meat in an
ovenproof dish
instead of on
skewers. Serve with
freshly boiled rice.

1 (5 fl oz/142 ml)
 carton natural
 yoghourt
1 small onion, grated
1 level tablespoon
 curry powder
$\frac{1}{4}$ level teaspoon
 each ground
 ginger, ground
 cinnamon and
 ground cloves
1 tablespoon oil
1 tablespoon lemon
 juice
salt and pepper
1$\frac{1}{2}$ lb/750 g skirt
 steak
watercress for
 garnish

Mix all the ingredients apart from
the steak in a large bowl. Cut the
steak into 1 inch/25 mm cubes and
add it to the mixture. Marinate the
steak overnight, turning occasionally. Thread the steak onto skewers.
Cook the kebabs under a hot grill,
turning frequently, for 10–15 minutes or until the meat is cooked.
Baste occasionally with the marinade. Heat any remaining marinade
in a saucepan and serve it as a
sauce. Garnish with watercress.

Beef Goulash

Serves: 4–6 people
Preparation time:
20 minutes
Cooking time:
2 hours

A good dish for a hot
buffet. Serve with rice
or mashed potatoes.

1$\frac{1}{2}$ lb/$\frac{3}{4}$ kg stewing
 beef
2 tablespoons oil
2 onions, sliced
1 clove garlic,
 crushed
1 level tablespoon
 paprika pepper
$\frac{1}{2}$ level tablespoon
 cayenne pepper
1 oz/25 g plain flour
1 pint/6 dl beef stock
 or water and beef
 stock cube
2 tablespoons tomato
 purée
salt and pepper
1 (5 fl oz/142 ml)
 carton natural
 yoghourt

Cut the meat into 1 inch/25 mm
cubes. Heat the oil in a large
saucepan, add the pieces of beef
and fry them until browned all over.
Remove the meat from the pan. Add
the onion, garlic, the paprika and
cayenne peppers and fry gently for 3
minutes. Stir in the flour and
continue cooking for 2 minutes.
Remove from the heat and gradually
blend in the stock. Add the meat and
tomato purée. Return to the heat
and bring to the boil, stirring
continuously, add salt and pepper
to taste. Cover the pan and simmer
gently for 2 hours. Remove from
the heat, leave to cool and keep in
the refrigerator or cool place overnight. The next day, simmer the
goulash for a further $\frac{1}{2}$–1 hour, until
the meat is tender. Stir in the
yoghourt just before serving.

133

Belgian Beef

Serves: 6 people
Preparation time:
20 minutes
Cooking time:
2 hours

A filling and warming beef stew. Use brown ale if stout is not available.

2 lb/1 kg chuck
  steak
1½ oz/40 g butter
  or dripping
1 large onion, finely
  chopped
1 clove garlic,
  crushed
¾ pint/4 dl stout
2 level teaspoons
  prepared mustard
2 level teaspoons
  brown sugar
2 teaspoons malt
  vinegar
1 level teaspoon salt
1 bay leaf
pinch of dried thyme
2 oz/50 g white
  breadcrumbs

Cut the steak into 1 inch/25 mm cubes. Heat the butter or dripping in a large saucepan and fry the onion and garlic until softened. Add the meat and fry until browned all over. Stir in all the remaining ingredients except the breadcrumbs. Bring to the boil, stirring constantly. Cover tightly, then simmer very gently for 2 hours. Remove the bay leaf, stir in the breadcrumbs and serve.

Beef and Orange Stew

Serves: 4 people
Preparation time:
20 minutes
Cooking time:
2–2½ hours

For real economy, use shin of beef. Cook it for at least 3 hours to ensure that the meat is tender.

1½ lb/¾ kg stewing
  beef
1 oz/25 g plain flour
salt and pepper
1½ oz/40 g dripping
1 onion, sliced
8 oz/225 g carrots,
  sliced
1 orange
2 beef stock cubes

Cut the beef into 1 inch/25 mm pieces. Mix the flour with salt and pepper on a plate. Coat the pieces of beef with the seasoned flour. Heat the dripping in a large saucepan, add the beef, onion and carrot and fry until the meat is browned all over. Cut 2 or 3 thin strips of rind from the orange with a potato peeler, then cut these into matchstick strips. Squeeze the juice from the orange and stir it into the stew with 1 pint/6 dl water. Crumble in the stock cubes. Bring to the boil, cover and simmer for 2–2½ hours or until the meat is tender. Stir the strips of orange rind into the stew 1 hour before the cooking is completed. Serve straightaway or allow to cool, then cover and store in the refrigerator or cool place until needed. Bring to the boil again and serve.

Veal Salad Ring

Serves: 4 people
Preparation time:
20 minutes plus
setting time
Cooking time:
None

A refreshing salad mould for hot days. It is an ideal way to use up leftover cooked veal. Make the aspic jelly from a packet of crystals.

8 oz/225 g cooked
  veal
2 level teaspoons
  chopped parsley
salt and pepper
4 small tomatoes,
  skinned
¼ cucumber, peeled
¾ pint/4·5 dl aspic
  jelly
salad vegetables
  for serving

Dice the veal and put into a bowl with the chopped parsley and salt and pepper. Chop the tomatoes and dice the cucumber. Mix all the ingredients, including the aspic, together, then put them into a ring or other mould. Put in a cool place until set. Unmould onto a serving plate and serve garnished with salad vegetables.

Osso Buco

Serves: 4 people
Preparation time:
20 minutes
Cooking time:
1½ hours

An inexpensive and delicious dish which can be served for family meals and when entertaining. If the budget is very tight leave out the wine.

2 oz/50 g plain flour
1 level teaspoon salt
½ level teaspoon
  pepper
4 thick slices shin
  of veal or 4 veal
  shanks
4 tablespoons oil
1 onion, chopped
1 carrot, chopped
1 clove garlic,
  chopped
¼ pint/1.5 dl chicken
  stock or water
  and chicken stock
  cube
3 fl oz/.75 dl white
  wine
3 level tablespoons
  tomato purée
grated rind and juice
  of 1 lemon
¼ level teaspoon
  dried thyme
2 bay leaves
8 oz/225 g long
  grain rice
1 level teaspoon
  turmeric
2 level tablespoons
  chopped parsley

Mix the flour and salt and pepper together. Coat the veal with the seasoned flour. Heat the oil in a large saucepan or flameproof casserole. Add the veal and brown all over. Remove from the pan and drain. Add the onion, carrot and garlic to the pan. Fry, stirring occasionally, for 3–4 minutes until the onion is soft. Stir in the stock, wine, tomato purée, lemon rind and juice, thyme and bay leaves. Bring to simmering point, cover and simmer for 1½ hours until the veal is tender. Remove the bay leaves. Meanwhile, cook the rice with the turmeric in boiling salted water for 12–15 minutes or until tender. Drain. Serve the osso buco on the rice, garnished with parsley.

Spicy Chicken and Pineapple

Serves: 4–6 people
Preparation time:
20 minutes plus
marinating time
Cooking time:
30 minutes

1 (3 lb/750 g)
  chicken
¾ level teaspoon
  chilli powder
1 level teaspoon salt
3 cloves garlic,
  crushed
10 spring onions,
  thinly sliced
2 level teaspoons
  tomato purée

3 tablespoons oil
1 (12 oz/340 g) can
  pineapple pieces,
  drained
2 level teaspoons
  grated lemon rind
2 tablespoons lemon
  juice
½ pint/3 dl coconut
  milk
2 teaspoons soy
  sauce

Cut the chicken meat from the carcase and chop into 1 inch/25 mm pieces. In a large bowl mix together the chilli powder, salt, garlic, spring onions (reserve a few slices for garnish) and tomato purée. Add the chicken pieces, mix well and leave for at least 1 hour. Heat the oil in a large saucepan and fry the chicken and pineapple until the chicken is lightly browned. Add the lemon rind and juice, coconut milk and soy sauce to the saucepan. Cover and simmer very gently for 30 minutes or until the chicken is tender. Serve immediately, garnished with the few reserved spring onion slices and accompanied by freshly cooked rice and hot spicy chutney.

To make coconut milk: Place 6 oz/175 g desiccated coconut in a saucepan with 1 pint/6 dl water. Bring to the boil, then cover the pan and remove it from the heat. When lukewarm, strain the milk through several thicknesses of muslin. A second extract can also be made, and the two extracts mixed together.

Creamy Chicken Salad

Serves: 4–6 people
Preparation time:
15 minutes plus
cooling and setting
time
Cooking time:
None

A filling lunch or
supper salad for
using up cold
cooked chicken.

1 (15 oz/½ litre) can
  cream of chicken
  soup
¼ pint/1.25 dl milk
2 level tablespoons
  gelatine
6 oz/150 g cold
  chicken
1 (10 oz/285 g)
  can sweetcorn
1 onion, grated
2 tomatoes, skinned
  and chopped
2 sticks celery,
  chopped
salt and pepper
salad for serving

Put the cream of chicken soup into a saucepan with the milk and heat gently. Stir the gelatine with 4 tablespoons hot water until dissolved. Add it to the soup and stir well. Do not boil. Allow the soup to cool. Cut the chicken into bite-sized pieces and stir it into the soup with the drained sweetcorn, onion, tomato and celery. Taste and season if necessary. Put the salad into a 2 pint/1 litre mould and chill until set. Unmould the chicken salad onto a serving plate and serve with a green salad.

Oven-Fried Chicken

Serves: 8–12 people
Preparation time:
20 minutes
Cooking time:
45 minutes
Oven temperature:
375°F/190°C Mark 5

This can be served hot with a mushroom sauce, savoury rice and peas, or cold with a salad.

2 (3 lb/1½ kg) chickens
4 oz/100 g cornflakes, crushed
1 level teaspoon salt
1 level teaspoon pepper
1 level teaspoon paprika pepper
4 tablespoons oil
1 egg, beaten

Cut the chicken into 8–12 pieces. Mix together the crushed cornflakes, salt, pepper and paprika pepper on a large plate. Combine the oil and egg in a bowl. Coat the chicken pieces in the egg mixture and then the cornflake crumbs, pressing them on well with a knife.

Place the chicken in a roasting pan, cover and leave in the refrigerator or cool place overnight. Next day, bake in a moderately hot oven (375°F/190°C Mark 5) for 45 minutes or until rich golden brown in colour.

Chicken Cacciatora

Serves: 4 people
Preparation time:
15 minutes
Cooking time:
1 hour
Oven temperature:
350°F/180°C Mark 4

A good casserole for entertaining as it can be made ahead of time and left to cook. Use red wine instead of the chicken stock if the budget will allow.

1 (3 lb/1½ kg) chicken
2 level tablespoons plain flour
salt and pepper
6 tablespoons oil
1 onion, chopped
1 clove garlic, crushed
2 oz/50 g mushrooms, sliced
2 carrots, peeled and sliced
1 (15 oz/426 g) can tomatoes
2 tablespoons chicken stock

Cut the chicken into 8 small pieces. Mix the flour with the salt and pepper and sprinkle over each chicken piece. Heat the oil in a large frying pan and fry the chicken until golden, transfer to an oven-proof casserole. Add the onion and garlic to the pan and cook until softened. Add the mushrooms and

carrot and continue frying, stirring occasionally, until the onion is lightly browned. Add the tomatoes and chicken stock. Bring to the boil then pour over the chicken. Cover the casserole and cook in a moderate oven (350°F/180°C Mark 4) for about 45 minutes or until the chicken is tender.

Chicken with Oranges

Serves: 4–6 people
Preparation time:
20 minutes
Cooking time:
55 minutes
Oven temperature:
400°F/200°C Mark 6

Use fresh orange segments instead of canned if you prefer. For special occasions try adding one chopped red pepper with the sweetcorn.

1 cooked chicken
1 tablespoon oil
1 onion, chopped
8 oz/225 g long grain rice
½ pint/3 dl water
½ pint/3 dl orange juice
1 level teaspoon salt
freshly ground pepper
7 oz/200 g frozen or canned sweetcorn, drained
2 tomatoes, quartered
1 small can mandarin oranges

Cut the chicken into 4–6 portions. Heat the oil in a large saucepan, add the onion and rice and fry for 5 minutes, stirring frequently with a wooden spoon. Stir in the water, orange juice, salt and pepper. Bring to the boil and simmer for 20 minutes. Pour into an ovenproof casserole, add the corn and chicken pieces. Bake in a hot oven (400°F/200°C Mark 6) for 30 minutes. Garnish with the mandarin segments and tomato quarters. Serve immediately.

Chicken Country-Style

Serves: 4 people
Preparation time:
20 minutes
Cooking time:
50 minutes
Oven temperature:
400°F/200°C Mark 6

A substantial dish which is a meal in itself. Serve with a green salad if liked.

1 small cooked chicken
3 oz/75 g margarine
2 carrots, diced
1 small turnip, diced
1 leek, sliced
1 onion, chopped
2 sticks celery, sliced
salt and pepper
1 level teaspoon sugar
¼ pint/1·5 dl chicken stock or water and chicken stock cube
1 oz/25 g plain flour
½ pint/2·5 dl milk
2 oz/50 g Cheddar cheese, grated
¼ teaspoon dry mustard
parsley for garnish

Cut the chicken into pieces and remove the meat from the bones. Heat 2 oz/50 g of the margarine in a saucepan. Add the prepared vegetables, salt and pepper and sugar. Fry very gently, stirring occasionally, for 10 minutes. Add the chicken stock, cover the pan, bring to the boil then simmer gently for 20 minutes. Melt the remaining 1 oz/25 g margarine in a saucepan, stir in the flour and cook, stirring, for 2 minutes. Add the milk gradually, then bring to the boil, stirring until the sauce is thickened and smooth. Stir the grated cheese into the sauce with the mustard. Put the drained vegetables in an ovenproof dish, arrange the chicken on top and pour the sauce over the top. Bake in a hot oven (400°F/200°C Mark 6) for 20 minutes. Serve garnished with parsley.

Chicken Pie with Herb Topping

Serves: 4 people
Preparation time:
20 minutes
Cooking time:
20 minutes
Oven temperature:
400°F/200°C Mark 6

This is an excellent recipe for converting a little leftover cooked chicken into a delicious and satisfying meal for a family.

2 oz/50 g streaky bacon, chopped
2 oz/50 g mushrooms, sliced
4 oz/100 g cooked chicken
2 carrots, cooked and sliced
½ pint/3 dl chicken stock or water and chicken stock cube
1 level tablespoon cornflour
salt and pepper
6 oz/175 g self raising flour
3 oz/75 g margarine
2 level tablespoons chopped parsley
cold water to mix

Fry the bacon in a saucepan until the fat runs. Add the mushrooms and fry until softened. Add the chicken, cut into bite-sized pieces, then the carrots and the stock, Mix the cornflour with a little of the stock then return it to the pan. Bring to the boil, stirring constantly, until thickened. Season with salt and pepper. Pour into a shallow ovenproof dish. Sift the self raising flour into a bowl and rub in the margarine until it resembles fine breadcrumbs. Stir in the parsley and a pinch of salt then enough cold water to make a soft dough. Roll out the dough to fit the dish and place it on the chicken mixture. Mark with a knife to make a diamond pattern. Bake in a hot oven (400°F/200°C Mark 6) for 15—20 minutes or until well risen and golden.

Chicken and Mushroom Soufflé Omelette

Serves: 4 people
Preparation time:
15 minutes
Cooking time:
3–5 minutes

A lunch or supper for any occasion. A soufflé omelette is very impressive. This filling is very good but any leftover meat could be used instead of chicken. Serve with a green vegetable.

8 oz/225 g cooked chicken
2 oz/50 g margarine
2 oz/50 g mushrooms
8 eggs, separated
2 tablespoons water
salt and pepper

Mince the chicken. Heat half the margarine and fry the chicken, and mushrooms until softened. Whisk the egg whites until stiff. Beat the egg yolks together in a small bowl with the water and salt and pepper. Stir the yolks into the whites. Heat ¼ oz/7 g of the margarine in a 7 inch/18 cm omelette pan. Cook a quarter of the egg mixture quickly until the bottom is set. Place the pan under a hot grill for about 30 seconds or until set. Put a quarter of the chicken mixture on the omelette, fold in half and serve on a hot plate with a vegetable. Cook 3 more omelettes in the same way, fill with the remaining chicken mixture and serve as soon as possible.

Chicken and Mushroom Pie

Serves: 6 people
Preparation time:
20 minutes
Cooking time:
1½–2 hours
Oven temperature:
400°F/200°C Mark 6

A good recipe for 'stretching' an already inexpensive meat to serve a number of people.

Filling:
1 small boiling fowl
salt and pepper
1 bay leaf
1½ oz/40 g margarine
1½ oz/40 g plain flour
2 tablespoons top-of-the-milk
4 oz/100 g mushrooms, sliced
Pastry:
8 oz/200 g plain flour
pinch of salt
2 oz/50 g margarine
2 oz/50 g lard
cold water to mix
milk for glazing

Make the filling: Place the boiling fowl in a saucepan with water to cover, salt and pepper and the bay leaf. Bring to the boil, cover and simmer for 1–1½ hours or until the chicken is tender. Strain the stock and reserve ¾ pint/4 dl. Cut the chicken into 1 inch/25 mm pieces. Melt the margarine in a saucepan, stir in the flour and cook for 2–3 minutes, stirring constantly. Remove from the heat and blend in the reserved stock and top-of-the-milk. Return to the heat and bring to the boil, stirring constantly. Boil until the sauce has thickened (about 2–3 minutes). Stir in the mushrooms and chicken pieces. Add salt and pepper to taste. Pour into a 2 pint/1 litre pie dish.
Make the pastry: Sift the flour and salt into a bowl, add the margarine and lard, cut into small pieces. Rub in the fat with your fingertips until the mixture resembles fine breadcrumbs. Stir in sufficient water with a round-bladed knife until a firm dough is formed. Roll out the pastry on a lightly floured surface to the size of the pie dish. Cover the pie and decorate with pastry trimmings. Brush with milk and bake in a hot oven (400°F/200°C Mark 6) for 25–30 minutes until golden brown.

Chicken Pilau

Serves: 4 people
Preparation time:
15 minutes
Cooking time:
30 minutes

This delicious dish is an excellent way of making a little leftover chicken serve a number of people. Despite this, it is an ideal dish to serve when entertaining.

1 tablespoon oil
1 onion, chopped
6 oz/175 g long grain rice
1 pint/6 dl white stock or water and chicken stock cubes
½ teaspoon tabasco sauce
1 green pepper, coarsely chopped (optional)
2 oz/50 g raisins
2 oz/50 g peanuts
6 oz/175 g cooked chicken, diced
salt and pepper
rind of ½ orange

Heat the oil in a large frying pan or saucepan, add the onion and fry gently, stirring, for about 5 minutes or until it is tender. Add the rice and cook, stirring, for 1 minute. Stir in the stock, tabasco sauce, green pepper and raisins. Bring to the boil then cover the pan and simmer for 15 minutes. Stir in the peanuts, diced chicken and salt and pepper to taste. Cover and simmer for a further 10 minutes or until all the liquid is absorbed. Meanwhile peel off the orange rind (avoiding the pith) with a potato peeler and cut it into thin strips. Place in a pan of water, bring to the boil and drain immediately. Serve the chicken mixture on a warmed serving dish and sprinkle on the orange strips.

Waldorf Chicken Salad

Serves: 4 people
Preparation time:
15 minutes
Cooking time:
None

A versatile salad that uses up leftover chicken. It can be served as a light lunch or supper or as part of a buffet when entertaining. If the apples have a red skin, do not peel them as the colour is very attractive.

4 dessert apples
juice of $\frac{1}{2}$ lemon
$\frac{1}{4}$ pint/1·5 dl mayonnaise
salt and pepper
8 oz/225 g cooked chicken, diced
2 sticks celery, chopped
1 tablespoon chopped walnuts
lettuce leaves for serving

Peel, core and dice the apples. Mix the apple with lemon juice to prevent it discolouring. Season the mayonnaise with salt and pepper and put in a bowl with the diced apple, chicken, celery and walnuts. Mix lightly. Arrange the lettuce on a serving plate, place the prepared salad in the middle and serve.

Chicken Curry with Grapes

Serves: 4 people
Preparation time:
20 minutes
Cooking time:
1 hour 20 minutes

Make this curry for special occasions. Watch out for cheap grapes, especially in the summer and autumn. $\frac{3}{4}$ pint/4·5 dl fresh milk may be used in place of evaporated milk and water, if preferred.

3 oz/75 g margarine
2 onions, finely chopped
1 (3 lb/1$\frac{1}{2}$ kg) chicken
2 level tablespoons curry powder
$\frac{3}{4}$ pint/4·5 dl chicken stock or water and chicken stock cube
2 carrots, grated
1 small can evaporated milk
2 level tablespoons plain flour
8 oz/225 g white grapes
freshly boiled rice for serving
parsley for garnish

Melt the margarine in a large saucepan and fry the onion gently until softened. Chop the chicken into 4 portions, add them to the pan and fry until golden. Remove the chicken. Stir in the curry powder and cook for 2–3 minutes. Gradually add the stock, stirring constantly. Bring to the boil, add the carrot and return the chicken to the pan. Cover and simmer for 1 hour. Pour the evaporated milk into a jug and whisk in $\frac{1}{2}$ pint/3 dl water and the flour. Place the chicken on a serving dish. Stir the milk mixture into the saucepan, add the grapes and bring to the boil. Simmer for 5 minutes. Pour the sauce over the chicken. Spoon the rice round the curry and garnish with a sprig of parsley.

Spiced Duck with Fruit and Mushroom Sauce

Serves: 4 people
Preparation time:
20 minutes
Cooking time:
1 hour
Oven temperature:
350°F/180°C Mark 4

This dish can also be made with chicken but the fruit is especially good with duck. Serve with boiled rice.

1 (4 lb/1¾ kg) duck
salt and pepper
3 oz/75 g margarine
2 level tablespoons
  plain flour
pinch each ground
  nutmeg and
  ground ginger
1 small can
  pineapple rings
1 orange
¼ pint/1·5 dl chicken
  stock or water and
  chicken stock
  cube
1 tablespoon
  sultanas
4 oz/100 g button
  mushrooms

Cut the duck into serving portions, wipe with a damp cloth and sprinkle with salt and pepper. Heat the margarine in a large frying pan and fry the duck until golden all over (about 10 minutes). Put the duck in a casserole. Mix the flour with the nutmeg and ginger and stir into the frying pan, cook gently for 2 minutes. Blend in ¼ pint/1 dl pineapple syrup from the can and the juice of half the orange with the chicken stock. Bring to the boil, stirring, simmer for 2—3 minutes. Add the sultanas and the mushrooms, and pour the sauce over the duck. Cover the casserole and cook in a moderate oven (350°F/180°C Mark 4) for 1 hour. Add slices of pineapple and orange to the casserole 15 minutes before the cooking time is complete.

Curried Turkey

Serves: 4 people
Preparation time:
20 minutes
Cooking time:
30 minutes

A good way of serving leftover turkey. Serve with hot, freshly boiled rice and side dishes such as sliced tomatoes, mango chutney, peanuts, sliced banana and desiccated coconut.

12 oz/350 g cooked
  turkey
juice of ½ lemon
2 oz/50 g margarine
1 clove garlic,
  crushed
½ level teaspoon
  ground ginger
1 onion, chopped
1 level tablespoon
  plain flour
1 level tablespoon
  curry powder, or
  to taste
½ pint/3 dl chicken
  stock or water and
  chicken stock cube
1 tablespoon tomato
  purée
1 small dessert apple,
  peeled, cored and
  chopped
1 tablespoon
  sultanas
pinch of sugar
salt and pepper

Cut the turkey into bite-sized pieces and mix with the lemon juice in a bowl. Heat the margarine in a saucepan, add the garlic, ginger, onion, flour and curry powder. Fry gently, stirring, for 3—4 minutes. Stir in the chicken stock, bring to the boil. Add the tomato purée, apple, sultanas, sugar and salt and pepper to taste. Cover the pan and simmer for 15 minutes. Stir in the turkey and cook for a further 10 minutes.

Rabbit in Sultana Sauce

Serves: 4 people
Preparation time:
15 minutes
Cooking time:
1 hour 20 minutes
Oven temperature:
325°F/170°C Mark 3

Rabbit is an economical buy at most times of the year. Cooked this way, it is suitable to serve when entertaining. It is also a good recipe for slimmers, being low in calories.

4 rabbit joints
1 onion, finely chopped
2 rashers streaky bacon, diced
2 oz/50 g sugar
1 level teaspoon dry mustard
2 level teaspoons cornflour
4 tablespoons vinegar
¾ pint/4·5 dl chicken stock or water and chicken stock cube
3 tablespoons sultanas

Rinse the rabbit in cold water. Put the rabbit in a saucepan with cold water to cover, bring to the boil, simmer for 2 minutes then drain. Put the rabbit in a casserole. Mix all the remaining ingredients together in a saucepan. Bring to the boil, stirring, simmer for 2–3 minutes. Pour the sauce over the rabbit, cover the casserole and cook in a moderately slow oven (325°F/170°C Mark 3) for 1¼ hours or until the rabbit is tender.

Chicken Liver Risotto

Serves: 4 people
Preparation time:
15 minutes
Cooking time:
15–20 minutes

Chicken livers have a more delicate flavour than other livers. This recipe makes a dish which is a meal in itself and is very inexpensive.

2 tablespoons oil
1 onion, peeled and chopped
2 rashers streaky bacon, chopped
10 oz/300 g long grain rice
1 pint/6 dl chicken stock or water and chicken stock cube
1 oz/25 g margarine
4 oz/100 g mushrooms, sliced
8 oz/225 g chicken livers
chopped parsley for garnish
grated cheese for serving

Heat the oil in a large saucepan, fry the onion and bacon until softened, then add the rice and cook, stirring, until lightly browned. Add the chicken stock and bring to the boil. Cover the pan tightly and simmer for 15 minutes. Do not lift the lid until the end of the cooking time when all the liquid will have been absorbed and the rice is tender.

Meanwhile, heat the margarine in a frying pan and cook the mushrooms and chicken livers until the livers are browned all over. Add the mushrooms and livers to the cooked rice and reheat if necessary. Serve in a hot dish, garnished with chopped parsley. Serve a bowl of grated cheese separately.

Lambs' Tongues in Sweet and Sour Sauce

Serves: 4 people
Preparation time:
20 minutes
Cooking time:
About 1¾ hours

Use cider instead of stock for special occasions.

8 lambs' tongues
salt and pepper
2 level tablespoons
  cornflour
½ pint/3 dl stock
  or water and beef
  stock cube
4 level tablespoons
  brown sugar
2 level tablespoons
  redcurrant jelly
2 tablespoons soy
  sauce
4 tablespoons
  vinegar
8 oz/225 g long
  grain rice

Wash the tongues, blanch them by cooking in boiling salted water for 3–5 minutes. Drain. Put in a saucepan of fresh salted water, bring to the boil and simmer, covered, for about 1½ hours or until very tender. Drain. As soon as the tongues are cool enough to handle, remove the skins (if necessary) and cut off any gristle and bones from the root. Blend the cornflour with a little of the stock in a saucepan, stir in the remaining stock, brown sugar. redcurrant jelly and soy sauce. Bring slowly to the boil, stirring continuously, then simmer for 5–10 minutes. Stir in the vinegar and add the cooked tongues. Reheat gently. Meanwhile cook the rice in boiling salted water for about 15 minutes or until tender. Drain well. Serve the tongues on a bed of rice.

Stuffed Hearts

Serves: 4 people
Preparation time:
20 minutes plus
soaking time
Cooking time:
1½ hours
Oven temperature:
325°F/170°C Mark 3

For special occasions use ¼ pint/1·5 dl sweet sherry instead of that amount of stock. Serve with fresh vegetables.

4 lambs' hearts
2 oz/50 g cooked
  ham
4 oz/100 g fresh
  breadcrumbs
1 level tablespoon
  chopped parsley
pinch each dried
  sage, rosemary
  and thyme
salt and pepper
1 egg, beaten
juice of ½ lemon
¾ pint/4 dl stock or
  water and beef
  stock cube

Wash the hearts in cold running water. Remove any fat and skin surrounding the hearts. Inside the hearts cut the dividing walls to make one cavity. Place the hearts in a bowl of cold salted water to cover and soak for 45 minutes. Rinse them well, drain and pat dry with absorbent kitchen paper. Chop the ham and mix it in a bowl with the breadcrumbs, parsley, herbs, salt and pepper to taste, the beaten egg and lemon juice. Mix well with a fork. Pack the stuffing into the hearts and press down well. Put the hearts into a casserole, pour on the stock, cover with the lid and bake in a moderate oven (325°F/ 170°C Mark 3) for 1½ hours. Baste the hearts frequently during cooking. Serve hot.

Kidney Ragout

Serves: 4 people
Preparation time:
15 minutes
Cooking time:
20 minutes

Kidneys are relatively inexpensive, especially as there is the minimum of waste. They are a good source of some vitamins and minerals essential for good health and they have very little fat content.

1 lb/½ kg lambs' kidneys, without fat
1 large onion
1 tablespoon corn oil
1 oz/25 g plain flour
½ pint/3 dl stock or water and chicken stock cube
1 bay leaf
½ level teaspoon dried thyme
1 teaspoon tomato purée
salt and pepper
chopped parsley for garnish

Slice the kidneys in half lengthwise and remove the core and any skin. Rinse in salted water. Peel and chop the onion. Heat the oil in a saucepan and fry the kidneys until almost tender (about 4 minutes). Keep hot. Fry the onion until softened, then stir in the flour and cook, stirring constantly for 2–3 minutes. Blend in the stock gradu-ally, stirring until the sauce is thickened and smooth. Add the bay leaf, thyme and tomato purée. Cover and simmer for 10 minutes. Remove the bay leaf. Add the kidneys to the pan and reheat. Taste and adjust seasoning. Serve on a heated dish, sprinkled with chopped parsley.

Liver and Bacon in Tomato Sauce

Serves: 6 people
Preparation time:
20 minutes
Cooking time:
30 minutes
Oven temperature:
375°F/190°C Mark 5

A variation on a popular dish – this one is cooked in the oven.

1½ lb/750 g lambs' liver
2 oz/50 g plain flour
salt and pepper
1 oz/25 g margarine
1 onion, chopped
¾ pint/4 dl tomato juice
6 rashers streaky bacon

Slice the lambs' liver into ¼–½ inch/12–25 mm slices. Put the flour onto a plate and season it with salt and pepper. Coat the slices of liver with the seasoned flour. Heat the margarine in a flameproof casserole, add the onion and fry for 3–5 minutes or until soft but not browned. Add the liver and fry lightly on both sides. Stir in the tomato juice and salt and pepper to taste. Remove the rind from the bacon, cut the rashers in half and roll them up. Place the bacon rolls on top of the casserole and bake, uncovered, in a moderately hot oven (375°F/190°C Mark 5) for 30 minutes. Serve as soon as possible.

Ox Liver Stew

Serves: 4 people
Preparation time:
20 minutes
Cooking time:
1 hour

A very inexpensive but satisfying stew. Kidneys could be used instead of liver.

1 lb/½ kg ox liver
salt and pepper
1 oz/25 g plain flour
½ level teaspoon mixed herbs
4 rashers streaky bacon, chopped
1 tablespoon oil
1 lb/½ kg onions, sliced
1 lb/½ kg carrots, chopped
½ pint/3 dl beef stock or water and beef stock cube
chopped parsley for garnish

Cut the liver into strips. Season the flour, add the herbs and use to coat the liver. Fry the bacon in the oil in a saucepan, until softened. Add the liver and flour. Fry, stirring, until beginning to brown. Add the onions, carrots and stock. Bring to the boil, stirring continuously. Cover the pan and simmer gently for 1 hour. Stir once or twice during cooking. Taste and adjust the seasoning. Serve hot, garnished with chopped parsley.

French Country Liver

Serves: 4 people
Preparation time:
15 minutes
Cooking time:
20–25 minutes
Oven temperature:
350°F/180°C Mark 4

A delicious and quick to prepare casserole using an inexpensive cut of meat. Pigs' liver can also be used but the flavour is stronger.

1 lb/½ kg lambs' liver
2 level tablespoons cornflour
2 tablespoons corn oil
1 (1½ pint/840 ml) packet French country vegetable soup
1 pint/6 dl water
2 level tablespoons tomato purée
fried bread and parsley for garnish

Wash the liver and cut into ½ inch/ 12 mm wide strips. Coat the strips in cornflour. Heat the oil in a heat-proof casserole, add the liver and fry until browned all over. Add the soup, water and tomato purée. Bring to the boil, stirring constantly. Put the casserole into a moderate oven (350°F/180°C Mark 4) and cook for 20–25 minutes. Serve garnished with fried bread croûtes and chopped parsley.

Bacon and Egg Charlotte

Serves: 4 people
Preparation time:
20 minutes
Cooking time:
30—35 minutes
Oven temperature:
375°F/190°C Mark 5

A very economical dish. It needs only a salad or green vegetable to make a complete meal.

6 slices bread and butter
6 rashers streaky bacon
4 oz/100 g cheese, grated
3 eggs
¾ pint/4·5 dl milk
¼ level teaspoon dry mustard
salt and pepper
watercress for garnish

Cut the bread and butter into ½ inch/12 mm squares. Remove the rinds and bones from the bacon rashers. Chop roughly. Starting with the bread, make layers of bread, bacon and cheese in a greased ovenproof dish. Beat the eggs in a bowl and add the milk, mustard and season-ings. Pour the egg custard over the bacon and bread. Allow to stand for 10—15 minutes. Bake in a moderately hot oven (375°F/190°C Mark 5) for 30—35 minutes or until well risen and golden. Serve as soon as possible, garnished with watercress.

Tortilla

Serves: 4 people
Preparation time:
15 minutes
Cooking time:
30 minutes

This traditional Spanish dish is a complete meal in itself. Add tomatoes and peppers for a special occasion.

¼ pint/1.5 dl olive oil
1 lb/½ kg old potatoes
1 large onion, finely chopped
3 oz/75 g Spanish stuffed green olives, sliced
4 eggs
salt and pepper

Heat the oil in a large saucepan. Cut the potato into ⅛ inch/3 mm slices and add to the pan. Stir to coat the potato in oil, then cook gently for about 10 minutes. Add the onion and continue cooking until the potato is tender and golden brown. Put the mixture into a colander to drain off any excess oil. Reserve the oil. Add the olives to the potato. Beat the eggs in a large bowl with salt and pepper. Add the potato mixture to the eggs. Heat about 2 tablespoons of the drained oil in a large frying pan. Add the omelette mixture and spread it out evenly. Cook gently until browned underneath. Place a plate over the frying pan and invert the omelette onto it. Slide the omelette back into the pan, browned-side upper-most. Cook for 2—3 minutes to brown the underneath. Serve im-mediately, cut into 4 pieces.

147

Creamy Vegetable and Cheese Pie

Serves: 4 people
Preparation time:
15 minutes
Cooking time:
45 minutes
Oven temperature:
375°F/190°C Mark 5

An inexpensive pie which makes an excellent lunch or supper dish. If it is to be eaten straightaway, brown the top under a hot grill. Mash the potato with a little margarine and milk.

1 oz/25 g margarine
1 large onion, sliced
4 oz/100 g
  mushrooms, sliced
1 oz/25 g plain flour
½ pint/3 dl milk
1 (8 oz/226 g) packet
  mixed frozen
  vegetables
4 oz/100 g cheese,
  grated
salt and pepper
1 lb/½ kg potatoes,
  boiled and mashed
1 level tablespoon
  chopped parsley

Heat the margarine in a saucepan, add the onion and fry gently for 5 minutes, add the mushrooms and fry for a further 2–3 minutes. Stir in the flour and cook for 2 minutes, stirring constantly. Remove from the heat and blend in the milk. Return to the heat and bring to the boil, stirring constantly until thickened. Stir in the mixed vegetables and simmer gently for 5 minutes, stirring occasionally. Remove from the heat, stir in the cheese and salt and pepper to taste. Put the mixture into a 2 pint/1 litre ovenproof dish. Place the mashed potato in a piping bag with a large star pipe and pipe it onto the vegetable mixture. Alternatively, spread on the potato with a round-bladed knife. Cover and keep in the refrigerator or cool place overnight. The next day, place the casserole in a moderately hot oven (375°F/190°C Mark 5) for 30 minutes until heated through and golden brown on top. Sprinkle with chopped parsley before serving.

Cheese Potato Crown

Serves: 6 people
Preparation time:
15 minutes
Cooking time:
60–70 minutes
Oven temperature:
375°F/190°C Mark 5

Serve this recipe for a very inexpensive supper or snack. It also makes an impressive vegetable for special occasions.

1½ lb/¾ kg potatoes
1 lb/½ kg onions
2 oz/50 g margarine
8 oz/225 g cheese,
  shredded or
  coarsely grated
salt and pepper
½ level teaspoon
  ground nutmeg
parsley for garnish

Peel the potatoes and onions and shred them into long thin strips, or grate coarsely. Melt the margarine and add the potato, onion, 6 oz/175 g cheese, plenty of salt and pepper and the ground nutmeg. Mix lightly. Line a 9 inch/23 cm ring tin (or 8 inch/20 cm deep round cake tin) with a piece of foil. Grease well. Put the potato mixture into the tin, press down well. Cover with a piece of greased foil and bake in a moderately hot oven (375°F/190°C Mark 5) for about 50–55 minutes. Turn the ring carefully out of the tin onto an ovenproof dish. Sprinkle the remaining cheese over the top and return to the oven for 5–10 minutes or until the cheese has melted. Serve hot, garnished with sprigs of parsley.

Cheese Flan

Serves: 4 people
Preparation time:
20 minutes
Cooking time:
50 minutes
Oven temperature:
400°F/200°C Mark 6

This is a real money-saving dish. Serve it hot, or cold with salad. Use the asparagus spears when entertaining.

Pastry:
6 oz/170 g plain
   flour
salt and pepper
1½ oz/40 g margarine
1½ oz/40 g lard
Filling:
3 eggs
¼ pint/1·5 dl milk
3 oz/75 g Cheddar
   cheese, grated
1 tomato, sliced
1 (7 oz/198 g) can
   asparagus spears
   (optional)

Make the pastry: Sift the flour and pinch of salt into a mixing bowl. Add the margarine and lard, cut into small pieces. Rub the fat into the flour with your fingertips until the mixture resembles fine breadcrumbs. Using a round-bladed knife, mix in enough cold water to make a firm dough. Roll out the pastry on a lightly floured surface and use to line an 8 inch/20 cm flan ring standing on a baking tray. Prick the base with a fork. Place a piece of greaseproof paper in the flan and fill with baking beans. Bake the flan case in a hot oven (400°F/200°C Mark 6) for about 20 minutes.
Make the filling: Beat the eggs and the milk together in a bowl. Stir in the cheese and salt and pepper. Remove the flan ring, paper and beans from the cooked flan. Arrange the tomato and asparagus spears (if used) on the base of the flan and pour in the cheese mixture. Bake for a further 20—30 minutes or until firm and golden.

Cheese and Walnut Loaf

Serves: 8 people
Preparation time:
20 minutes
Cooking time:
1 hour
Oven temperature:
375°F/190°C Mark 5

An inexpensive and delicious cheese loaf which makes a good alternative to meat. Vegetarians can omit the bacon rashers.

12 rashers streaky
   bacon
2 oz/50 g margarine
2 onions, chopped
4 oz/100 g fresh
   breadcrumbs
12 oz/350 g cheese,
   grated
6 oz/175 g walnuts,
   roughly chopped
4 tomatoes, skinned
   and chopped
salt and pepper
4 eggs, beaten
½ pint/3 dl milk

Lightly grease a 2 lb/1 kg loaf tin. Remove the rinds from the bacon, spread the rashers with a round-bladed knife and use them to line the loaf tin. Heat the margarine in a saucepan and fry the onion for about 3 minutes or until tender but not brown. Remove from the heat and stir in the breadcrumbs, cheese, walnuts, tomatoes and salt and pepper according to taste. Add the eggs and milk and mix well together. Pour into the prepared tin and cover with greased greaseproof paper. Bake in a moderately hot oven (375°F/190°C Mark 5) for 1 hour or until firm. When cold, turn out of the tin, slice the loaf and pack in an airtight container ready for the picnic.

Mixed Vegetable Flan

Serves: 4–6 people
Preparation time:
20 minutes
Cooking time:
45 minutes
Oven temperature:
400°F/200°C Mark 6
then 350°F/180°C
Mark 4

A delicious and inexpensive vegetable flan which is easy to carry on a picnic. Pack it in an airtight container.

Pastry:
6 oz/170 g plain flour
¼ level teaspoon salt
1½ oz/40 g margarine
1½ oz/40 g lard
cold water to mix
Filling:
2 potatoes, peeled
2 tomatoes, skinned
1 onion
2 oz/50 g peas
1½ oz/35 g margarine
¼ pint/1·5 dl milk
2 eggs
¼ level teaspoon dried mixed herbs
salt and pepper

Make the pastry: Sift the flour and salt into a mixing bowl, add the fat and rub it in with your fingertips until the mixture resembles fine breadcrumbs. With a round-bladed knife stir in sufficient cold water to form a firm dough. Turn it onto a lightly floured surface and knead gently. Roll out the pastry to fit an 8 inch/20 cm flan ring. Line the flan ring standing on a baking tray. Fill the pastry with a sheet of grease-proof paper and some baking beans. Bake in a hot oven (400°F/200°C Mark 6) for 10 minutes, remove the baking beans and bake for a further 5 minutes.

Make the filling: Cut the potatoes and tomatoes into ½ inch/1 cm dice, chop the onion. Fry the potatoes, onion and peas in the margarine for 5 minutes. Beat together the milk, eggs, herbs, salt and pepper. Stir in the cooled vegetables and tomatoes. Pour the mixture into the cooled flan case. Bake in a moderate oven (350°F/180°C Mark 4) for 25–30 minutes or until the filling is set. Remove the flan ring for the last 10 minutes of cooking time to brown the pastry. Leave on a wire rack to cool.

Colcannon Supper

Serves: 4 people
Preparation time:
20 minutes
Cooking time:
1 hour
Oven temperature:
400°F/200°C Mark 6

Colcannon is traditionally made with kale or kohl rabi so use these if available. Brussels sprout tops are also good. Omit the bacon and cheese if it is to be served as a vegetable.

1 lb/½ kg potatoes
½ medium-sized cabbage
2 oz/50 g margarine
2 rashers streaky bacon, chopped
salt and pepper
2 oz/50 g cheese, grated
extra margarine

Peel the potatoes and cook in boiling salted water to cover for 20 minutes or until tender. Drain and mash well. Cook the cabbage in a little boiling salted water until tender (about 15 minutes). Drain and chop finely. Melt the margarine in a large saucepan and fry the bacon until softened. Add the vegetables and season well with salt and pepper. Mix thoroughly. Put into an ovenproof dish, sprinkle the cheese on top, dot with margarine and put into a hot oven (400°F/200°C Mark 6) for 20 minutes or until golden. Serve piping hot.

Mediterranean Pasta Salad

Serves: 4–6 people
Preparation time:
15 minutes plus
cooling time
Cooking time:
12 minutes

Serve this salad with crusty French bread. It makes a good lunch dish or meal starter. This interesting combination of ingredients makes a filling and economical salad without meat.

salt
8 oz/225 g pasta wheels or shells
1 clove garlic, crushed
$\frac{1}{4}$ pint/1·5 dl French dressing
3 hard-boiled eggs
1 lettuce
$\frac{1}{4}$ pint/1·5 dl mayonnaise
6 anchovy fillets
1 ($7\frac{1}{2}$ oz/212 g) can tuna
2 ripe tomatoes
8 black olives
8 green stuffed olives

Put 4 pints/2 litres water in a large saucepan with 4 level teaspoons salt. Bring to the boil. Sprinkle in the pasta and cook, uncovered, for 12 minutes or until tender but still in shape. Drain well in a colander. Add the garlic to the French dressing and mix lightly with the pasta until well coated. Leave to cool. Arrange the lettuce on a flat serving plate. Cut the eggs in half length-ways and place on the lettuce; put a little mayonnaise and an anchovy fillet on each one. Place a line of pasta each side of the eggs. Flake the tuna, mix with a little mayonnaise and place beside the pasta. Put the remaining pasta down the edge of the plate. Cut the tomatoes into wedges and arrange them on the pasta. Garnish with the olives.

Cider Vegetable Hot Pot

Serves: 4 people
Preparation time:
20 minutes
Cooking time:
$1\frac{1}{2}$–2 hours
Oven temperature:
350°F/180°C Mark 4
then 400°F/200°C
Mark 6

This dish will keep in a cool place overnight. Add the cheese before placing the casserole in the oven and reheat for about 30 minutes.

2 oz/50 g margarine
1 large onion, sliced
1 large leek, sliced
8 oz/225 g carrots, sliced
8 oz/225 g swede, cubed
8 oz/225 g turnip, cubed
$1\frac{1}{2}$ oz/40 g plain flour
$\frac{3}{4}$ pint/4.5 dl dry cider
2 teaspoons Worcestershire sauce
1 level tablespoon tomato ketchup
salt and pepper
1 chicken stock cube
1 lb/450 g potatoes, sliced
oil for brushing
3 oz/75 g cheese, grated

Heat the margarine in a saucepan, add the onion, leek, carrot, swede, and turnip, fry gently, stirring occasionally, for 10 minutes. Lift the vegetables out of the pan, draining the margarine back into the saucepan, and place them in a casserole. Return the saucepan to the heat, stir in the flour and cook for 2–3 minutes. Remove from the heat and slowly blend in the cider. Return to the heat, stir in the Worcestershire sauce, tomato ketchup, salt and pepper to taste and crumbled stock cube. Boil, stirring continuously, for 5 minutes. Pour the sauce onto the vegetables in the casserole. Arrange the potato slices on top. Brush the potato liberally with oil. Cover the casserole and bake in a moderate oven (350°F/180°C Mark 4) for $1\frac{1}{2}$–2 hours or until the vegetables are cooked. Remove the casserole from the oven, sprinkle with the cheese and place uncovered in a hot oven (400°F/200°C Mark 6) until the cheese is melted and golden.

Stuffed Tomatoes

Serves: 4 people
Preparation time:
15 minutes
Cooking time:
35–40 minutes
Oven temperature:
350°F/180°C Mark 4

This is a very attractive way of using up any leftover cooked meat. This recipe is good enough to serve when entertaining.

8 large tomatoes
4 oz/100 g cold cooked meat, minced
1 level teaspoon chopped parsley
1 small onion, finely chopped or grated
½ level tablespoon breadcrumbs
salt and pepper
1 egg, beaten
2½ oz/65 g margarine
10 oz/300 g long grain rice
1 pint/6 dl water
1 level teaspoon salt
2 level teaspoons mixed dried herbs

Cut the tops off the tomatoes and reserve. Very carefully scoop out the insides of the tomatoes, being careful not to break the skins. Reserve the tomato pulp. Turn the tomatoes upside down on absorbent kitchen paper to drain. Put the meat in a mixing bowl with the reserved pulp, parsley, onion, breadcrumbs, salt and pepper. Mix all together with enough egg to bind, then fill the drained tomatoes with the mixture. Put the tops back on the tomatoes, if liked, and dot with 2 oz/50 g margarine. Place the tomatoes on a baking tray and cook in a moderate oven (350°F/180°C Mark 4) for 20–25 minutes.

Meanwhile, put the rice, water and 1 level teaspoon salt into a saucepan. Bring to the boil, stir once. Cover the pan and simmer gently for 15 minutes or until the rice is tender and all the liquid absorbed. Stir in the remaining ½ oz/15 g margarine and the mixed herbs, with a fork. Put the rice in a serving dish and arrange the tomatoes on top.

Stuffed Marrow

Serves: 4–6 people
Preparation time:
20 minutes
Cooking time:
1 hour 20 minutes
Oven temperature:
325°F/170°C Mark 3

Serve stuffed marrow as a complete supper dish or as a part of a main course with other vegetables. Marrows are in season in the late summer and autumn. Use other leftover cold meat, as available.

1 onion
2 rashers streaky bacon
1 oz/25 g margarine
8 oz/225 g cooked lamb, minced
2 oz/50 g breadcrumbs
½ level teaspoon each ground nutmeg and cinnamon
salt and pepper
chicken stock or water and chicken stock cube
1 medium-sized marrow
½ oz/15 g butter, melted
4 tomatoes, for serving
parsley for garnish

Chop the onion and bacon finely. Fry them in the margarine in a saucepan until beginning to brown. Stir in the lamb, breadcrumbs, spices, seasonings and enough chicken stock to bind the mixture together. Peel the marrow, then cut off the ends and remove the pith and pips. Pile the stuffing into the marrow and wrap in foil. Put on a baking tray and bake in a moderately slow oven (325°F/170°C Mark 3) for about 1 hour or until the marrow is tender when tested with a skewer. Unwrap the foil, brush the marrow with melted butter and cook for a further 15 minutes or until it begins to brown. Wipe the tomatoes, cut a cross on top of each and bake on the tray beside the marrow for the last 15 minutes. Serve garnished with parsley.

Desserts

Prune Cream

Serves: 4–6 people
Preparation time:
15 minutes plus
setting time
Cooking time:
30 minutes

A store cupboard
dessert. Keep all the
ingredients ready in
case of unexpected
guests. Use other
fruit if liked.

6 oz/175 g dried
   prunes
castor sugar
juice and finely
   grated rind of 1
   lemon
1 level tablespoon
   gelatine
1 small can
   evaporated milk,
   chilled
whipped cream,
   extra prunes and
   almonds for
   decoration

Put the prunes into a saucepan with water to cover. Bring to the boil and simmer, covered, until the prunes are tender (about 30 minutes). Remove the stones. Put the liquid and the prunes into an electric blender and blend until puréed. Alternatively, press the prunes through a sieve with a wooden spoon. Sweeten the purée to taste, add the lemon juice and rind, measure and make up to 1 pint/5·5 dl with water. Put 3 tablespoons hot water into a bowl, sprinkle in the gelatine and stir until dissolved. Place the bowl over a saucepan of hot water if you have difficulty in dissolving the gelatine. Stir the gelatine into the prune purée. Cool. Whip the evaporated milk until thickened and stir into the prune mixture. Put aside until set. Spoon the mixture into individual serving dishes and decorate with cream, almonds and extra prunes.

Mandarin Yoghourt Ambrosia

Serves: 4–6 people
Preparation time:
15 minutes plus
setting time
Cooking time:
None

A delicious recipe
which turns canned
creamed rice into a
party dessert fit for
any occasion.

2 (1 pint/569 ml)
   packets orange
   jelly
¾ pint/4·5 dl water
1 (15½ oz/440 g)
   can creamed rice
2 (6 fl oz/170 ml)
   cartons mandarin
   and lemon
   yoghourt
2 egg whites
1 mandarin orange

Put 1 jelly in a saucepan with the water. Heat gently, stirring until the jelly is dissolved. Cool slightly, then measure ¼ pint/1·5 dl of the jelly. Spoon this into 4–6 serving glasses. Leave in a cool place until set. Add the second jelly to the pan with the remaining melted jelly. Bring slowly to the boil, stirring until all the jelly is dissolved. Put the creamed rice in a bowl and add half the jelly, mixing well. Divide between the serving glasses. Return to a cool place to set. Allow the remaining jelly to cool but not set, then stir in the yoghourt. Whisk the egg whites until stiff, then fold into the yoghourt mixture. Spoon into the glasses. When set, decorate with mandarin orange segments.

Apple and Orange Whip

Serves: 4–6 people
Preparation time:
20 minutes plus
chilling time
Cooking time:
10 minutes

Apples are plentiful all the year round but are at their cheapest and best in the autumn and winter Try using soft fruit when in season, instead of apple, with the appropriate flavour of jelly and yoghourt

1 lb/½ kg cooking apples
¼ pint/1·5 dl water
1 (1 pint/569 ml) orange jelly
1 (5 fl oz/142 ml) carton mandarin orange yoghourt
2 egg whites

Peel, core and slice the apples. Put them into a saucepan with the water and cook gently until soft and pulpy. Beat thoroughly. Measure the pulp and make up to ¾ pint/4·5 dl with water if necessary. Break the jelly into pieces and stir it into the hot pulp until dissolved. Allow to cool then stir in half the yoghourt. Chill until syrupy and beginning to set around the edges. Whisk the egg whites until stiff. Whisk the jelly mixture until frothy then fold in the egg whites. Spoon into serving dishes or a mould and chill until set. Serve the extra yoghourt poured over the whip.

Frozen Christmas Pudding

Serves: 6 people
Preparation time:
15 minutes plus
freezing time
Cooking time:
None

Try making this recipe as a change from the conventional Christmas pudding. It can be served at any time of year. Chill the can of evaporated milk in the refrigerator overnight.

1 level teaspoon gelatine
2 level teaspoons instant coffee powder
3 tablespoons hot water
1 small can evaporated milk, chilled
1 level tablespoon soft brown sugar
9 oz/250 g mincemeat
4 oz/100 g mixture of glacé cherries, angelica and walnuts
1 teaspoon vanilla essence

Turn the refrigerator to its coldest setting. Dissolve the gelatine and coffee in the hot water in a small bowl. Place the bowl in a saucepan of hot water if you have difficulty in dissolving the gelatine. Whisk the evaporated milk until thick. Stir in the sugar and dissolved gelatine mixture. Whisk again until stiff. Stir in the remaining ingredients. Lightly oil a 1 pint/6 dl mould, pour in the ice cream mixture and place it in the freezing compartment of the refrigerator until firm. Unmould onto a plate and serve as soon as possible.

Chilled Lemon Fluff

Serves: 4 people
Preparation time:
20 minutes plus
cooling and chilling
time
Cooking time:
None

An inexpensive and
delicious lemon
dessert which
improves with
chilling overnight.

3 lemons
¾ pint/4.5 dl water
8 oz/225 g sugar
3 oz/75 g cornflour
2 eggs, separated
freshly ground
nutmeg

Cut fine strips of rind from the lemons with a potato peeler. Squeeze out the juice. Place the water, sugar, lemon juice and pieces of rind in a saucepan. Heat gently, stirring, until the sugar has dissolved. Blend the cornflour with a little cold water in a bowl and stir into the saucepan. Bring to the boil, stirring constantly until thickened. Remove from the heat, discard the lemon rind and beat in the egg yolks. Whisk the egg whites in a clean bowl until stiff. Whisk the cooled sauce until smooth. Fold the egg whites into the sauce with a tablespoon. Put into a glass serving bowl, cover and leave in the refrigerator or cool place to chill overnight. Serve sprinkled with freshly ground nutmeg.

Gooseberry Sparkle

Serves: 8 people
Preparation time:
20 minutes plus
cooling and setting
time
Cooking time:
None

An inexpensive but
spectacular cold
dessert which must
be made the day
before needed. The
jelly must be almost
set before adding the
gooseberries
otherwise they will all
sink to the bottom.

1½ (1 pint/569 ml)
   packets lime jelly
1 (1 lb 3 oz/540 g)
   can gooseberries
1 small can cream or
   ¼ pint/1.5 dl
   whipping cream
1 oz/25 g glacé
   cherries, chopped
1 oz/25 g crystallised
   ginger, chopped

Dissolve the jelly in ½ pint/3 dl boiling water in a measuring jug. Drain the syrup from the gooseberries into the jug, then make the jelly up to 1½ pints/9 dl with cold water. Leave until almost set. Stir the gooseberries into the almost set jelly. Rinse out a 2 pint/1 litre jelly mould with water. Pour the jelly into the mould and leave in a cool place overnight to set completely. Just before serving turn out the jelly onto a serving dish. Pipe some of the cream round the jelly, mix the rest with the glacé cherries and ginger and pile it into the centre of the ring.

Gooseberry Mist

Serves: 6 people
Preparation time:
15 minutes plus
chilling time
Cooking time:
None

Gooseberries are in season during the summer; they can be used instead of the canned variety, cooked with a little water and sugar to taste until tender. This is a low-calorie dessert—good for slimmers. Fresh milk can also be used if you have plenty to spare.

1 oz/25 g skimmed milk powder
1 packet chilled dessert mix, vanilla flavour
1 (1 lb 3 oz/540 g) can gooseberries
1 egg white
green food colouring
grated chocolate for decoration

Put the skimmed milk powder into a measuring jug and make up to ¼ pint/1·25 dl with cold water. Make up the chilled dessert mix with the reconstituted milk as directed on the side of the packet. Pour into a large bowl. Press the gooseberries through a sieve with a wooden spoon or blend until smooth in an electric blender. Stir into the dessert mix. Whisk the egg white until stiff and fold it into the gooseberry mixture with a metal spoon. Gently mix in a few drops of green food colouring. Place the mixture in the freezing compartment of your refrigerator until set. Remove it from the refrigerator 5 minutes before serving. Spoon into 6 glasses, sprinkle with a little grated chocolate and serve.

Rhubarb and Raspberry Fool

Serves: 4–6 people
Preparation time:
20 minutes plus
cooling time
Cooking time:
None

Use rhubarb to make the more expensive raspberries go further. Both these fruits are in season in the summer – use canned or frozen fruit at other times of the year

1 lb/½ kg rhubarb
4 oz/100 g raspberries
sugar to taste
2 level tablespoons custard powder
½ pint/3 dl milk
whipped cream, optional
extra raspberries for decoration

Prepare the rhubarb, cut it into 1 inch/25 mm pieces and cook it in very little water until tender. Press the rhubarb and raspberries through a sieve or purée in an electric blender. Sweeten the fruit purée to taste. Blend the custard powder with a little of the milk in a bowl. Put the milk in a saucepan, bring to the boil, then pour onto the custard powder, stirring. Return to the pan and simmer, stirring, for 2 minutes. Leave until cold. Blend the fruit purée with the custard. Put the fool into individual serving dishes and chill until needed. Serve decorated with whipped cream, if liked, and the extra raspberries.

Yoghourt Fruit Jellies

Serves: 4–6 people
Preparation time:
20 minutes plus
soaking and setting
times
Cooking time:
20–25 minutes

These deliciously
different jellies can
also be made with
raspberries or
strawberries. Use
8 oz/225 g fresh
or frozen fruit and
make it into a purée.

4 oz/100 g dried
   apricots
2 level teaspoons
   gelatine
3 (5 fl oz/142 ml)
   cartons natural
   yoghourt
1 oz/25 g castor
   sugar (optional)
2 egg whites
fruit for decoration

Put the apricots in a bowl with
water to cover and leave to soak
overnight. Next day, tip the apricots
and the water into a saucepan,
bring to the boil and simmer for
20–25 minutes or until tender. Put
the apricots with $\frac{1}{2}$ pint/3 dl of the
water in an electric blender and
blend until smooth. Alternatively,
rub the apricots through a sieve to
make a purée, then add the water.
Dissolve the gelatine in 2 tablespoons hot water and stir into the
apricot purée. Stir in the yoghourt
and castor sugar. Whisk the egg
whites until stiff and fold in gently.
Spoon the jellies into 4 individual
serving dishes and chill until set.
Serve decorated with pieces of
fruit.

Pineapple Pancakes

Serves: 6 people
Preparation time:
15 minutes
Cooking time:
15 minutes

A delicious dish
which is most
impressive. Make the
pancakes and the
fruit mixture well
ahead of time.
Assemble the dessert
at the last minute.

Pancakes:
4 oz/100 g plain
   flour
$\frac{1}{2}$ level teaspoon salt
1 egg
$\frac{1}{2}$ pint/3 dl milk
$\frac{1}{2}$ oz/15 g butter
oil for frying
Filling:
$\frac{1}{2}$ pint/3 dl double
   cream
6 rings fresh or
   canned pineapple,
   chopped
1 small can peaches
   or 2 fresh oranges,
   segmented

Make the pancakes: Sift the flour
and salt together into a mixing
bowl. Make a well in the centre
and add the egg. Mix in the egg,
then gradually add half the milk,
beating well until smooth. Stir
in the remaining milk and melted
butter. Chill the batter for 15
minutes. Heat a little oil in a frying
pan, then add a little of the batter
to make a paper-thin pancake. Fry
until golden, turn the pancake over
and cook the other side. Continue
until all the batter is used.
Make the filling: Lightly whip the
cream and fold in the chopped
pineapple and peaches or oranges.
Fold each pancake into four to
form a triangle and fill with the
cream and fruit mixture.

157

Peasant Girl in a Veil

Serves: 4 people
Preparation time:
20 minutes plus
cooling time
Cooking time:
None

For speed, grate the apples into the pan. Both the breadcrumbs and the apple purée can be made the day before. Use canned apple purée if liked.

3 oz/75 g margarine
8 oz/225 g fresh
 white breadcrumbs
2 oz/50 g demerara
 sugar
1½ lb/675 g cooking
 apples
juice of 1 lemon
2 tablespoons water
2 oz/50 g castor
 sugar
¼ pint/1.5 dl
 whipped cream
1 oz/25 g plain
 chocolate, grated

Heat the margarine in a frying pan, add the breadcrumbs and fry slowly until crisp and golden, stirring occasionally. Remove from the heat, stir in the demerara sugar and leave until cold. Peel, core and slice the apples into a saucepan with the lemon juice, water and castor sugar, bring to the boil, cover and simmer for about 10 minutes or until tender and pulpy. Mash them with a fork, leave until cold. Divide half of the apple purée between 4 individual glasses, top with half the breadcrumbs. Repeat the layers of apple and breadcrumbs. Leave to chill before serving. Decorate with the whipped cream and grated chocolate.

Meringues Glacées Chantilly

Serves: 6 people
Preparation time:
15 minutes
Cooking time:
1½–2 hours
Oven temperature:
200°F/100°C Mark ¼
or the lowest
temperature setting

Omit the rosette of cream on top of each meringue if the budget is tight.

2 egg whites
4 oz/100 g castor
 sugar
1 family-sized block
 (17 fl oz/½ litre)
 vanilla ice cream
¼ pint/1·5 dl
 whipped cream
6 maraschino or
 glacé cherries
1 oz/25 g walnuts,
 chopped

Whisk the egg whites until stiff. Add half the sugar and continue whisking until the meringue is stiff again. Gently fold in the remaining sugar with a metal spoon. Place a piece of greased greaseproof paper on a baking tray. Draw six 3 inch/7 cm circles on the paper. Using a ½ inch/12 mm fluted icing pipe, pipe on the meringue. Bake in a cool oven (200°F/100°C Mark ¼) for 1½–2 hours until dry but still white. Remove the greaseproof paper and cool on a wire rack. Place a scoop of ice cream on each meringue. Pipe a large rose of cream on the top of the ice cream. Decorate with chopped cherries and chopped walnuts. Serve immediately.

Creamy Apricot Ring

Serves: 4–6 people
Preparation time:
15 minutes plus
setting time
Cooking time:
None

A store cupboard
dessert. Try other
combinations of fruit
and jelly for variety

1 (1 lb 3 oz/540 g)
   can apricot halves
1 (1 pint/569 ml)
   orange jelly
1 (15½ oz/440 g)
   can creamed rice
¼ pint/1·5 dl
   whipped cream
   (optional)

Drain the juice from the apricot halves into a measuring jug. Make up to ¼ pint/1·5 dl, if necessary, with water. Pour the juice into a saucepan and add the jelly, broken into pieces. Heat gently, stirring until the jelly is dissolved. Remove from the heat and stir in the creamed rice. Arrange about 8 apricot halves in the base of an 8 inch/20 cm ring mould. Reserve 4–6 halves, then purée the remainder by rubbing them through a sieve or blending them in an electric blender. Stir the apricot purée into the creamed rice mixture. Allow to set slightly before pouring the mixture into the ring mould. Leave in a cool place until set. Just before serving, unmould the ring onto a serving plate. Chop the reserved apricots roughly, fold them into the whipped cream (if used) and pile them into the centre of the ring.

Hawaiian Dreams

Serves: 6 people
Preparation time:
15 minutes plus
setting time
Cooking time:
None

An excellent party
dessert. Chocolate
ice cream could be
used instead of
vanilla for variety.
Use other nuts,
walnuts or peanuts,
for family meals.

1 (8 oz/226 g) can
   crushed pineapple
½ oz/15 g gelatine
2 teaspoons lemon
   juice
1 family-sized
   block (17 fl oz/
   ½ litre) vanilla
   ice cream
2 oz/50 g almonds,
   chopped and
   toasted
¼ pint/1·5 dl
   whipped cream
6 glacé cherries

Place the crushed pineapple, pine-apple syrup and lemon juice in a measuring jug and make up to 1 pint/6 dl with water. Pour a little of the liquid into a heatproof bowl, stir in the gelatine. Place the bowl in a saucepan of simmering water and stir to dissolve the gelatine. Return it to the crushed pineapple. Pour into 6 serving glasses and leave in a cool place to set. Just before serving, place a scoop of ice cream in each glass on top of the jelly. Sprinkle with the toasted almonds. Decorate with whipped cream and top with a glacé cherry.

Strawberry Alaska

Serves: 6 people
Preparation time:
15 minutes plus
chilling time
Cooking time:
2–3 minutes
Oven temperature:
450°F/230°C Mark 8

Fresh strawberries
are in season for
most of the summer.
Use them in
preference to the
canned or frozen
varieties as they have
a better flavour. Keep
a packet of chilled
dessert mix in store
for unexpected
guests.

1 packet chilled
   dessert mix,
   strawberry flavour
¼ pint/1·25 dl cold
   milk
1 (7–8 inch/
   18–20 cm) sponge
   flan case
1 (15 oz/428 g) can
   strawberries
2 egg whites
4 oz/100 g castor
   sugar

Make up the chilled dessert mix with the milk as directed on the side of the packet and place in the freezing compartment of the refrigerator until firm. Place the flan case on a baking tray. Drain the strawberries and arrange them in tne base of the flan case. Whisk the egg whites until stiff, add half the sugar and whisk again until stiff; carefully fold in the remaining sugar with a tablespoon. Cover the strawberries in the flan case with spoonfuls of the set chilled dessert mix. Completely cover this with the meringue, making sure that there are no holes and that it meets the sponge flan all the way round. Place in a very hot oven (450°F/230°C Mark 8) for 2–3 minutes until lightly browned. Lift gently onto a plate and serve immediately.

Strawberry Fluff Charlotte

Serves: 4–6 people
Preparation time:
15 minutes plus
setting time
Cooking time:
None

A speedy dessert for a
very special occasion.
Make it ahead of time
to allow for setting.

1 (15 oz/426 g) can
   strawberries
1 (1 pint/569 ml)
   strawberry jelly
1 sachet dessert
   topping mix
¼ pint/1.5 dl milk
1 packet sponge
   fingers
2 egg whites

Drain the strawberries from the syrup. Make the jelly using the strawberry syrup made up to ¾ pint/4.5 dl with water. Pour ¼ pint/1.5 dl of the jelly into a 6 inch/15 cm diameter deep round cake tin or charlotte mould and leave it to set. Make up the dessert topping mix with the milk as directed on the side of the packet. When the remaining jelly is syrupy and beginning to set, whisk in the cream topping and drained strawberries. Trim one end off the sponge fingers and arrange them round the inside of the tin or mould. Whisk the egg whites in a clean bowl until stiff and stir gently into the strawberry mixture. Pour the mixture into the lined tin or mould and allow to set. Unmould when ready to serve.

Tropical Flash

Serves: 4–6 people
Preparation time:
15 minutes
Cooking time:
35 minutes
Oven temperature:
300°F/150°C Mark 2

A dessert to tempt the most fastidious eater. It appeals to most children and is very good for them!

1 (15 oz/428 g) can pineapple chunks
2 oz/50 g dried skimmed milk powder
2 oz/50 g cornflour
4 oz/100 g castor sugar
2 eggs, separated

Drain the syrup from the pineapple chunks through a sieve into a measuring jug and make up to ¾ pint/4 dl with water. Stir in the dried milk until it has all dissolved. Place the cornflour and 2 oz/50 g of the castor sugar into a small bowl and blend together with a little of the milk mixture. Pour the remaining liquid into a saucepan and stir in the blended cornflour. Bring to the boil, stirring continuously, and boil for about 2 minutes or until thickened. Leave to cool slightly. Stir in the pine-apple chunks (reserving a few for decoration), then the egg yolks. Pour the mixture into a 1½ pint/9 dl ovenproof dish. Place the egg whites in a clean bowl and whisk them until stiff. Fold in the remaining 2 oz/50 g castor sugar. Pile the meringue on top of the pineapple mixture. Place in a slow oven (300°F/150°C Mark 2) for 30 minutes or until the meringue is slightly browned. Decorate the top with the reserved pineapple chunks and serve.

Georgian Syllabub

Serves: 6–8 people
Preparation time:
20 minutes
Cooking time:
None

Only small portions of this very rich dessert will be needed. Serve with crisp biscuits.

2 oranges
¼ pint/1.5 dl white wine
1 oz/25 g castor sugar
½ pint/3 dl whipping cream
3 tablespoons marmalade

Place the grated rind and juice of one of the oranges into a bowl. Add the wine, sugar and cream. Whisk the mixture well until it is standing in peaks. Fold in the marmalade with a metal spoon. Divide the mixture between 6 or 8 individual serving glasses. Chill until required. Cut the remaining orange into thin slices and decorate each glass of syllabub with a twist of orange before serving.

Yoghourt Jelly Fluff

Serves: 2 people
Preparation time:
10 minutes plus
setting time
Cooking time:
None

A special dessert,
just right for a
dinner for two.

1 (1 pint/569 ml)
packet black-
currant jelly
1 (6 fl oz/170 ml)
carton black-
currant yoghourt
1 egg white

Put half the jelly in a small saucepan with ½ pint/3 dl water. Bring to the boil, stirring until the jelly is dissolved. Cool slightly, then pour into 2 large serving glasses. Put in a cool place until set. Put the remaining jelly in a saucepan and add 6 tablespoons water. Heat gently, stirring until the jelly is dissolved. Cool slightly, then stir in the yoghourt. Whisk the egg white until stiff and fold into the yoghourt mixture. Spoon onto the set jelly. Leave in a cool place until firm.

Mousse au Chocolat Basque

Serves: 4 people
Preparation time:
20 minutes plus
setting time
Cooking time:
None

A rich and delicious
dessert.

8 oz/225 g plain
chocolate
1 level tablespoon
instant coffee
powder
1 teaspoon vanilla
essence
½ pint/3 dl boiling
water
½ oz/15 g gelatine
3 tablespoons warm
water
¼ pint/1.5 dl
whipping cream
Decoration:
crystallised rose
petals or glacé
cherries
4 sponge fingers

Break the chocolate into pieces and put it in a heatproof bowl over a saucepan of hot water, or in the top of a double saucepan. Add the coffee, vanilla essence and boiling water. Whisk over gently simmering water until it has all melted. Dissolve the gelatine in the warm water in a bowl over hot water. Stir into the chocolate mixture. Leave to cool. Whip the cream. When the chocolate mixture is just beginning to set round the edges, fold in most of the whipped cream, reserving a little for decoration. Divide the mousse between 4 individual serving glasses. Leave to set. Decorate with the crystallised rose petals or cherries and the sponge fingers.

Tahitian Coconut Ice Cream

Serves: 6 people
Preparation time:
20 minutes plus
freezing time
Cooking time:
None

Bought vanilla ice cream may be used in place of the evaporated milk mixture if speed is important. Beat in the coconut and refreeze the ice cream. Toast the coconut by heating it under a hot grill, stirring occasionally, until golden.

1 level teaspoon
   gelatine
½ large can
   (13 fl oz/368 ml)
   evaporated
   milk, chilled
3 oz/75 g castor
   sugar
1 teaspoon vanilla
   essence
3 tablespoons
   desiccated
   coconut, toasted
1 (7¾ oz/220 g) can
   pineapple pieces
6 canned apricot
   halves

Turn the refrigerator to its coldest setting. Dissolve the gelatine in 2 tablespoons hot water in a small bowl. Make sure it is thoroughly dissolved, standing the bowl in a pan of hot water if necessary. Whisk the evaporated milk in a large bowl until thick enough for the whisk to leave a trail. Add the dissolved gelatine, castor sugar and vanilla essence, whisking continuously. Pour into 2 refrigerator ice cube trays (dividers removed) and leave in the freezing compartment until it becomes firm round the edges. Turn the ice cream into a large bowl and stir in the toasted desiccated coconut. Return to the trays and freeze until firm. Divide the ice cream between 6 serving glasses, top each with some pineapple and syrup and finish with half an apricot. Serve immediately.

Orange Turnabouts

Serves: 5 people
Preparation time:
20 minutes plus
setting time
Cooking time:
None

This is always a popular dessert with children.

1 (1 pint/569 ml)
   packet orange jelly
1 (11 oz/311 g)
   can mandarin
   oranges
1 small can
   evaporated milk,
   chilled
1 chocolate flake bar
¼ pint/1·5 dl
   whipped cream
   (optional)
5 chocolate buttons

Rinse individual moulds or cups, each of ¼ pint/1·5 dl capacity, in cold water. Put half of the jelly in a measuring jug and dissolve it in ½ pint/3 dl boiling water. Divide it equally between the 5 moulds and leave in a cool place until set. Put ¼ pint/1.5 dl of the mandarin orange syrup in a saucepan with the remaining jelly. Heat gently, stirring, until the jelly is dissolved. Cool. Whisk the evaporated milk until thick, then stir in the jelly. Mix in the crushed chocolate flake bar, chop the mandarin oranges (reserving a few whole segments for decoration) and add to the jelly. Pour the mixture into the moulds on top of the set jelly and put in a cool place until firm. Unmould the jellies just before serving. Dip each mould quickly into hot water, then turn out the pudding onto individual plates. Decorate with whipped cream if liked and top with chocolate buttons and mandarin orange segments.

Fruit Flan

Serves: 4–6 people
Preparation time:
15 minutes
Cooking time:
35 minutes
Oven temperature:
375°F/190°C Mark 5
then 325°F/170°C
Mark 3

Use fresh fruit in
season (such as
strawberries in the
summer), frozen or
well drained canned
fruit at other times.
A little fruit syrup can
be used instead of
the red currant jelly.

Pastry:
6 oz/150 g plain flour
pinch of salt
1½ oz/40 g margarine
1½ oz/40 g lard
1 oz/25 g castor
  sugar
1 egg yolk
cold water to mix
Filling:
6–8 oz/175–225 g
  strawberries
½ oz/15 g castor
  sugar
1 level teaspoon
  arrowroot
1 tablespoon water
3 level tablespoons
  red currant jelly
2 teaspoons lemon
  juice

Lightly grease an 8 inch/20 cm flan ring and stand it on a greased baking tray. Make the pastry (see Apple Dumplings page 167). Place a piece of greaseproof paper on the pastry and fill with baking beans. Bake in a moderately hot oven (375°F/190°C Mark 5) for 20 minutes. Carefully remove the flan ring and the greaseproof paper with the baking beans. Reduce the oven temperature to moderately slow (325°F/170°C Mark 3) and bake the flan case for a further 10 minutes. Remove it from the baking tray and cool on a wire rack.
Make the filling: Arrange the strawberries in the flan case and sprinkle with castor sugar. Blend the arrowroot with the water in a small bowl. Place the red currant jelly in a saucepan over a low heat, bring to the boil, and stir in the blended arrowroot and lemon juice. Continue boiling for 2 minutes, stirring constantly. Glaze the fruit while the mixture is still warm. Serve the flan when quite cold.

French Pancakes

Serves: 4 people
Preparation time:
20 minutes
Cooking time:
10–15 minutes
Oven temperature:
425°F/220°C Mark 7

Inexpensive but
very delicious.
Stewed fruit can be
used as a filling
instead of jam.

4 oz/100 g
  margarine
4 oz/100 g castor
  sugar
grated rind of
  1 lemon
2 eggs, separated
4 oz/100 g plain
  flour
½ level teaspoon
  baking powder
½ pint/3 dl milk
castor sugar
4 tablespoons
  raspberry jam

Lightly grease 8 old saucers. Cream the margarine and sugar together with a wooden spoon, until light and fluffy. Beat in the lemon rind and egg yolks. Sift the flour and baking powder and fold it into the creamed mixture alternately with the milk. Whisk the egg whites until stiff and fold them in. Divide the mixture between the 8 prepared saucers, place them on baking trays and bake in a hot oven (425°F/220°C Mark 7) for 10–15 minutes or until well risen and browned. Turn the pancakes out onto sugared kitchen paper. Heat the jam in a saucepan, then place 1 tablespoon on each pancake. Fold them over and serve very hot sprinkled with a little more castor sugar.

Fruit Kebabs

Serves: 4 people
Preparation time:
15 minutes
Cooking time:
5–10 minutes

Use fruit which is in season if possible. The fruits mentioned here would make a good autumn or winter selection.

2 small oranges
3 firm bananas
2 apples
3 level tablespoons honey
2 oz/50 g butter
½ level teaspoon ground ginger
1 teaspoon lemon juice

Peel the oranges with a sharp knife, removing all the peel, pith and skin. Cut the oranges into chunks. Cut the bananas into quarters. Peel and core the apples and cut them into chunks. Thread the pieces of fruit onto 4 skewers. Put the honey, butter, ground ginger and lemon juice into a small saucepan. Heat gently, stirring, until the butter is melted and the ingredients combined. Brush the kebabs with the butter mixture. Cook over a hot fire or under a hot grill, basting frequently, for 5–10 minutes or until the banana is lightly browned.

Eggnog Pie

Serves: 6 people
Preparation time:
20 minutes plus setting time
Cooking time:
None

A really delicious dessert for family meals and when entertaining. Use 1 teaspoon rum essence instead of the rum or brandy if the budget is tight.

8 oz/225 g shortbread biscuits
2 oz/50 g walnuts, finely chopped
4 oz/100 g butter, melted
4 oz/100 g castor sugar
4 eggs, separated
½ pint/3 dl milk
1 level tablespoon gelatine
4 tablespoons hot water
1 small can evaporated milk, chilled
1 tablespoon rum or brandy
extra walnuts for decoration

Put the biscuits into a polythene bag and crush them with a rolling pin to fine crumbs. Put the crumbs into a bowl, add the walnuts and melted butter. Mix thoroughly. Press the biscuits over the base and up the sides of an 8 inch/20 cm spring form tin or deep round cake tin lined with greased greaseproof paper. Put in a cool place. Put the castor sugar in a heatproof mixing bowl with the 4 egg yolks. Warm the milk and stir it into the sugar and egg yolks. Put the bowl over a saucepan of simmering water; it should not touch the water. Cook, stirring, until the custard coats the back of the spoon. Sprinkle the gelatine into the hot water and stir until dissolved. Stir the warm gelatine into the warm custard. Cool, then chill until syrupy. Whip the evaporated milk until thickened and stir it into the custard with the rum or brandy. Whisk the egg whites until stiff and fold in. Pour the mixture into the biscuit crumb crust and chill until set. Serve decorated with extra walnuts.

Hot Gooseberry Trifle

Serves: 4 people
Preparation time:
15 minutes
Cooking time:
30 minutes
Oven temperature:
350°F/180°C Mark 4

An inexpensive but popular pudding, and a good way to use up leftover sponge cake. Other canned fruit, or even stewed fruit, can be used for variation.

1 sponge cake or packet sponge cakes
2 tablespoons jam
1 (12½ oz/355 g) can gooseberries
2 level tablespoons custard powder
2 eggs, separated
1 level tablespoon granulated sugar
1 pint/6 dl milk
4 oz/100 g castor sugar

Break the sponge cake into pieces and spread with the jam. Arrange the cake and gooseberries with the syrup in a 1½ pint/9 dl ovenproof dish. Blend the custard powder, egg yolks, granulated sugar and a little of the milk in a large bowl. Heat the rest of the milk until boiling, pour it onto the custard mixture, stirring continuously. Return to the saucepan and bring to the boil, stirring for about 3 minutes. When thick, pour over the gooseberries and leave to cool. Whisk the egg whites in a clean bowl until stiff, fold in the castor sugar, then pile on top of the custard. Bake in a moderate oven (350°F/180°C Mark 4) for 20 minutes or until the meringue is slightly browned.

Blackberry and Apple Crunchy Pie

Serves: 6 people
Preparation time:
20 minutes plus cooling time
Cooking time:
1 minute

A very unusual and delicious pie. The fresh fruits are available in the autumn, otherwise use frozen or canned.

6 oz/175 g digestive biscuits
2 oz/50 g brown sugar
3 oz/75 g butter or margarine, melted
1 tablespoon golden syrup
1½ lb/¾ kg cooking apples
6 oz/175 g blackberries
¼ pint/1·5 dl whipping cream (optional)
4 oz/100 g demerara sugar

Put the biscuits into a polythene bag and crush them with a rolling pin. Put the crumbs in a bowl, stir in the brown sugar, melted butter or margarine and syrup. Mix until thoroughly combined. Press the crumb mixture over the base and sides of a lightly greased 8–9 inch/20–23 cm pie plate. Put in a cool place until firm. Peel, core and slice the apples. Cook with the minimum of water until tender. Put aside until cold. Spread the apples onto the biscuit crust case. Whip the cream (if used) and spread over the apple. Arrange the blackberries on top, then sprinkle with the demerara sugar. Place under a hot grill until the sugar is caramelised (about 1 minute). Serve immediately or leave until cold.

Apple Dumplings

Serves: 4 people
Preparation time:
20 minutes
Cooking time.
40 minutes
Oven temperature:
375°F/190°C Mark 5
then 350°F/180°C
Mark 4

If you want to vary
the number of
servings, a basic
guide is to allow
2 oz/50 g shortcrust
pastry (made with
2 oz/50 g plain flour,
1 oz/25 g fat etc.)
per apple per person.

Pastry:
8 oz/200 g plain flour
pinch of salt
2 oz/50 g margarine
2 oz/50 g lard
1½ oz/40 g castor
   sugar
1 egg yolk
cold water to mix
Filling:
2 oz/50 g dates,
   chopped
1 oz/25 g sultanas
1 oz/25 g currants
1 level tablespoon
   soft brown sugar
4 cooking apples,
   peeled and cored

Make the pastry: Sift the flour and salt into a mixing bowl. Add the margarine and lard and rub in with your fingertips until the mixture resembles fine breadcrumbs. Stir in the sugar, egg yolk and sufficient water to make a firm dough. Divide the pastry into 4 and roll out each piece on a lightly floured surface to a round about ⅛ inch/3 mm thick, and large enough to wrap around an apple without stretching.
Make the filling: Combine the dates, sultanas, currants and sugar in a bowl. Place an apple on each round of pastry. Fill the apples with the dried fruit mixture. Damp the edges of the pastry with a little cold water, then bring it up around the apple and seal the edges together on top. Place the apple dumplings on a greased baking tray with the pastry joins underneath. Make a small hole in the pastry on top for the steam to escape. Brush with milk and bake in a moderately hot oven (375°F/190°C Mark 5) for 20 minutes, then reduce to 350°F/180°C Mark 4 for a further 20 minutes or until the apples are cooked.

Rhubarb Meringue Tart

Serves: 4 people
Preparation time:
20 minutes
Cooking time:
40 minutes
Oven temperature:
400°F/200°C Mark 6

An excellent way of
using up seasonal
fruit to make a
dessert for a special.
occasion. Use
rhubarb, goose-
berries or plums in
the summer.

Pastry:
8 oz/200 g plain flour
½ level teaspoon salt
2 oz/50 g margarine
2 oz/50 g lard
2–3 tablespoons cold
   water
Filling:
1 lb/450 g rhubarb
¼ pint/1.5 dl water
6 oz/175 g brown
   sugar
1 oz/25 g cornflour
pinch of salt
½ level teaspoon
   ground cinnamon
¼ level teaspoon
   ground cloves
¼ level teaspoon
   ground nutmeg
1 oz/25 g margarine
   or butter
1 egg, separated
2 oz/50 g castor
   sugar

Make the pastry (see Frosted Apple Pie page 245). Put it onto a lightly floured surface and roll out to line an 8 inch/20 cm pie plate; keep the trimmings.
Make the filling: Put the prepared rhubarb, water and brown sugar into a saucepan. Cook for 15 minutes or until the rhubarb is tender. Remove from the heat and stir in the cornflour, salt, cinnamon, cloves, nutmeg and margarine. Return to the heat and cook, stirring, for about 3 minutes or until thickened. Stir in the egg yolk. When cooled, pile the filling into the prepared pie plate. Roll out the pastry trimmings and arrange them across the pie. Bake in a hot oven (400°F/200°C Mark 6) for 20 minutes. Whisk the egg white until stiff, add the castor sugar and beat again until stiff. Place teaspoonfuls of the meringue on the pie and return it to the oven for 5–10 minutes or until the meringue is lightly browned.

167

Honey Rice Apples

Serves: 4 people
Preparation time:
15 minutes
Cooking time:
45 minutes
Oven temperature:
350°F/180°C Mark 4

A delicious way to serve simple ingredients. Apples are at their best and cheapest in the autumn.

4 medium-sized cooking apples
3 tablespoons honey
1 tablespoon sultanas
1 tablespoon raisins
1 tablespoon chopped walnuts
6 oz/175 g cooked long grain rice (2 oz/50 g uncooked)
3 pieces preserved ginger, thinly sliced (optional)
1 oz/25 g butter
1 level teaspoon ground cinnamon

Wash and dry the apples, remove the cores. Put the honey, sultanas, raisins, walnuts, rice and ginger in a bowl and mix well. Place the apples in a shallow ovenproof dish and put some of the mixture into each one. Dot with butter and sprinkle with cinnamon. Bake in a moderate oven (350°F/180°C Mark 4) for 45 minutes or until the apples are tender. Serve hot or cold, with any remaining rice mixture.

Cheddar Apple Crumble

Serves: 6 people
Preparation time:
20 minutes
Cooking time:
40–50 minutes
Oven temperature:
375°F/190°C Mark 5

A delicious variation on a traditional recipe. Serve with custard or cream. Apples are at their best and cheapest in the autumn.

2 lb/1 kg cooking apples
8 oz/225 g Cheddar cheese, grated
3 oz/75 g soft brown sugar
½ level teaspoon ground nutmeg
2 oz/50 g sultanas
8 oz/200 g plain flour
4 oz/100 g margarine
2 oz/50 g demerara sugar

Lightly grease a 1½ pint/9 dl capacity ovenproof dish. Peel, core and slice the apples. Mix 6 oz/175 g of the cheese with the soft brown sugar, nutmeg and sultanas. Layer the apple slices with the cheese mixture into the dish. Put the flour in a mixing bowl and add the margarine, cut into small pieces. Rub the margarine into the flour with your fingertips until the mixture resembles fine breadcrumbs. Stir in the demerara sugar and remaining 2 oz/50 g grated cheese. Spread the crumble mixture on top of the apple and cheese layers. Bake in a moderately hot oven (375°F/190°C Mark 5) for 40–50 minutes or until golden and crisp on top. Serve hot.

Rhubarb and Ginger Compote

Serves: 4–6 people
Preparation time:
15 minutes
Cooking time:
12–15 minutes

A delicious variation on what can be a very monotonous stewed fruit.

1½ lb/675 g rhubarb
4 oz/100 g
  granulated sugar
½ pint/3 dl water
2 tablespoons
  preserved ginger
  syrup
2 thin lemon slices
1 tablespoon
  chopped
  preserved ginger

Cut the rhubarb into 1 inch/ 25 mm pieces. Place the sugar and water in a saucepan and stir over a low heat until the sugar has dissolved, then boil rapidly for 5 minutes. Stir in the ginger syrup, rhubarb and lemon slices, cover the pan and simmer for 7 minutes or until the rhubarb is tender. Remove the lemon slices, pour the compôte into a warmed serving dish, sprinkle with the chopped preserved ginger and serve.

Quick Cherry Strudel

Serves: 6 people
Preparation time:
20 minutes
Cooking time:
35–40 minutes
Oven temperature:
450°F/230°C Mark 8
then 375°F/190°C
Mark 5

This is an easier and quicker version of the traditional strudel recipe.

1 (15 oz/428 g) can
  cherries
3 oz/75 g walnuts,
  finely chopped
2 oz/50 g castor
  sugar
1 tablespoon grated
  lemon rind
1 level teaspoon
  ground cinnamon
2 oz/50 g margarine
1 slice bread,
  crumbed
1 (7½ oz/213 g)
  packet frozen puff
  pastry
extra margarine
icing sugar, sifted

Drain the cherries, cut them in half, removing any stones. Mix together the walnuts, castor sugar, lemon rind and ground cinnamon in a bowl. Melt the margarine in a pan, remove from the heat and stir in the breadcrumbs until well combined. Thaw the pastry according to the instructions on the side of the packet. Roll out the pastry on a clean, floured tea-towel to a thin rectangle 14 × 20 inches/35 × 50 cm, with the longer side of the pastry towards you. Brush with the extra melted margarine and sprinkle the breadcrumbs evenly over the surface, leaving a 2 inch/5 cm margin of pastry all round. Arrange the cherries and the walnut mixture down the centre, parallel with the longer edge. Fold in the sides of the pastry and brush them with melted margarine. Roll up the strudel and place it on a damp baking tray. Brush all over with melted margarine and bake in a very hot oven (450°F/230°C Mark 8) for 10 minutes. Reduce the oven temperature to moderately hot (375°F/ 190°C Mark 5) for a further 25–30 minutes or until golden brown. Brush with more melted margarine every 10 minutes. Sprinkle with icing sugar and serve warm.

Swiss Meringue

Serves: 4 people
Preparation time:
15 minutes
Cooking time:
5 minutes

A 'store cupboard' dessert which can be made extremely quickly but is good enough for the most special occasion. Other sponge cakes can be used instead of a Swiss roll; spread with jam

4 ($\frac{1}{2}$ inch/1 cm) slices Swiss roll
1 small can pineapple rings
1 egg white
2 oz/50 g castor sugar
Decoration:
2 glacé cherries, quartered
few angelica leaves

Place a slice of Swiss roll in 4 individual ovenproof dishes. Drain the pineapple rings and use the syrup to sprinkle over the Swiss roll. Place a pineapple ring on each slice. Whisk the egg white in a clean bowl until very stiff and dry. Whisk in half the sugar, then fold in the remainder with a tablespoon. Pile the meringue on top of the pineapple, then place under a low grill for 5 minutes, until golden brown on top. Decorate with glacé cherries and angelica leaves. Serve hot or cold.

Caramel Queen Pudding

Serves: 4–5 people
Preparation time:
20 minutes plus cooling time
Cooking time:
1 hour 10 minutes
Oven temperature:
325°F/170°C Mark 3
then 275°F/140°C
Mark 1

A very inexpensive pudding which can be made with ingredients from your store cupboard.

3 oz/75 g golden syrup
$\frac{1}{2}$ oz/15 g butter
$\frac{1}{2}$ pint/3 dl milk
2 oz/50 g fresh breadcrumbs
2 eggs, separated
few drops vanilla essence
2 oz/50 g castor sugar
extra castor sugar for sprinkling

Lightly grease a 1 pint/6 dl pie dish. Place the syrup and butter in a saucepan, stir over a low heat until it has turned a deep golden brown. Slowly stir in the milk and return to the boil. Place the crumbs in a mixing bowl, pour in the syrup mixture and allow to cool slightly. Beat in the egg yolks and vanilla essence. Pour the mixture into the prepared dish and bake in a moderately slow oven (325°F/170°C Mark 3) for 30 minutes. Allow to cool slightly. Whisk the egg whites until stiff but not dry, add 1 tablespoon of sugar and whisk again until very stiff. Fold in the remaining sugar with a tablespoon. Spread or pipe the meringue onto the pudding. Sprinkle with a little extra castor sugar. Bake in a slow oven (275°F/140°C Mark 1) for 30–40 minutes or until golden brown on top. Serve immediately.

Belgian Gozette

Serves: 6 people
Preparation time:
20 minutes
Cooking time:
40 minutes
Oven temperature:
425°F/220°C Mark 7
then 350°F/180°C
Mark 4

A spicy fruit turnover which is very quick to make, especially when you use a pastry mix.

12 oz/350 g flaky pastry mix or home-made flaky pastry, using 8 oz/200 g flour etc.
1 lb/½ kg cooking apples, peeled, cored and sliced
3 oz/75 g soft brown sugar
1 oz/25 g raisins, chopped
1 level teaspoon ground cinnamon
milk for brushing
little castor sugar for sprinkling

Make up the flaky pastry mix in a mixing bowl according to the instructions on the side of the packet. Roll out the pastry on a lightly floured surface to about ⅛ inch/3 mm thick and cut out a circle of 14 inches/35 cm diameter. Combine the apples, sugar, raisins and cinnamon well together and pile onto half the circle of pastry. Damp the edges with cold water, then fold over the other half of the pastry. Seal the edges by pinching them together. Use the pastry trimmings to decorate the top. Place on a baking tray, brush with milk and sprinkle with castor sugar. Bake in a hot oven (425°F/220°C Mark 7) for 10 minutes, then reduce the oven temperature to moderate (350°F/180°C Mark 4) and cook for a further 30 minutes or until well risen and golden.

Orange Princess Pudding

Serves: 2 people
Preparation time:
20 minutes
Cooking time:
50–55 minutes
Oven temperature:
325°F/170°C Mark 3

A very inexpensive pudding. For four people, double all the ingredients.

½ pint/3 dl milk
½ oz/15 g margarine
finely grated rind and juice of 1 orange
1½ oz/40 g castor sugar
2 oz/50 g soft white breadcrumbs
1 egg, separated
2 tablespoons apricot jam

Put the milk, margarine, orange rind and ½ oz/15 g castor sugar into a saucepan. Heat gently, stirring occasionally, until the margarine and sugar have melted. Stir in the breadcrumbs, remove from the heat and put aside for 15 minutes. Beat the egg yolk into the breadcrumb mixture. Pour into a 1 pint/6 dl capacity ovenproof dish. Cook in a moderately slow oven (325°F/170°C Mark 3) for 30–35 minutes or until firm. Mix the apricot jam with the orange juice and spread over the pudding. Whisk the egg white until stiff and fold in the remaining castor sugar. Spread the meringue over the jam and put the pudding back into the oven for about 20 minutes or until the meringue is lightly browned. Serve hot.

171

Fruit Pie

Serves: 4–6 people
Preparation time:
20 minutes
Cooking time:
40 minutes
Oven temperature:
400°F/200°C Mark 6
then 350°F/180°C
Mark 4

Use whatever fruit is in season and cheap. Drained canned fruit can also be used; reduce the cooking time accordingly.

Filling:
1½ lb/700 g prepared fruit
4 oz/100 g sugar, or to taste
2 tablespoons water
Pastry:
6 oz/150 g plain flour
1½ oz/50 g margarine
1½ oz/25 g lard
cold water to mix
little castor sugar

Prepare the fruit of your choice: Peel, core and slice apples and pears; cut rhubarb into 1 inch/25 mm pieces; stone cherries, plums, damsons etc. Fill a 1½ pint/9 dl pie dish with layers of prepared fruit and sugar, finishing with a layer of fruit. Add the water.

Make the pastry: Sift the flour into a mixing bowl and add the margarine and lard; rub the fat in with your fingertips until the mixture resembles fine breadcrumbs. Stir in sufficient water (about 1–2 tablespoons) with a round-bladed knife to make a firm dough. Roll out on a lightly floured surface. Cover the pie with pastry, flute the edge by pinching the pastry between thumb and forefinger. Brush the pastry with a little water and sprinkle with castor sugar. Make a small cut in the top to allow steam to escape. Bake in a hot oven (400°F/200°C Mark 6) for 20 minutes. Reduce the oven temperature to moderate (350°F/180°C Mark 4) and cook the pie for a further 20 minutes or until the pastry is golden and the fruit tender.

Apple and Date Triangles

Makes: 4 pastries
Preparation time:
20 minutes
Cooking time:
20–25 minutes
Oven temperature:
400°F/200°C Mark 6

These pastries can also be deep-fried. Heat the oil to 375°F/190°C and fry for 10 minutes or until golden brown. Drain on absorbent kitchen paper.

Pastry:
8 oz/200 g plain flour
pinch of salt
2 oz/50 g margarine
2 oz/50 g lard
cold water to mix
Filling:
1 cooking apple
2 oz/50 g castor sugar
3 oz/75 g dates, finely chopped
castor sugar for sprinkling

Lightly grease a baking tray. Make the pastry: Sift the flour and salt into a bowl, add the margarine and lard and rub in with your fingertips until the mixture resembles fine breadcrumbs. Stir in sufficient cold water to make a firm dough. Gently knead the pastry on a lightly floured surface. Roll out thinly to a 16 inch/40 cm square and cut into 4 squares.

Make the filling: Peel, core and finely chop the apple, place in a bowl with the sugar and dates. Stir well to combine thoroughly. Divide the filling between the pastry squares. Damp the edges with water. Fold into triangles, pressing down the edges firmly to seal them. Brush with water and sprinkle with castor sugar. Place on the prepared baking tray and bake in a hot oven (400°F/200°C Mark 6) for 20–25 minutes or until cooked. Serve immediately with custard or cream.

Banana Twists

Serves: 4 people
Preparation time:
20 minutes
Cooking time:
20–25 minutes
Oven temperature:
425°F/220°C Mark 7

A quick to make
dessert for special
occasions. Serve as
soon as baked.

8 oz/225 g flaky
  pastry mix
4 bananas
milk to glaze
2 level teaspoons
  castor sugar
¼ level teaspoon
  ground cinnamon

Prepare the flaky pastry mix according to the instructions on the side of the packet. Roll out the dough on a lightly floured surface to a rectangle about 2 × 20 inches/5 × 50 cm. Cut the pastry into 4 strips, 20 inches/ 50 cm long, ½ inch/1 cm wide. Peel the bananas, then twist 1 pastry strip round each banana.

Place them on a greased baking tray. Brush with milk and bake in a hot oven (425°F/220°C Mark 7) for 20–25 minutes, until the pastry is well risen and golden brown. Mix together the sugar and ground cinnamon, then sprinkle over the banana twists. Serve hot.

Syrup Layer Pudding

Serves: 4 people
Preparation time:
20 minutes
Cooking time:
2½–3 hours

An economical
pudding which is
equally delicious
made with a filling
of jam, mincemeat or
marmalade. Serve
with extra syrup.

Pastry:
8 oz/200 g plain flour
2 level teaspoons
  baking powder
½ level teaspoon salt
4 oz/100 g shredded
  suet
about ¼ pint/1.25 dl
  cold water to mix
Filling:
8 oz/200 g golden
  syrup
2 oz/50 g fresh white
  breadcrumbs
grated rind of
½ lemon

Make the pastry: Sift the flour, baking powder and salt into a bowl. Add the suet, then enough water to make a soft dough, stirring with a round-bladed knife. Turn onto a lightly floured surface and knead gently to a smooth dough. Divide the dough into 4 unequal portions, the smallest being just big enough to cover the base of a 2 pint/1 litre pudding basin, and the largest being about one-third of the total amount.
Make the filling: Place the syrup in a small pan over a low heat to soften it. Remove from the heat and stir in the breadcrumbs and lemon rind. Grease the pudding basin and cover the base with the smallest piece of pastry. Spoon over one-third of the syrup. Roll out the second smallest piece of pastry and place over the syrup in the basin. Top with half the remaining syrup,

then the third piece of pastry. Pour on the remaining syrup and final layer of pastry. Cover the pudding with a double layer of well greased greaseproof paper with a pleat in it to allow the pudding to rise. Tie the greaseproof paper securely with string round the top. Place the basin in a steamer over boiling water or in a saucepan of boiling water with the water coming a third to halfway up the side of the pudding. Cover tightly and steam for 2½–3 hours. Turn the pudding out of the bowl onto a serving plate. Serve hot.

173

Viennoise Pudding

Serves: 4 people
Preparation time:
15 minutes plus
standing time
Cooking time:
1½ hours
Oven temperature:
325°F/170°C Mark 3

An excellent but
economical recipe
for special occasions
or family meals. It
transforms leftover
bread into a light
and delicious
pudding.

1 oz/25 g granulated
  sugar
½ pint/3 dl milk
3 oz/75 g leftover
  white bread
2 oz/50 g sultanas
1 oz/25 g mixed
  peel, chopped
1½ oz/40 g castor
  sugar
1 level teaspoon
  grated lemon rind
2 eggs
1 tablespoon sherry
  (optional)
custard for serving

Put the granulated sugar in a small saucepan with 4 tablespoons water. Heat the pan, stirring only until the sugar is dissolved and the syrup is golden. Add the milk and heat gently, stirring until the caramel is dissolved. Cut the crusts off the bread and cut into ¼ inch/6 mm dice. Put the bread into a bowl and mix in the sultanas, mixed peel, castor sugar and lemon rind. Beat the eggs together in a bowl and add the caramel milk and sherry, if used. Strain the egg and milk mixture onto the bread. Cover and put aside for 30 minutes. Spoon the mixture into a lightly greased 1 pint/ 6 dl pudding bowl. Cover the top with a piece of foil and stand the bowl in a larger pan with 1 inch/ 25 mm warm water. Bake in a moderately slow oven (325°F/ 170°C Mark 3) for about 1½ hours or until firm. Turn the hot pudding out of the bowl onto a serving plate. Serve with custard.

Blackberry Layer Pudding

Serves: 6 people
Preparation time:
20 minutes
Cooking time:
2 hours

Other fresh fruit
can be used in this
recipe. Blackberries
are in season in the
autumn.

Pastry:
8 oz/200 g self
  raising flour
1 level teaspoon
  salt
4 oz/100 g shredded
  suet
about ¼ pint/1·5 dl
  cold water to mix
Filling:
1½ lb/675 g
  blackberries
4 oz/100 g sugar
  or to taste

Make the pastry: Sift the flour and salt into a bowl. Add the suet, then enough water to make a soft dough, stirring with a round-bladed knife. Divide the dough into 4 unequal portions, the smallest being just big enough to cover the base of a 2 pint/1 litre pudding basin and the largest being one-third of the total amount.
Make the filling: Place the black-berries and sugar in a bowl and mix together. Grease the pudding basin and cover the base with the smallest piece of pastry. Spoon in one-third of the blackberries. Roll out the second smallest piece of pastry and place it on top. Continue layering with the filling and dough, finishing with a layer of dough. Cover the pudding with a double layer of greased greaseproof paper with a pleat in it to allow the pudding to rise. Tie securely with string round the rim of the basin. Place the basin in a steamer over boiling water or in a saucepan of boiling water with water coming halfway up the sides of the basin. Cover tightly and steam for about 2 hours. Turn the pudding out of the bowl onto a serving plate. Serve as soon as possible.

30 Minute Dishes

With more time on your side there are many exciting dishes to choose from which are especially good for entertaining. Ratatouille is delicious hot or cold, and inexpensive when the vegetables are in season. Fritto Misto di Mare is a popular Italian dish which can be made with a wide variety of fish and Stuffed Mushrooms are always a success. Take advantage of the extra time available to prepare unusual stuffings and roasts such as Lamb with Apricot and Prune Stuffing, a Crown of Pork with Orange Rice, garnished with grapes, or Roast Duck with Celery Stuffing. The desserts are particularly spectacular. Many small cakes and gâteaux traditionally served with coffee or hot chocolate are firm favourites as desserts also, such as the classic Linzertorte and Käsetorte from Austria, Apple Palmiers or Chocolate Dessert Roll. In the autumn when fresh fruits are available serve a Four Fruit Pie made with plums, pears, apples and blackberries, or raid the store-cupboard for the ingredients to make a Winter Fruit Pie. Whichever dishes you choose, you are sure to earn lots of praise.

Savoury Pancakes

Serves: 4 people
Preparation time: 30 minutes
Cooking time: 15 minutes
Oven temperature: 350°F/180°C Mark 4

Pancakes:
4 oz/100 g plaïn flour
pinch of salt
1 egg
½ pint/2.5 dl water
lard for frying

Mushroom filling:
1 small onion, chopped
½ oz/15 g butter
2 tablespoons tomato purée
8 mushrooms
2 tablespoons chopped parsley
salt and pepper

Sweetcorn filling:
4 oz/100 g bacon, chopped
1 oz/25 g butter
1 (7 oz/198 g) can sweetcorn
½ oz/15 g flour
¼ pint/1.5 dl milk
salt and pepper
2 tablespoons chopped parsley
pinch of cayenne pepper

Make the pancakes: Sift the flour into a bowl with the salt. Make a well in the centre, add the egg and mix in. Gradually add the water, beating well. Melt a little lard in a 6 inch/15 cm frying pan and make 6 pancakes. Cool, then wrap loosely in foil, with a piece of greaseproof paper between each one. Reheat in a moderate oven (350°F/180°C Mark 4) when needed.
Mushroom filling: Fry the onion in the melted butter until soft. Stir in the tomato purée and mushrooms. Cook for 3–4 minutes. Add the parsley and seasoning.
Bacon and sweetcorn filling: Fry the bacon in half the butter until crisp. Add the drained can of sweetcorn. Melt the remaining butter in a separate pan, remove from the heat and stir in the flour. Return the pan to the heat and cook for 1 minute, stirring all the time. Gradually add the milk and bring to the boil. Season and add the chopped parsley and cayenne pepper. Stir in the bacon and sweetcorn. Fill the pancakes and roll up.

Potato Nests

Serves: 4–6 people
Preparation time:
30 minutes
Cooling time:
50 minutes
Oven temperature:
400°F/200°C Mark 6

You can put almost any savoury filling in these nests.

1½ lb/¾ kg potatoes
1 oz/25 g margarine
1 egg, separated
salt and pepper
hot milk
Filling:
1 small packet
    frozen peas
6 rashers streaky
    bacon

Peel then cook the potatoes in boiling salted water for 20–30 minutes or until tender. Cool slightly. Mash with the margarine, egg yolk, salt and pepper, and enough hot milk to make a firm mixture. Pipe the potato nests onto a lightly greased baking tray. Brush with the egg white. Cook in a hot oven (400°F/200°C Mark 6) for 20 minutes or until beginning to brown.

Make the filling: Cook the peas according to the instructions on the packet and drain. Chop 3 rashers of the bacon and make the remaining ones into 6 bacon rolls. Grill the bacon and mix the chopped bacon with the peas. Place a little of the mixture in each potato nest. Place a bacon roll on top of each one. Serve hot.

Chicken and Egg Balls

Serves: 4 people
Preparation time:
25 minutes plus
chilling time
Cooking time:
None

These are a very good meal starter. Make the balls smaller if they are to be served with drinks before the meal.

6 hard-boiled eggs
2 tablespoons
    chopped chives
8 oz/225 g cooked
    chicken, minced or
    very finely chopped
mayonnaise to mix
2 oz/50 g browned
    breadcrumbs
lettuce and tomatoes
for serving

Chop the eggs and put them into a bowl with the chives and chicken. Add enough mayonnaise to bind the mixture together. Divide the mixture into 12 and roll each portion into a ball. Roll each ball in breadcrumbs and chill. Place a bed of lettuce on a serving plate and arrange the chicken and egg balls on top. Garnish with tomato wedges.

Fish and Mushroom Bundles

Serves: 4 people
Preparation time:
25 minutes
Cooking time:
20–25 minutes
Oven temperature:
450°F/230°C Mark 8

Serve these little fish pies as a starter or for a light lunch or supper. Serve with a little salad and garnish with parsley.

4 oz/100 g white
    fish
salt and pepper
¼ pint/1·5 dl milk
1¼ oz/35 g margarine
¾ oz/20 g plain flour
1 oz/25 g
    mushrooms,
    chopped
1 level tablespoon
    chopped parsley
1 teaspoon lemon
    juice
1 (7½ oz/112 g)
    packet frozen puff
    pastry, thawed
extra milk for glazing

Put the fish into a saucepan, season well with salt and pepper, then add the milk. Bring to the boil, then simmer for 15–20 minutes or until the fish flakes easily. Drain and reserve the cooking liquid. Heat ¾ oz/20 g of the margarine in a saucepan, stir in the flour and cook, stirring, for 2 minutes. Add the reserved cooking liquid and bring to the boil, stirring all the time. Cook for 2 minutes. Melt the remaining margarine in a frying pan and fry the mushrooms until cooked. Flake the cooked fish, removing all the skin and bones. Add the fish to the sauce with the mushrooms, parsley and lemon juice. Allow the mixture to become cold. Roll out the pastry thinly on a lightly floured surface. Cut into eight 5 inch/13 cm circles. Place each pastry circle in a patty tin (the pastry should stand well above the edges of the tin). Put a dessert spoonful of the fish mixture into each circle. Damp the inside edges of the pastry, bring to the centre and press firmly together to seal. Make a small slit in the top of each bundle. Brush with milk and bake in a very hot oven (450°F/ 230°C Mark 8) for 20–25 minutes or until golden. Serve the hot bundles, 2 per person, with salad.

Golden Vegetable Hors d'Oeuvre

Serves: 6–8 people
Preparation time:
30 minutes plus
cooling time
Cooking time:
5–10 minutes

A vegetable hors d'oeuvre is a good economical choice of appetiser.

1 egg yolk
golden syrup
salt and pepper
curry powder
oil
vinegar
dry mustard
½ small chopped
    onion
8 oz/225 g broad
    beans
1 cauliflower
8 oz/225 g tomatoes
4 oz/100 g
    mushrooms
½ cucumber
2 cooked beetroot
red pepper strips
chopped gherkins
onion rings
ground nutmeg

For curried mayonnaise: Put the egg yolk, 1 teaspoon golden syrup, salt and pepper and ½ level teaspoon curry powder into a bowl and beat until blended. Add ¼ pint/1·5 dl oil drop by drop, beating well all the time until the mixture is thick. Add 1 teaspoon or more vinegar as necessary.
For sweet-sour dressing: Put 4 tablespoons vinegar and 1 tablespoon golden syrup in a saucepan and heat till the syrup is liquid. Put the mixture and ¼ pint/1·5 dl oil, 1 level teaspoon salt, 1 level teaspoon dry mustard, pinch of pepper and the onion in a screw-top jar; shake well and leave for 1 hour. Cook the broad beans and cauliflower in boiling salted water until just cooked. Drain and cool. Slice the tomatoes and mushrooms, dice the cucumber and beetroot. Toss the mushrooms, beans and cauliflower pieces separately in the mayonnaise. Toss the tomatoes, cucumber and beetroot separately in the sweet-sour dressing. Arrange the vegetables in dishes, garnishing with pepper, gherkins and onion; sprinkle the mushrooms with nutmeg (see picture).

Orange Terrine

Serves: 6–8 people
Preparation time:
30 minutes
Cooking time:
2 hours 45 minutes
Oven temperature:
325°F/170°C Mark 3

Transform some of the cheaper cuts of pork into this delicious pâté. 3 tablespoons single cream can be used instead of the evaporated milk if you have some available.

12 oz/350 g belly pork
8 oz/225 g pigs' liver
4 oz/100 g lean veal
2 oz/50 g bacon scraps
½ oz/15 g butter
1 onion, chopped
1 small clove garlic, crushed
2 level teaspoons salt
¼ level teaspoon each pepper, mixed spice and dried thyme
1 tablespoon honey
1 tablespoon orange juice
½ small can evaporated milk
1 large orange, peeled and sliced
4 oz/100 g chicken livers

Remove any bones, skin and sinews from the pork, pigs' liver, veal and bacon. Mince them all together finely and put into a mixing bowl. Heat the butter in a frying pan and fry the onion and garlic until softened. Add them to the minced meats with the seasoning, mixed spice, thyme, honey, orange juice and evaporated milk. Mix all together very thoroughly. Line a 2 lb/1 kg capacity loaf tin with foil. Grease lightly, then arrange slices of orange over the base. Place half the meat mixture into the tin, place the chicken livers on top and cover with the remaining meat. Cover with greased foil. Place the tin in a roasting pan with hot water to come halfway up the sides. Cook in a moderately slow oven (325°F/170°C Mark 3) for 2 hours 45 minutes. Allow to become completely cold before turning the meat out of the tin. Serve sliced.

Raisin-Stuffed Bananas

Serves: 4 people
Preparation time:
15 minutes
Cooking time:
20–25 minutes
Oven temperature:
425°F/220°C Mark 7

An interesting dish which can be served as a snack or light supper dish. Watch out for cheap, loose bananas.

4 ripe, firm bananas
lemon juice
2 oz/50 g seedless raisins
4 rashers streaky bacon
2 tomatoes, for serving

Peel the bananas and scoop out the centre of each one, lengthways, with a small spoon. Dip the bananas in lemon juice to prevent them discolouring. Chop the raisins, divide them evenly between the 4 bananas and use to fill the hollowed-out centres. Remove the rinds from the bacon rashers. Place the rashers on a flat surface and spread each one with the back of knife until half as long again. Hold a stuffed banana in one hand, and wrap a rasher of bacon around it; repeat with the other bananas. Either place the bananas in an ovenproof dish and cook in a hot oven (425°F/220°C Mark 7) for 20–25 minutes, together with the tomatoes, cut in half. Or, wrap each banana in foil and cook over a hot fire for 20–25 minutes with the tomatoes.

Fruity Coleslaw

Serves: 4–6 people
Preparation time:
25 mlnutes
Cooking time:
None

Serve the coleslaw in a 'cabbage bowl' for a party. Toss in a few caraway seeds for a change of flavour.

1 small cabbage
mayonnaise
1 orange
1 red-skinned apple
juice of 1 lemon
1 onion
2 tablespoons
   sultanas
grated rind of 1
   orange

Shred the cabbage very finely. Put into a bowl, mix with enough mayonnaise to moisten. Peel the orange, removing all the pith. Cut into segments, removing all the skin. Core the apple, slice and put the slices in the lemon juice. Peel and slice the onion finely. Put the orange, grated orange rind, apple, lemon juice, onion and sultanas in the bowl with the cabbage. Mix well. Chill before serving.

Vegetable Pasties

Serves: 4 people
Preparation time:
30 minutes
Cooking time:
35–40 minutes
Oven temperature:
400°F/200°C Mark 6

Buy mushroom stalks for economy. If you buy whole mushrooms, use the caps for making soup or a mushroom salad. Serve with a green salad.

Pastry:
8 oz/200 g plain
   flour
½ level teaspoon
   salt
2 oz/50 g margarine
2 oz/50 g lard
2 oz/50 g Cheddar
   cheese, grated
cold water to mix
Filling:
1 oz/25 g margarine
1 level teaspoon
   meat extract
1 onion, finely
   chopped
1 carrot, diced
1 large potato, diced
2 oz/50 g mushroom
   stalks, chopped
salt and pepper

Make the pastry: Sift the flour and salt together into a mixing bowl. Cut the margarine and lard into pieces and rub them into the flour with your fingertips until the mixture resembles fine breadcrumbs. Stir in the cheese, then enough cold water to make a stiff dough. Roll out the pastry and cut out 8 large or 16 small rounds.
Make the filling: Melt the margarine and meat extract in a saucepan. Add the prepared vegetables and stir until the mixture is thoroughly combined. Season. Pile the vegetable mixture equally on the pastry rounds. Damp the edges and fold the pastry upwards to make small pasties. Press the edges together firmly. Put the pasties on a greased baking tray and bake in a hot oven (400°F/200°C Mark 6) for 35–40 minutes or until golden. Serve hot.

Egg and Potato Rolls

Makes: 8 large or
24 small savouries
Preparation time:
30 minutes
Cooking time:
10 minutes

A tasty and
substantial hot
savoury. The rolls
or balls can be made
well in advance and
fried just before
needed.

1½ lb/750 g potatoes
salt and pepper
1 oz/25 g
  margarine
milk
6 hard-boiled eggs
3 oz/75 g cheese,
  grated
6 spring onions,
  finely chopped
2 eggs, beaten
2–4 oz/50–100 g
  breadcrumbs
oil for deep-frying
cocktail sticks for
  serving

Peel the potatoes and cook them in boiling salted water until tender. Mash them with the margarine and enough milk to make a firm mixture. Finely chop the hard-boiled eggs and place them in a bowl with the mashed potato, grated cheese, salt, pepper and spring onions. Beat well together. Mould the mixture into 8 (4 inch/10 cm long) rolls or about 24 (1 inch/25 mm dia-meter) balls. Put the beaten egg onto one plate and the bread-crumbs onto another. Coat the rolls or balls in egg, then bread-crumbs. Heat the oil in a deep pan to 375°F/190°C (a 1 inch/25 mm cube of bread will brown in 30 seconds). Fry the rolls or balls for 10 minutes or until golden brown. Drain on absorbent kitchen paper and serve on cocktail sticks.

Potted Pork

Serves: 4 people
Preparation time:
30 minutes plus
cooling time
Cooking time:
3–4 hours
Oven temperature:
300°F/150°C Mark 2

A delicious and
inexpensive appetiser,
made with a cheap
cut of pork. Serve
with French bread.
For speed, blend the
pork for a short time
in an electric blender.

1½ lb/¾ kg fat belly
  pork
1 clove garlic, crushed
1 level teaspoon dried
  mixed herbs
½ level teaspoon salt
¼ level teaspoon
  black pepper
3 tablespoons water

Remove the rind and any bones from the pork and cut into short thin strips. Mix the pork with all the remaining ingredients and place in an ovenproof dish. Cover with a lid or foil and cook in a slow oven (300°F/150°C Mark 2) for 3–4 hours. The pork should be very tender and swimming in its own fat. Drain off the fat and reserve.

Mash the pork thoroughly with a fork, pulling it into fine shreds. Taste and adjust the seasoning if necessary. Pack the pork into small china or earthenware pots and pour a little of the reserved fat on top to seal. Store in the refrigerator to chill. Remove the fat from the top before serving.

Individual Onion and Herb Pies

Serves: 4 people
Preparation time:
30 minutes
Cooking time:
25 minutes
Oven temperature:
400°F/200°C Mark 6
then 350°F/180°C
Mark 4

These pies are best
eaten very fresh,
while still warm if
possible.

Pastry:
6 oz/150 g plain
    flour
pinch of salt
2 oz/50 g margarine
1 oz/25 g lard
cold water to mix
Filling:
1 oz/25 g margarine
12 oz/350 g onions,
    grated
2 eggs
4 tablespoons milk
salt and pepper
1 level teaspoon
    dried mixed herbs

Make the pastry: Sift the flour and salt into a bowl. Rub in the margarine and lard until the mixture resembles fine breadcrumbs. Mix in enough cold water to make a firm dough. Roll out the pastry and line small tart cases. If you wish to make a large pie, line a 7 inch/ 18 cm tin or plate.
Make the filling: Melt the margarine in a saucepan and fry the onions very gently until soft, stirring occas-

ionally. The onions should not brown. Beat the eggs, milk, seasonings and herbs together. Divide the onions equally between the pastry cases and pour over the egg and milk mixture. Bake in a hot oven (400°F/200°C Mark 6) for 10 minutes, then reduce the oven temperature to moderate (350°F/ 180°C Mark 4) for a further 15 minutes or until cooked.

Tourta

Serves: 4–6 people
Preparation time:
25 minutes
Cooking time:
35–40 minutes
Oven temperature:
350°F/180°C Mark 4

Serve tourta cut into
1½ inch/2 cm
squares. It is a good,
economical hot
savoury to serve with
drinks before a meal.

4 oz/100 g long
    grain rice
salt and pepper
3 tablespoons oil
2 onions, sliced
2 eggs, beaten
4 oz/100 g Cheddar
    cheese, grated
1 level teaspoon dried
    basil
1 tablespoon
    chopped parsley
2 tomatoes, skinned
    and sliced
½ oz/15 g grated
    Parmesan cheese

Put the rice into a saucepan with 8 fl oz/2 dl salted water. Bring to the boil, stir, then cover the pan and simmer for 15 minutes or until the rice is cooked and the water absorbed. Meanwhile, heat the oil in a frying pan and fry the onion until softened. Drain the rice and the onion well and mix together. Add the eggs, Cheddar cheese,

basil, parsley and salt and pepper. Spread the mixture into a lightly greased tin about 7 inches/18 cm square. Arrange the tomato slices on top and sprinkle with the Parmesan cheese. Bake in a moderate oven (350°F/180°C Mark 4) for 35–40 minutes or until golden on top. Serve cut into squares.

Fritto Misto di Mare

Serves: 6 people
Preparation time:
30 minutes
Cooking time:
5–10 minutes

Use as many different fish as possible for an interesting flavour. Serve with tartare sauce.

2 lb/1 kg assorted fish (sole, red mullet, prawns, whitebait etc.)
1 egg, beaten
2 oz/50 g fresh breadcrumbs
Batter:
4 oz/100 g plain flour
pinch of salt
1 egg
$\frac{1}{4}$ pint/1·5 dl water
oil for deep frying
1 lemon
parsley for garnish

Ask your fishmonger to skin and fillet the fish if necessary or do this yourself. Cut the larger fish into bite-sized pieces. Shell the prawns. Dip half the fish in beaten egg, then press on a coating of breadcrumbs. Make the batter: Sift the flour and salt into a mixing bowl, make a well in the centre, add the egg, then slowly beat in half the water. Beat until smooth, then stir in the remaining water. Coat the remaining pieces of fish with the batter. Half fill a deep frying pan with oil and heat to 350°F/180°C (a $\frac{1}{2}$ inch/1 cm cube of bread will brown in 1 minute). Fry the fish for 5–10 minutes or until cooked through and golden brown. Drain on absorbent kitchen paper and serve in a hot dish garnished with lemon quarters and sprigs of parsley.

Egg Pizzas

Makes: 6 pizzas
Preparation time:
25 minutes
Cooking time:
20 minutes
Oven temperature:
425°F/220°C Mark 7
then 375°F/190°C
Mark 5

Very inexpensive picnic pizzas which are easy to make and pack for carrying. Use airtight containers for taking on the picnic.

Pizza base:
8 oz/225 g plain flour
2 level teaspoons baking powder
salt and pepper
$2\frac{1}{2}$ oz/65 g margarine
$\frac{1}{4}$ pint/1·5 dl milk
Topping:
1 onion, finely chopped
3 level tablespoons tomato purée
$\frac{1}{4}$ level teaspoon oregano or marjoram
3 hard-boiled eggs
$\frac{1}{2}$ can anchovy fillets (optional)
8 oz/225 g cheese, grated
2 eggs, beaten
$1\frac{1}{2}$ level teaspoons prepared mustard

Make the pizza base: Sift the flour, baking powder, salt and pepper into a mixing bowl. Rub the margarine into the flour. Add the milk and mix to a soft dough and knead it gently until smooth. Divide the mixture into 6 equal portions and roll out each to a round, 4–5 inches/10–12 cm in diameter, and place on a baking tray.
Make the topping: Combine the onion, tomato purée, oregano or marjoram, salt and pepper in a bowl and spread the mixture equally over the pizza bases. Slice the hard-boiled eggs and divide the slices between the pizzas. Arrange the anchovy fillets, if liked, over the top. Mix the cheese, eggs and mustard and put on top. Bake in a hot oven (425°F/220°C Mark 7) for 10 minutes, then reduce the oven temperature to moderately hot (375°F/190°C Mark 5) for a further 10 minutes.

Swiss Cheese Flan

Serves: 6 people
Preparation time:
30 minutes
Cooking time:
1 hour
Oven temperature:
375°F/190°C Mark 5
then 350°F/180°C
Mark 4

Serve while still hot and puffed up, if possible.

Pastry:
6 oz/170 g plain flour
pinch of salt
1½ oz/40 g margarine
1½ oz/40 g lard
cold water to mix
Filling:
4 oz/100 g streaky bacon
1 onion, chopped
7 oz/200 g Gruyère or Emmenthal cheese, grated
6 fl oz/1·75 dl milk
1 (5 fl oz/142 ml) carton natural yoghourt
2 oz/50 g plain flour
2 egg yolks
1 level teaspoon salt
½ level teaspoon pepper
¼ level teaspoon ground nutmeg
1 egg white
Garnish:
6 bacon rolls, grilled

Make the pastry (see Fruit Pie page 172). Knead lightly on a lightly floured surface. Roll out the pastry and line a lightly greased 8 inch/20 cm flan ring standing on a greased baking tray.

Make the filling: Fry the bacon cut into small strips. Add the onion and fry until tender. Spread the mixture over the base of the flan. Sprinkle with the grated cheese. Place the milk, yoghourt, flour, egg yolks, salt, pepper and nutmeg in a bowl and beat together. Whisk the egg white until stiff, then fold into the yolk mixture. Pour into the flan case. Bake in a moderately hot oven (375°F/190°C Mark 5) for 20 minutes. Reduce the oven temperature to moderate (350°F/180°C Mark 4) and cook for a further 40 minutes or until set. Remove the flan ring 20 minutes before the end of the cooking time. Garnish with bacon rolls.

Stuffed Mushrooms

Serves: 4 people
Preparation time:
30 minutes
Cooking time:
15—20 minutes
Oven temperature:
350°F/180°C Mark 4

Use open, flat mushrooms for this recipe. Serve as a first course or with drinks before a meal.

4 large or 8 smaller mushrooms
2 oz/50 g margarine
1 small onion, chopped
½ oz/15 g plain flour
¼ pint/1·5 dl milk
½ small red pepper
2 oz/50 g cooked ham, chopped
1 level tablespoon parsley, chopped
salt and pepper
3 oz/75 g fresh breadcrumbs

Wipe the mushrooms, remove the stalks and reserve. Put the mushroom caps, upside down, in a shallow greased ovenproof dish. Dot with 1 oz/25 g of the margarine and bake in a moderate oven (350°F/180°C Mark 4) for 10 minutes. Meanwhile, heat the remaining margarine in a saucepan and fry the onion until softened. Stir in the flour and cook, stirring, for 2—3 minutes. Blend in the milk and bring to the boil, stirring all the time. Boil for 2 minutes. Chop the reserved mushroom stalks and half the pepper (slice the remainder of the pepper for garnish). Add the pepper and mushroom stalks to the sauce with the ham, parsley, salt and pepper and the breadcrumbs. Pile some stuffing into each mushroom cap. Return to the oven and bake for a further 15—20 minutes. Serve hot, garnished with strips of red pepper.

Savoury Cheese and Onion Flan

Serves: 4–6 people
Preparation time:
30 minutes
Cooking time:
45 minutes
Oven temperature:
400°F/200°C Mark 6
then 375°F/190°C
Mark 5

An inexpensive and very tasty pie. Use leftover stale cheese if available.

Pastry:
6 oz/170 g plain
  flour
½ level teaspoon salt
1½ oz/40 g margarine
1½ oz/40 g lard
cold water to mix
Filling:
½ oz/15 g margarine
1 onion, chopped
3 tomatoes, sliced
5 oz/150 g cheese,
  grated
2 eggs
¼ pint/1·5 dl milk
1 level teaspoon salt
½ level teaspoon
  pepper

Make the pastry: Sift the flour and salt into a mixing bowl. Cut the margarine and lard into small pieces and add to the flour. Rub in with your fingertips until the mixture resembles fine breadcrumbs. Stir in enough water to form a firm dough. Knead gently on a lightly floured surface. Roll out to line an 8 or 9 inch/20–23 cm diameter foil plate. Place on a baking tray.
Make the filling: Heat the margarine in a frying pan and fry the onion for about 3 minutes over low heat or until soft but not browned. Drain on absorbent kitchen paper and leave to cool. Arrange the onion, tomato slices (reserving 3) and three-quarters of the grated cheese in the flan case. Beat the eggs in a bowl and beat in the milk, salt and pepper. Pour the milk mixture into the flan and bake in a hot oven (400°F/200°C Mark 6) for 15 minutes, then reduce the oven to moderately hot, (375°F/190°C Mark 5) for a further 20 minutes. Put the remaining cheese and tomato slices on the top and return to the oven for 10 minutes. Leave to cool.

Blintz

Serves: 6 people
Preparation time:
25 minutes
Cooking time:
20–25 minutes
Oven temperature:
400°F/200°C Mark 6

A good recipe for making a little cheese into a substantial lunch or supper dish.

2 oz/50 g plain flour
1 oz/25 g margarine,
  melted
2 eggs
¼ pint/1·5 dl water
margarine for frying
8 oz/225 g cottage
  cheese
grated rind of ½ lemon
salt and pepper
1 (5 fl oz/142 ml)
  carton soured
  cream
1 onion, very finely
  chopped
1 tablespoon
  chopped parsley

Sift the flour into a mixing bowl. Make a well in the centre and add the melted margarine and eggs. Beat some of the flour into the eggs, then gradually add the water, beating well until a smooth batter is formed. Heat a little margarine in a small frying pan and add enough batter to thinly cover the base of the pan. Cook until the underside of the pancake is browned and the top dry. Remove from the pan and continue cooking the remaining batter in the same way. Place the pancakes, browned-side uppermost, flat on a clean work surface. Mix the cottage cheese with the grated lemon rind and season to taste. Divide the cheese equally between the pancakes and roll up. Place the pancakes in an ovenproof dish. Bake in a hot oven (400°F/200°C Mark 6) for 20–25 minutes, until browned. Pour the soured cream over the top and serve hot, sprinkled with the onion and parsley.

Cauliflower Fritters

Serves: 4 people
Preparation time:
30 minutes
Cooking time:
15 minutes

Cauliflower fritters can be served as a supper dish or as part of a main course. The creamy cauliflower goes well with the crisp coating. Omit the sauce if time is short.

1 small cauliflower
salt and pepper
1 oz/25 g margarine
5 oz/125 g plain flour
½ pint/2·5 dl milk
¼ level teaspoon mixed dried herbs
1 egg
¼ pint/1·5 dl water
oil for deep-frying

Wash the cauliflower well, break into flowerets then cook in boiling salted water for 5 minutes. Drain well. Melt the margarine in a saucepan, stir in 1 oz/25 g of the flour. Cook, stirring, for 2–3 minutes. Add the milk and bring to the boil, stirring. Boil for 2–3 minutes. Season and add herbs. Dip the cauliflower into the sauce then put aside to get cold. Sift the remaining 4 oz/100 g plain flour into a mixing bowl with a pinch of salt. Make a 'well' in the centre and add the egg. Mix in the egg, then the water, gradually mixing in the flour from around the bowl. Heat the oil until a ½ inch/12 mm cube of bread will brown in less than 1 minute (375°F/190°C). Dip the cauliflower into the batter then deep-fry until golden. Drain well on absorbent kitchen paper and serve as soon as possible.

Spinach Flan

Serves: 6 people
Preparation time:
30 minutes
Cooking time:
35–40 minutes
Oven temperature:
375°F/190°C Mark 5

This flan has all the ingredients for a very nourishing light lunch, supper or meal starter. Use 1 lb/450 g fresh spinach when in season.

Pastry:
6 oz/170 g plain or wholewheat flour
pinch of salt
1½ oz/40 g margarine
1½ oz/40 g lard
cold water to mix
Filling:
1 (11 oz/311 g) packet frozen spinach
2 eggs
¼ pint/1.5 dl milk
4 oz/100 g cheese, grated
salt and pepper
tomato slices and sprigs of parsley for garnish

Make the pastry: Sift the flour and salt into a mixing bowl. Add the margarine and lard and rub in with your fingertips until the mixture resembles fine breadcrumbs. Stir in sufficient cold water to make a firm dough. Knead the dough very gently with your hand. Roll out on a lightly floured surface to line an 8 inch/20 cm plain flan ring standing on a baking tray.
Make the filling: Cook the spinach in boiling salted water according to the instructions on the side of the packet. Leave it to cool. Meanwhile, beat the eggs in a bowl, beat in the milk, grated cheese and salt and pepper to taste. Spread the cooked spinach onto the base of the flan case. Pour the milk mixture over it. Bake in a moderately hot oven (375°F/190°C Mark 5) for 35–40 minutes or until cooked. Garnish the flan with tomato slices and sprigs of parsley.

Gnocchi

Serves: 4 people
Preparation time:
25 minutes plus
resting time
Cooking time:
15 minutes
Oven temperature:
400°F/200°C Mark 6

A very inexpensive
supper or light lunch.
It is also good served
as a starter to a meal.

1 pint/6 dl milk
4 oz/125 g semolina
1 level teaspoon salt
½ level teaspoon
  pepper
¼ level teaspoon
  ground nutmeg
5 oz/150 g cheese,
  grated
2 eggs, beaten
1 oz/25 g margarine
parsley for garnish

Lightly grease a 10 inch/25 cm square shallow cake tin. Pour the milk into a saucepan and bring to the boil. Sprinkle in the semolina and cook, stirring with a wooden spoon until sufficiently thick to support the spoon. Remove from the heat and beat in the salt, pepper, nutmeg, 3 oz/75 g of the grated cheese and the beaten eggs. Spread the mixture into the prepared cake tin in a layer ¼ inch/6 mm thick.

Leave until cold and set, preferably overnight as this makes it easier to handle. With a 1½ inch/4 cm pastry cutter, cut out circles of the gnocchi; alternatively, cut out triangles with a knife. Arrange the shapes in a greased ovenproof dish, overlapping. Dot with the margarine and sprinkle with the remaining cheese. Bake in a hot oven (400°F/200°C Mark 6) for 15 minutes. Serve hot, garnished with chopped parsley.

Courgettes (Zucchini) and Tomatoes with Cheese

Serves: 4 people
Preparation time:
30 minutes
Cooking time:
45 minutes
Oven temperature:
350°F/180°C Mark 4

Courgettes and
tomatoes are at their
best and cheapest in
the summer. Serve
this as a lunch or
supper dish, or as a
vegetable with the
main course.

4 courgettes
2 oz/50 g margarine
1 small onion,
  chopped
12 oz/350 g
  tomatoes, skinned
3 oz/75 g Cheddar
  cheese, grated
salt and pepper

Cut the courgettes into ½ inch/12 mm slices. Heat the margarine in a frying pan and fry the onion and courgettes together for about 10 minutes, without browning. Drain. Cut the tomatoes into ½ inch/12 mm slices. Add the tomatoes to the frying pan and cook for a further

1–2 minutes. Grease an ovenproof dish and starting with the tomatoes, layer the vegetables, sprinkling each layer with cheese and salt and pepper. Finish with a layer of tomato sprinkled with cheese. Bake in a moderate oven (350°F/180°C Mark 4) for 45 minutes.

Ratatouille

Serves: 4 people
Preparation time:
30 minutes
Cooking time:
1–1¼ hours

A ratatouille is a vegetable stew from the Mediterranean region of France. The vegetables used are at their best and cheapest in the summer and early autumn. Serve for a starter or for a light supper.

2 red or green
  peppers
2 aubergines
  (eggplants)
salt and pepper
2 onions
3 courgettes
  (zucchini)
5 tomatoes, skinned
1–2 cloves garlic
¼ pint/1·5 dl olive
  oil

Wipe the peppers, slice thinly, removing the seeds and membranes. Wipe the aubergines and cut into ¼ inch/6 mm slices. Put the aubergine slices in layers in a colander and sprinkle each layer with salt. Put a plate on top and put aside for 20 minutes. Slice the onions thinly. Wipe the courgettes and slice. Slice the tomatoes. Crush the garlic. Heat the olive oil in a large saucepan and fry the onion until softened but not browned. Drain the aubergines and rinse off excess salt, pat dry with absorbent kitchen paper. Add the aubergines to the saucepan with the other vegetables and the garlic. Cover the pan and cook very gently for 1–1¼ hours. Stir, then season to taste. Serve straightaway or keep until later—ratatouille can be reheated successfully.

Stuffed Courgettes (Zucchini)

Serves: 2 people or
4 people as a meal
starter
Preparation time:
25 minutes
Cooking time:
15–20 minutes
Oven temperature:
375°F/190°C Mark 5

A very attractive dish which is most inexpensive in the summer when courgettes are in season.

4 medium-sized
  courgettes
salt and pepper
1 tablespoon oil
4 rashers streaky
  bacon, diced
1 small onion,
  chopped
1 clove garlic,
  crushed (optional)
1 oz/25 g
  mushrooms,
  chopped
1 level tablespoon
  tomato purée
grated rind and juice
  of ½ lemon
2 level teaspoons
  chopped parsley
1 tomato for garnish

Cut each courgette in half lengthways. Carefully scoop out the flesh with a teaspoon and reserve, leaving a ¼ inch/6 mm shell. Cook the courgettes in a pan of boiling salted water for 2 minutes. Drain well. Heat the oil in a saucepan and fry the bacon and onion until softened. Add the garlic, mushrooms, tomato purée, grated rind and juice of the lemon, parsley and reserved courgette flesh. Season well. Place the courgette shells in a lightly greased ovenproof dish, pile the stuffing in the centres. Cook in a moderate oven (375°F/190°C Mark 5) for 15–20 minutes. Serve hot, garnished with thin slices of tomato.

Cheesy Egg Tarts

Serves: 4–6 people
Preparation time:
25 minutes plus
resting time
Cooking time:
10–15 minutes
Oven temperature:
375°F/190°C Mark 5

These tarts are made
with a special cream
cheese pastry.

Pastry:
4 oz/100 g flour
salt and pepper
2 oz/50 g cream
  cheese
2 oz/50 g margarine
Filling:
1 (8 oz/226 g) can
  tomatoes, drained
4 hard-boiled eggs
1 tablespoon lemon
  juice
3 level tablespoons
  salad cream or
  mayonnaise

Make the pastry: Sift the flour and a pinch of salt into a bowl. Add the cream cheese and margarine, cut into small pieces. Rub them into the flour with your fingertips until the mixture resembles fine breadcrumbs. Using a round-bladed knife add enough cold water to make a firm dough. Put the pastry in a polythene bag and put it in a cool place for about 1 hour. Roll out the pastry on a lightly floured surface and use to line 4–6 large patty tins or 12 smaller tins. Prick the bases and bake in a moderately hot oven (375°F/190°C Mark 5) for 10–15 minutes until crisp and golden brown.

Make the filling: Chop the tomatoes and hard-boiled eggs, reserving a few slices for garnish, heat gently with the lemon juice and salad cream in a saucepan. Add seasoning to taste. Put into the pastry cases. Serve garnished with slices of the remaining hard-boiled egg.

Crowned Cream of Spinach Soup

Serves: 4–6 people
Preparation time:
30 minutes
Cooking time:
55 minutes
Oven temperature:
400°F/200°C Mark 6

A spectacular soup
for special occasions.

2 oz/50 g
  margarine
1 onion, chopped
1 (6 oz/170 g)
  packet frozen
  chopped spinach,
  thawed
1¼ pints/7 dl
  chicken stock or
  water and chicken
  stock cubes
pinch of ground
  nutmeg
1 oz/25 g plain
  flour
1 large (13 fl oz/
  368 ml) can
  evaporated milk
salt and pepper
Potato rings:
8 oz/225 g cold
  cooked potato
salt and pepper
evaporated milk to
  mix

Melt the margarine in a saucepan, add the onion and fry gently, covered, for 10 minutes. Add the spinach and fry for a further 15 minutes. Stir in the stock and nutmeg. Bring to the boil, then cover the pan and simmer for 10 minutes. Whisk the flour into the evaporated milk and gradually stir it into the soup. Bring to the boil, stirring all the time. Simmer for 5 minutes. Taste and adjust the seasoning. Meanwhile, make the potato rings: Sieve the cooked potato, season, then beat in enough evaporated milk to make a soft piping consistency. Pipe rings onto a greased baking tray. Bake in a hot oven (400°F/200°C Mark 6) for about 10–15 minutes or until golden. Serve the soup with the potato rings placed gently on top.

Main Courses

Smoked Haddock and Egg Pie

Serves: 4–6 people
Preparation time:
25 minutes
Cooking time:
50 minutes
Oven temperature:
375°F/190°C Mark 5

A satisfying and tasty pie for any time of the year. It can be eaten hot or cold.

Pastry:
10 oz/250 g plain
  flour
pinch of salt
2 oz/50 g lard
3 oz/75 g margarine
cold water to mix
beaten egg for
  glazing
Filling:
1 oz/25 g margarine
1 oz/25 g plain flour
½ pint/2·5 dl milk
salt and pepper
8 oz/200 g cooked
  smoked haddock
3 hard-boiled eggs
8 oz/200 g frozen
  mixed vegetables

Make the pastry: Sift the flour and salt into a mixing bowl. Add the margarine and lard, cut into small pieces. Rub the fat into the flour until the mixture resembles fine breadcrumbs. Using a round-bladed knife, mix in enough cold water to make a firm dough. Divide into 2 pieces, one-third and two-thirds of the total amount. Knead lightly on a floured surface, then roll out the larger piece and line a deep 8 inch/20 cm pie plate. Roll out the smaller piece to make a lid.
Make the filling: Melt the margarine, stir in the flour and cook for 2–3 minutes. Blend in the milk and seasonings, bring to the boil, stirring,

and boil for 2–3 minutes. Flake the fish and remove any bones and skin. Chop the eggs roughly. Stir into the sauce with the fish and vegetables. Taste and adjust seasoning. Pour into the pastry case. Damp the edges of the pastry, cover with the lid and decorate. Glaze with beaten egg and bake in a moderately hot oven (375°F/190°C Mark 5) for 35–40 minutes or until golden.

Normandy Mackerel

Serves: 4 people
Preparation time:
30 minutes
Cooking time:
About 40 minutes
Oven temperature:
350°F/180°C Mark 4

Fresh fish and apples are both plentiful in Normandy. Herrings can be used instead of mackerel.

4 mackerel
1½ oz/40 g margarine
1 onion, chopped
4 oz/100 g bread-
  crumbs
2 medium-sized
  cooking apples,
  peeled, cored and
  chopped
1 level tablespoon
  chopped parsley
pinch of dried basil
grated rind of ½
  lemon
salt and pepper
Garnish:
1 dessert apple
1 oz/25 g butter

Clean the mackerel, fillet and remove the heads or ask your fishmonger to do it for you. Heat the margarine in a frying pan, add the onion and fry gently for 3–5 minutes or until softened. Stir in the breadcrumbs and chopped apple, continue cooking until tender. Stir in the herbs, lemon rind and salt and pepper to taste. Fill the mackerel with the stuffing and secure with small skewers or wooden cocktail sticks. Wrap each fish in foil and place on

a baking tray. Bake in a moderate oven (350°F/180°C Mark 4) for about 40 minutes. Unwrap the foil for the last 15 minutes of cooking time. Meanwhile, make the garnish. Core the apple but do not peel it, and cut into slices ¼ inch/6 mm thick. Heat the butter in a frying pan and fry the apple rings until golden brown on both sides. Serve the mackerel garnished with the apple slices and sprigs of parsley.

Herring Crumb Bake

Serves: 4 people
Preparation time:
25 minutes
Cooking time:
20 25 minutes
Oven temperature:
350°F/180°C Mark 4

Other whole fish can be substituted for herrings if they are not available. Mackerel or mullet would be ideal.

4 large herrings
salt and pepper
1 level tablespoon French mustard
3 oz/75 g margarine or butter
1 onion, finely chopped
3 sticks celery, finely chopped
2 oz/50 g breadcrumbs
3 oz/75 g Cheddar cheese, grated
4 tomatoes and lemon wedges for serving
parsley for garnish

Ask your fishmonger to scale, clean and bone the herrings or do this yourself. Season the prepared fish and spread mustard sparingly inside each one. Melt 2 oz/50 g of the margarine in a saucepan and fry the onion and celery gently until softened. Stir in the breadcrumbs, cheese and salt and pepper. Mix well. Stuff the fish, leaving a little stuffing for garnish if liked. Reshape each fish with the stuffing inside and place them in an ovenproof dish. Dot the fish with the remaining margarine, and sprinkle with any remaining filling. Bake the fish in a moderate oven (350°F/180°C Mark 4) for 20–25 minutes. Serve with grilled tomato halves and lemon wedges. Garnish with parsley.

Fish Sticks

Serves: 4 people
Preparation time:
30 minutes
Cooking time:
6 minutes

Make the fish sticks the day before needed or at least 2–3 hours in advance. Cover and keep in a cool place — the coating will be firmer.

1 lb/$\frac{1}{2}$ kg cod, haddock, coley or snapper fillets
1 egg
1 teaspoon water
$\frac{1}{2}$ level teaspoon curry powder
$\frac{1}{4}$ level teaspoon celery salt
$\frac{1}{4}$ level teaspoon onion salt
2 oz/50 g plain flour
4 oz/100 g dried breadcrumbs
oil for frying

Cut the fish into rectangles ($\frac{1}{2} \times 3$ inches/1×8 cm), removing any bones at the same time. Break the egg into a bowl, whisk in the water, curry powder, celery and onion salts. Coat the fish with flour, the egg mixture, then with breadcrumbs. Press the coating on firmly. Heat a little oil in a frying pan, add the fish sticks and fry on each side for 2–3 minutes. Drain on absorbent kitchen paper.

Stuffed Fish Rolls

Serves: 4 people
Preparation time:
30 minutes
Cooking time:
15 minutes

Use plaice, flounder or flathead fillets. These rolls can also be served as an appetiser. The stuffing and egg and breadcrumb coating make the fish more substantial.

8 small fish fillets
2 oz/50 g margarine
1 small onion, finely chopped
2 level tablespoons chopped parsley
2 oz/50 g mushrooms, chopped
4 level tablespoons breadcrumbs
salt and pepper
plain flour
2 eggs, beaten
extra breadcrumbs
oil for deep-frying

Trim the fillets. Heat the margarine in a saucepan and fry the onion until softened. Add the parsley, mushrooms, breadcrumbs, salt and pepper. Continue cooking gently, stirring, until the ingredients are thoroughly mixed. Spread a little of the stuffing on each fish fillet and roll up. Secure each roll with a wooden cocktail stick. Coat the rolls in flour, then in beaten egg and breadcrumbs. Press the coating on firmly. Fill a deep frying pan one-third to half full of oil. Heat the oil to 350°F/180°C (a ½ inch/1 cm cube of bread will brown in 1 minute). Fry the rolls until golden and cooked (about 10 minutes). Drain on absorbent kitchen paper and serve as soon as possible.

Baked Fish with Vegetables

Serves: 4 people
Preparation time:
20–30 minutes
Cooking time:
1 hour
Oven temperature:
350°F/180°C Mark 4

A complete meal in one dish which is high in protein and low in calories.

4 small herrings
salt and pepper
juice of ½ lemon
2 onions
2 potatoes
2 carrots
2 sticks celery
4 oz/100 g mushrooms
oil for frying
chopped parsley for garnish

Gut and clean the fish or ask your fishmonger to do this for you. Place them in a greased ovenproof dish and sprinkle with salt and pepper and lemon juice. Clean and slice the vegetables and fry each vegetable separately in the oil for a few minutes. Drain well and arrange them round the fish. Cover the dish and bake in a moderate oven (350°F/180°C Mark 4) for 1 hour. Serve sprinkled with chopped parsley.

Marinated Australian Lamb Cutlets

Serves: 4 people
Preparation time:
30 minutes plus
overnight marinating
Cooking time:
About 8 minutes

For special
occasions, use wine
instead of the vinegar
and stock. If only
dried herbs are
available, use half
these amounts.

8 middle neck lamb
  cutlets
6 tablespoons oil
4 tablespoons
  vinegar
1 onion, finely
  chopped
1 clove garlic,
  crushed
salt and pepper
1 level teaspoon
  chopped mint
3 oz/75 g margarine
4 level teaspoons
  chopped sage
4 level teaspoons
  chopped parsley
1 lb/½ kg carrots
½ pint/3 dl stock or
  water and beef
  stock cube
5 tablespoons olive
  oil
2 spring onions,
  chopped
1 level teaspoon
  sugar
1 bay leaf
1 level teaspoon
  chopped thyme
2 oz/50 g walnuts

Mix together the oil, vinegar, onion, garlic, pepper and mint, then pour over the cutlets. Leave overnight. Soften the butter in a bowl and beat in the sage and parsley.
Prepare the vegetables: Cut the carrots into strips. Mix together the stock, oil, spring onions, sugar, bay leaf, thyme and salt and pepper in a saucepan. Bring to the boil, then add the carrots and cook for 5 minutes. Leave to cool overnight with the carrots still in the liquid. Spread each cutlet with the herb butter and place them under a hot grill for 3–4 minutes on each side. Add the chopped walnuts to the carrots. Bring to the boil, simmer for 3 minutes. Strain and serve with the cutlets.

Lamb Plait

Serves: 4 people
Preparation time:
30 minutes
Cooking time:
45 minutes
Oven temperature:
425°F/220°C Mark 7
then 350°F/180°C
Mark 4

A very impressive
way of making a
little lamb into
good-sized servings.
Serve hot with peas,
tomatoes, and new
potatoes or cold with
a salad.

12 oz/350 g boned
  shoulder of lamb
2 onions
1 oz/25 g fresh
  breadcrumbs
1 level tablespoon
  tomato purée
1 tablespoon
  Worcestershire
  sauce
1 egg, beaten
salt and pepper
8 oz/225 g frozen
  puff pastry
milk for glazing

Mince or finely chop the lamb; chop the onions. Combine the lamb, onions, breadcrumbs, tomato purée, Worcestershire sauce, egg and salt and pepper to taste, and mix well together. Roll out the pastry on a lightly floured surface to a rectangle approximately 12 × 6 inches/30 × 15 cm. Place on a baking tray and pile the lamb mixture down the centre. Cut diagonal strips of pastry from near the filling to the edge, down either side of the filling. Damp the edges of the pastry with water. Fold over the pastry at the top. Place the strips over the filling, alternate sides overlapping (see picture). Brush the plait with a little milk and bake in a hot oven (425°F/220°C Mark 7) for 15 minutes, then reduce the oven temperature to moderate (350°F/180°C Mark 4) for a further 30 minutes or until the meat is cooked.

Curried Shepherd's Pie

Serves: 4 people
Preparation time:
30 minutes
Cooking time:
About 1 hour 20
minutes
Oven temperature:
425°F/220°C Mark 7

A warming lunch or
supper. Serve with
a green salad for a
complete meal.

2 lb/1 kg potatoes
2 oz/50 g butter or
  margarine
little milk
2 tablespoons oil
2 onions, chopped
2 level tablespoons
  curry powder
1½ lb/¾ kg shoulder
  of lamb, minced
1 level tablespoon
  cornflour
¼ pint/1·5 dl stock
  or water and beef
  stock cube
salt and pepper

Peel the potatoes and cook them in boiling salted water until tender (about 20 minutes). Mash them well, removing all the lumps; beat in the butter or margarine and sufficient milk to give a soft consistency. Heat the oil in a large saucepan and fry the chopped onion for about 3 minutes. Stir in the curry powder and cook for a further 2 minutes. Add the minced lamb, stirring to brown it all over. Blend the cornflour to a paste with a little of the stock. Add the remainder of the stock to the pan and season. Cover the pan and simmer for 15 minutes. Stir in the blended cornflour and bring to the boil again. Turn the meat into an ovenproof dish. Cover with the mashed potato and smooth the surface with a fork. Bake in a hot oven (425°F/220°C Mark 7) for 25—35 minutes, or until the potato is well browned.

Braised Lamb Roll

Serves: 4 people
Preparation time:
30 minutes
Cooking time:
1½ hours
Oven temperature:
375°F/190°C Mark 5

Almost a complete
meal in a casserole.
Serve with a green
vegetable for a family
meal or when
entertaining.

2 lb/1 kg boned
  breast of lamb
4 rashers streaky
  bacon
1 cooking apple
1 level tablespoon
  brown sugar
¼ level teaspoon
  dried thyme
2 level tablespoons
  fresh breadcrumbs
1 lb/½ kg potatoes
2 sticks celery
1 onion
1 level teaspoon
  plain flour
salt and pepper
¼ pint/1·5 dl stock or
  water and beef
  stock cube

Put the lamb, boned side uppermost, on the work surface. Lay the bacon rashers on top. Peel, core and slice the cooking apple and spread over the bacon. Mix together the sugar, thyme and breadcrumbs and sprinkle them over the meat. Roll up the meat and secure it at 2—3 inch/5—7 cm intervals with string. Place the roll in a casserole. Thinly slice the potatoes and chop the celery and onion. Place the vegetables round the meat in the casserole, sprinkle with the flour and salt and pepper and pour in the stock. Cover the casserole and bake in a moderately hot oven (375°F/190°C Mark 5) for 45 minutes. Remove the lid and cook for a further 45 minutes. Serve the meat and vegetables together.

Lamb and Kidney Pudding

Serves: 6 people
Preparation time:
30 minutes
Cooking time:
3 hours

A filling meal for the hungriest diner.

Filling:
2 oz/50 g plain flour
salt and pepper
1 lb/½ kg boned
  shoulder of lamb
8 oz/225 g lambs'
  kidneys, cored and
  skinned
1 oz/25 g margarine
1 onion, chopped
4 oz/100 g
  mushrooms, sliced
3 tablespoons stock
  or water
Pastry:
8 oz/225 g plain
  flour
2 level teaspoons
  baking powder
½ level teaspoon salt
4 oz/100 g shredded
  suet
about ¼ pint/1·25 dl
  cold water to mix

Make the filling: Season the flour well with salt and pepper. Cut the lamb into 1 inch/25 mm cubes and the prepared kidneys into ½ inch/1cm pieces. Coat the meat with the seasoned flour. Heat the margarine in a large saucepan, add the onion and fry gently for 3 minutes or until soft. Stir in the floured meat and fry the pieces until browned all over. Add the mushrooms and stock. Leave to cool.

Make the pastry: Sift the flour, baking powder and salt into a bowl. Add the suet, then enough water to make a soft dough, stirring with a round-bladed knife. Turn onto a lightly floured surface and knead gently to a smooth dough. Line a 1½ pint/9dl basin reserving enough dough to make a lid. Pile the filling into the lined basin. Make a pastry lid. Damp the edges and fit on the lid. Press the edges together to seal them and trim away excess pastry. Cover the basin with a double layer of well-greased greaseproof paper or foil, with a pleat to allow the pudding to rise, tie securely with string Steam for 3 hours. Serve hot.

Lamb Spare Ribs in Barbecue Sauce

Serves: 4 people
Preparation time:
30 minutes
Cooking time:
About 1 hour

These spare ribs are best eaten with your fingers so you will need finger bowls. Ideal with rice, green vegetables or a green salad.

3 lb/1½ kg breast of
  lamb
1 onion, chopped
1 clove garlic,
  crushed
3 level tablespoons
  tomato ketchup
2 tablespoons
  vinegar
1 tablespoon
  Worcestershire
  sauce
1 level tablespoon
  chutney
1 level tablespoon
  brown sugar
1½ level teaspoons
  salt
1½ level teaspoons
  pepper
¼ pint/1·5 dl water
chopped parsley for
  garnish

Cut the lamb into individual chops or ask your butcher to do this for you. Trim off excess fat. Place a large heavy-based saucepan on the cooker over a low heat. When it is hot, add the ribs and fry them slowly on all sides until browned all over. Remove the meat. Add the onion and garlic to the lamb fat in the saucepan. Fry them for about 3 minutes until soft. Stir in the tomato ketchup, vinegar, Worcestershire sauce, chutney, brown sugar, salt, pepper and water. Return the ribs to the saucepan, cover and simmer for 45 minutes to 1 hour or until the meat is tender. Add more water if necessary. Skim off any fat. Serve garnished with chopped parsley.

Lamb with Apricot and Prune Stuffing

Serves: 8 people
Preparation time:
30 minutes
Cooking time:
25 minutes per lb/
½ kg plus 25 minutes
over
Oven temperature:
350°F/180°C Mark 4

A spectacular dish.
Use boned breast of
lamb for an
economical meal. If
you are using dried
prunes, soak them in
water overnight.

8 oz/225 g prunes
1 (1 lb 13 oz/823 g)
  can apricot halves
1 oz/25 g margarine
  or butter
1 onion, chopped
1 level teaspoon
  chopped dried
  thyme
1 level teaspoon
  chopped dried
  sage
1 level tablespoon
  chopped parsley
6 oz/175 g fresh
  breadcrumbs
1 egg, beaten
salt and pepper
3 lb/1½ kg boned
  shoulder of lamb
1 (10 oz/283 g) can
  butter beans

Chop the prunes. Reserve one-third of the apricot halves and roughly chop the rest. Heat the butter or margarine in a frying pan, add the onion and fry gently for 3–5 minutes or until soft but not browned. Place the cooked onion in a bowl with the prunes, apricots, herbs, breadcrumbs, egg and salt and pepper to taste. Mix together with a fork until well-combined. Reserve one-third of the mixture. Use the rest to stuff the boned shoulder of lamb. Tie string round the meat at intervals to secure it. Weigh the meat. Roast in a moderate oven (350°F/180°C Mark 4) for 25 minutes for each lb/½ kg plus 25 minutes over. Roll the reserved stuffing into small balls and place them round the meat for the last 20 minutes of cooking time. Before serving secure the stuffing balls and reserved apricot halves together with cocktail sticks (see picture) and arrange round the meat. Heat the butter beans and serve them with the lamb, sprinkled with more chopped parsley.

Casseroled Lamb

Serves: 6 people
Preparation time:
25 minutes
Cooking time:
1–1½ hours
Oven temperature:
325°F/170°C Mark 3

An inexpensive
family meal. Serve
with baked potatoes,
cooked in the oven
at the same time, and
a green vegetable.

2 oz/50 g plain flour
salt and pepper
2 lb/1 kg middle
  neck of lamb
2 tablespoons oil
2 onions, chopped
2 carrots, chopped
1 stick celery,
  chopped
1 cooking apple,
  cored and
  chopped
1 pint/6 dl stock or
  water and beef
  stock cube

Place the flour in a bowl and season it with salt and pepper. Cut the meat into 1 inch/25 mm cubes and coat them with the seasoned flour. Heat the oil in a large saucepan, add the meat and fry until browned all over. Stir in the chopped vegetables and apple and fry for a further 5 minutes. Add the stock and bring to the boil. Transfer to a casserole and cook in a moderately slow oven (325°F/170°C Mark 3) for 1–1½ hours or until tender.

Spicy Meat Loaf

Serves: 4 people
Preparation time:
25 minutes
Cooking time:
1 hour
Oven temperature:
350°F/180°C Mark 4

An especially
popular meal with
children. Also good
for a cold lunch or
supper.

8 oz/225 g streaky
bacon rashers
1 lb/½ kg boned
shoulder of lamb
salt and pepper
2 teaspoons tabasco
sauce
¼ level teaspoon
marjoram
1 level teaspoon dry
mustard
1 teaspoon honey
4 oz/100 g fresh
breadcrumbs
2 tomatoes for
garnish

Lightly grease a 1 lb/½ kg loaf tin. Remove the rinds from the bacon rashers and spread them with a round-bladed knife, then use them to line the loaf tin. Trim excess fat from the lamb, then mince it. Combine the minced lamb, salt and pepper to taste, tabasco sauce, marjoram, mustard, honey and breadcrumbs in a mixing bowl. Knead together well with your hands. Pack the mixture into the prepared loaf tin and press down well. Bake in a moderate oven (350°F/180°C Mark 4) for 1 hour or until cooked. Turn out of the tin, garnish with tomato slices and serve hot or cold.

Hungarian Lamb Casserole

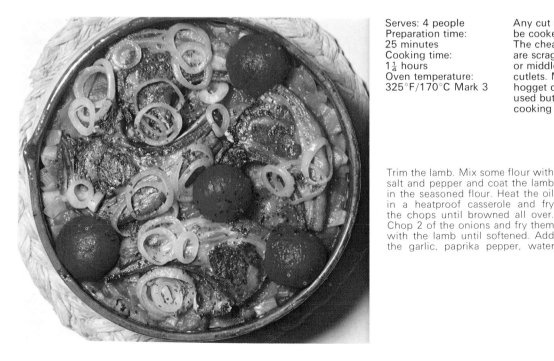

Serves: 4 people
Preparation time:
25 minutes
Cooking time:
1¼ hours
Oven temperature:
325°F/170°C Mark 3

Any cut of lamb can
be cooked this way.
The cheapest cuts
are scrag end of neck
or middle neck
cutlets. Mutton or
hogget could be
used but extend the
cooking time.

1½ lb/¾ kg stewing
lamb
plain flour
salt and pepper
1 tablespoon oil
3 onions
1 clove garlic,
crushed (optional)
1 level tablespoon
paprika pepper
½ pint/3 dl water
4 tomatoes, skinned
parsley for garnish

Trim the lamb. Mix some flour with salt and pepper and coat the lamb in the seasoned flour. Heat the oil in a heatproof casserole and fry the chops until browned all over. Chop 2 of the onions and fry them with the lamb until softened. Add the garlic, paprika pepper, water and tomatoes. Bring to the boil. Slice the remaining onion and scatter it over the meat. Cover the casserole and cook in a moderately slow oven (325°F/170°C Mark 3) for 1¼ hours or until meat is tender. Serve garnished with chopped parsley.

Lamb and Butterbean Casserole

Serves: 4–6 people
Preparation time:
25 minutes plus
soaking time for the
beans
Cooking time:
2 hours
Oven temperature:
325°F/170°C Mark 3

Choose an
inexpensive cut of
lamb, which is as
lean as possible.
Shoulder is ideal.
Serve with a fresh
green vegetable in
season. Soak dried
butterbeans in cold
water overnight.

2 lb/1 kg lamb
2 tablespoons oil
6 small onions,
   peeled
1 (14 oz/396 g)
   can tomatoes
1 beef stock cube
4 oz/100 g butter-
   beans or 1 large
   can butterbeans
salt and pepper

Cut the lamb into 1 inch/25 mm
cubes. Heat the oil in a heatproof
casserole and add the onions and
meat. Fry, stirring occasionally,
until they are well browned. Add
the tomatoes, crumble in the beef
stock cube. Bring to the boil, add
the butterbeans and salt and pepper
to taste. Cover the casserole and
cook in a moderately slow oven
(325°F/170°C Mark 3) for 2 hours
or until the lamb is tender.

Crown Roast of Lamb with Onion and Apple Stuffing

Serves: 6–12 people
Preparation time:
20–30 minutes
Cooking time:
20 minutes per lb/
$\frac{1}{2}$ kg plus 20 minutes
over
Oven temperature:
375°F/190°C Mark 5

This spectacular dish
is really roast lamb
'with-a-difference'.
Stuffing always
makes meat 'stretch'
to serve more
portions. Serve with
gravy.

2 racks (6 or 7 bones
   each) best end of
   neck lamb cutlets,
   chined
1 oz/25 g margarine
1 onion, chopped
2 dessert apples,
   peeled and diced
1 level teaspoon salt
$\frac{1}{4}$ level teaspoon
   pepper
1 level teaspoon
   dried sage
3 oz/75 g soft white
   breadcrumbs
1 egg
water to mix

Make the 2 racks of cutlets into a
'crown' or ask your butcher to do
this for you. (Order the 'crown' well
in advance and the butcher will be
more obliging.) If you are doing it
at home, cut and scrape the meat
away from the bones 1 inch/25 mm
from the top. Wrap the tops in foil
to prevent them becoming too
brown. Stitch the 2 racks of cutlets
together with thin string to make a
circle. Melt the margarine in a
saucepan and fry the onion and
apple until softened. Stir in the
remaining ingredients, adding
enough water to moisten the
stuffing. Put the crown of lamb
onto a baking tray and pile the
stuffing into the centre. Weigh the
meat and stuffing. Roast in a
moderately hot oven (375°F/190°C
Mark 5) for 20 minutes per lb/$\frac{1}{2}$ kg
plus 20 minutes over. Remove the
foil and replace with cutlet frills if
liked.

Lamb Curry with Prunes

Serves: 4–6 people
Preparation time:
30 minutes plus
soaking time for the
prunes
Cooking time:
1½ hours

The flavour of this
curry mellows when
stored overnight.
Serve with boiled
rice. For special
occasions, use dried
apricots instead of
prunes.

6 oz/150 g prunes
1½ lb/¾ kg boned
shoulder of lamb
1 oz/25 g margarine
2 onions, chopped
1 clove garlic,
crushed
1 level tablespoon
curry powder or to
taste
1 level teaspoon
ground ginger
salt and pepper

Put the prunes in a bowl and cover with ¾ pint/4.5 dl boiling water. Leave to soak for 2 hours. Cut the meat into 1 inch/25 mm cubes. Heat the margarine in a heavy-based saucepan, add the onion and garlic and fry gently until tender, stirring frequently. Stir in the lamb and fry until browned all over. Stir in the curry powder and ginger and fry gently for 3 minutes, stirring continuously. Stir in the prunes, the soaking water and salt and pepper to taste. Bring to the boil, cover the pan and simmer gently for 1½ hours or until the meat is tender, stirring occasionally. Leave to cool, then place in the refrigerator or cool place overnight. Next day, reheat thoroughly before serving.

September Lamb

Serves: 4 people
Preparation time:
25 minutes
Cooking time:
About 1 hour
Oven temperature:
325°F/170°C Mark 3

A hearty casserole
for family meals or
when entertaining.
The cider gives an
interesting flavour.

1 oz/25 g margarine
or butter
1 onion, sliced
8 oz/225 g carrots,
sliced
1 medium-sized
turnip, diced
4 oz/100 g button
mushrooms,
halved
1 lb/½ kg boneless
lamb
1 oz/25 g plain flour
¼ pint/1·5 dl dry
cider
½ pint/3 dl chicken
stock or water and
chicken stock cube
¼ level teaspoon
dried marjoram
salt and pepper
2 tablespoons thin
cream or top-of-
the-milk
parsley for garnish

Melt the margarine in a heatproof casserole. Add the onion, carrots and turnip and cook, stirring, for 2–3 minutes. Add the mushrooms and the lamb, cut into 1 inch/25 mm cubes, and cook for a further 1 minute. Sprinkle in the flour and cook, stirring, for 2–3 minutes. Add the cider and stock and bring to the boil, stirring constantly. Add the marjoram and seasoning to taste. Cover the casserole and cook in a moderately slow oven (325°F/ 170°C Mark 3) for about 1 hour or until the lamb and vegetables are tender. Stir in the cream just before serving. Garnish with chopped parsley.

Spanish Lamb Chops

Serves: 4 people
Preparation time:
25 minutes
Cooking time:
45 minutes
Oven temperature:
350°F/180°C Mark 4

Use lamb chops or lamb shoulder, cut into cubes. If fresh tomatoes are too expensive, use 1 (14 oz/396 g) can of tomatoes.

4 lamb chops
1 tablespoon olive oil
2 onions, sliced
1 clove garlic, crushed
1 lb/½ kg tomatoes, skinned
1 level tablespoon tomato purée
1 level teaspoon ground cinnamon
¼ pint/1·5 dl chicken stock or water and chicken stock cube
1 bay leaf
salt and pepper

Trim excess fat from the chops. Heat the oil in a heatproof casserole and fry the chops until brown, remove and drain. Fry the onion and garlic until softened. Chop the tomatoes and add to the pan with the tomato purée, cinnamon, stock, bay leaf and salt and pepper. Bring to the boil. Return the chops to the casserole. Cover and cook in a moderate oven (350°F/180°C Mark 4) for 45 minutes or until the chops are just tender.

Breast of Lamb with Sausage Stuffing

Serves: 4–6 people
Preparation time:
30 minutes
Cooking time:
25 minutes per lb/ ½ kg plus 25 minutes over
Oven temperature:
350°F/180°C Mark 4

One of the tastiest and most inexpensive roasting joints. It is also delicious served cold.

1 large breast of lamb
8 oz/225 g sausagemeat
2 level tablespoons dried sage and onion stuffing
½ level teaspoon mixed herbs
1 tablespoon chutney
salt and pepper

Bone, skin and remove any excess fat from the breast of lamb or ask your butcher to do this for you. Combine the sausagemeat, dried stuffing, herbs, chutney and salt and pepper to taste, in a bowl. Mix well together with a fork. Lay the meat, skin-side downwards, on a surface. Spread the sausagemeat mixture on the lamb. Roll up the meat and tie it in several places to prevent it unrolling. Weigh the joint. Place the stuffed breast of lamb in a roasting tin and roast in a moderate oven (350°F/180°C Mark 4) for 25 minutes per lb/½ kg plus 25 minutes over. Serve immediately.

Pork and Onion Pasties

Serves: 4 people
Preparation time:
30 minutes
Cooking time:
25–30 minutes
Oven temperature:
400°F/200°C Mark 6

A very tasty way of using up leftover pork. Serve hot, or cold for outdoor meals and picnics.

Pastry:
8 oz/200 g plain flour
pinch of salt
4 oz/100 g lard
milk for glazing
Filling:
8 oz/200 g cold cooked pork
1 oz/25 g margarine
1 onion, sliced
1 oz/25 g plain flour
½ pint/3 dl milk
salt and pepper

Make the pastry: Sift the flour and salt into a mixing bowl. Add the lard and rub it into the flour with your fingertips until the mixture resembles fine breadcrumbs. Add enough water to make a firm dough. Knead lightly on a floured surface and divide into 4 pieces. Roll each piece into a round about 5 inches/13 cm in diameter.
Make the filling: Cut the pork into small pieces. Melt the margarine in a saucepan, add the onion and fry gently until softened. Add the flour and cook, stirring, for a further 2–3 minutes. Blend in the milk and bring to the boil, stirring all the time. Simmer for 2 minutes. Add the pork and season to taste. Cool slightly. Divide the filling between the 4 pastry circles. Damp the edges, then fold the pastry to make 4 pasties. Press the edges together firmly, fluting them with your fingers. Stand the pasties on a lightly greased baking tray and brush with milk. Bake in a hot oven (400°F/200°C Mark 6) for 25–30 minutes or until golden. Serve hot or cold.

Honeyed Kebabs with Apple

Serves: 4 people
Preparation time:
25 minutes plus marinating time
Cooking time:
15–20 minutes

A more unusual way of serving pork as a main course, accompanied by rice and a green salad, or as a starter. Leave the pork pieces in the marinade for as long as possible to absorb the flavour.

2 tablespoons soy sauce
5 tablespoons honey
1 level teaspoon ground ginger
juice of ½ lemon
1 lb/½ kg boneless pork, cut into 1 inch/25 mm cubes
1 large green pepper, cut into squares
4 small onions, halved
2 apples, quartered and cored
8 medium-sized mushrooms

Combine the soy sauce, honey, ground ginger and lemon juice in a large bowl. Add the pork pieces to the marinade and leave to marinate for 3–4 hours or overnight. Thread the meat on 4 skewers, alternating with pieces of green pepper, onion, apple and the mushrooms. Place the kebabs under a hot grill, turning frequently until cooked through; baste with the remaining marinade.

Spiced Pork Balls

Serves: 6 people
Preparation time:
25 minutes
Cooking time:
30 minutes
Oven temperature:
350°F/180°C Mark 4

Use up leftover pork by making these delicious meatballs. Serve with noodles or rice.

10 oz/275 g cooked pork
1 small onion, grated
2 cloves garlic, crushed
½ level teaspoon ground cinnamon and ground nutmeg
¼ level teaspoon ground cloves
salt and pepper
2 oz/50 g bread-crumbs
1 egg
1 tablespoon oil
Sauce:
1 onion, thinly sliced
1 (8 oz/226 g) can tomatoes
¼ pint/1·5 dl water
salt and pepper
pinch of sugar
parsley for garnish

Mince the pork then put it into a mixing bowl with the onion, garlic, ground spices, salt and pepper, breadcrumbs and egg. Mix very thoroughly. Divide the mixture into 12 pieces and roll each piece into a ball. Heat the oil in a frying pan and fry the meatballs until browned all over. Remove the meatballs, drain and put into an ovenproof dish. Make the sauce: Add the sliced onion to the frying pan and fry until softened. Add the tomatoes, water, salt, pepper and sugar. Bring to the boil, stirring frequently. Pour the sauce over the meatballs. Cook in a moderate oven (350°F/180°C Mark 4) for 30 minutes. Serve hot, garnished with parsley.

Pork Epigrammes

Serves: 4 people
Preparation time:
30 minutes
Cooking time:
10 minutes

This is a particularly economical dish. The egg and breadcrumb coating helps a small quantity of inexpensive meat to serve a number of people. Serve with tomato sauce.

1 lb/½ kg belly pork
2 eggs, beaten
1 oz/25 g margarine, melted
3 oz/75 g fine white breadcrumbs
½ level teaspoon chopped dried rosemary
2 level teaspoons finely grated lemon rind
salt and pepper
oil for frying
watercress for garnish

Remove the skin and bones from the pork or ask your butcher to do this for you. Cut the pork into slices (across the grain of the meat) about 2 inches/5 cm long and ½ inch/12 mm thick. Beat the eggs with the melted margarine. Mix the breadcrumbs with the rosemary, lemon rind and salt and pepper. Dip the pork slices into the egg then into the breadcrumbs. Press the coating on firmly then recoat if necessary. Heat ½ inch/12 mm oil in a frying pan and fry the pork until crisp and golden. Drain on absorbent kitchen paper. Serve piping hot, garnished with watercress.

Roast Stuffed Pork

Serves: 6 people
Preparation time:
30 minutes
Cooking time:
30 minutes per lb/
½ kg plus 30
minutes over
Oven temperature:
450°F/230°C Mark 8
then 350°F/180°C
Mark 4

Almost any cut of
pork can be roasted.
The cheaper cuts
make a delicious and
inexpensive meal.
Serve with roast
potatoes and gravy.
Apple sauce could be
served instead of the
apples.

1 (3 lb/1½ kg)
   boned pork joint
1 oz/25 g margarine
1 onion, chopped
2 oz/50 g soft
   breadcrumbs
1 level teaspoon
   dried sage
salt and pepper
3 red dessert apples
1 tablespoon oil

Ask your butcher to bone the joint and to score the skin at regular ¼–½ inch/6–12 mm intervals to make crackling. Heat the margarine in a saucepan and fry the onion until softened but not browned. Stir in the breadcrumbs, sage and plenty of salt and pepper. Place the pork skin-side down and spread it with the stuffing. Reserve a little stuffing for garnish. Roll the meat up and tie securely in shape with string. Weigh the joint and calculate the cooking time, allowing 30 minutes for each lb/½ kg plus 30 minutes over. Cut the apples in half, remove the cores. Brush a little oil over each and top with some of the reserved stuffing, rolled into small balls. Rub the remaining oil into the skin of the pork and sprinkle with salt. Put the pork on a rack in a roasting pan and roast in a very hot oven (450°F/230°C Mark 8) for 30 minutes. Reduce the oven temperature to moderate (350°F/180°C Mark 4) for the remainder of the cooking time. Arrange the apples round the meat for the last 45 minutes of cooking.

Pork and Prunes with Spaghetti

Serves: 4 people
Preparation time:
30 minutes plus
soaking time for the
prunes
Cooking time:
30–35 minutes

This is a good dish
to serve when
entertaining. Use red
wine instead of
stock if the budget
will allow.

8 large prunes
½ pint/3 dl chicken
   stock or water and
   chicken stock cube
1 lb/½ kg boneless
   pork
2 level tablespoons
   flour
salt and pepper
3½ oz/90 g margarine
   or butter
8 oz/225 g
   spaghetti
salt and freshly
   ground black
   pepper
1 level tablespoon
   chopped chives
¼ pint/1·5 dl cream
1 tablespoon
   redcurrant jelly
lemon juice to taste

Soak the prunes in the stock overnight, then cook in the stock for 20 minutes. Trim the pork of excess fat and cut into thin slices. Mix the flour with some salt and pepper and coat the pork. Heat 2 oz/50g of the margarine or butter in a large frying pan and fry the pork until browned all over. Drain off excess fat and add ¼ pint/1·5 dl of the stock from the prunes. Cover the pan and simmer gently for 15 minutes or until the pork is tender. Meanwhile, put 4 pints/2 litres of salted water in a large saucepan. Bring to the boil, then add the spaghetti and cook for 10–15 minutes or until tender. Drain well in a colander. Return to the pan, toss with the remaining margarine or butter and chives. Put in a serving dish and keep hot. Blend 2 tablespoons of the liquid from the meat into the cream with the redcurrant jelly. Add to the meat, and cook gently, without boiling, stirring until the sauce is smooth and glossy. Taste and add lemon juice, salt and pepper. Add the prunes and pour over the spaghetti.

Pork Paprika

Serves: 4 people
Preparation time:
30 minutes
Cooking time:
1½ hours

This casserole is good enough to serve when entertaining. The soured cream makes a good contrast to the pork both in colour and flavour.

1½ lb/¾ kg lean boneless pork
1 oz/25 g lard
1 onion, chopped
1 oz/25 g plain flour
1 level tablespoon paprika pepper
½ pint/3 dl white stock or water and chicken stock cube
1 (2½ oz/71 g) can tomato purée
salt and pepper
6 oz/175 g small button mushrooms
1 (5 fl oz/142 ml) carton soured cream
extra paprika pepper for garnish

Cut the pork into 1½ inch/3 cm cubes. Melt half the lard in a saucepan or flameproof casserole dish. Add the pork and fry, stirring, until the meat starts to brown. Remove from the pan and drain on absorbent kitchen paper. Add the onion to the pan and fry for 2 minutes. Add the remaining amount of lard to the pan and stir in the flour and paprika pepper and cook for 2 minutes. Gradually stir in the stock and tomato purée. Return the pork to the pan, season well with salt and pepper. Cover the pan and simmer very gently for 1½ hours or until the pork is tender. Add the mushrooms to the pan 5 minutes before the cooking time is complete. Taste and adjust the seasoning, place in a serving dish if necessary. Pour the soured cream over the top, sprinkle with extra paprika pepper and serve immediately.

Crown of Pork with Orange Rice

Serves: 12 people
Preparation time:
30 minutes
Cooking time:
30 minutes per lb/½ kg plus 30 minutes over
Oven temperature:
350°F/180°C Mark 4

For a really special occasion, serve this crown of pork loin chops. Your butcher will probably prepare the crown if you ask him in good time.

2 (6 bone) pieces loin end of pork
salt and pepper
2 oz/50 g butter or margarine
8 oz/225 g celery, finely chopped
1 large onion, chopped
1 lb/450 g long grain rice
1¼ pints/7 dl chicken stock or water and chicken stock cube
½ pint/3 dl orange juice
4 oz/100 g raisins
1 level tablespoon grated orange rind
grapes and watercress for garnish

Ask your butcher to remove the chine bones then cut up 1 inch/25 mm between the chops. Scrape the meat away from the top 1 inch/25 mm of the bones. Form the loins into a circle, sewing them together with fine string and tieing a double piece of string around to keep it in shape. Wrap the ends of the bones in foil. Sprinkle the pork with salt and pepper and put in a roasting pan. Roast in a moderate oven (350°F/180°C Mark 4) for 30 minutes per lb/½ kg plus 30 minutes over.
Make the orange rice: Heat the butter in a saucepan, and stir in the celery, onion, rice and 2 level teaspoons salt. Add the stock and orange juice. Bring to the boil, stir, then cover the pan tightly. Simmer the rice gently for 15 minutes, or until it is tender and all the liquid absorbed. Stir in the raisins and orange rind. Put the cooked pork on a serving plate and spoon the orange rice into the centre. Remove the foil from the bones and garnish with grapes and watercress.

Cassoulet

Serves: 4 people
Preparation time:
20 minutes plus
soaking time for the
beans
Cooking time:
2½–3 hours
Oven temperature:
300°F/150°C Mark 2

A very inexpensive
meal. Use fresh pork
if pickled pork is
not available. The
sausage should be of
the spicy Continental
variety.

8 oz/225 g dried
   haricot beans
8 oz/225 g pickled
   pork
2 cloves garlic,
   crushed
2 tablespoons oil
1 onion, sliced
bouquet garni
1 level teaspoon salt
½ level teaspoon
   pepper
2 oz/50 g pork or
   garlic sausage
2 tomatoes, skinned
   and chopped
chopped parsley for
   garnish

Soak the haricot beans, in water to cover, overnight. Drain. Place the pork and garlic in a saucepan and cover with cold water. Bring to the boil and simmer for 5–7 minutes. Drain and slice the pork. Heat the oil in a flameproof casserole, add the onion and pork, and fry until golden brown. Stir in the soaked beans, bouquet garni, salt, pepper and boiling water to cover. Cover the casserole and cook in a slow oven (300°F/150°C Mark 2) for 1½–2 hours. Add the sliced sausage and tomatoes and cook for a further 1 hour. Remove the bouquet garni and serve sprinkled with chopped parsley.

Chopped Belly of Pork Pie

Serves: 4 people
Preparation time:
25 minutes
Cooking time:
25–30 minutes
Oven temperature:
425°F/220°C Mark 7

An economical and
nourishing pie which
can be served hot or
cold.

1 lb/½ kg belly pork,
   boned and skinned
2 level teaspoons
   dried basil
salt and pepper
1 egg, beaten
1 (13 oz/368 g)
   packet frozen puff
   pastry, thawed

Mince or finely chop the pork and put it into a mixing bowl with the basil, salt, pepper and half the beaten egg. Mix thoroughly. Roll out the pastry thinly on a lightly floured surface to an oblong about 10 inches/25 cm long. Form the pork into a 4 inch/10 cm wide roll and place it down the centre of the oblong. Brush the edges of the pastry with beaten egg. Fold the pastry over the filling and press the edges together firmly. Put the pie, join underneath, on a greased baking tray. Brush with beaten egg. Bake in a hot oven (425°F/220°C Mark 7) for 25–30 minutes or until cooked and golden.

Raised Pork and Orange Pie

Serves: 6 people
Preparation time.
30 minutes
Cooking time:
1¼–1½ hours
Oven temperature:
375°F/190°C Mark 5

A delicious variation
on a traditional
British pie. Ideal
picnic fare.

Pastry:
10 oz/275 g plain
  flour
½ level teaspoon salt
6 tablespoons water
4 oz/110 g lard
milk for glazing
Filling:
1 onion, grated
1½ lb/600 g pork
  shoulder, chopped
rind and juice of 1
  orange
little water and half a
  chicken stock cube
1 level teaspoon
  gelatine

Make the pastry: Sift the flour and salt into a mixing bowl. Put the water and lard into a saucepan and heat until the lard has melted and the liquid is boiling. Pour the lard and water into the flour and stir well with a wooden spoon to make a soft dough. Allow the dough to cool slightly, then knead until smooth. Cut off a quarter of the dough and put it in a warm bowl; cover with a tea-towel. Press the remainder into a thick round, then mould it up around the outside of a large jam jar.

Make the filling. Mix the onion, pork and orange rind together thoroughly in a bowl. Pack the pork mixture into the prepared pastry case. Flatten out the remaining pastry to make a lid. Press the edges together firmly. Make a hole in the centre (large enough to pour stock through). Put the pie on a baking tray and brush with milk. Bake in a moderately hot oven (375°F/190°C Mark 5) for 1¼–1½ hours or until the pastry is golden and the meat cooked. If the pastry becomes over-browned place a piece of foil over it. Allow to cool. Place the orange juice into a measuring jug and make up to ¼ pint/1.25 dl with chicken stock. Dissolve the gelatine in the stock and orange juice and pour it through the hole in the top of the pie when cold. Put aside until jellied.

Pork Rashers with Potato and Apples

Serves: 4 people
Preparation time:
25 minutes
Cooking time:
1 hour 10 minutes
Oven temperature:
400°F/200°C Mark 6

An inexpensive and
hearty meal. The
flavour of apples
goes very well with
pork.

1 lb/½ kg medium-
  sized potatoes
3 dessert apples,
  peeled and cored
2 onions
salt and pepper
¼ pint/1·5 dl chicken
  stock or water and
  chicken stock cube
melted butter
4 thick belly pork
  rashers
tomato wedges and
  parsley for garnish

Peel and slice the potatoes into ¼ inch/6 mm slices. Slice the apples and onions. Layer the potatoes, apples and onions in a well greased casserole. Season each layer well with salt and pepper. Finish with a layer of potatoes. Pour over the stock and brush the top with melted butter. Bake in a hot oven (400°F/200°C Mark 6) for 30 minutes. Place the pork rashers on the casserole and continue for a further 40 minutes or until the meat is cooked and browned. Garnish with tomato wedges and parsley.

Stuffed Streaky Bacon Joint

Serves: 6–8 people
Preparation time:
25–30 minutes plus
1 hour soaking time
and chilling time
Cooking time:
2 hours 15 minutes
Oven temperature:
350°F/180°C Mark 4

An inexpensive
bacon joint which is
even better value
when stuffed. Serve
cold with salad,
boiled potatoes and
hard-boiled eggs.

3 lb/1½ kg streaky
    bacon joint, boned
4 oz/100 g fresh
    white bread-
    crumbs
2 level tablespoons
    chopped parsley
1 level teaspoon
    mixed dried herbs
salt and pepper
1 oz/25 g butter or
    margarine, melted
1 oz/25 g walnuts,
    chopped
1 egg, beaten
2 level teaspoons
    soft brown sugar
2 level teaspoons
    plain flour
walnut halves and
    parsley for garnish

Put the bacon in a large bowl, cover with cold water and leave for about 1 hour. Cut the joint in half and remove any gristle. Mix the breadcrumbs, parsley, herbs, salt and pepper, melted butter and walnuts together in a bowl. Add enough egg to bind the mixture. Spread the stuffing over the rib side of one half of the bacon. Cover with the other half of the joint and press together firmly. Tie securely then wrap in foil. Put into a roasting pan and cook in a moderate oven (350°F/180°C Mark 4) for 2 hours. Remove the foil and the top rind from the bacon. Score the fat in a criss-cross pattern. Mix the brown sugar with the flour and sprinkle over the fat. Return the bacon to the oven and cook for a further 10–15 minutes or until browned and crisp. Remove from the oven, cut off the bottom rind and place a heavy weight on the bacon. Leave until cold. Remove the rind from the underside of the joint. Serve sliced, garnished with walnut halves and sprigs of parsley.

Bacon and Egg Pie

Serves: 2 people
Preparation time:
25 minutes
Cooking time:
50 minutes
Oven temperature:
400°F/200°C Mark 6
then 350°F/180°C
Mark 4

An easy and
inexpensive pie
which is delicious
served hot or cold.

4 oz/100 g plain
    flour
pinch of salt
1 oz/25 g lard
1 oz/25 g margarine
3 oz/75 g streaky
    bacon, chopped
2 eggs
1 small can
    evaporated milk
salt and pepper
1 tomato and sprig
    of parsley for
    garnish

Sift the flour into a mixing bowl. Add the lard and margarine. Cut into pieces and rub into the flour with your fingertips until the mixture resembles fine breadcrumbs. Using a round-bladed knife, mix in enough cold water to make a soft dough. Roll out the pastry on a lightly floured surface and line a 7 inch/18 cm flan ring standing on a baking tray. Place a piece of greaseproof paper in the flan and fill with baking beans. Bake in a hot oven (400°F/200°C Mark 6) for 20 minutes. Meanwhile, fry the bacon in its own fat until softened. Beat the eggs with the evaporated milk and salt and pepper. Remove the paper and beans. Arrange the bacon over the base of the flan and pour in the egg mixture. Bake in a moderate oven (350°F/180°C Mark 4) for about 30 minutes or until firm and browned. Serve garnished with tomato slices and parsley.

Bacon and Cabbage Casserole

Serves: 4–6 people
Preparation time:
25 minutes
Cooking time:
30 minutes
Oven temperature:
350°F/180°C Mark 4

A very inexpensive casserole which can be served for lunch or supper. Use belly pork instead of bacon for a variation.

8 oz/225 g piece streaky bacon
2 oz/50 g dripping or lard
2 onions, sliced
8 oz/225 g tomatoes, skinned
½ medium-sized cabbage
salt and pepper

Cut the rind off the bacon in one piece. Put the rind to one side, dice the bacon. Heat the dripping in a saucepan and fry the bacon and onion until the onion is softened but not browned. Slice the tomatoes. Shred the cabbage and cook in a covered saucepan with a little boiling salted water and the bacon rind, until tender (about 10 minutes). Drain well and discard the rind. In a deep casserole put layers of cabbage, bacon and onion and tomatoes. Season the layers with pepper and finish with a layer of tomato. Cook in a moderate oven (350°F/180°C Mark 4) for 30 minutes.

Baked Ham and Pasta Mould

Serves: 4 people
Preparation time:
25 minutes
Cooking time:
20 minutes
Oven temperature:
400°F/200°C Mark 6

This mould makes a good lunch or supper dish. It can also be served as an appetiser at the start of a meal. Serve with tomato sauce and a green salad.

salt and freshly ground pepper
8 oz/225 g short cut macaroni or noodles
2 oz/50 g butter
1 small onion, chopped
8 oz/225 g lean ham, diced
2 oz/50 g cheese, grated
7 fl oz/2 dl soured cream
1 egg
parsley and green peas for garnish

Put 4 pints/2 litres salted water in a large saucepan and bring to the boil. Add the macaroni or noodles and cook for about 7–10 minutes or until just tender. Drain well in a colander. Melt the butter in a saucepan, fry the onion until softened but not browned. Put the ham in a bowl with the cheese, soured cream and egg. Mix well, then add to the pasta. Stir well, then season to taste. Line the base of a greased 2 pint/1 litre mould or cake tin with greased greaseproof paper. Put the pasta mixture into the mould and bake in a hot oven (400°F/200°C Mark 6) for about 20 minutes or until set. Cool slightly, then turn the mould onto a hot plate. Serve garnished with parsley and green peas.

207

Gouda Savoury Flan

Serves: 4 people
Preparation time:
25 minutes
Cooking time:
45 minutes
Oven temperature:
400°F/200°C Mark 6

A really delicious flan which is good for both family meals and entertaining. Peppers are cheapest in the summer.

Pastry:
6 oz/150 g flour
salt and pepper
1½ oz/40 g margarine
1½ oz/40 g lard
Filling:
3 tablespoons oil
2 green peppers, thinly sliced, or 1 small head celery, chopped
4 oz/100 g mushrooms, sliced
2 level teaspoons dried oregano
3 oz/75 g Gouda cheese, grated
6—8 rashers bacon

Make the pastry: Sift the flour and a pinch of salt into a mixing bowl, add the margarine and lard, cut into small pieces. Rub the fat into the flour until the mixture resembles fine breadcrumbs. Using a round-bladed knife, mix in enough cold water to make a soft dough. Roll out the pastry on a lightly floured surface and use to line an 8 inch/20 cm flan ring standing on a baking tray or an 8 inch/20 cm shallow round cake tin. Prick the base with a fork. Place a piece of greaseproof paper in the flan and fill it with baking beans. Bake the flan case in a hot oven (400°F/200°C Mark 6) for 20 minutes.
Meanwhile make the filling: Heat the oil in a saucepan and fry the peppers, or celery, and mushrooms until softened. Drain, then mix in the oregano, salt, pepper and cheese. Remove the flan ring, paper and beans from the cooked pastry. Put the vegetable and cheese mixture into the flan case. Remove the rinds and any bones from the bacon and roll up. Arrange the bacon rolls on the flan. Return to the oven and bake for 20—25 minutes or until the bacon is just beginning to crisp. Serve hot or cold.

Bacon Casserole

Serves: 6—8 people
Preparation time:
30 minutes
Cooking time:
20—25 minutes per lb/½ kg plus 20—25 minutes over
Oven temperature:
350°F/180°C Mark 4

Use an inexpensive bacon joint; collar or forehock are very good and economical as there is no waste. Mild cured bacon does not need soaking.

2—3 lb/1—1½ kg bacon joint, boned and tied in shape
2 bay leaves
1 large onion, sliced
4 small onions, peeled
3 carrots, sliced
3 small leeks
1½ oz/40 g margarine

Put the bacon in a large saucepan with cold water to cover. Bring to the boil then remove from the heat, drain and add fresh cold water to cover. Add the bay leaves. Bring the water to the boil again then reduce the heat and simmer the joint for half the cooking time. Prepare the vegetables; clean the leeks, cut each in half lengthwise. Heat the margarine in a large frying pan and fry the vegetables gently for 10 minutes. Put the vegetables in a large deep casserole.

Remove the half-cooked bacon from the pan, remove the rind and put the joint on top of the vegetables. Add ½ pint/3 dl of the bacon cooking liquid. Cover with a lid or piece of foil and cook in a moderate oven (350°F/180°C Mark 4) for the remaining half of the cooking time. Uncover the bacon for the last 15 minutes to allow the fat to brown. Serve the bacon surrounded by the vegetables with the cooking liquid separately.

Potato Coated Meat Loaf

Serves: 4 people
Preparation time:
30 minutes
Cooking time:
1 hour
Oven temperature:
350°F/180°C Mark 4

A meat loaf with a difference. Ideal to serve with a green salad for an easy and economical meal.

1 lb/½ kg minced steak
4 oz/100 g fresh breadcrumbs
¼ pint/1·5 dl cold milk
1 egg, beaten
salt and pepper
¼ level teaspoon cayenne pepper
¼ level teaspoon dry mustard
1 onion, finely chopped or grated
1 lb/½ kg potatoes
1 oz/25 g butter or margarine
hot milk to mix
2 level tablespoons chopped parsley

Put the minced steak in a mixing bowl with the breadcrumbs, cold milk, egg, 1 level teaspoon salt, cayenne pepper, mustard and onion. Mix all together very thoroughly. Put in a greased 1 lb/ ½ kg loaf tin and bake in a moderate oven (350°F/180°C Mark 4) for 45 minutes. Meanwhile, peel the potatoes and cook in boiling salted water until tender (about 15–20 minutes). Mash well with the butter and enough hot milk to make creamy mashed potatoes. Beat in salt, pepper and 1 tablespoon parsley. Turn the cooked meat loaf out of the tin and put it on a baking tray. Coat the loaf in mashed potatoes and return it to the oven for about 15 minutes or until beginning to brown. Serve garnished with chopped parsley.

Steak and Kidney Pie

Serves: 4–6 people
Preparation time:
25 minutes
Cooking time:
1 hour 45 minutes
Oven temperature:
425°F/220°C Mark 7
then 350°F/180°C
Mark 4

Pastry mixes are a very useful stand-by to have in your cupboard. If you have the time, however, make your own using 6 oz/150 g flour etc. This recipe freezes well; make it in a foil dish and freeze before cooking the pastry.

1 oz/25 g margarine
1 onion, chopped
1½ lb/675 g braising steak
8 oz/225 g ox kidney
1 oz/25 g plain flour
½ pint/3 dl beef stock or water and beef stock cube
2 level tablespoons tomato purée
1 level teaspoon salt
½ level teaspoon pepper
1 bay leaf
¼ level teaspoon mixed herbs
12 oz/350 g flaky pastry mix
little milk for glazing

Heat the margarine in a large saucepan and fry the onion gently for 5 minutes or until tender, but not browned. Cut the steak and kidney into 1 inch/25 mm cubes, then toss them in the flour. Add the meat and any remaining flour to the saucepan and fry gently, turning occasionally, until browned. Stir in the stock, tomato purée, seasoning and herbs, bring to the boil, cover and simmer for 1 hour. Pour into a 1½ pint/9 dl pie dish, remove the bay leaf and allow to cool. Make up the pastry according to the instructions on the side of the packet. Roll out the pastry on a lightly floured surface and put a top on the pie. Make a small hole in the pastry to allow steam to escape. Brush the surface with milk. Bake in a hot oven (425°F/220°C Mark 7) for 25 minutes, then reduce the oven temperature to moderate (350°F/ 180°C Mark 4)' for a further 15 minutes. Serve hot.

Steak and Kidney with Dumplings

Serves: 4–6 people
Preparation time:
30 minutes
Cooking time:
2 hours
Oven temperature:
325°F/170°C Mark 3

Ox kidney is a cheaper cut of meat than stewing steak so besides adding flavour it makes this casserole very economical.

12 oz/350 g chuck steak
8 oz/225 g ox kidney
1 oz/25 g plain flour
salt and pepper
2 tablespoons oil
1 onion, chopped
2 carrots, chopped
1 level teaspoon mixed dried herbs
¾ pint/4 dl beef stock or water and beef stock cube
chopped parsley for garnish
Dumplings:
8 oz/225 g self raising flour
½ level teaspoon salt
pinch of dried thyme
½ onion, grated
2 oz/50 g shredded suet
water to mix

Remove excess fat from the steak and cut it into 1 inch/25 mm cubes. Trim any sinews from the kidney, wash well and cut into ½ inch/12 mm pieces. Mix the flour with salt and pepper. Coat the beef and kidney in the seasoned flour. Heat the oil in a heatproof casserole and fry the meat, stirring, until browned. Add the vegetables and continue cooking until the onion is softened. Add the herbs and stock. Bring to the boil, stirring. Cover the casserole and cook in a moderately slow oven (325°F/170°C Mark 3) for 1½ hours.
Meanwhile, make the dumplings: Sift the flour and salt into a mixing bowl. Add the thyme, onion and suet. Stir in enough water to make a soft dough. Form the dough into 4 or 6 small balls. Place the dumplings in the stew. Cover and continue cooking for 30 minutes. Serve sprinkled with chopped parsley.

Chilli Beef with Vegetables

Serves: 4–6 people
Preparation time:
30 minutes
Cooking time:
2 hours
Oven temperature:
325°F/170°C Mark 3

This casserole is a complete meal in a dish. It will cook by itself in the oven while you are elsewhere.

1½ lb/¾ kg chuck steak
1 oz/25 g plain flour
salt and pepper
1 level teaspoon chilli powder or to taste
2 tablespoons oil
12 small onions, peeled
2 carrots, sliced
1 parsnip or 1 turnip, sliced
1 lb/½ kg potatoes, sliced
1 pint/6 dl beef stock or water and beef stock cubes

Remove excess fat from the meat and cut into 1 inch/25 mm cubes. Season the flour with salt and pepper and chilli powder. Coat the meat in the flour. Heat the oil in a saucepan and fry the meat until browned. Add the onions, carrots, parsnip or turnip, potatoes and stock. Bring to the boil, stirring occasionally. Pour the mixture into a casserole and cook in a moderately slow oven (325°F/170°C Mark 3) for 2 hours or until the meat and vegetables are tender.

Beef Turnovers

Serves: 4–6 people
Preparation time:
30 minutes
Cooking time:
20 minutes
Oven temperature:
400 F/200 C Mark 6

A very good recipe for using up leftover beef, but canned corned beef may be used instead, if liked. Serve with tomato sauce. These turnovers may be deep-fried in hot oil if preferred.

1 tablespoon oil
1 rasher streaky bacon, chopped
1 small onion, chopped
4 oz/100 g cold cooked beef or veal, minced or finely chopped
2 tomatoes, skinned and chopped
1 level teaspoon mixed dried herbs
salt and pepper
Pastry:
8 oz/200 g plain flour
pinch of salt
2 oz/50 g lard
2 oz/50 g margarine

Heat the oil in a saucepan, and fry the bacon and onion until softened and beginning to brown. Stir in the beef, tomatoes, herbs, salt and pepper. Cook, stirring, until hot and thoroughly mixed.
Make the pastry: Sift the flour and salt into a mixing bowl and rub in the lard and margarine with your fingertips until the mixture resembles fine breadcrumbs. Add enough cold water to make a firm dough. Roll out the pastry on a lightly floured surface and cut out twelve 4½ inch/11 cm diameter rounds. Divide the beef mixture between the rounds, damp the edges and fold over to make 12 small turnovers. Press the edges together firmly. Cook in a moderately hot oven (400°F/200°C Mark 6) for 20 minutes. Serve.

Beef Jarratt

Serves: 4 people
Preparation time:
25 minutes
Cooking time:
2½ hours
Oven temperature:
325°F/170°C Mark 3

A delicious casserole which is good for family meals or entertaining.

8 oz/225 g rashers streaky bacon
1½ lb/¾ kg chuck steak
1 large onion, sliced
3 carrots, sliced
3 sticks celery, sliced
2 level tablespoons plain flour
¾ pint/4·5 dl beef stock or water and beef stock cube
salt and pepper
2 tablespoons Worcestershire sauce

Cut the rinds off the bacon rashers, then stretch each one with the back of a knife until doubled in length. Cut each rasher in half. Cut the steak into fingers about 2 inches/5 cm long and 1 inch/25 mm wide. Wrap each finger of meat in a piece of bacon. Fry the beef and bacon gently in a frying pan for 5–6 minutes, turning once. Remove carefully and place in a casserole. Add the onion, carrots and celery to the frying pan and fry them in the remaining bacon fat for 5 minutes. Add extra fat if necessary. Stir in the flour, remove from the heat and blend in the stock. Bring to the boil, stirring. Add salt and pepper to taste and the Worcestershire sauce. Pour over the meat. Cover the casserole and cook in a moderately slow oven (325°F/170°C Mark 3) for about 2½ hours or until the meat is tender.

Surprise Baked Beefburgers

Serves: 4 people
Preparation time:
25 minutes
Cooking time:
25–30 minutes
Oven temperature:
350 F/180 C Mark 4

Make this recipe as
one large hamburger
if liked. Cook it for
45–50 minutes.

1 lb/½ kg minced
   steak
4 oz/100 g
   breadcrumbs
1 clove garlic,
   crushed (optional)
salt and pepper
1 (8 oz/226 g) can
   tomatoes
1 tablespoon oil
1 large onion, thinly
   sliced
1 red or green
   pepper, chopped
4 large baps or rolls

Put the minced steak into a bowl with the breadcrumbs, garlic, salt and pepper. Add the juice from the can of tomatoes. Divide the mixture into 8 pieces and shape them into thin rounds, about 2½ inches/6 cm in diameter. Heat the oil in a frying pan and fry the onion until softened. Add the tomatoes and pepper and cook gently for 2–3 minutes. Put a little of the vegetable mixture on 4 of the rounds and top with the remaining 4 rounds. Press the edges together firmly and make the beefburgers an even shape. Put the beefburgers on a lightly greased baking tray and cook in a moderate oven (350°F/180°C Mark 4) for 25–30 minutes or until cooked. Serve each beefburger in a bap or roll. Top with some of the remaining vegetable mixture.

Rouladen

Serves: 6 people
Preparation time:
30 minutes
Cooking time:
About 1¼ hours

Serve with red
cabbage and
dumplings or boiled
potatoes.

2 lb/1 kg topside
   or silverside beef
6 level teaspoons
   prepared mustard
1 small onion, finely
   chopped
6 rashers streaky
   bacon
6 gherkins
1 oz/25 g lard
¾ pint/4.5 dl beef
   stock or water and
   beef stock cube
4 sticks celery,
   chopped
1 carrot, chopped
1 leek, chopped
1 parsnip, chopped
1 level teaspoon salt
½ oz/15 g margarine
½ oz/15 g plain flour

Ask your butcher to cut the meat into 6 steaks. Hammer each steak with the end of a rolling pin or back of a wooden spoon to flatten it to about a ¼ inch/6 mm thickness. Spread each steak with 1 teaspoon of prepared mustard, sprinkle on some chopped onion and place a rasher of bacon down the centre of each one. Cut the gherkins in half, lengthways, and place the halves on top of the bacon. Roll up the steaks like a Swiss roll and tie each end with a piece of fine string. Heat the lard in a large saucepan, add the beef rolls and fry until browned all over. Drain. Pour off excess fat, then add the stock to the pan with the celery, carrot, leek, parsnip and salt, bring to the boil, add the beef rolls, cover and simmer for 1 hour. Remove the rolls. Strain the cooking liquor, press the vegetables through a sieve to make a purée. Return to the pan and boil rapidly until ¾ pint/4.5 dl of liquid is left. Heat the margarine in a saucepan, stir in the flour and cook for 2 minutes. Remove from the heat and stir in the stock and vegetable purée. Bring to the boil, stirring all the time, and boil for 2–3 minutes. Add the beef rolls to the sauce and slowly heat through. Serve hot.

Beef Olives with Onion Rice

Serves: 4 people
Preparation time:
30 minutes
Cooking time:
1½ hours
Oven temperature:
325°F/170°C Mark 3

Serve this onion rice with almost any meat or fish casserole. Beef olives are particularly good for a change, when you entertain.

1 lb/½ kg braising steak in one flat piece
1 packet sage and onion stuffing mix
1 oz/25 g lard or dripping
¾ pint/4 dl beef stock or water and beef stock cube
1 (1 pint/569 ml) packet French onion soup mix
8 oz/225 g long grain rice
1 level teaspoon dried mixed herbs
1 level tablespoon cornflour

Cut the steak into eight 3 inch/7 cm squares. Place between 2 pieces of polythene and beat well until ⅛–¼ inch/3–6 mm thick. Make the stuffing mix according to the directions on the packet. Spread some stuffing on each piece of steak. Roll up and secure with wooden cocktail sticks. Heat the lard or dripping in a heatproof casserole. Brown the beef olives all over. Pour off the excess fat and add the beef stock. Bring to the boil then put into a moderately slow oven (325°F/170°C Mark 3) for 1½ hours or until tender. Meanwhile place the onion soup, rice and herbs in a saucepan with 1 pint/5 5 dl water. Bring to the boil, stir once and cover the pan with a tight-fitting lid. Simmer gently for 15 minutes or until the rice is tender and the liquid absorbed. Put on a serving dish and keep hot. Place the cooked beef olives on the rice. Blend the cornflour with a little water then add to the beef stock. Bring to the boil, stirring continuously, cook for 2 minutes. Pour a little of the gravy over the beef olives and serve the rest separately.

Kofta Curry

Serves: 4 people
Preparation time:
30 minutes
Cooking time:
30 minutes

Although apples are not generally used in Indian cookery, they are particularly good in this recipe. Use more curry powder if you prefer a stronger flavour.

1 lb/½ kg lean minced beef
1 egg, beaten
1 level teaspoon salt
1 tablespoon oil
2 onions, chopped
1 cooking apple, peeled, cored and chopped
2 level tablespoons curry powder or to taste
1 oz/25 g plain flour
1 pint/6 dl beef stock or water and beef stock cube
2 tablespoons mango chutney
1 oz/25 g sultanas

Place the minced beef, egg, and salt in a mixing bowl and mix together well. Divide the mixture into 16–20 pieces, then shape into small balls. Heat the oil in a large frying pan and fry the meatballs until browned all over. Remove from the pan, then fry the onions and apple, stirring occasionally, for about 5 minutes or until softened. Stir in the curry powder and flour and cook gently for 1 minute. Remove from the heat and slowly blend in the stock. Add the chutney and sultanas and bring to the boil stirring continuously. Add the fried meatballs and simmer gently for 30 minutes. Serve on a bed of boiled rice.

Beef Stew with Celery

Serves: 4 people
Preparation time:
25 minutes
Cooking time:
2–2½ hours
Oven temperature:
325°F/170°C Mark 3

This is a good winter stew when celery is at its best. Use chuck, blade or other inexpensive stewing steak.

1 lb/½ kg stewing steak
1 oz/25 g flour
salt and pepper
1 oz/25 g margarine or beef dripping
8 small onions, peeled
1 carrot, sliced
1 small head celery chopped
½ pint/3 dl beef stock or water and beef stock cube
1 level tablespoon tomato paste
chopped parsley for garnish

Trim the steak and cut into 1 inch/ 25 mm cubes. Mix the flour with the salt and pepper and coat the cubes of meat. Melt the margarine or dripping in a heatproof casserole. Add the meat and fry until browned, stirring constantly. Add the onions, carrot and celery. Cover the pan and cook very gently until softened (about 10 minutes). Add the stock and tomato paste. Bring to the boil, stirring all the time. Cover the casserole and cook in a moderately slow oven (325°F/170°C Mark 3) for 2–2½ hours or until the meat is tender. Serve garnished with chopped parsley.

Polder Pie

Serves: 4–6 people
Preparation time:
30 minutes
Cooking time:
25–30 minutes
Oven temperature:
400°F/200°C Mark 6

Use best mince, i.e. with the minimum of fat. Health food addicts will like to use organically grown vegetables.

2 tablespoons oil
1 large onion, chopped
1 clove garlic, crushed
1 lb/½ kg minced beef
2 level teaspoons dried chopped basil
1 oz/25 g wholewheat plain flour
¼ pint/1.5 dl beef stock or water and beef stock cube
salt and pepper
1 aubergine (eggplant), sliced
8 oz/225 g tomatoes, skinned and sliced
1 lb/½ kg potatoes, cooked and mashed
3 oz/75 g Edam cheese, grated

Heat 1 tablespoon of the oil in a large frying pan and fry the onion and garlic for 3–5 minutes, until soft. Stir in the minced beef and fry for 10 minutes, stirring occasionally, until browned all over. Stir in the basil, flour, then stock, and cook gently, stirring until thickened slightly. Add salt and pepper to taste. Pour the mixture into an ovenproof dish. Heat the remaining oil in a frying pan, add the aubergine slices and fry until browned on both sides. Drain and arrange them in the dish with the tomato slices. Beat together the mashed potato and cheese, then pipe or spoon the mixture round the edge of the dish and bake in a hot oven (400°F/200°C Mark 6) for 25–30 minutes, until golden brown. Serve hot.

Oxtail Casserole

Serves: 4–6 people
Preparation time:
25 minutes plus
soaking time for
the beans
Cooking time:
3 hours
Oven temperature:
325°F/170°C Mark 3

Oxtail makes a
delicious casserole.
Make it the day
before if possible
as it improves with
being kept overnight.
Remove any fat
before reheating.

8 oz/225 g butter-
  beans
1 large oxtail
2 oz/50 g plain flour
salt and pepper
2 tablespoons oil or
  beef dripping
2 onions, chopped
2 rashers streaky
  bacon, chopped
2 carrots, sliced
1 level teaspoon
  mixed dried herbs
1 pint/6 dl water
1 small packet
  frozen peas

Soak the butterbeans overnight in cold water to cover. Ask your butcher to chop the oxtail in pieces. Season the flour with salt and pepper and coat the oxtail pieces. Heat the oil or dripping in a saucepan and fry the onion, bacon and carrot, stirring, until softened. Drain and put into an ovenproof casserole. Fry the oxtail until browned all over. Drain and put into the casserole. Sprinkle with the herbs and add the water and butterbeans. Cover the casserole and put into a moderately slow oven (325°F/170°C Mark 3) for 2½ hours. Add the peas and continue cooking for a further 30 minutes. Serve.

Veal Goulash

Serves: 4 people
Preparation time:
30 minutes
Cooking time:
1½ hours
Oven temperature:
325°F/170°C Mark 3

Use stewing veal or
'pie' veal. Pork could
be used as a
substitute if veal is
unavailable or too
expensive.

1½ lb/¾ kg lean veal
1 level tablespoon
  paprika pepper
1 level teaspoon salt
pinch of pepper
2 level tablespoons
  cornflour
2 tablespoons oil
1 onion, chopped
1 (6 oz/170 g) can
  tomatoes
½ level teaspoon
  chilli powder
½ level teaspoon
  caraway seeds
1 level teaspoon
  mixed dried herbs
2 sticks celery,
  chopped
½ pint/3 dl chicken
  stock or water and
  chicken stock cube

Trim the veal and cut into 1 inch/ 25 mm cubes. Mix the paprika pepper with the salt, pepper and cornflour and coat the veal. Heat the oil in a heatproof casserole and fry the meat and onion together until the onion is softened and the veal lightly browned. Add all the remaining ingredients. Bring to the boil, stirring, then put into a moderately slow oven (325°F/ 170°C Mark 3) for 1½ hours.

Stuffed Cold Chicken

Serves: 6–8 people
Preparation time:
30 minutes
Cooking time:
1 hour

Not only does the stuffing make the chicken go further but a boned chicken can be sliced very economically.

1 (3¾ lb/1¾ kg)
  chicken
3 oz/75 g margarine
4 oz/100 g streaky
  bacon, chopped
4 oz/100 g chicken
  livers, chopped
1 onion, chopped
1 clove garlic,
  crushed
2 oz/50 g fresh
  breadcrumbs
grated rind of 1 lemon
salt and pepper
1 egg, beaten

Bone the chicken or ask your butcher to do this for you. Heat 1 oz/25 g of the margarine in a large frying pan. Add the bacon, livers, onion, and garlic and fry gently for 5 minutes, stirring continuously. Remove from the heat and stir in the breadcrumbs, lemon rind, salt and pepper to taste, and sufficient beaten egg to bind the mixture. Fill the boned chicken with the stuffing, then sew up the opening with a needle and strong thread. Grease a piece of foil with the remaining margarine and wrap it securely round the chicken. Place the chicken in a saucepan of water and simmer for 1 hour. Leave to cool in the water. Drain and leave in the refrigerator or cool place overnight. Serve in slices.

Devilled Chicken Casserole

Serves: 4–6 people
Preparation time:
25 minutes
Cooking time:
1–1¼ hours
Oven temperature:
325°F/170°C Mark 3

A spicy casserole which will quickly become a favourite. If you are slimming use liquid artificial sweetener to taste instead of sugar; the family certainly won't notice the difference.

1 (3 lb/1½ kg)
  chicken
1 tablespoon oil
1 small onion, finely
  chopped
1 clove garlic,
  crushed
1 stick celery,
  chopped
1 level tablespoon
  brown sugar
2 tablespoons
  Worcestershire
  sauce
2 tablespoons
  vinegar
1 level teaspoon
  French mustard
½ pint/3 dl tomato
  juice
¼ pint/1·5 dl chicken
  stock or water and
  chicken stock cube
salt and pepper

Cut the chicken into joints. Heat the oil in a frying pan and fry the chicken until browned all over. Drain well and put into an ovenproof casserole. Mix all the remaining ingredients together in a bowl and pour them over the chicken. Cover the casserole and cook in a moderately slow oven (325°F/170°C Mark 3) for 1–1¼ hours or until the chicken is tender.

Chicken Vol-au-Vent

Serves: 4 people
Preparation time:
25 minutes
Cooking time:
35 minutes
Oven temperature:
425°F/220°C Mark 7
then 350°F/180°C
Mark 4

1 (13 oz/368 g)
   packet frozen puff
   pastry
little milk
1½ oz/40 g margarine
1½ oz/40 g plain flour
¾ pint/4 dl white
   stock or water and
   chicken stock cube
1 level teaspoon salt

½ level teaspoon
   pepper
few drops lemon
   juice
8 oz/225 g cooked
   chicken, cut into
   ½ inch/12 mm
   cubes
2 oz/50 g button
   mushrooms
parsley sprigs for
   garnish

Roll out the prepared pastry on a lightly floured surface to a rectangle 8 × 16 inches/20 × 40 cm. From the rectangle of pastry cut two 8 inch/20 cm diameter circles. Place one on a baking tray and cut another circle, 5 inches/13 cm in diameter, from the centre of the second circle. Roll out the 5 inch/13 cm circle until it measures 6 inches/15 cm across. Brush a little milk on the pastry on the baking tray, taking care not to spill any over the edges. Lay the second piece of pastry, with the centre removed, on top of the first, again brush with milk and prick the base with a fork. Place the 6 inch/15 cm circle also on the baking tray and brush with milk.

Make lattice marks with a sharp knife on the pastry. Bake in a hot oven (425°F/220°C Mark 7) for 20 minutes. Remove the pastry lid and reduce the oven to moderate (350°F/180°C Mark 4) and bake for a further 5 minutes. Melt the margarine in a saucepan, stir in the flour and cook for 2–3 minutes, stirring continuously. Remove the pan from the heat and blend in the stock. Return to the heat, bring to the boil and cook for 2–3 minutes, stirring continuously. Stir in the remaining ingredients and reheat gently. Pile the chicken mixture into the hot vol-au-vent case, top with the pastry lid and garnish with parsley.

Chicken Maryland

Serves: 4 people
Preparation time:
30 minutes
Cooking time:
30 minutes

This is a traditional American way of serving chicken. The joints are deep-fried and served with sweetcorn fritters. Young people in particular like the combination of sweet and savoury flavours.

1 (2–2½ lb/1–1¼ kg)
   chicken
1 oz/25 g plain
   flour
salt and pepper
1 egg, beaten
soft white
   breadcrumbs
oil for deep-frying
2 bananas
2 oz/50 g margarine
2 oz/50 g self raising
   flour
1 egg
6 tablespoons water
8 oz/225 g
   sweetcorn (canned
   or frozen)

Cut the chicken into 4 serving portions. Mix the flour and salt and pepper together. Coat the chicken in the flour, then beaten egg and finally breadcrumbs. Press the coating on firmly. Heat the oil for deep-frying until hot (375°F/190°C or until a ½ inch/12 mm cube of bread will brown in less than a minute). Fry the chicken for 20–30 minutes or until cooked. The temperature may be reduced slightly if the coating becomes over-browned. Meanwhile, prepare the bananas by cutting them in half and frying in the margarine for 2–3 minutes.

Make the sweetcorn fritters: Sift the flour into a bowl with a pinch of salt. Make a 'well' in the centre and add the egg. Mix in with a wooden spoon then gradually add the water. Beat until smooth. Stir in the sweetcorn. Fry tablespoonfuls of the mixture in the margarine until browned, turning once. Drain the cooked bananas, fritters and chicken on absorbent kitchen paper and keep hot until needed.

Chicken with Apricots

Serves: 4–6 people
Preparation time:
25 minutes
Cooking time:
1 hour
Oven temperature:
375°F/190°C Mark 5

This is a most spectacular way of serving a roast chicken. It is an ideal recipe for entertaining.

1 (3 lb/1½ kg)
  chicken
1 (15½ oz/440 g) can
  apricot halves
1 oz/25 g walnuts,
  chopped
1 level teaspoon
  dried rosemary
2 oz/50 g fresh
  white breadcrumbs
1 lemon
salt and pepper
1 oz/25 g butter or
  margarine
1 oz/25 g plain flour
1 (13 oz/369 g) can
  asparagus spears
  for garnish
  (optional)
parsley for garnish

Prepare the chicken, make stock from the giblets. Drain the can of apricots and reserve the juice. Chop 4 of the apricot halves and put into a bowl with 1 tablespoon of the syrup, the chopped walnuts, rosemary, breadcrumbs, ½ teaspoon grated lemon rind, 2 teaspoons lemon juice, salt and pepper. Mix thoroughly then stuff the chicken and truss. Rub the outside of the chicken with the juice of ½ lemon and the butter or margarine. Season with salt and pepper. Roast the chicken in a moderately hot oven (375°F/190°C Mark 5) for 15 minutes per lb/½ kg plus 15 minutes over. Keep hot. Pour 1 tablespoon of the fat from the pan into a saucepan, add the flour and cook, stirring, for 2–3 minutes. Add 1 pint/5 dl of the giblet stock and a little apricot syrup. Bring to the boil, stirring, cook for 2–3 minutes. Serve the chicken garnished with apricot halves, asparagus (if used) and parsley. Serve the gravy separately.

Chicken and Ham Mould

Serves: 4 people
Preparation time:
30 minutes plus setting time
Cooking time:
None

Other leftover cooked cold meats can be used in this recipe. Ideal for special occasion picnics.

8 oz/225 g cooked
  chicken
4 oz/100 g ham
8 spring onions,
  chopped
1 level tablespoon
  chopped parsley
1 (1 pint/575 ml)
  packet aspic jelly
½ cucumber, thinly
  sliced
salt and pepper

Mince or finely chop the cooked chicken and ham, mix them together with the spring onions and parsley in a large bowl. Make up the aspic jelly as directed on the side of the packet. When cold and beginning to set, pour a little into the bottom of a 2 pint/1 litre container with an airtight lid. Swirl it round the sides to coat them. Dip slices of cucumber into the aspic and arrange them on the base and around the sides of the container. Mix the rest of the aspic and salt and pepper to taste into the chicken and ham mixture, and mix well together. When the cucumber has set in the mould, pile the aspic mixture into it and press down well. Place the lid on the container and leave it to set. Take the mould on the picnic in the airtight container. Unmould before serving.

218

Hawaiian Barbecued Chicken

Serves: 4 people
Preparation time:
30 minutes plus 2
hours marinating
time
Cooking time:
10–20 minutes

Although these
kebabs are most
suitable for
barbecuing, they can
also be cooked under
the grill. Onions and
tomato halves can
be used instead of
peppers if they are
very expensive.
Serve with a salad.

1 (3 lb/1½ kg)
  chicken
1 red pepper
1 green pepper
1 clove garlic,
  crushed
1 small onion, grated
2 level teaspoons
  brown sugar
1 level teaspoon
  curry powder
½ pint/3 dl tomato
  juice
½ level teaspoon
  each ground
  ginger, cayenne
  pepper and salt
1 tablespoon lemon
  juice

Cut all the meat from the chicken and cut into bite-sized pieces. Wash the peppers, remove all the seeds and membranes and cut into squares. Thread the chicken and peppers alternately onto 4 skewers. Place the kebabs in a shallow bowl. Mix all the remaining ingredients in a bowl and whisk thoroughly together. Pour the marinade over the kebabs and leave in a cool place for up to 2 hours, turning occasionally. Grill the kebabs for 10–20 minutes or until the chicken is cooked. Baste occasionally with the marinade.

Golden Harvest Casserole

Serves: 4–6 people
Preparation time:
30 minutes plus
marinating time
Cooking time:
1 hour 20 minutes
Oven temperature:
375°F/190°C Mark 5

If you are looking
for something to
serve for a special
occasion, try this
recipe. Make it
ahead of time and
leave it to cook.

1 (3–3½ lb/1½–1¾ kg)
  chicken
1 level tablespoon
  clear honey
1 tablespoon cider
  vinegar
1 tablespoon soy
  sauce
12 fl oz/3·5 dl dry
  cider
1½ oz/40 g margarine
  or butter
2 onions, sliced
1 green pepper,
  seeds removed,
  and sliced
2 level tablespoons
  plain flour
salt and pepper
1 (15½ oz/440 g)
  can peach halves
parsley for garnish

Divide the chicken into joints, wipe them with a damp cloth and put into a shallow dish. Mix together the honey, vinegar, soy sauce and 4 tablespoons of the cider. Pour the mixture over the chicken joints and put in a cool place overnight, or for 12 hours. Turn the chicken once or twice. Remove, drain and dry. Melt 1 oz/25 g of the margarine in a large frying pan and brown the chicken quickly, all over. Remove and drain. Fry the onion and pepper for 1–2 minutes. Remove and drain. Melt the remaining margarine in the frying pan, then stir in the flour. Cook, stirring, for 1–2 minutes. Measure the marinade and make up to ½ pint/3 dl with more dry cider. Blend the cider mixture into the frying pan. Bring to the boil, stirring constantly, and season to taste. Put the chicken, onion and pepper into a deep casserole. Pour over the cider sauce. Cover and cook in a moderately hot oven (375°F/190°C Mark 5) for 1 hour. Drain the peach halves, add them to the casserole and cook for a further 20 minutes. Garnish with chopped parsley.

Chicken and Mushrooms on Rice

Serves: 4–6 people
Preparation time:
25 minutes
Cooking time:
30 minutes

Chicken cooked this way is particularly good served with rice. Add white wine to the chicken, instead of stock, if the budget allows.

1 (2½ lb/1¼ kg) chicken
2 oz/50 g margarine or butter
1 large onion, sliced
salt and pepper
4 large tomatoes, skinned and chopped
1½ pints/8·5 dl chicken stock or water and chicken stock cubes
8 oz/225 g mushrooms, sliced
12 oz/350 g long grain rice

Cut the chicken into 4–6 portions. Heat the margarine or butter in a large saucepan and fry the chicken until browned all over. Remove the chicken from the pan. Add the onion and fry, stirring, until browned. Pour off any fat. Replace the chicken in the pan, sprinkle with salt and pepper and add the tomatoes and ¼ pint/1·5 dl chicken stock. Bring to the boil and cook, uncovered, for 15 minutes. Add the mushrooms to the pan, cover, and cook for a further 15 minutes. Meanwhile, put the rice in a saucepan with the remaining 1¼ pints/7 dl chicken stock. Bring to the boil, stir and cover the pan tightly. Simmer for 15 minutes or until the rice is tender and the liquid absorbed. Put the rice on a serving plate and arrange the chicken and vegetables on top.

Curried Chicken Flan

Serves: 4 people
Preparation time:
30 minutes
Cooking time:
45 minutes
Oven temperature:
400°F/200°C Mark 6
then 350°F/180°C
Mark 4

A delicious and creamy flan which is especially good on hot days. Pack in an airtight container for a picnic.

Pastry:
5 oz/140 g plain flour
¼ level teaspoon salt
1½ oz/40 g margarine
1 oz/30 g lard
cold water to mix
Filling:
1 onion, chopped
1 oz/25 g margarine
1 oz/25 g plain flour
2 level teaspoons curry powder
¼ pint/1·25 dl milk
¼ pint/1·25 dl chicken stock or water and a chicken stock cube
6 oz/150 g cooked chicken
2 oz/50 g peas
2 tablespoons plain yoghourt
salt and pepper

Make the shortcrust pastry (see Picnic fare recipe 3). Roll out the pastry on a lightly floured surface and line a 7 inch/18 cm flan ring, standing on a baking tray. Place a piece of greaseproof paper in the flan and fill with baking beans. Bake the flan case in a hot oven (400°F/200°C Mark 6) for about 25 minutes, reduce the oven temperature to moderate (350°F/180°C Mark 4) and remove the baking beans and flan ring for the last 10 minutes.

Make the filling: Fry the onion in the margarine until soft. Stir in the flour and curry powder and cook for 2–3 minutes, stirring constantly. Remove from the heat and slowly blend in the milk and chicken stock. Return to the heat and bring to the boil, stirring constantly. Boil, stirring until thickened. Cut the chicken into 1 inch/25 mm pieces and stir into the sauce with the peas and yoghourt. Add salt and pepper according to taste. Pour the filling into the cooked flan case. Leave to cool.

Farmhouse Chicken

Serves: 4 people
Preparation time:
25 minutes
Cooking time:
1¼ hours
Oven temperature:
350°F/180°C Mark 4

For a really delicious chicken, cook it this way. Put all the vegetables in the pot with the chicken to make a complete meal. Potatoes and other root vegetables can be used instead of or as well as carrots. The chicken can be fried in oil to brown it all over if liked.

1 (3 lb/1½ kg) chicken
8 oz/225 g sausagemeat
2 oz/50 g soft white breadcrumbs
salt and pepper
½ level teaspoon each dried parsley and thyme
chicken stock or water and chicken stock cubes
1 large onion, sliced
1 lb/½ kg carrots, sliced
parsley for garnish

Prepare the chicken and wipe inside with a clean damp cloth. Put the sausagemeat, breadcrumbs, salt and pepper and herbs into a bowl and mix together thoroughly. Stuff the chicken and truss. Put the chicken into a casserole. Add enough stock to come three-quarters of the way up the sides of the chicken. Put the casserole, uncovered, into a moderate oven (350°F/180°C Mark 4) for 45 minutes. Add the onion and carrot. cover the casserole and continue cooking for 30 minutes or until the carrot is tender. Serve garnished with parsley.

Paella

Serves: 6 people
Preparation time:
30 minutes
Cooking time:
45 minutes
Oven temperature:
375°F/190°C Mark 5

This Spanish dish is a complete meal in itself. Use a boiling fowl for economy and cook it before starting the recipe below.

1 (4 lb/2 kg) chicken
2 tablespoons oil
2 oz/50 g margarine
2 onions, chopped
2 cloves garlic, crushed
6 oz/175 g long grain rice
1 pint/6 dl chicken stock or water and chicken stock cube
½ level teaspoon turmeric
salt and pepper
4 oz/100 g green beans, cooked
3 tomatoes, skinned and chopped
4 oz/100 g prawns, mussels or other shellfish
few whole prawns for garnish

Cut the chicken into 6 portions. Heat the oil and margarine in a large frying pan, add the chicken and brown it all over. Remove from the pan, drain and put it into a casserole. Add the onions and garlic, fry for 3–4 minutes until tender. Add the rice and cook, stirring, for 1 minute. Add the stock, turmeric, and salt and pepper to taste, bring to the boil, then pour over the chicken. Cover the casserole. Cook in a moderately hot oven (375°F/190°C Mark 5) for 35 minutes. Stir in the beans, tomatoes and shellfish. Cook for a further 10 minutes. Serve piled on a hot dish. Garnish with a few whole prawns, if liked.

Turkey Loaf

Serves: 4 people
Preparation time:
25 minutes
Cooking time:
1 hour
Oven temperature:
350°F/180°C Mark 4

An ideal way to use up the turkey at Christmas. Chicken or other poultry can also be used instead of turkey.

2 eggs
10 oz/275 g cooked turkey, ham and stuffing (as available)
8 oz/225 g streaky bacon
1 oz/25 g margarine
1 oz/25 g plain flour
½ pint/2·5 dl milk
salt and pepper to taste
watercress and tomatoes for garnish

Cook the eggs in boiling water to cover for 10 minutes. Cool in cold water, crack the shells. Cut the turkey, ham and stuffing into small pieces. Remove the bacon rinds and any small bones. Using the back of a knife, stretch the rashers until they are doubled in length. Arrange the rashers over the base and sides of a 1 lb/½ kg capacity loaf tin. Reserve some rashers for the top. Melt the margarine in a saucepan, add the flour and cook gently, stirring, for 2–3 minutes. Blend in the milk. Bring to the boil, stirring constantly, then add the salt and pepper. Stir in the prepared turkey, etc. Put half the mixture into the tin, place the eggs on top, cover with remaining mixture. Press down firmly. Cover with the reserved bacon. Cover the tin with foil and place it in a larger tin with enough water to come halfway up the sides. Bake in a moderate oven (350°F/180°C Mark 4) for 1 hour. Leave the loaf in the tin to cool, then chill in the refrigerator. Turn the loaf out of the tin onto a serving plate and garnish with watercress and tomatoes.

Boned Duck with Orange Stuffing

Serves: 8–10 people
Preparation time:
30 minutes
Cooking time:
2 hours
Oven temperature:
375°F/190°C Mark 5

This is an ideal dish for a large number of people. Hot or cold, it will slice easily and give many more portions than an unboned duck.

1 (5 lb/2¼ kg) duck
salt and pepper
2 oz/50 g margarine
1 large onion, chopped
4 sticks celery, finely chopped
12 oz/350 g pork sausagemeat
¼ level teaspoon ground nutmeg
4 oz/100 g soft white breadcrumbs
1 orange
beaten egg to mix
watercress for garnish

Bone the duck or ask your butcher to do this for you. Season the inside with salt and pepper. Melt the margarine in a saucepan and fry the onion and celery until soft and golden. Stir in the sausagemeat, nutmeg, breadcrumbs, 1 teaspoon finely grated orange rind and enough egg to bind. Peel the orange and cut into quarters. Place one-third of the stuffing in the duck arrange the orange quarters evenly on top, then cover with the remaining stuffing. Make the duck into a neat parcel and sew the opening together with fine string. Place the duck on a rack in a roasting pan and cook in a moderately hot oven (375°F/190°C Mark 5) for 2 hours. Cover the duck with foil if it becomes too brown. Serve hot or cold, garnished with watercress.

Roast Duck with Celery Stuffing

Serves: 4 people
Preparation time:
30 minutes
Cooking time:
15 minutes per
lb/½ kg plus 15
minutes over
Oven temperature:
375°F/190°C Mark 5

Make this delicate and unusual stuffing when celery is readily available.

1 (4 lb/1¾ kg) duck
salt and pepper
4 oz/100 g streaky
    bacon, chopped
liver from the duck
2 onions, chopped
2 sticks celery,
    chopped
8 oz/225 g soft
    white breadcrumbs
¼ pint/1·5 dl milk
2 tablespoons
    chopped parsley
¼ teaspoon each
    dried sage and
    thyme
beaten egg to bind
extra celery, canned
    cherries and
    watercress for
    garnish

Prepare the duck, wipe the inside with a clean damp cloth. Sprinkle with salt and pepper. Fry the bacon in a saucepan, add the liver, then chop when cooked. Fry the onions and celery until soft, then stir in the breadcrumbs, milk, herbs, salt and pepper and enough beaten egg to bind. Pile the stuffing into the duck and truss. Roast the duck in a moderately hot oven (375°F/190°C Mark 5) for 15 minutes per lb/½ kg plus 15 minutes over. To prepare the garnish, cut some celery into 1 inch/25 mm lengths, cook in boiling salted water until tender. Heat the cherries in their own syrup. Place the duck on a large serving dish and arrange the garnish round it. Add watercress to complete the garnish.

German Rabbit Casserole

Serves: 4 people
Preparation time:
25 minutes
Cooking time:
1½ hours
Oven temperature:
325°F/170°C Mark 3

Rabbit makes a welcome change to routine family fare. This recipe is particularly delicious so serve it to visitors as well.

4 rabbit joints
2 tablespoons oil
1 oz/25 g plain flour
salt and pepper
½ pint/3 dl chicken
    stock or water and
    chicken stock cube
4 cloves
1 small onion
1 bay leaf
1 slice lemon about
    ¼ inch/6 mm thick
juice of ½ lemon
1 (5 fl oz/142 ml)
    carton soured
    cream
1 level tablespoon
    capers

Wipe the rabbit and dry well. Heat the oil in a saucepan and fry the rabbit until lightly browned all over. Remove, drain and put the rabbit in a casserole. Add the flour to the saucepan with salt and pepper. Cook very gently, stirring, for 3 minutes. Blend in the stock and bring to the boil, stirring constantly. Simmer for 2 minutes. Pour over the rabbit in the casserole. Stick the cloves in the peeled onion and add it to the casserole with the bay leaf, lemon slice and lemon juice. Cover and cook in a moderately slow oven (325°F/170°C Mark 3) for 1½ hours or until the rabbit is tender. Remove the onion, lemon slice and bay leaf. Pour a little of the liquid into a bowl, and stir in the soured cream and capers. Return to the casserole and mix lightly. Serve as soon as possible.

Gougère with Chicken Livers

Serves: 4 people
Preparation time:
25 minutes
Cooking time:
50 minutes
Oven temperature:
400 °F/200 °C Mark 6

Choux pastry:
2½ oz/65 g plain flour
¼ pint/1.25 dl water
2 oz/50 g margarine
2 eggs, beaten
2½ oz/65 g cheese,
  grated
salt and pepper

Filling:
1 oz/25 g margarine
4 oz/100 g chicken
  livers
1 onion, sliced
2 oz/50 g
  mushrooms, sliced
1 level tablespoon
  plain flour
¼ pint/1.25 dl stock
  or water and beef
  stock cube
1 tomato, skinned
  and chopped
1 level tablespoon
  breadcrumbs
chopped parsley

Grease an 8 inch/20 cm pie plate. Make the pastry: Sift the flour. Put the water and margarine into a pan, melt the margarine, then bring to the boil. Remove from the heat, beat in the flour until smooth, then cook for 1 minute. Cool for 5 minutes. Beat in the eggs gradually, then stir in 2 oz/50 g of the cheese and season. Spoon the mixture round the edge of the prepared plate.
Make the filling: Heat the margarine in a pan and fry the chicken livers,

drain. Fry the onion until softened, add the mushrooms and fry for 2 minutes. Stir in the flour, then blend in the stock. Cook, stirring, for 2–3 minutes. Stir in the livers and tomato, then cool. Pile the filling into the pastry. Mix together the remaining cheese and breadcrumbs and sprinkle on the filling. Bake in a hot oven (400 °F/200 °C Mark 6) for 30–40 minutes or until golden brown. Sprinkle with parsley.

Kidney Stew with Onions

Serves: 4 people
Preparation time:
30 minutes
Cooking time:
1 hour

An economical and delicious stew for family meals. Wash the kidneys well in salted water before using as they can be very strong in flavour.

1 lb/500 g pigs'
  kidneys
2 level tablespoons
  plain flour
salt and pepper
2 tablespoons oil
4 rashers streaky
  bacon, chopped
4 onions, sliced
½ pint/3 dl brown
  stock or water and
  beef stock cube
pinch of ground
  ginger
8 oz/225 g small
  pasta (bows,
  shells, rings etc.)
chopped parsley and
  diced pepper
  (optional) for
  garnish

Wash the kidneys well, remove any skin and membranes. Snip out the cores with scissors. Slice them lengthwise. Season the flour with salt and pepper and coat the kidney halves. Heat the oil in a saucepan and fry the bacon and onion until softened. Add the kidneys and any excess flour and continue cooking for 2–3 minutes, stirring well. Add the stock and ginger and bring to the boil, stirring all the time. Cover the pan and simmer gently for 1

hour. Meanwhile, cook the pasta in a large saucepan of boiling salted water for 15 minutes or until just tender. Drain well and keep hot. To serve, put the pasta round the edges of a heated serving dish and pile the kidney stew in the centre. Garnish with chopped parsley and diced pepper, if available.

Pissaladière

Serves: 6 people
Preparation time:
30 minutes plus
rising time
Cooking time:
25–30 minutes
Oven temperature:
425°F/220°C Mark 7

This is a French
version of an Italian
pizza. If you use
dried yeast, mix
¼ oz/7 g with half
the warm liquid and
1 teaspoon sugar.
Put aside until frothy.

8 oz/225 g plain
flour
pinch of salt
1 oz/25 g butter or
margarine
½ oz/15 g yeast
¼ pint/1.5 dl milk
and water, mixed
3 tablespoons olive
oil
1¼ lb/575 g onions,
thinly sliced
1 clove garlic,
crushed
3 large ripe tomatoes,
skinned and sliced
salt and pepper
1 small can anchovy
fillets
black olives
chopped parsley for
garnish

Sift the flour and salt into a mixing bowl and rub in the butter. Mix the yeast with a little of the milk and water and stir until dissolved. Beat the remaining liquid into the flour with the yeast mixture. Put the dough on a lightly floured surface and knead well. Put the dough inside an oiled polythene bag and leave in a warm place until it has doubled in size. Meanwhile, heat 3 tablespoons oil in a large frying pan and fry the onion gently for about 15 minutes, stirring occasionally, until pale gold. Add the garlic and tomato and cook, stirring, until thickened. Season to taste. Roll out the dough to a 9 inch/23 cm round or 8 inch/20 cm square and put it on a greased baking tray.

Spread the tomato mixture over the dough. Crisscross the top with anchovy fillets and place olives in the squares. Leave in a warm place for 20 minutes, then bake in a hot oven (425°F/220°C Mark 7) for 25–30 minutes. Serve hot or cold, garnished with chopped parsley.

Cheese and Onion Custard

Serves: 4–6 people
Preparation time:
25 minutes
Cooking time:
35 minutes
Oven temperature:
375°F/190°C Mark 5

An inexpensive and
tasty lunch or supper.
Serve with a salad
and crusty bread.

2 oz/50 g margarine
1½ lb/¾ kg onions,
sliced
¾ pint/4·5 dl milk
3 eggs
2 oz/50 g Cheddar
cheese, grated
salt and pepper
pinch of dry mustard
tomato slices and
parsley for garnish

Melt the margarine in a large saucepan and fry the onion very gently until softened (about 20 minutes), stirring occasionally. Put the onion into a 2 pint/1 litre capacity ovenproof dish. Put the milk into a bowl with the eggs, cheese, salt, pepper and mustard. Beat together until just mixed. Pour the egg custard over the onions. Put the dish in a roasting pan with enough hot water to come halfway up the sides. Cook in a moderately hot oven (375°F/190°C Mark 5) for 35 minutes or until the tip of a knife inserted in the middle comes out clean. Serve as soon as possible, garnished with tomato slices and a sprig of parsley.

Cottage Cheese and Smoked Haddock Soufflé Pudding

Serves: 4–6 people
Preparation time:
30 minutes
Cooking time:
25–30 minutes
Oven temperature:
425°F/220°C Mark 7

A lunch or supper
dish to impress.
Serve with a green
salad.

1 (7½ oz/215 g)
  packet frozen
  smoked haddock
  fillets
½ oz/15 g margarine
1 onion, chopped
2 level tablespoons
  chopped parsley
2 oz/50 g fresh
  white breadcrumbs
12 oz/350 g
  cottage cheese
½ pint/3 dl milk
2 eggs, separated
salt and freshly
  ground black
  pepper

Cook the smoked haddock according to the instructions on the side of the packet. Drain and flake. Heat the margarine in a saucepan and fry the onion gently for 3–4 minutes. Put the onion in a mixing bowl and mix with the parsley, breadcrumbs, cottage cheese and flaked smoked haddock. Beat the milk with the egg yolks and seasoning. Stir it into the cheese mixture. Put aside for 15 minutes. Whisk the egg whites until just stiff. Fold into the cheese mixture. Put into a greased 1½ pint/9 dl capacity ovenproof dish. Bake in a hot oven (425°F/220°C Mark 7) for 25–30 minutes, or until the pudding has risen and browned. Serve immediately.

Cottage Cheese Casserole

Serves: 4 people
Preparation time:
30 minutes
Cooking time:
45–50 minutes
Oven temperature:
350°F/180°C Mark 4

A very high-protein/
low-calorie lunch
or supper. Serve with
a salad for a complete
meal.

8 oz/225 g smoked
  haddock
¼ pint/1.5 dl milk
½ oz/15 g margarine
2 oz/50 g
  mushrooms, sliced
1 small green pepper
  (optional)
3 eggs
3 oz/75 g fresh
  breadcrumbs
12 oz/350 g cottage
  cheese
salt and pepper

Put the smoked haddock and milk into a saucepan. Bring the milk to the boil, then cover the pan and simmer gently for 15 minutes or until the fish is cooked. Drain the fish and reserve the milk. Flake the fish. Melt the margarine in a frying pan and fry the mushrooms for 2–3 minutes; put some aside for garnish. Cut a few slices of pepper for garnish, chop the rest. Beat the eggs together in a bowl, add the cooking milk and breadcrumbs. Put aside for 10 minutes, then stir in the fish, cottage cheese and salt and pepper to taste. Lightly oil a 2 pint/1 litre ovenproof dish and pour the mixture into it. Arrange the reserved mushrooms and green pepper slices on top. Place the dish in a roasting pan with enough warm water to come halfway up the sides. Bake in a moderate oven (350°F/180°C Mark 4) for 45–50 minutes or until set. Serve hot.

Dutch Vegetable Flan

Serves: 6 people
Preparation time:
25 minutes
Cooking time:
45 minutes
Oven temperature:
375°F/190°C Mark 5

Serve the flan hot with vegetables in season or a green salad, or cold on a picnic. This pastry is very good to eat.

Pastry:
6 oz/150 g plain flour
$\frac{1}{2}$ level teaspoon mustard
$\frac{1}{4}$ level teaspoon salt
few shakes pepper
3 oz/75 g butter
cold water to mix
Filling:
1 oz/25 g butter
1 onion, chopped
3 carrots, chopped
4 oz/100 g mushrooms, sliced
1 level teaspoon salt
$\frac{1}{2}$ level teaspoon pepper
2 eggs
$\frac{1}{4}$ pint/1.5 dl milk
4 oz/100 g grated cheese

Make the pastry: Sift the flour, mustard, salt and pepper into a mixing bowl, add the butter and rub in with your fingertips until the mixture resembles fine breadcrumbs. Stir in sufficient water with a round-bladed knife to make a firm dough. Knead it lightly with your hands. Roll out the pastry, on a lightly floured surface, and line an 8 inch/20 cm flan ring standing on a baking tray.
Make the filling: Heat the butter in a large frying pan, add the onion and carrots. Fry gently for 8 minutes. Stir in the mushrooms and fry for a further 2 minutes. Leave to cool. Add the salt and pepper. Beat the eggs in a bowl and beat in the milk, then the cheese. Spread the vegetables over the base of the flan and pour over the cheese mixture. Bake in a moderately hot oven (375°F/190°C Mark 5) for 35 minutes. Remove the flan from the oven and carefully lift off the flan ring. Cook for a further 10 minutes.

Vegetable Curry

Serves: 4 people
Preparation time:
30 minutes
Cooking time:
50 minutes

Serve with a selection of side salads, for example: sliced banana, melon cubes, tomato and onion salad. Poppadoms, cashew nuts and peanuts, and chutney are also good curry accompaniments.

1 tablespoon oil
2 large onions, coarsely chopped
2 cloves garlic, crushed
1 level teaspoon chilli powder or to taste
2–3 level tablespoons curry powder
4 carrots
1 small turnip
2 potatoes
8 oz/225 g green beans
1 (14 oz/396 g) can tomatoes
sea salt
1 cooking apple
2 oz/50 g sultanas
8 oz/225 g brown rice

Heat the oil in a large, heavy-based pan. Add the onion and garlic and fry gently for 5 minutes, stirring frequently. Stir in the chilli powder and curry powder and cook for 1 minute. Cut the carrots, turnip, potatoes and green beans into 1 inch/25 mm pieces. Add these vegetables to the pan and stir to coat them with the curry mixture. Add the can of tomatoes and salt to taste. Cover and simmer for 30 minutes, stirring occasionally. Peel, core and cut the apple into $\frac{1}{2}$ inch/1 cm cubes. Gently stir the apple cubes and sultanas into the curry, taking care not to break up the cooked vegetables. Cook, uncovered, for a further 10 minutes. Meanwhile, cook the brown rice in boiling salted water for about 50 minutes or until cooked. Arrange the rice round the edge of a serving dish and pour the curry into the middle.

Spiced Vegetable Casserole

Serves: 4–6 people
Preparation time:
30 minutes plus
soaking time for
the beans
Cooking time:
1 hour
Oven temperature:
350°F/180°C Mark 4

This inexpensive
casserole can be
served as a main
dish accompanied by
rice or as a vegetable
with grilled, fried or
roast meat.

4 oz/100 g kidney or
  haricot beans
1 oz/25 g margarine
1 level teaspoon
  ground ginger
½ level teaspoon
  ground cinnamon
1 oz/25 g plain flour
¾ pint/4 dl beef
  stock or water and
  beef stock cube
8 oz/225 g carrots,
  sliced
8 oz/225 g parsnips,
  cut in small pieces
8 oz/225 g swede,
  cut in small pieces
2 onions, sliced
4 tomatoes, skinned
  and chopped
1 clove garlic,
  crushed
1 bay leaf
salt and pepper

Soak the beans overnight in cold water. Melt the margarine in a heatproof casserole, stir in the ginger, cinnamon and flour. Cook, stirring, for 2–3 minutes. Blend in the stock, the drained beans, the prepared vegetables and bay leaf.

Season to taste. Bring to the boil, stirring frequently. Cover the casserole and cook in a moderate oven (350°F/180°C Mark 4) for 1 hour or until all the vegetables are tender. Remove the bay leaf and serve.

Vegetable Cheese Pie

Serves: 4 people
Preparation time:
30 minutes
Cooking time:
30 minutes

Makes an inexpensive
supper or
vegetable with a meat
course. An ideal
winter dish, when
root vegetables are
good value for
money. Serve with
mashed potato, piped
round the edge, for
special occasions.

2 lb/1 kg mixed
  root vegetables
  (carrots, parsnips,
  swede, turnip)
1 large onion
salt
2 oz/50 g margarine
2 oz/50 g plain flour
½ pint/3 dl milk
4 oz/100 g Cheddar
  cheese, grated
pinch of dry mustard
pepper
tomato for garnish
  (optional)

Peel all the vegetables and chop into 1–2 inch/3–5 cm cubes. Cut the onion into eighths. Put them in a large saucepan, cover with cold salted water. Bring to the boil and cook for about 20 minutes or until all the vegetables are tender. Drain, reserving the cooking liquid, and put into a heatproof serving dish. Meanwhile, melt the margarine in a saucepan, add the flour and cook, stirring, for 2–3 minutes. Put the milk into a measuring jug and make up to 1 pint/6 dl with some

of the cooking water from the vegetables. Add the liquid to the saucepan and bring to the boil, stirring constantly. Boil for 2–3 minutes. Remove the pan from the heat and stir in 3 oz/75 g of the cheese with the mustard and salt and pepper to taste. Pour the sauce over the hot vegetables and sprinkle with the remaining cheese. Arrange the tomato slices on top, if used, and cook under a hot grill until golden.

Desserts

Baked Orange and Ginger Cheesecake

Serves: 6–8 people
Preparation time:
30 minutes
Cooking time:
35 minutes
Oven temperature:
375°F/190°C Mark 5

Cottage cheese makes a very good and inexpensive cheesecake. Use artificial sweetener if you have slimming in mind.

Crumb crust:
8 oz/200 g ginger biscuits
4 oz/100 g butter
Filling:
8 oz/225 g cottage cheese
1 oz/25 g cornflour
3 eggs, separated
2 oz/50 g castor sugar
1 orange
icing sugar for decoration
1 (11 oz/311 g) can mandarin oranges for decoration

Put the biscuits in a polythene bag and crush them with a rolling pin until they become fine crumbs. Put the crumbs into a mixing bowl. Melt the butter and stir it into the biscuit crumbs until well mixed. Press the crumbs over the base and up the sides of an 8 inch/20 cm round cake tin.
Make the filling: Sieve the cottage cheese into a bowl and mix in the cornflour. Add the egg yolks, sugar, grated orange rind and orange juice, and beat well. Whisk the egg whites until stiff and fold in gently. Pour the filling into the case. Bake in a moderately hot oven (375°F/190°C Mark 5) for 35 minutes or until golden. Turn off the oven and allow the cheesecake to cool in the oven. Serve cold, liberally sprinkled with icing sugar and decorated with mandarin orange segments.

Meringue Puff

Serves: 6 people
Preparation time:
30 minutes
Cooking time:
1 hour 50 minutes
Oven temperature:
400°F/200°C Mark 6
then 350°F/180°C
Mark 4 then
275°F/140°C Mark 1

This can be served hot or cold. It is equally good served as a dessert as it is as a sticky pastry at tea-time.

8 oz/225 g flaky pastry mix
2 tablespoons apricot jam
4 oz/100 g margarine
8 oz/200 g castor sugar
juice of 2 lemons
4 eggs, separated

Prepare the flaky pastry mix according to the instructions on the side of the packet. Line an 8 inch/20 cm flan ring standing on a baking tray with the dough. Prick the base well with a fork. Line with a sheet of greaseproof paper and fill with baking beans. Bake in a hot oven (400°F/200°C Mark 6) for 20 minutes, remove the greaseproof paper and baking beans and bake for a further 10 minutes. Remove from the oven and spread the jam on the base of the pastry. Melt the margarine in a saucepan, stir in 4 oz/ 100 g sugar and lemon juice, leave to cool. Beat in the egg yolks. Pour the mixture into the flan case on top of the jam. Bake in a moderate oven (350°F/180°C Mark 4) for 20 minutes. Remove from the oven and cool again. Whisk the egg whites in a clean bowl until stiff and standing in peaks. Fold in the remaining sugar with a tablespoon. Spread the meringue over the filling and bake in a slow oven (275°F/140°C Mark 1) for 1 hour, until dry. Remove from the baking tray and cool on a wire rack.

Coffee Soufflé

Serves: 4 people
Preparation time:
30 minutes
Cooking time:
None

An impressive dessert when served in a soufflé dish. It can also be served in a bowl or individual bowls; the flavour will be just as good!

3 eggs, separated
3 oz/75 g castor sugar
2 level teaspoons instant coffee
½ oz/15 g gelatine
3 tablespoons hot water
¼ pint/1·5 dl evaporated milk or whipping cream
chocolate vermicelli or toasted coconut
whipped cream for decoration (optional)

Lightly grease a 5 inch/13 cm diameter soufflé dish. Make a double folded strip of greaseproof paper, grease it lightly and then secure it around the soufflé dish with an elastic band. It should stand about 2 inches/5 cm higher than the top of the dish all round. Put the egg yolks in a mixing bowl with the sugar. Place the bowl over a saucepan of hot water. Whisk the egg yolks and sugar together until light in colour and thick enough for the whisk to leave a trail. Dissolve the coffee and the gelatine in the hot water. Cool. Add to the egg and sugar mixture. Whip the evaporated milk or cream until thickened. Whisk the egg whites until stiff. Fold the cream into the coffee mixture then the egg whites. Carefully pour the mixture into the prepared soufflé dish and put in a cold place to set. Before serving, peel off the paper and press chocolate vermicelli or toasted coconut around the sides. Decorate with whipped cream if liked.

Creamy Chocolate Pie

Serves: 6–8 people
Preparation time:
25 minutes plus chilling time
Cooking time:
20 minutes
Oven temperature:
425°F/220°C Mark 7

Pastry:
8 oz/200 g plain flour
pinch of salt
2 oz/50 g margarine
2 oz/50 g lard

Filling:
8 oz/200 g castor sugar
pinch of salt
2 egg yolks
¼ pint/1·5 dl milk
4 level teaspoons gelatine
4 oz/100 g cooking chocolate
1 large (13 fl oz/ 368 ml) can evaporated milk, chilled
vanilla essence
1 egg white
¼ pint/1·5 dl whipping cream

Make the pastry: Sift the flour and salt into a mixing bowl. Add the margarine and lard and rub in with your fingertips until the mixture resembles fine breadcrumbs. Add sufficient cold water to make a firm dough. Knead lightly and roll out on a lightly floured surface. Line a 9 inch/23 cm pie plate. Prick the base with a fork, fill with grease-proof paper and baking beans and bake blind in a hot oven (425°F/ 220°C Mark 7) for 10 minutes. Remove the paper and beans and cook for a further 10 minutes or until golden.
Make the filling: Put 6 oz/150 g sugar in a heatproof bowl with the salt, egg yolks and milk. Sprinkle in the gelatine. Place the bowl over hot water and cook until the mixture coats the back of a spoon.

Melt half the chocolate in a bowl over hot water and add to the egg custard. Cool until syrupy. Whisk the evaporated milk until thick and fold into the egg custard with a few drops vanilla essence. Pour into the pastry case and chill until firm. Whisk the egg white until stiff, beat in the remaining castor sugar. Whip the cream until thick, fold in the egg white and spread over the pie. Grate the remaining chocolate on top.

French Fruit Tartlets

Makes: about 18 tartlets
Preparation time: 30 minutes plus resting time for the pastry
Cooking time: 20 minutes
Oven temperature: 400°F/200°C Mark 6

French flan pastry is tricky to make, but the flavour is extremely good so it is worth persevering. It is very crumbly in texture. Rich shortcrust pastry could be used as an alternative.

Pastry:
8 oz/200 g plain flour
4 oz/100 g butter
4 oz/100 g castor sugar
1 egg
1 egg yolk
Filling:
2 pears
juice of 1 lemon
6 black grapes
6 white grapes
3 oz/75 g apricot jam

Lightly grease 18 patty tins. Make the pastry: Sift the flour onto a cold surface, add the butter, sugar, egg and egg yolk. Work all the ingredients together to make a firm dough. Put the pastry into a polythene bag and leave to rest in a cool place for at least 30 minutes. Roll out the pastry on a lightly floured surface and use it to line 18 patty tins. Prick each one well with a fork. Bake in a hot oven (400°F/200°C Mark 6) for 20 minutes or until cooked and golden. Remove from the tins and cool on a wire rack.
Make the filling: Peel, core and thinly slice the pears, sprinkle with a little lemon juice to prevent them discolouring. Halve the grapes and remove the pips. Put the apricot jam and remaining lemon juice in a saucepan and heat gently, stirring until liquid. Arrange the pear slices and grape halves in the pastry cases and brush with the apricot glaze.

Orange Roll

Makes: one Swiss roll
Preparation time: 30 minutes plus cooling time
Cooking time: 7–10 minutes
Oven temperature: 400°F/200°C Mark 6

For rolling the cake, place a damp tea-towel on a work surface with a piece of sugared greaseproof paper on top. Turn the cooked cake out of the tin onto the paper so that it will stay moist and, if you work quickly, be easy to roll.

3 large eggs
3 oz/75 g castor sugar
3 oz/75 g self raising flour
1 sachet powdered dessert topping mix
¼ pint/1·5 dl milk
2 teaspoons orange squash
1 (11 oz/312 g) can mandarin oranges, drained

Grease a 12 × 9 inch/30 × 22 cm Swiss roll tin and line with greased greaseproof paper. Put the eggs and castor sugar into a bowl and place over a pan of hot water. Whisk until thick and creamy and the whisk leaves a trail. Remove the bowl from the heat. Sift in the flour and fold in with a tablespoon. Pour into the prepared tin. Bake in a hot oven (400°F/200°C Mark 6) for 7–10 minutes or until golden. Roll up while still hot, incorporating the sugared greaseproof paper in the roll. Leave to cool. Make up the powdered topping mix with the milk, add the orange squash. Unroll the now cold roll, remove the paper. Spread half the topping onto the cake. Chop half the mandarins and put them on the cake. Roll up again. Decorate as illustrated.

Apple and Apricot Dessert Cake

Makes one 7 inch/
18 cm cake
Preparation time:
25 minutes
Cooking time:
1–1¼ hours
Oven temperature:
350°F/180°C Mark 4

This can be served either with tea or as a dessert with a main meal.

3 oz/75 g margarine
3 oz/75 g castor
 sugar
1 level teaspoon
 lemon rind
1 egg, beaten
5 oz/125 g plain
 flour
½ level teaspoon
 baking powder
milk to mix
3 apples, skinned
 and thinly sliced
3 level tablespoons
 apricot jam, sieved

Grease a 7 inch/18 cm deep cake tin, with a loose base. Beat together the margarine and sugar with the lemon rind in a mixing bowl until light and fluffy. Gradually beat in the egg. Sift the flour and baking powder and fold them into the mixture. Fold in sufficient milk to form a soft dropping consistency. Spoon the mixture into the pre-pared tin and arrange the apple slices over the top. Bake in a moderate oven (350°F/180°C Mark 4) for 1–1¼ hours or until cooked. Turn the cake out of the tin onto a wire rack to cool. When cold, spread the top with the sieved apricot jam. Pack in an airtight container ready for the picnic.

Blackberry Gâteau

Serves: 6–8 people
Preparation time:
30 minutes
Cooking time:
35–40 minutes
Oven temperature:
350°F/180°C Mark 4

This light Genoese sponge helps to 'stretch' the fruit and cream to serve more people. Use other fruit if preferred. Blackberries are at their best and cheapest in the autumn.

4 eggs
4 oz/100 g
 castor sugar
3 oz/75 g margarine,
 melted
3 oz/75 g plain
 flour, sifted
¼ pint/1·5 dl
 whipped cream
12 oz/350 g
 blackberries

Grease and flour a 7 inch/18 cm deep round cake tin. Put the eggs into a mixing bowl with the sugar. Place the bowl over a saucepan of simmering water. Whisk the eggs and sugar together until thick, light and creamy. Remove the bowl from the heat and continue whisking until the mixture is cool. Fold in half the margarine, then half the sifted flour. When well mixed, fold in the remaining margarine and flour. Put the mixture into the prepared tin and bake in a moderate oven (350°F/180°C Mark 4) for 35–40 minutes or until well risen and firm. Turn the cake out of the tin and cool on a wire rack. When cold, spread a little of the cream over the top of the sponge and pipe the remainder round the edge in rosettes. Arrange the black-berries on the cream. Keep the gateau in the refrigerator until ready to serve.

Pineapple Gâteau

Serves: 6 people
Preparation time:
25 minutes
Cooking time:
10–15 minutes
Oven temperature:
450°F/230°C Mark 8

Serve this gateau as soon as possible after making it.

1 oz/25 g cornflour
½ pint/3 dl pineapple drink
½ oz/15 g margarine
1 egg, beaten
1 (7½ oz/213 g) packet frozen puff pastry
1 (8 oz/226 g) can pineapple slices, drained
¼ pint/1.5 dl whipping cream
icing sugar for sprinkling

Place the cornflour in a saucepan and slowly blend in the pineapple drink. Bring to the boil and cook, stirring continuously, until thickened. Remove from the heat and beat in the margarine and egg. Leave to cool. Roll out the pastry on a lightly floured surface to a 10 inch/25 cm square. Cut into 2 strips, each 10 × 5 inches/25 × 13 cm and place them on a damp baking tray. Bake in a hot oven (450°F/230°C Mark 8) for 10–15 minutes or until well risen and golden brown. Remove from the baking tray. Leave to cool on a wire rack. Spread the pineapple custard onto one slice and arrange the pineapple slices on top. Whip the cream until stiff and pipe or spoon it onto the pineapple. Top with the other slice of pastry. Sprinkle with sifted icing sugar.

Galaxy Fruit Tart

Serves: 4–6 people
Preparation time:
25 minutes plus cooling time
Cooking time:
35 minutes
Oven temperature:
400°F/200°C Mark 6

A custard tart with a difference. Use other fruit if liked.

4 oz/100 g plain flour
pinch of salt
1 oz/25 g lard
1 oz/25 g margarine
4 level tablespoons custard powder
1 egg, separated
¾ pint/4.5 dl milk
2 oz/50 g sugar
raspberry jam
1 (8 oz/226 g) can pineapple rings
cherries and angelica for decoration

Sift the flour and salt into a bowl. Add the lard and margarine and rub into the flour with your fingertips until the mixture resembles fine breadcrumbs. Add enough cold water to make a firm dough. Roll the pastry out on a lightly floured surface and use to line a 7 inch/18 cm flan ring standing on a baking tray. Line the pastry with grease-proof paper and fill with baking beans; bake in a hot oven (400°F/200°C Mark 6) for 15 minutes. Remove the paper and beans; cook for 15 minutes or until golden. Cool. Put the custard powder and egg yolk in a bowl and mix to a smooth cream with a little of the milk. Heat the remaining milk in a saucepan, pour onto the blended custard powder, stirring all the time. Return to the saucepan and bring to the boil, stirring constantly. Put aside until cold, stirring frequently. Beat well. Whisk the egg white until stiff and whisk in the sugar until smooth and stiff again. Fold into the cold custard. Spread a thin layer of raspberry jam onto the flan case. Pour the custard filling over the jam. Arrange the drained pineapple rings on top and decorate with cherries and angelica.

233

Meringue Nests

Serves: 4 people
Preparation time:
30 minutes
Cooking time:
About 2 hours
Oven temperature:
200°F/100°C Mark ¼
or the lowest
temperature setting

A very attractive
but economical
dessert. The filling
can be varied
according to your
taste and your
budget. Serve with
cream.

2 egg whites
4 oz/100 g castor
sugar
1 (15 oz/428 g) can
mixed fruit salad

Whisk the egg whites until stiff. Add half the sugar and continue whisking until the meringue is stiff again. Add the remaining sugar and fold in gently with a metal spoon. Place a sheet of greased grease-proof paper on a baking tray and mark 4 small circles on it, each about 3 inches/7 cm in diameter.

Pipe the meringue to make a flat base then build up the sides to make a 'nest'. Place the nests in the coolest part of a very slow oven (200°F/100°C Mark ¼) for about 2 hours or until dry but still white. Cool on a wire rack. Drain the fruit salad well and divide between the nests, just before serving.

Honey Cheese Tart

Serves: 6–8 people
Preparation time:
30 minutes
Cooking time:
1 hour
Oven temperature:
400°F/200°C Mark 6
then 325°F/170°C
Mark 3

A dessert made with
the best of health-
giving foods, natural
and unrefined. Make
the day before
needed if possible.
Raw sugar can be
bought in health food
shops.

Pastry:
6 oz/150 g
wholewheat plain
flour
pinch of salt
1 oz/25 g castor
sugar
2 oz/50 g margarine
2 oz/50 g lard
cold water to mix
Filling:
12 oz/350 g cottage
cheese
4 oz/100 g honey
2 level teaspoons
raw sugar
2 eggs
ground cinnamon for
decoration

Make the pastry: Put the flour, salt and sugar into a bowl. Add the margarine and lard and rub in with your fingertips until the mixture resembles fine breadcrumbs. Stir in sufficient cold water to make a firm dough. Roll out the pastry on a lightly floured surface to line an 8 inch/20 cm fluted flan ring standing on a baking tray. Line the flan case with greaseproof paper and fill with baking beans. Bake in a hot oven (400°F/200°C Mark 6) for 10 minutes, remove the baking beans and cook for a further 10 minutes. Leave the flan case to cool. Make the filling: Beat together the cottage cheese, honey, sugar and eggs. Pour the mixture into the flan case and bake in a moderate oven (325°F/170°C Mark 3) for 40 minutes, until the filling is set. Leave the tart to cool. Sprinkle liberally with ground cinnamon and serve.

Frangipane Flan

Serves: 4 people
Preparation time:
30 minutes
Cooking time:
30 minutes
Oven temperature:
350°F/180°C Mark 4

A cheaper substitute for ground almonds is sold in some health food shops.

Make the pastry: Sift the flour and salt together into a mixing bowl. Rub in the margarine and lard with your fingertips until the mixture resembles fine breadcrumbs. Stir in the sugar and mix to a firm dough with a little beaten egg. Roll out the pastry on a floured surface and line a 7 inch/18 cm flan ring standing on a baking tray.
Make the filling: Put the margarine, sugar and honey into a mixing bowl and cream them together until light and fluffy. Beat in the egg, then stir in the ground almonds and almond essence. Fold in the flour. Spread the lemon curd over the base of the pastry case and spoon the filling on top. Bake in a moderate oven (350°F/180°C Mark 4) for about 30 minutes or until firm and golden. Cool. Sift the icing sugar and add enough lemon juice to make a stiff icing. Ice the flan and decorate as illustrated.

Pastry:
4 oz/100 g plain flour
pinch of salt
1 oz/25 g margarine
1 oz/25 g lard
½ oz/15 g castor sugar
egg to bind
Filling:
2 oz/50 g margarine
1 oz/25 g castor sugar
1 tablespoon honey
1 egg
3 oz/75 g ground almonds
4 drops almond essence
½ oz/15 g self raising flour
1 tablespoon lemon curd
Decoration:
6 oz/175 g icing sugar
lemon juice
2 glacé cherries, halved
angelica

Lemon Apricot Roll

Makes: one Swiss roll
Preparation time:
25 minutes
Cooking time:
10 minutes
Oven temperature:
400°F/200°C Mark 6

This roll will keep well in an airtight container. It is easy enough to make for everyday family fare.

4 oz/100 g self raising flour
2 oz/50 g margarine
4 oz/100 g castor sugar
1 level teaspoon grated lemon rind
2 eggs
2 tablespoons warm water
extra castor sugar
apricot jam
lemon juice

Line an 8 x 12 inch/20 x 30 cm Swiss roll tin with greased greaseproof paper. Sift the flour. Put the softened margarine into a mixing bowl with the castor sugar and lemon rind. Cream them together until light and fluffy. Beat the eggs together lightly in a small bowl. Gradually beat the eggs into the creamed mixture, beating well after each addition. Fold in the flour and the water. Spread the mixture evenly in the prepared tin. Bake in a hot oven (400°F/200°C Mark 6) for 10 minutes or until golden and firm to the touch. Meanwhile, fold a wet tea-towel in half on the work top. Put a piece of greaseproof paper on top and dredge with the extra castor sugar. Warm some apricot jam in a small saucepan and add a little lemon juice to soften it. Turn the cake out of the tin on to the greaseproof paper. Remove the paper lining and spread quickly with the apricot jam. Roll the cake up tightly. Cool on a wire rack. Trim the ends of the roll when cold.

Chocmallows

Makes: about 17–18 cakes
Preparation time: 30 minutes
Cooking time: 25 minutes
Oven temperature: 425°F/220°C Mark 7

Cakes:
1½ oz/40 g margarine
1½ oz/40 g castor sugar
1 egg
3 oz/75 g self raising flour
½ level tablespoon cocoa
1 level teaspoon ground cinnamon
¼ level teaspoon salt
1 tablespoon milk

Marshmallows:
5 oz/150 g granulated sugar
¼ pint/1.5 dl water
½ oz/15 g gelatine
1 egg white
few drops vanilla essence

Filling:
apricot jam

Make the cakes: Grease and dust with flour 18 small patty cake tins. Cream the margarine and sugar together in a bowl with a wooden spoon for about 5 minutes or until light and fluffy. Beat the egg, then gradually add it to the margarine and sugar, beating well. Sift the flour, cocoa, cinnamon and salt together and fold in with the milk. Spoon the mixture into the prepared patty cake tins and bake in a hot oven (425°F/220°C Mark 7) for 15 minutes. Remove the cakes from the tins and leave to cool on a wire rack. Wash the patty tins and grease them lightly.

Make the marshmallows: Boil together the sugar and half the water in a saucepan for 4 minutes, then allow to cool. Place the remaining water and gelatine in a bowl over hot water and dissolve the gelatine, stirring. Whisk the egg white until stiff, add the sugar syrup, vanilla and gelatine. Whisk again until the mixture is white and spongy and beginning to set. Fill the patty tins with the mixture and leave it to set in the refrigerator. Unmould and sandwich them together with the cake portion with the apricot jam.

Manchester Pudding

Serves: 4–6 people
Preparation time: 30 minutes
Cooking time: 55 minutes
Oven temperature: 350°F/180°C Mark 4

This is an extremely inexpensive dessert. For special occasions use 1 tablespoon brandy instead of the vanilla essence.

Pastry:
4 oz/100 g plain flour
pinch of salt
2 oz/50 g butter
cold water to mix
Filling:
½ pint/2·5 dl milk
grated rind of 1 lemon
2 oz/50 g white breadcrumbs
2 eggs, separated
2 oz/50 g butter
4 oz/100 g castor sugar
1 teaspoon vanilla essence
3 level tablespoons raspberry jam
lemon slices for decoration

Make the pastry: Sift the flour and salt into a mixing bowl. Add the butter, cut into small pieces, and rub into the flour until the mixture resembles fine breadcrumbs. Add enough water to make a firm dough. Roll out the pastry on a lightly floured surface and line an 8 inch/20 cm pie plate. Trim the edges. Make the filling: Pour the milk into a saucepan and bring to the boil. Stir in the lemon rind, breadcrumbs, egg yolks, butter, 1 oz/25 g sugar and vanilla essence. Mix well. Spread the jam over the base of the pastry case and pour the breadcrumb mixture on top. Bake in a moderate oven (350°F/180°C Mark 4) for 45 minutes. Whisk the egg whites until stiff and fold in the remaining sugar. Pile the meringue on top of the cooked pudding, making sure that it touches the pastry all round. Return the pudding to the oven for 5–10 minutes or until the meringue is lightly browned. Serve hot or chill and serve cold. Decorate with slices of lemon.

Linzertorte

Serves: 6–8 people
Preparation time:
30 minutes plus
resting and cooling
time
Cooking time:
35–40 minutes
Oven temperature:
375°F/190°C Mark 5

A classic Austrian
cake, named after the
town of Linz. In
Austria it is
traditionally served
with coffee, but it
also makes a good
dessert.

4 oz/100 g plain
  flour
1 level tablespoon
  cocoa
½ level teaspoon
  ground cinnamon
½ level teaspoon
  baking powder
pinch of salt
2 oz/50 g castor
  sugar
4 oz/100 g ground
  almonds
4 oz/100 g margarine
little milk (if
  necessary)
1 lb/450 g raspberry
  or strawberry jam
icing sugar for
  sprinkling
few raspberries or
  strawberries for
  decoration
  (optional)

Grease an 8 inch/20 cm deep round cake tin with a loose base or a spring form tin. Sift the flour, cocoa, cinnamon, baking powder and salt into a mixing bowl. Stir in the castor sugar and ground almonds. Add the margarine and rub it in with your fingertips until the mixture resembles fine breadcrumbs. Knead lightly to combine the dough, adding a little milk if necessary. Wrap in a polythene bag and leave to rest in the refrigerator for 30 minutes. Roll out two-thirds of the dough on a lightly floured surface to fit the prepared tin. Press the dough well into the tin. Spread the jam over the top. Roll out the remaining pastry and make ½ inch/1 cm wide lattice strips as illustrated. Finally, lay a strip right round the edge of the cake. Press down lightly. Chill for 15 minutes in the refrigerator. Bake in a moderate oven (350°F/180°C Mark 4) for 35–40 minutes. Allow to cool, and when completely cold remove from the tin and serve.

Choux Coffee Gâteau

Makes: one 6 inch/
15 cm ring cake
Preparation time:
30 minutes plus
cooling time
Cooking time:
About 35 minutes
Oven temperature:
400°F/200°C Mark 6

To make a perfect
choux ring draw a
6 inch/15 cm circle on
a piece of greaseproof
paper. Place this,
upside down, on the
baking tray and
grease lightly.

Choux pastry:
2½ oz/65 g flour
¼ pint/1.5 dl water
2 oz/50 g margarine
2 eggs, beaten
1 oz/25 g flaked
  almonds
Filling:
4 oz/100 g unsalted
  butter
8 oz/200 g icing
  sugar
2 tablespoons strong
  black coffee
extra icing sugar for
  decoration

Lightly grease a baking tray. Make the choux pastry: Sift the flour onto a piece of kitchen paper and put it in a warm place. Place the water and margarine in a saucepan, heat until the margarine has melted, then bring to the boil. Immediately add the flour, all at once, then cook gently, beating well until the mixture forms a smooth ball that leaves the sides of the pan clean. Remove the pan from the heat and cool slightly. Beat in the eggs a little at a time. Spoon the choux pastry into a 6 inch/15 cm ring on the prepared tray. Sprinkle with the flaked almonds. Bake in a hot oven (400°F/200°C Mark 6) for about 35 minutes or until golden brown, well risen and crisp. Remove the cooked ring from the baking tray, slice it in half horizontally and leave to cool on a wire rack.
Make the icing: Cream the unsalted butter and sugar together in a bowl until light and fluffy. Beat in the coffee. Pipe or spoon the icing into the lower half of the choux ring and replace the top half. Sift icing sugar over the top for decoration.

Apple Palmiers

Makes: 18–20 pastries
Preparation time: 30 minutes plus cooling time
Cooking time: 20 minutes
Oven temperature: 425°F/220°C Mark 7

Other types of fruit, such as gooseberries, rhubarb and apricots, can be used instead of apples.

12 oz/350 g flaky pastry mix
3 oz/75 g castor sugar
Filling:
1 lb/450 g cooking apples, peeled, cored and sliced
1 tablespoon water
2 oz/50 g castor sugar
2 level teaspoons custard powder
¼ pint/1.5 dl milk
¼ pint/1.5 dl whipped cream

Make up the flaky pastry mix according to the instructions on the side of the packet. Roll out to a rectangle 18 × 10 inches/45 × 25 cm. Sprinkle 1 oz/25 g sugar over the pastry, fold the 2 narrow ends into the middle, press down firmly. Sprinkle with another 1 oz/25 g sugar and fold to the centre again. Sprinkle with the remaining sugar and place the 2 folded portions together. Press down well. Cut the strip into ¼ inch/6 mm slices. Place, cut-side down, well spaced, on a lightly greased baking tray. Bake in a hot oven (425°F/220°C Mark 7) for about 5 minutes, until golden brown. Turn them over and bake for a further 5–7 minutes. Leave on a wire rack to cool.

Make the filling: Cook the apples with the water and sugar until soft. Beat with a wooden spoon. Blend the custard powder with a little of the milk, then stir it into the apples with the rest of the milk. Bring to the boil, stirring constantly, then cook for a few minutes. Leave until cold. Fold 2 tablespoons cream into the cold apple mixture with a tablespoon. Spread the mixture onto half the slices, then top with the remaining slices. Decorate with the rest of the whipped cream.

Two-Layer Chocolate Honeycomb Mould

Serves: 4 people
Preparation time: 25 minutes plus setting time
Cooking time: None

A two-layer mould which is a firm favourite with children.

1 pint/6 dl milk
2 oz/50 g cooking chocolate
1½ level tablespoons gelatine
4 tablespoons hot water
2 eggs, separated
2 oz/50 g castor sugar
few drops vanilla essence
chocolate buttons for decoration

Put the milk into a saucepan. Add the chocolate, broken into small pieces. Heat gently, stirring, until the chocolate is dissolved. Dissolve the gelatine in the hot water, in a small bowl. Place the bowl over a pan of hot water to help dissolve the gelatine, if necessary. Put the egg yolks and sugar in a heatproof bowl and whisk together until thick. Rest the bowl over a saucepan of simmering water and stir in the warm chocolate milk. Cook, stirring, until the mixture coats the back of the spoon. Stir in the dissolved gelatine and vanilla essence. Whisk the egg whites until stiff and fold in. Put the whole mixture into a saucepan and bring almost to boiling point. Pour into a lightly oiled mould, cool and chill. Unmould before serving. Decorate with chocolate buttons.

Apricot Almond Slices

Makes: about 20 pastries
Preparation time: 30 minutes
Cooking time: 30—40 minutes
Oven temperature: 350°F/180°C Mark 4

Use other ground nuts if preferred or, if more economical, add extra almond essence for flavour.

6 oz/175 g shortcrust pastry mix
4 tablespoons apricot jam
4 oz/100 g margarine
4 oz/100 g castor sugar
2 eggs, beaten
4 oz/100 g ground almonds
1 oz/25 g plain flour
few drops almond essence

Prepare the shortcrust pastry mix according to the instructions on the side of the packet. Roll out the pastry on a lightly floured surface to line a rectangular tin 7 × 11 × 1½ inches/18 × 28 × 4 cm. Reserve the pastry trimmings for lattice decoration. Spread the jam over the pastry. Place the margarine and sugar in a mixing bowl and beat together until light and fluffy. Slowly add the eggs, beating well after each addition. Fold in the ground almonds, flour and almond essence. Spread the mixture over the jam in the tin. Roll out the reserved pastry and cut it into strips. Lay the strips in a lattice pattern over the almond mixture. Bake in a moderate oven (350°F/180°C Mark 4) for 30—40 minutes or until well risen and golden brown. Turn out of the tin and cool on a wire rack. Cut into slices or squares.

Raspberry Meringue Basket

Serves: 6 people
Preparation time: 25 minutes
Cooking time: 2½—3 hours
Oven temperature: 200°F/100°C Mark ¼ or the lowest temperature setting

Serve this dessert for special occasions. Use other fruit for variety.

2 egg whites
4 oz/100 g castor sugar
¼ pint/1·5 dl whipping cream
1 tablespoon milk
sugar to taste
8 oz/225 g fresh or frozen raspberries

Place a piece of lightly greased greaseproof paper on a baking tray. Draw an 8 inch/20 cm diameter circle on the paper. Put the egg whites in a mixing bowl and whisk until stiff. Add half the castor sugar and continue whisking until the meringue is shiny and stiff again. Fold in the remaining castor sugar. Spread the meringue over the 8 inch/20 cm circle. Make the edges slightly higher than the centre with a spoon or by piping rosettes. Bake in a very slow oven (200°F/100°C Mark ¼) for 2½—3 hours. Remove the paper, cool on a wire rack, then place on a serving plate. Whip the cream and milk together until thick. Sweeten to taste and stir in half the raspberries. Just before serving pile the fruit and cream into the basket and decorate with the remaining raspberries.

Käsetorte

Serves: 6–8 people
Preparation time:
30 minutes plus
setting time
Cooking time:
None

A special occasion
dessert cake.

Base:
7 oz/200 g digestive
  biscuits
4 oz/100 g margarine
1 oz/25 g castor
  sugar
2 oz/50 g plain
  chocolate
Filling:
8 oz/225 g cream
  cheese
2 tablespoons lemon
  juice
1 egg, separated
1 oz/25 g castor
  sugar
$\frac{1}{4}$ pint/1.5 dl milk
few drops vanilla
  essence
$\frac{1}{2}$ oz/15 g gelatine
1 tablespoon water
Decoration:
1 oz/25 g plain
  chocolate
lemon twists

Crush the biscuits in a polythene bag with a rolling pin. Melt the margarine, stir in the sugar and crushed biscuits. Press the mixture into an 8 inch/20 cm round, loose-bottomed cake tin, into the bottom and up the sides. Melt the chocolate in a bowl over a pan of hot water, then spread it over the biscuit crust. Leave in a cool place until hard.
Make the filling: Beat the cream cheese and lemon juice until smooth. Beat the egg yolk with the sugar and milk. Cook gently, stirring, until slightly thickened. Stir into the cream cheese mixture with the vanilla essence. Dissolve the gelatine in a tablespoon of water in a bowl over hot water. Stir into the cream cheese mixture. Whisk the egg white until stiff. When the mixture is just beginning to set round the edges, fold in the whisked egg white. Quickly pour the mixture into the biscuit base and leave it to set in a cool place. Melt the chocolate and decorate as illustrated.

Raspberry Shortcake

Makes: one 8 inch/
20 cm round cake
Preparation time:
20 minutes plus
cooling time
Cooking time:
30–40 minutes
Oven temperature:
325°F/170°C Mark 3

Serve this for a
dessert or a special
tea party. Use whole
raspberries for
decoration when they
are in season.

8 oz/225 g butter
6 oz/175 g castor
  sugar
12 oz/350 g plain
  flour
$\frac{1}{4}$ pint/1.5 dl milk
1 ($\frac{1}{2}$ pint/283 g)
  packet raspberry
  dessert mix
1 (5 fl oz/142 ml)
  carton raspberry
  yoghourt
little castor or
  icing sugar for
  sprinkling

Grease 2 baking trays. Beat the butter and castor sugar together in a bowl until light and fluffy. Mix in the flour. Knead the dough with a warm hand to bind it. Halve the dough and shape it into two 8 inch/20 cm diameter circles. Place one on each baking tray. Crimp the edges, prick the surface with a fork and mark one into 8 wedges. Bake in a moderately slow oven (325°F/ 170°C Mark 3) for 30–40 minutes or until pale gold. Remove the cakes from the trays and leave to cool on a wire rack. Place the milk in a bowl, whisk in the dessert mix, then stir in the yoghourt. Place the unmarked cake on a serving plate, spread on the raspberry mixture and arrange the wedges of the remaining shortcake on top. Sprinkle the top with castor or icing sugar.

Monte Bianco

Serves: 6 people
Preparation time:
30 minutes
Cooking time:
3–4 hours
Oven temperature:
200°F/100°C Mark ¼
or the lowest oven
setting

Monte Bianco is the
Italian name for
Mont Blanc, the
highest peak of the
Alps. The meringues
can be made well in
advance and stored
in an airtight
container.

2 egg whites
4 oz/100 g castor
  sugar
4 oz/100 g plain
  chocolate
1 (8 oz/227 g) can
  sweetened
  chestnut purée
rind of 1 orange
¼ pint/1.5 dl
  whipped cream

Grease and flour 2 baking trays. Whisk the egg whites in a clean bowl until stiff and standing in peaks. Whisk in half the sugar and whisk again until very stiff. Fold in the remaining sugar with a tablespoon. Place the meringue in a piping bag with a star nozzle. Pipe 6 rounds, 2½ inches/6 cm in diameter, on the prepared baking trays, or spread the meringue into circles with a spoon. Cook in a cool oven (200°F/100°C Mark ¼) for 3–4 hours until dried out. Remove the meringues from the baking trays and cool on a wire rack. Break the chocolate into a heatproof bowl over a saucepan of hot water and allow it to melt. Stir in the chestnut purée, grated rind of half the orange and 1 tablespoon of the whipped cream. Make a piping bag from greaseproof paper, fill it with the chocolate mixture, cut off the tip. Pipe the mixture unevenly over each meringue as shown in the picture. Alternatively, carefully spoon it over the meringue. Pile the rest of the whipped cream in the centre of each meringue. Cut the rind of the remaining half orange into thin strips and use for decoration.

Chilled Lemon Cheesecake

Serves: 6–8 people
Preparation time:
30 minutes
Cooking time:
7 minutes

A particularly
popular cheesecake.

Crumb crust:
8 oz/225 g digestive
  biscuits
4 oz/100 g margarine
½ level teaspoon
  ground cinnamon
Filling:
8 oz/225 g cottage
  cheese, sieved
4 oz/100 g castor
  sugar
3 eggs, separated
4 tablespoons milk
½ oz/15 g gelatine
4 tablespoons hot
  water
2 large lemons

Put the biscuits in a polythene bag and crush them with a rolling pin until they become fine crumbs. Put into a bowl. Melt the margarine and stir into the crumbs with the cinnamon; mix well. Press the crumbs over the base and sides of an 8 inch/20 cm spring form tin. Make the filling: Put the cottage cheese into a heatproof bowl and beat in 2 oz/50 g of the sugar then the egg yolks, one at a time. Stir in the milk, then place the bowl over a pan of simmering water. Cook for 5–7 minutes or until beginning to thicken, stirring frequently. Put the mixture aside to cool. Dissolve the gelatine in the hot water. Pour into the cottage cheese mixture with the juice of both lemons and the finely grated rind of one. Cool until syrupy. Whisk the egg whites until stiff; gradually beat in the remaining castor sugar. Fold the egg whites into the cottage cheese mixture. Pour into the biscuit crumb case. Chill until set. Decorate with finely grated lemon rind.

Caramel Creams

Serves: 10–12 people
Preparation time:
25 minutes
Cooking time:
45–60 minutes
Oven temperature:
325°F/170°C Mark 3

An inexpensive but impressive sweet. It is comparatively easy to make and can be prepared the day before needed. It is a good dessert to serve if you are entertaining a lot of people.

6 oz/175 g
  granulated sugar
4 tablespoons water
9 large eggs
1½ pints/9 dl
  warmed milk
3 oz/75 g castor
  sugar
1 teaspoon vanilla
  essence

Heat the granulated sugar and the water in a heavy-based saucepan over a low heat. Allow the syrup to become golden brown. Lightly grease three 1 pint/6 dl ovenproof moulds or 10–12 small ones. Carefully pour some of the caramel into each mould. Beat the eggs in a large bowl, beat in the warmed milk, castor sugar and vanilla essence. Mix well together to dissolve the sugar. Divide the mixture equally between the moulds, stand them in a roasting pan with enough water to come halfway up the sides. Cook in a moderately slow oven (325°F/170°C Mark 3) for 45–60 minutes, until the custard is set. The small moulds will only take 35–40 minutes. To test the custard, insert the tip of a knife in the centre; it should come out clean. Cool, then chill until needed. Remove from the moulds just before serving by running the edge of a sharp knife round the edge of the custard before turning upside down.

Fruit in Lemon Jelly

Serves: 4–6 people
Preparation time:
25 minutes plus
setting time
Cooking time:
None

This delicious home-made jelly teams well with most fresh fruit to make a spectacular dessert

¼ pint/1·5 dl lemon
  juice
thinly peeled rind of
  2 lemons
4 oz/100 g
  granulated sugar
2 level tablespoons
  gelatine
1 lb/½ kg fresh fruit
  (cherries, grapes,
  apple and banana
  slices, orange
  segments etc.)
extra lemon juice
whipped cream for
  decoration

Put the lemon juice in a heatproof bowl with 1 pint/6 dl water and the lemon rind. Place the bowl over a saucepan of hot water, sprinkle in the sugar and the gelatine. Heat gently, stirring occasionally, until the sugar and gelatine are dissolved. Put aside until cold. Strain. Pour a little of the liquid into the base of a lightly oiled 2 pint/1 litre mould. Leave until set. Meanwhile, prepare the fruit. Remove any pips and stones, wash carefully and dry if necessary. Arrange a layer of fruit on the set jelly, making sure that it does not touch the mould. Pour more jelly over the fruit so that it is just covered. Allow this to set and then repeat the procedure to fill the mould. Put aside until very firm. Unmould the jelly just before serving and top with any remaining fruit. Decorate with whipped cream if liked.

Chocolate Dessert Roll

Serves: 4–6 people
Preparation time: 25 minutes plus overnight standing and chilling time
Cooking time: 15–20 minutes
Oven temperature: 350°F/180°C Mark 4

A spectacular dessert for a special dinner party. Make it the day before and complete it well in advance so that it is properly chilled before serving.

4 oz/100 g plain chocolate
4 eggs, separated
4 oz/100 g castor sugar
1 tablespoon orange juice
1 teaspoon vanilla essence
icing sugar
$\frac{1}{4}$ pint/1.5 dl whipping cream
grated rind of $\frac{1}{2}$ orange

Lightly grease an 8 × 12 inch/20 × 30 cm Swiss roll tin and line it with greased greaseproof paper. Break the chocolate into a heatproof bowl and place it over a pan of hot water; stir occasionally until melted. Put the egg yolks into a bowl with the sugar, beat them together until thick and pale in colour. Stir in the melted chocolate, orange juice and vanilla essence. Whisk the egg whites until stiff and fold them into the chocolate mixture with a tablespoon. Spread the mixture into the prepared tin. Bake in a moderate oven (350°F/180°C Mark 4) for 15–20 minutes. Cool, then cover and leave in a cool place overnight. The next day, sprinkle icing sugar onto a sheet of greaseproof paper, turn the cooked mousse out onto the paper. Whip the cream until fairly thick, stir in the orange rind and spread it over the mousse. Roll up like a Swiss roll, using the paper to help. Leave the roll to chill in the refrigerator for 3 hours. Sprinkle with icing sugar before serving. Cut into slices with a knife dipped in hot water.

Apricot Gâteau

Serves: 8 people
Preparation time: 30 minutes plus cooling time
Cooking time: 20–25 minutes
Oven temperature: 350°F/180°C Mark 4

If liked, the apricots can be glazed with 1 level teaspoon arrowroot boiled in a little of the syrup.

3 eggs
3 oz/75 g castor sugar
3 oz/75 g self raising flour
4 oz/100 g apricot jam
$\frac{1}{4}$ pint/1.5 dl whipped cream
chocolate vermicelli
1 (15$\frac{1}{2}$ oz/439 g) can apricot halves, drained

Line an 8 inch/20 cm deep round cake tin with greased greaseproof paper. Whisk the eggs with the sugar in a heatproof bowl over a saucepan of hot water until creamy and thick enough for the whisk to leave a trail. Sift the flour into the bowl and fold in with a tablespoon. Spoon the mixture into the prepared tin. Bake in a moderate oven (350°F/180°C Mark 4) for 20–25 minutes. Turn the cake out of the tin onto a wire rack to cool. Cut the cake through and sandwich the halves together with the apricot jam. Spread a little cream all over the cake, press on the chocolate vermicelli around the sides. Decorate as illustrated.

Iced Layer Pastry

Serves: 4–6 people
Preparation time: 30 minutes plus resting time for the pastry
Cooking time: 5–7 minutes
Oven temperature: 375°F/190°C Mark 5

Pastry:
8 oz/200 g plain flour
4 oz/100 g butter, softened
4 oz/100 g castor sugar
1 egg
1 egg yolk

Icing:
8 oz/225 g icing sugar
1 egg white
1 teaspoon lemon juice
1 level tablespoon cocoa
Filling:
½ pint/3 dl whipped cream

Lightly grease 3 baking trays. Make the pastry: Sift the flour onto a cold surface, add the butter, sugar, egg and egg yolk. Work all the ingredients together with your fingertips to make a firm dough. Put the pastry in a polythene bag and leave in a cool place for at least 30 minutes before using. Cut the dough into 3 equal portions. Roll out each portion on a lightly floured surface to an oblong 6 × 10 inches/15 × 25 cm. Place each oblong on a prepared baking tray and bake in a moderately hot oven (375°F/190°C Mark 5) for 5–7 minutes or until cooked and golden. Remove the pastry from the baking tray and cool on a wire rack.
Make the icing: Sift the icing sugar. Put the egg white into a bowl and mix lightly with a wooden spoon. Add the lemon juice and enough icing sugar to make a soft icing. Place 3 tablespoons of the icing in a small bowl and sift in the cocoa. Beat well. Spread the whipped cream on 2 of the pastry oblongs, then layer them one on top of the other. Fill a piping bag with a small icing pipe with the chocolate icing. Pipe the icing in a lattice pattern over the top of the pastry. Cut into slices for serving.

Dulverton Fruit Tart

Serves: 6 people
Preparation time: 25 minutes
Cooking time: 35 minutes
Oven temperature: 375°F/190°C Mark 5 then 350°F/180°C Mark 4

Pastry:
6 oz/150 g plain flour
pinch of salt
2 oz/50 g margarine
1 oz/25 g lard
1 oz/25 g castor sugar
1 egg yolk
cold water to mix

Filling:
2 dessert apples
2 oz/50 g raisins
2 oz/50 g sultanas
1 oz/25 g glacé cherries, chopped
1 oz/25 g chopped mixed peel
1 teaspoon grated lemon rind
½ level teaspoon ground mixed spice
1 level tablespoon soft brown sugar
3–4 drops rum essence
2 oz/50 g margarine
2 oz/50 g castor sugar
2 eggs
2 oz/50 g ground almonds
few flaked almonds

Lightly grease an 8 inch/20 cm flan ring and stand it on a greased baking tray. Make the rich shortcrust pastry (see Pastry and pies recipe 9). Line the prepared flan ring. Make the filling: Peel, core and slice one of the apples and spread the slices over the pastry. Peel and grate the other apple and mix it with the next 8 ingredients in a bowl, stir well together, then spread on top of the apple slices. Cream the margarine and sugar well together with a wooden spoon until light and fluffy. Gradually add the eggs, beating well after each addition. Stir in the ground almonds. Spread it over the fruit and sprinkle with flaked almonds. Bake in a moderately hot oven (375°F/190°C Mark 5) for 15 minutes, then reduce to moderate (350°F/180°C Mark 4) for a further 20 minutes.

Pear Pastries

Makes: 6 pastries
Preparation time:
30 minutes
Cooking time:
10–15 minutes
Oven temperature:
375°F/190°C Mark 5

Pears are at their best and cheapest in the autumn but canned pear halves may also be used. Use other nuts if preferred.

4 oz/100 g butter, softened
1½ oz/40 g icing sugar, sifted
½ egg, beaten
few drops vanilla essence
7 oz/200 g plain flour
3 large, ripe pears
4 tablespoons apricot jam
1 oz/25 g hazelnuts

Make the pastry: Put the butter and icing sugar into a bowl and cream them together until light in colour. Beat in the egg and vanilla essence. Add the sifted flour and work it in to make a firm dough. Turn the pastry onto a lightly floured surface and knead very gently. Divide the pastry into 6 equal portions. Using your floured fingers, press each portion into the shape of a pear, about ½ inch/1 cm larger than the actual pears; flute the edges. Put the shaped pastry pieces onto a lightly greased baking tray and bake in a moderately hot oven (375°F/190°C Mark 5) for about 10–15 minutes or until golden brown. Remove from the oven and cool on the baking tray. Peel the pears, cut them in half and remove the cores. Place one half pear on each piece of pastry. Sieve the apricot jam into a saucepan and heat it gently. Brush the jam over the pear pastries. Put the hazelnuts onto a baking tray and leave them in the hot oven for 10 minutes, then rub them in a clean tea-towel to remove the outer skins. Chop the nuts and place them under a hot grill to toast and become golden brown. Sprinkle them onto the pears.

Frosted Apple Pie

Serves: 6 people
Preparation time:
30 minutes
Cooking time:
30 minutes
Oven temperature:
375°F/190°C Mark 5

A very special apple pie. Apples are cheapest in the autumn. Use canned apple pie filling for emergencies.

Pastry:
8 oz/200 g plain flour
pinch of salt
2 oz/50 g margarine
2 oz/50 g lard
cold water to mix
Filling:
1 lb/½ kg cooking apples
2 level teaspoons plain flour
1 level teaspoon ground cinnamon
4 oz/100 g soft brown sugar
2 level teaspoons grated lemon rind
Frosting:
4 oz/100 g icing sugar, sifted
lemon juice
1 oz/25 g demerara sugar

Make the pastry: Sift the flour and salt into a mixing bowl. Add the margarine and lard and rub into the flour until the mixture resembles breadcrumbs. Stir in enough cold water to make a firm dough.
Make the filling: Peel, core and slice the apples. Put into a saucepan with 2 or 3 tablespoons water. Cook gently, shaking the pan occasionally, until just tender. Stir in the flour, cinnamon, sugar, and lemon rind. Roll out two-thirds of the pastry on a lightly floured surface and line an 8 inch/20 cm pie plate. Put the apple filling on the pastry then roll out the remaining pastry to cover. Damp the edges and press them together firmly. Bake in a moderately hot oven (375°F/190°C Mark 5) for about 30 minutes or until the pastry is cooked and golden.

Meanwhile, make the icing: Mix the icing sugar to a stiff consistency with lemon juice. Spread over the pie immediately it comes out of the oven and sprinkle with the demerara sugar.

Hot Chocolate Soufflé

Serves: 4–6 people
Preparation time:
25 minutes
Cooking time:
40–45 minutes
Oven temperature:
400°F/200°C Mark 6

An inexpensive but spectacular dessert for special occasions. Serve it at once before it sinks, accompanied by custard.

3 oz/75 g margarine
2 oz/50 g plain flour
½ pint/3 dl milk
2 oz/50 g castor sugar
2 oz/50 g plain chocolate, grated
4 eggs, separated

Grease a 2 pint/1·25 litre soufflé dish. Melt the margarine in a saucepan, stir in the flour. Cook for 2–3 minutes, stirring all the time. Remove from the heat, blend in the milk. Return to the heat and cook, stirring, until thickened. Remove from the heat and stir in the sugar and chocolate. Beat in the egg yolks, one at a time. Whisk the egg whites in a clean bowl until standing in peaks. Fold the whites into the mixture with a tablespoon. Turn into the prepared soufflé dish. Bake in a hot oven (400°F/200°C Mark 6) for 40–45 minutes or until a skewer pushed into the centre comes out clean. Serve at once.

Mixed Fruit Slice

Serves: 6–8 people
Preparation time:
25 minutes
Cooking time:
30 minutes
Oven temperature:
350°F/180°C Mark 4

This fruit slice makes a delicious dessert or it can be served cold as a cake.

8 oz/225 g mixed dried fruit
2 oz/50 g margarine
3 slices bread
1 level teaspoon ground cinnamon
2 level teaspoons grated orange rind
juice of ½ orange
2 level teaspoons finely chopped preserved ginger
3 oz/75 g soft brown sugar
granulated sugar
Pastry:
12 oz/340 g plain flour
pinch of salt
3 oz/85 g margarine
3 oz/85 g lard
cold water to mix

Put the mixed dried fruit in a saucepan with the margarine and ½ pint/3 dl water. Simmer for 7 minutes. Cool. Cut the crusts off the bread and put the slices in a dish. Drain the water from the fruit onto the bread. When the bread is soaked, pour off the excess liquid. Mash the bread with the cinnamon, orange rind and juice, ginger and brown sugar. Stir in the fruit.
Make the pastry: Sift the flour and salt into a bowl, add the fat and rub in until the mixture resembles fine breadcrumbs. Mix with enough cold water to make a firm dough. Knead slightly, divide into 2 halves. Roll each half out to the size of an 8 × 12 inch/20 × 30 cm Swiss roll tin. Line the tin with one half, pile on the filling and cover with the remaining pastry. Crimp the edges together. Brush the pastry with water and sprinkle with granulated sugar. Bake in a moderate oven (350°F/180°C Mark 4) for about 30 minutes or until cooked and golden.

Lemon Meringue Pie

Serves: 6 people
Preparation time:
25 minutes
Cooking time:
30—35 minutes
Oven temperature:
400°F/200°C Mark 6

A traditional dessert which is always popular.

Pastry:
6 oz/150 g plain
    flour
pinch of salt
2 oz/50 g margarine
1 oz/25 g lard
cold water to mix
Filling:
1 oz/25 g butter
3 level tablespoons
    cornflour
grated rind and juice
    of 1 large lemon
2 oz/50 g sugar
2 egg yolks
Meringue:
2 egg whites
4 oz/100 g castor
    sugar

Make the pastry: Sift the flour and salt into a mixing bowl. Add the margarine and lard, cut into pieces. Rub the fat into the flour until the mixture resembles fine bread-crumbs. Add enough water to make a firm dough. Roll out the pastry on a floured surface and line an 8 inch/20 cm flan ring standing on a baking tray. Prick the pastry well, then line with greaseproof paper and fill with baking beans. Bake in a moderately hot oven (400°F/200°C Mark 6) for 10 minutes. Remove the flan ring and beans and cook for a further 10—15 minutes.
Make the filling: Place the butter, cornflour, lemon rind and juice made up to ½ pint/3 dl with water, and sugar in a saucepan. Whisking continuously over a moderate heat, bring the mixture to the boil and cook for 2—3 minutes until thickened and smooth. Cool slightly, then beat in the egg yolks. Pour into the cooked flan case.
Make the meringue: Whisk the egg whites until stiff and standing in peaks. Add the sugar and whisk until stiff once more. Pile over the lemon filling, making sure it is completely covered with meringue. Bake in a hot oven (400°F/200°C Mark 6) for 10 minutes.

Apricot and Orange Pancakes

Serves: 4 people
Preparation time:
30 minutes
Cooking time:
45 minutes
Oven temperature:
350°F/180°C Mark 4

These pancakes can be made well in advance and reheated just before serving. They are luxurious enough for the grandest dinner party.

Batter:
4 oz/100 g plain
    flour
pinch of salt
1 level tablespoon
    castor sugar
2 eggs
½ pint/3 dl milk and
    water, mixed
oil for frying
Filling:
8 oz/225 g dried
    apricots, soaked
    overnight in water
4 tablespoons
    orange marmalade
1 oz/25 g castor
    sugar
Decoration:
3—4 oranges

Sift the flour and salt into a bowl, add the castor sugar. Make a well in the centre, beat in the eggs, one at a time. Gradually beat in the milk and water mixture. Continue beating the batter until smooth. Heat a little oil in a small frying pan. Add sufficient batter to thinly cover the base of the pan, slant the pan to make an even layer. Lift the edges with a round-bladed knife to loosen them. When golden brown underneath toss or turn the pancake over in the pan and cook the other side. Turn out onto a wire rack to cool. Continue making pancakes until all the batter has been used.
Make the filling: Cook the soaked apricots until soft (about 30 minutes). Drain off the cooking water and rub the apricots through a sieve into a bowl. Stir in the marmalade and sugar. Spread the filling over the cooked pancakes and roll them up. Arrange them in an ovenproof dish, cover with foil and place in a moderate oven (350°F/180°C Mark 4) for 15 minutes to heat through. Decorate with orange slices and strips of peel as illustrated.

Coconut Pudding

Serves: 4 people
Preparation time:
30 minutes
Cooking time:
1 hour
Oven temperature:
325°F/170°C Mark 3

A light and fluffy hot pudding which uses up leftover sponge cake. If you have any leftover stewed fruit, use this under the pudding instead of jam.

3 oz/75 g desiccated coconut
½ pint/3 dl milk
1½ oz/40 g margarine
1½ oz/40 g castor sugar
3 eggs, separated
2 oz/50 g sponge cake, crumbled
2–3 level tablespoons jam
icing sugar for decoration

Put the coconut and milk into a saucepan, bring to the boil and simmer very gently for 10 minutes. Allow to cool. Cream the margarine and sugar together until light and fluffy. Beat in the egg yolks. Add the cooled coconut and milk mixture, gradually, then the cake crumbs. Whisk the egg whites until stiff and fold into the coconut mixture, carefully. Spread the jam over the base of a greased 1 pint/ 6 dl pie dish and pile the pudding mixture on top. Bake in a moderately slow oven (325°F/170°C Mark 3) for 1 hour or until well risen and golden. Serve sprinkled with icing sugar.

Spiced Pineapple Pudding

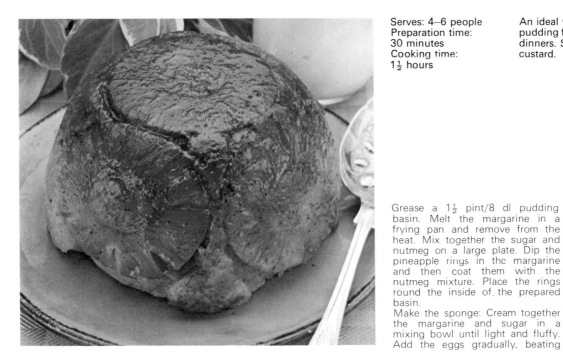

Serves: 4–6 people
Preparation time:
30 minutes
Cooking time:
1½ hours

An ideal winter pudding for special dinners. Serve with custard.

1 oz/25 g margarine
1 oz/25 g soft brown sugar
¼ level teaspoon ground nutmeg
1 small can pineapple rings
Sponge:
4 oz/100 g margarine
4 oz/100 g castor sugar
2 eggs, beaten
4 oz/100 g self raising flour, sifted
½ level teaspoon ground mixed spice

Grease a 1½ pint/8 dl pudding basin. Melt the margarine in a frying pan and remove from the heat. Mix together the sugar and nutmeg on a large plate. Dip the pineapple rings in the margarine and then coat them with the nutmeg mixture. Place the rings round the inside of the prepared basin.
Make the sponge: Cream together the margarine and sugar in a mixing bowl until light and fluffy. Add the eggs gradually, beating well after each addition. Fold in the sifted flour and spice. Carefully spread the mixture in the lined bowl, taking care not to disturb the pineapple. Cover with a double layer of greased greaseproof paper. Secure with a piece of string tied under the rim of the basin. Steam in a steamer over boiling water or in a large saucepan with water to come halfway up the sides of the basin, for 1½ hours. Turn out and serve.

Four Fruit Pie

Serves: 6 people
Preparation time:
30 minutes
Cooking time:
1 hour
Oven temperature:
425°F/220°C Mark 7
then 350°F/180°C
Mark 4

This is a good autumn pie when the fruit is in season. Use canned or frozen fruit at other times of the year. Pastry mixes are ideal for busy people.

8 oz/225 g cooking apples, peeled, cored and sliced
8 oz/225 g dessert pears, peeled, cored and sliced
8 oz/225 g blackberries
12 oz/350 g plums, stoned
1 tablespoon water
10 oz/275 g flaky pastry mix or home-made flaky pastry, using 8 oz/200 g flour etc.
castor sugar
little milk for glazing

Place the prepared fruit in a large saucepan with the tablespoon of water. Place over a low heat, cover and cook very gently for about 10 minutes or until almost tender. Drain the fruit but keep the juice; allow to cool. Make up the flaky pastry mix according to the instructions on the side of the packet. Halve the pastry dough and roll out one half on a lightly floured surface to fit an 8 inch/20 cm diameter pie plate. Pile the fruit onto the plate with a little of the juice and sprinkle on sugar to taste. Roll out the remaining pastry to fit over the pie. Damp the edges with cold water and cover the pie with the pastry. Seal the edges by pinching them together. Use the pastry trimmings to decorate the top. Brush the surface with milk, sprinkle with a little castor sugar and bake in a hot oven (425°F/ 220°C Mark 7) for 20 minutes, then reduce to moderate (350°F/ 180°C Mark 4) and bake for a further 25–30 minutes or until the pie is golden brown.

Bakewell Tart

Serves: 4–6 people
Preparation time:
30 minutes
Cooking time:
40–50 minutes
Oven temperature:
375°F/190°C Mark 5

An inexpensive and very good hot pudding which can also be served cold as a cake. Serve with custard.

Pastry:
8 oz/200 g plain flour
pinch of salt
2 oz/50 g lard
2 oz/50 g margarine
cold water to mix
Filling:
3–4 tablespoons jam
2 oz/50 g margarine
2 oz/50 g castor sugar
1 egg, beaten
2 oz/50 g ground almonds
milk for brushing

Make the pastry: Sift the flour and salt into a bowl. Add the lard and margarine and rub in with your fingertips until the mixture resembles fine breadcrumbs. Stir in sufficient water to make a firm dough. Knead lightly on a floured surface. Cut off two-thirds of the pastry and roll it out to fit an 8 inch/20 cm pie plate. Line the pie plate, trim the edges with a fluted pastry cutter if liked (as illustrated). Prick the pastry with a fork. Spread with the jam. Cream the margarine and sugar together in a mixing bowl until light and fluffy, beat in the egg. Stir in the ground almonds. Spread the mixture on the jam in the pie plate. Roll out the remaining pastry. Cut out lattice strips to go across the tart and around the edge. Brush with milk. Put the plate on a baking tray and bake in a moderately hot oven (375°F/ 190°C Mark 5) for 40–50 minutes or until golden brown.

Sticky Pear Gingerbread

Serves: 6 people
Preparation time:
30 minutes
Cooking time:
1¼–1½ hours
Oven temperature:
300°F/150°C Mark 2

A special hot
pudding which is
remarkably inexpensive.
Pears are at their
best in the autumn.
Serve with custard.

Topping:
2 pears
2 oz/50 g margarine
2 oz/50 g castor
  sugar
Gingerbread:
4 oz/100 g margarine
6 oz/175 g treacle
2 oz/50 g golden
  syrup
2 oz/50 g soft
  brown sugar
¼ pint/1·5 dl milk
2 eggs, beaten
8 oz/225 g plain
  flour
2 level teaspoons
  mixed spice
2 level teaspoons
  ground ginger
1 level teaspoon
  bicarbonate of
  soda
Decoration:
8 glacé cherries
angelica

Grease a 7 inch/18 cm deep round cake tin. Peel, core and slice the pears. Arrange the slices in a circle round the base of the tin. Cream together the margarine and sugar until light and fluffy. Spread the mixture over the pears.
Make the gingerbread: Heat the margarine, treacle, syrup and sugar in a saucepan over a low heat until melted. Stir in the milk, cool slightly, then stir in the beaten eggs. Sift together the flour, mixed spice, ginger and bicarbonate of soda. Blend in the egg mixture, then beat until smooth and pour onto the pears. Bake in a slow oven (300°F/150°C Mark 2) for 1¼–1½ hours or until cooked. Leave in the tin for 5 minutes before turning out, upside down, on a serving plate. Decorate with the glacé cherries and angelica.

Lemon Delicious

Serves: 4 people
Preparation time:
25 minutes
Cooking time:
45 minutes
Oven temperature:
350°F/180°C Mark 4

A tangy lemon
pudding which
makes its own sauce
underneath the
sponge while
cooking

2 oz/50 g
  margarine
4 oz/100 g
  castor sugar
grated rind and
  juice of 2 lemons
2 eggs, separated
2 oz/50 g self
  raising flour
pinch of salt
¼ pint/1·5 dl milk
icing sugar for
  decoration

Lightly grease a 1 pint/6 dl pie dish. Cream the margarine and sugar in a bowl with the finely grated lemon rind. Beat in the egg yolks one at a time. Stir in the sifted flour, salt and milk alternately. Stir in the lemon juice. Whisk the egg whites in a clean bowl until stiff and dry. Gently fold the creamed mixture into the whisked egg whites with a tablespoon, a little at a time. Pour the mixture into the prepared pie dish. Place the dish in a roasting pan with water to come halfway up the sides. Bake in a moderate oven (350°F/180°C Mark 4) for about 45 minutes. Serve sprinkled with icing sugar.

Apple and Cinnamon Layer Pudding

Serves: 6 people
Preparation time:
30 minutes
Cooking time:
2 hours

A delicious, inexpensive and filling pudding— ideal for cold days. Serve with custard.

8 oz/200 g self
   raising flour
pinch of salt
4 oz/100 g
   shredded suet
cold water to mix
Filling:
1 lb/½ kg cooking
   apples
2 oz/50 g sultanas
1 level teaspoon
   ground cinnamon
3 oz/75 g sugar

Grease a 1½ pint/8 dl pudding basin. Sift the flour and salt into a bowl. Stir in the suet, then sufficient water to make a firm dough. Place on a lightly floured surface and knead gently. Divide the dough into 4 unequal pieces, the smallest being just big enough to cover the base of a 2 pint/1 litre pudding basin and the largest being one-third of the total amount.
Make the filling: Peel, core and slice the apples, and mix with the sultanas, cinnamon and sugar. Roll out the smallest piece of dough to fit in the bottom of the prepared

basin. Spread on just under one-third of the apple filling. Roll out the next smallest piece of pastry and place in the basin. Continue layering with the filling and dough, finishing with a layer of dough. Cover the basin with a double layer of greased greaseproof paper with a pleat to allow the pudding to rise. Tie under the rim of the basin with string. Place in a steamer over boiling water or in a large saucepan with water to come halfway up the sides of the basin. Steam for 2 hours. Turn the pudding out of the basin and serve hot.

Epiphany Tart

Serves: 6–8 people
Preparation time:
30 minutes
Cooking time:
15–20 minutes
Oven temperature:
375°F/190°C Mark 5

A traditional English tart, made to celebrate Epiphany. Try to use as many different types of jam as you can to fill the pastry case. Make your own pastry if you have time.

8 oz/225 g shortcrust
   pastry mix
13 different flavours
   of jam, including
   lemon curd and
   honey

Make up the shortcrust pastry mix according to the instructions given on the packet. Roll out the pastry on a lightly floured surface to line a 9 inch/23 cm shallow tart plate. Trim the edge with a knife and keep the trimmings. Pinch the edges of the pastry decoratively. Lightly mark the surface of the pastry into 2 triangles to form a six-pointed star (see picture). Place 1 tablespoon of a

different kind of jam in each triangle, with 2 tablespoons in the central hexagon. Roll out the pastry trimmings and cut six ½ inch/1 cm wide strips, long enough to go over the tart. Moisten the pastry edge, then arrange the pastry strips over the jam to form the star. Bake in a moderately hot oven (375°F/ 190°C Mark 5) for 15–20 minutes or until cooked.

Winter Fruit Pie

Serves: 4–6 people
Preparation time:
30 minutes plus
overnight soaking
for the fruit
Cooking time:
45 minutes
Oven temperature:
425°F/220°C Mark 7

A delicious pie.
Keep all the
ingredients in store;
it is a useful recipe
to know when fresh
fruit is expensive.

12 oz/350 g dried
mixed fruit
(sultanas, raisins,
currants, apricots,
prunes)
8 oz/225 g flaky
pastry mix or
home-made flaky
pastry, using
6 oz/150 g flour
etc.
4½ oz/115 g castor
sugar
little milk for glazing

Place the dried fruit in a large bowl with 1¼ pints/7.5 dl water and leave covered to soak overnight. Make up the pastry according to the instructions on the side of the packet. Leave the pastry in the refrigerator, covered with polythene or foil, to 'rest' for 20 minutes. Place 4 oz/100 g of the sugar, the fruit and liquid into a saucepan.

Bring to the boil and simmer for 20 minutes. Pour into a 1½ pint/ 9 dl pie dish. Roll out the pastry on a lightly floured surface to cover the pie dish. Flute the edges. Brush with milk. Bake in a hot oven (425°F/220°C Mark 7) for 25 minutes. Sprinkle on the remaining ½ oz/15 g sugar and serve.

Apple Noodle Pudding

Serves: 4 people
Preparation time:
25 minutes
Cooking time:
45 minutes
Oven temperature:
350°F/180°C Mark 4

A deliciously different
family pudding.
Apples are at their
cheapest in the
autumn.

4 oz/100 g egg
noodles
salt
1 egg
4 oz/100 g castor
sugar
½ level teaspoon
ground cinnamon
2 oz/50 g sultanas
1 oz/25 g butter,
melted
1 lb/½ kg apples,
peeled, cored and
finely sliced

Cook the noodles in boiling salted water according to the directions on the packet. Drain well. Beat the egg and half the castor sugar together in a mixing bowl until thick and creamy. Stir in the cinnamon, sultanas, melted butter and noodles. Put the apples in a

2 pint/1 litre lightly greased oven-proof dish with 2 tablespoons water and the remaining castor sugar. Top with the noodle mixture and bake in a moderate oven (350°F/ 180°C Mark 4) for 45 minutes or until golden. Serve hot.

Store-cupboard Standbys

However well organised you are, there are bound to be times when you will have unexpected guests, or not be able to do the last-minute shopping. These are the occasions when a well-stocked store cupboard will prove invaluable. A freezer or the freezing compartment of a refrigerator can always be put to good use too. There are many recipes in this book which use basic standbys in addition to the basic ingredients – such as flour, rice, sugar, milk, margarine, dried herbs and spices, etc. – which are kept in most households. Following is a list of some recommended standbys.

Canned Vegetables

sweetcorn
mushrooms
tomatoes
tomato purée
baked beans
butterbeans
celery hearts
beansprouts
assorted soups
*(especially cream of celery,
asparagus and mushroom)*

Canned Fruit and Milk Products

apricots
pears
gooseberries
pineapple
peaches
mandarin oranges
fruit cocktail
creamed rice
semolina
evaporated milk

Canned Meat and Fish

corned beef
tuna
prawns
beef consommé
anchovy fillets

Packaged Foods

pasta in various shapes
instant potato
savory sauces
stuffings
shredded suet
fruit jellies
jelly cream desserts
dessert topping mixes
instant desserts
pastry mixes

Dried Foods

breadcrumbs
haricot beans
seedless raisins
sultanas
currants
apricots
prunes

Index

Alaska, Strawberry 160
Almond apricot slices 239
Ambrosia, Mandarin yoghourt 153
Apple:
    Apple and apricot dessert cake 232
    Apple and blackberry crunchy pie 166
    Apple and cinnamon layer pudding 251
    Apple and date triangles 172
    Apple dumplings 167
    Apple noodle pudding 252
    Apple and orange whip 154
    Apple palmiers 238
    Autumn apple mould 79
    Cheddar apple crumble 168
    Chicken livers with apple on rice 57
    Cider apple soup 106
    Frosted apple pie 245
    Honey rice apples 168
    Honeyed kebabs with apple 200
    Pork rashers with potato and apples 205
Apricot:
    Apple and apricot dessert cake 232
    Apricot almond slices 239
    Apricots with chicken 218
    Apricot gâteau 243
    Apricot lemon roll 235
    Apricot orange casserole 89
    Apricot and orange pancakes 247
    Apricot and prune stuffing with lamb 195
    Creamy apricot ring 159
Aubergine (eggplant) casserole 66
Autumn apple mould 79

Bacon:
    Bacon and cabbage casserole 207
    Bacon and egg charlotte 147
    Bacon and egg pie 206
    Bacon casserole 208
    Bacon olives 122
    Baked apricot bacon 47
    Butterbean and bacon soup 108
    Liver and bacon in tomato sauce 145
    Stuffed streaky bacon joint 206
Baked fish with pasta shells 33
Baked fish with vegetables 191
Baked ham and pasta mould 207
Baked lemon egg custard 88
Baked mushrooms in cheese sauce 101
Baked orange and ginger cheesecake 229
Bakewell tart 249
Banana:
    Banana and lemon delight 78
    Banana twists 173
    Chicken with bananas 56
    Frozen pineapple and banana snow 72
    Hawaiian barbecued chicken 219
    Indian banana fritters 86
    Raisin stuffed bananas 178
Barbecued chops with curry sauce 42
Barbecue sauce with meatballs 128
Beans, French vinaigrette 99
Beef:
    Beef, bacon and mushroom casserole 129
    Beef goulash 133
    Beef Jarratt 211
    Beef olives with onion rice 213
    Beef and orange stew 134
    Beef roll 132
    Beef stew with celery 214
    Beef turnovers 211
    Belgian beef 134
    Boiled salt (corned) beef 50
    Braised steak roll 132
    Chilli beef with vegetables 210
    Corned beef and onion hash 49
    Curried beef salad 130
    Poor man's beef stroganoff 131
    Russian cotletti with mushroom sauce 130
    Surprise baked beefburgers 212
Beer soup, German 27
Beetroot soup 32
Belgian gozette 171
Bermuda peaches 85
Bhugias 97
Blackberry and apple crunchy pie 166
Blackberry gâteau 232
Blackberry layer pudding 174
Blintz 184
Braised celery with mushrooms 65
Braised lamb roll 193
Braised lamb shanks 41

Braised oxtail 131
Braised steak roll 132
Brandy snaps, Iced 70
Breast of lamb with sausage stuffing 199
Broth, Supper vegetable 107
Butterbean and bacon soup 108
Butterbean and lamb casserole 197
Butterscotch creams 74

Caramel creams 241
Caramel queen pudding 170
Carrot and dill ring 97
Casseroles:
    Apricot orange 89
    Aubergine (eggplant) 66
    Bacon 208
    Bacon and cabbage 207
    Beef, bacon and mushroom 129
    Casseroled lamb 195
    Cheesy potato 61
    Cottage cheese 226
    Devilled chicken 216
    Fish with onions 113
    Golden harvest 219
    German rabbit 223
    Hungarian lamb 196
    Lamb and bean 116
    Lamb and butterbean 197
    Marmalade peach 87
    Oxtail 215
    Paprika pork 125
    Pork with herb scone topping 122
    Spiced vegetable 228
Cassoulet 204
Cauliflower cheese, Danish blue 66
Cauliflower fritters 185
Celery:
    Beef stew with celery 214
    Braised celery with mushrooms 65
    Celery with cheese 11
    Celery custard 64
    Quick curried celery soup 23
    Roast duck with celery stuffing 223
Charlotte, Strawberry fluff 160
Cheese:
    Baked mushrooms in cheese sauce 101
    Blintz 184
    Celery with cheese 11
    Cheddar apple crumble 168
    Cheddar cheese soup 31
    Cheese croquettes 100
    Cheese and cucumber salad 61
    Cheese flan 149
    Cheese and onion custard 225
    Cheese and onion flan, Savoury 184
    Cheese and onion topped cutlets 33
    Cheese and pineapple salad 13
    Cheese potato crown 148
    Cheese pudding 59
    Cheese walnut balls 103
    Cheese and walnut loaf 149
    Cheesy egg tarts 188
    Cheesy oven-fried chicken 52
    Cheesy potato casserole 61
    Chilled lemon cheesecake 242
    Cottage cheese casserole 226
    Courgettes (zucchini) and tomatoes with cheese 186
    Creamy vegetable and cheese pie 148
    Cucumber cheese barrels 98
    Danish blue savoury 104
    Dutch cheese and tomato medley 59
    Honey cheese tart 234
    Liptauer cheese 14
    Macaroni cheese special 60
    Potted cheese 100
    Sweet and sour cheese 60
    Swiss cheese flan 183
    Vegetable cheese pie 228
Cherry and pineapple mould 83
Cherry strudel, Quick 109
Chicken:
    Cheesy oven-fried chicken 52
    Chicken à la king 55
    Chicken with apricots 218
    Chicken cacciatora 137
    Chicken curry with grapes 141
    Chicken and egg balls 176
    Chicken and ham mould 218

Chicken:
    Chicken liver risotto 143
    Chicken liver savouries 8
    Chicken livers with apple on rice 57
    Chicken livers with peanuts 57
    Chicken Maryland 217
    Chicken and mushroom pie 140
    Chicken and mushrooms on rice 220
    Chicken and mushroom soufflé omelette 139
    Chicken with oranges 138
    Chicken pie with herb topping 139
    Chicken pilau 140
    Chicken rosemary 55
    Chicken surprise parcels 54
    Chicken vol-au-vent 217
    Country-style chicken 138
    Creamy chicken salad 136
    Curried chicken flan 220
    Devilled chicken 53
    Devilled chicken casserole 216
    Farmhouse chicken 221
    Fried chicken drumsticks 54
    Gougère with chicken livers 224
    Hasty sweet and sour chicken 56
    Hawaiian barbecued chicken 219
    Oven fried chicken 137
    Quick chicken liver pâté 7
    Spicy chicken 53
    Spicy chicken and pineapple 136
    Stuffed cold chicken 216
    Summer chicken 52
    Waldorf chicken salad 141
Chilled cauliflower and spring onion soup 24
Chilled cucumber and tomato soup 21
Chilled lemon cheesecake 242
Chilled lemon fluff 155
Chilled Spanish vegetable soup 23
Chilli beef with vegetables 210
Chilli con carne 51
Chinese pork 127
Chinese rice soup 25
Chinese roast pork 43
Chocolate:
    Chocmallows 236
    Chocolate dessert roll 243
    Chocolate and pear coronet 81
    Creamy chocolate pie 230
    Dreamy chocolate mallow 84
    Hot chocolate soufflé 246
    Rich chocolate delight 75
    Two-layer chocolate honeycomb mould 238
Chopped belly of pork pie 204
Choux coffee gâteau 237
Chowder, Thick chicken 31
Christmas pudding, Frozen 154
Christmas puffs 89
Cider apple soup 106
Cider vegetable hot pot 151
Coconut pudding 248
Coconut spiced eggs 63
Cod in yoghourt tartare sauce 112
Cod peppers 115
Coffee cloud dessert 75
Coffee soufflé 230
Colcannon supper 150
Cold spiced meat loaf 128
Coleslaw, Fruity 179
Compote, Rhubarb and ginger 169
Condé, Orange 80
Consommé brunois 20
Corn and haddock supper 115
Corned beef and onion hash 49
Cottage cheese and ham salad 48
Cottage cheese and smoked haddock soufflé pudding 226
Cottage cheese casserole 226
Cottage cheese ice cream 71
Cottage cheese stuffed tomatoes 98
Cottage strawberries 72
Country omelette 64
Country risotto 47
Country-style chicken 138
Country-style mushroom soup 27
Courgettes (zucchini) and tomatoes with cheese 186
Courgette (zucchini) and tomato special 99
Courgettes (zucchini), Stuffed 187
Cream of cucumber soup 26
Cream of leek soup 28
Cream of pea and ham soup 32
Creamed gooseberry mould 82
Creamed lamb with cucumber 120

Creamy apricot ring 159
Creamy chicken salad 136
Creamy chocolate pie 230
Creamy corn soup 30
Creamy lamb with mushrooms 120
Creamy vegetable and cheese pie 148
Crispy topped fish pie 35
Crowned cream of spinach soup 188
Crown of pork with orange rice 203
Crown roast of lamb with onion and apple stuffing 197
Crunchy ice cream mincemeat tarts 77
Crusted pineapple slices 85
Cucumber and tomato salad 102
Cucumber cheese barrels 98
Cucumber, tomato and yoghourt soup 22
Cucumber with creamed lamb 120
Curried beef salad 130
Curried chicken flan 220
Curried eggs 63
Curried shepherd's pie 193
Curried turkey 142
Curries:
    Chicken with grapes 141
    Gobi dahl 65
    Kofta 213
    Lamb with prunes 198
    Prawn 112
    Vegetable 227
Custard, Baked lemon egg 88
Custard, Celery 64
Custard, Cheese and onion 225

Danish blue cauliflower cheese 66
Danish blue savoury 104
Desserts:
    10 minute 69–90
    20 minute 153–174
    30 minute 229–252
Devilled chicken 53
Devilled chicken casserole 216
Devilled spare rib pork chops 46
Dreamy chocolate mallow 84
Dreamy raspberry nests 69
Duck:
    Boned with orange stuffing 222
    Roast with celery stuffing 223
    Spiced with fruit and mushroom sauce 142
Dulverton fruit tart 244
Dutch cheese and tomato medley 59
Dutch vegetable flan 227

Eastern fruit salad 78
Egg: see also Omelettes
    Cheesy egg tarts 188
    Coconut spiced eggs 63
    Curried eggs 63
    Egg and bacon charlotte 147
    Egg and bacon pie 206
    Egg and chicken balls 176
    Egg and onion pie 62
    Egg and potato rolls 180
    Egg pizzas 182
    Egg soup 30
    Eggnog pie 165
    Eggs en cocotte 12
    Eggs Lyonnaise and macaroni 62
    Eggs Mornay 12
    Stuffed eggs 101
    Tortilla 147
Epiphany tart 251

Family pâté 96
Farmhouse chicken 221
Fettucine all' Alfredo 8
Fish:
    Baked fish with vegetables 191
    Crispy topped fish pie 35
    Fish with bananas 36
    Fish casserole with onions 113
    Fish curls 94
    Fish curry 38
    Fish with egg and herb sauce 34
    Fish fritters 19
    Fish goulash with herbed rice 113
    Fish kebabs on curry rice 37
    Fish and mushroom bundles 177
    Fisherman's supper 110
    Fish in mustard mayonnaise 91
    Fish pâté, mixed 17

Index

Fish:
  Fish sticks 190
  Fish in sweet and sour sauce 19
  Fish sticks
  Fritto misto di mare 182
  German herring salad 110
  Herbed fish parcels 36
  Herring crumb bake 190
  Herrings with tomato sauce 38
  Kipper pâté 92
  Limed fish 92
  Mackerel in foil 109
  Mackerel with mustard sauce 114
  Mussels Aurora 18
  Mussels with parsley butter 18
  Paprika fish turbans 114
  Philippine Islands fish soup 105
  Pilchard special 16
  Prawn and potato appetiser 15
  Prawn curry 112
  Prawn risotto 37
  Salmon loaf 111
  Seafood cocktail 94
  Shrimp and mushroom cocktail 16
  Smoked haddock mousse 93
  Spinach ring with fish sauce 93
  Stuffed fish rolls 191
  Taramasalata 95
  Tuna shell pie 109
  Tuna and tomato toasts 15
  Whitebait fritters 95
  Whiting Meuniére 35
Flan:
  Cheese 149
  Curried chicken 220
  Dutch vegetable 227
  Frangipane 235
  Fruit 164
  Gouda savoury 208
  Mixed vegetable 150
  Savoury cheese and onion 184
  Spinach 185
  Swiss cheese 183
Fluff:
  Chilled lemon 155
  Pear and strawberry 70
  Yoghourt jelly 162
Fool, Rhubarb-raspberry 156
Four fruit pie 249
Frangipane flan 235
French beans vinaigrette 99
French country liver 146
French onion soup 104
French pancakes 164
Fricassee, Pork 125
Fried chicken drumsticks 54
Fritters:
  Cauliflower 185
  Indian banana 86
  Whitebait 95
Fritto misto di mare 182
Frosted apple pie 245
Frozen Christmas pudding 154
Frozen pineapple and banana snow 72
Fruit flan 164
Fruit in lemon jelly 241
Fruit in syrup 90
Fruit jellies, Yoghourt 157
Fruit kebabs 165
Fruit pie 172
Fruit pie, Four 249
Fruit pie, Winter 252
Fruit salad, Eastern 78
Fruit slice, mixed 246
Fruit tart, Dulverton 244
Fruit tart, Galaxy 233
Fruit tartlets, French 231
Fruity coleslaw 179
Fruity rice pudding 90

Galaxy fruit tart 233
Gâteau:
  Apricot 243
  Blackberry 232
  Choux coffee 237
  Pineapple 233
Georgian syllabub 161
German beer soup 27
German herring salad 110
German rabbit casserole 223
Ginger and rum dessert 82
Gingerbread, Sticky pear 250
Gingered pork chops with pineapple 44
Gnocchi 186
Gobi dahl curry 65

Golden harvest casserole 219
Golden lentil soup 29
Golden vegetable hors d'oeuvre 177
Gooseberry charlotte special 87
Gooseberry mist 156
Gooseberry mould, Creamed 82
Gooseberry sparkle 155
Gooseberry trifle, Hot 166
Gouda savoury flan 208
Gougère with chicken livers 224
Goulash:
  Beef 132
  Fish with herbed rice 113
  Veal 215
Granita di limone 73
Grilled pork Susanna 43

Haddock and corn supper 115
Haddock and egg pie, Smoked 189
Haddock cobbler, Smoked 111
Ham and chicken mould 218
Ham and cottage cheese salad 48
Ham and tomato pancake 48
Ham, Baked and pasta mould 207
Ham rolls 9
Hasty pudding 86
Hasty sweet and sour chicken 56
Hawaiian barbecued chicken 219
Hawaiian dreams 159
Hearts, Stuffed 144
Herbed fish parcels 36
Herbed rice with fish goulash 113
Herring, Crumb bake 190
Herring salad, German 110
Herrings with tomato sauce 38
Honey cheese tart 234
Honeyed kebabs with apple 200
Honey fruit fanfare 76
Honey rice apples 168
Hors d'oeuvre, Golden vegetable 177
Hot chocolate soufflé 246
Hot gooseberry trifle 166
Hot pot:
  Cider vegetable 151
  Lancashire 119
  Mince 51
Hungarian lamb casserole 196

Ice cream, Cottage cheese 71
Ice cream, Tahitian coconut 163
Ice, Orange water 73
Iced brandy snaps 70
Iced cucumber and yoghourt soup 22
Iced layer pastry 244
Iced tomato orange soup 21
Indian banana fritters 86
Individual onion and herb pies 181
Irish stew 117
Italian pears 79

Jarratt, Beef 211
Jellied pork brawn 124
Jellies, Yoghourt fruit 157
Jelly fluff, Yoghourt 162
Jelly fruit in lemon 241
Jelly, Rhubarb 80

Karti kebabs 133
Käsertorte 240
Kebabs:
  Fruit 165
  Honeyed with apple 200
  Karti 133
Kidney and lamb pudding 194
Kidney and steak pie 209
Kidney and steak with dumplings 210
Kidney ragout 145
Kidney stew with onions 224
Kidneys sauté turbigo 58
Kipper pâté 92
Kofta curry 213
Kromeskies 96

Lamb:
  Boiled lamb and caper sauce 118
  Braised lamb roll 193
  Braised lamb shanks 41
  Breast of lamb with sausage stuffing 199

Lamb:
  Casseroled lamb 195
  Creamed lamb with cucumber 120
  Creamy lamb with mushrooms 120
  Crown roast of lamb with onion and apple stuffing 197
  Curried shepherd's pie 193
  Hungarian lamb casserole 196
  Lamb with apricot and prune stuffing 195
  Lamb and bean casserole 116
  Lamb and butterbean casserole 197
  Lamb chops rosemary 40
  Lamb curry with prunes 198
  Lamb cutlets in pastry 119
  Lamb Florentine 39
  Lamb and kidney pudding 194
  Lamb paprika-style 41
  Lamb and peach bake 42
  Lamb plait 192
  Lamb in the round 118
  Lamb spare ribs in barbecue sauce 194
  Lamb and vegetable pie 116
  Lamb with yoghourt 39
  Marinated Australian lamb cutlets 192
  September lamb 198
  Spanish lamb chops 199
  Turmeric lamb chops 40
Lambs' tongues in sweet and sour sauce 144
Lancashire hot pot 119
Layer pastry, Iced 244
Leeks à la grecque 10
Lemon and banana delight 78
Lemon and raisin pudding 88
Lemon apricot roll 235
Lemon cheesecake, Chilled 242
Lemon delicious 250
Lemon egg custard, Baked 88
Lemon fluff, Chilled 155
Lemon meringue pie 247
Limed fish 92
Lime pear cream 83
Linzertorte 237
Liptauer cheese 14
Liver:
  French country liver 146
  Ox liver stew 146
  Liver and bacon in tomato sauce 145
  Liver with parsley and orange 58
Loaf:
  Cheese and walnut 149
  Potato coated meat 209
  Salmon 111
  Spicy meat 196
  Turkey 222
Lychee and sesame salad 14

Macaroni and eggs lyonnaise 62
Macaroni cheese special 60
Macaroni salad 68
Mackerel in foil 109
Mackerel, Normandy 189
Mackerel with mustard sauce 114
Main courses:
  10 minute 33-68
  20 minute 109-152
  30 minute 189-228
Malayan rice salad 67
Manchester pudding 236
Mandarin cream trifle 84
Mandarin yoghourt ambrosia 153
Marinated Australian lamb cutlets 192
Marmalade peach casserole 87
Marrow, Stuffed 152
Marshmallow sundae 76
Meatballs with barbecue sauce 128
Meat loaf:
  Cold spiced 128
  Potato coated 209
  Spicy 196
Mediterranean pasta salad 151
Meringue:
  Meringue nests 234
  Meringue puff 229
  Meringues glacées Chantilly 158
  Raspberry meringue baskets 239
  Swiss meringue 170
Mince hot pot 51
Minestrone 107
Mist, Gooseberry 156
Mixed fish pâté 17
Mixed fruit slice 246
Mixed vegetable flan 150
Monte bianco 242

Mould:
  Autumn apple 79
  Baked ham and pasta 207
  Cherry and pineapple 83
  Chicken and ham 218
  Creamed gooseberry 82
  Two-layer chocolate honeycomb 238

Mousse:
  au chocolat Basque 162
  Savoury luncheon 124
  Smoked haddock 93
Mushroom:
  Baked mushrooms in cheese sauce 101
  Braised celery with mushrooms 65
  Chicken and mushroom pie 140
  Chicken and mushrooms on rice 220
  Chicken and mushroom soufflé omelette 139
  Fish and mushroom bundles 177
  Mushroom and egg appetiser 13
  Mushroom risotto 9
  Mushroom soup 29
  Stuffed mushrooms 183
Mussels Aurora 18
Mussels with parsley butter 18

Nasi goreng 126
Nests, Meringue 234
Nests, Potato 176
Noodle, Apple pudding 252
Normandy mackerel 189

Olives, Bacon 122
Omelette, Chicken and mushroom soufflé 139
Omelette, Country 64
Onion:
  Beef olives with onion rice 213
  Cheese and onion custard 225
  Crown roast of lamb with onion and apple stuffing 197
  Egg and onion pie 62
  French onion soup 104
  Individual onion and herb pies 181
  Kidney stew with onions 224
  Pork and onion pasties 200
  Potato and onion soup 106
Orange:
  Apple and orange whip 154
  Apricot orange casserole 89
  Apricot and orange pancakes 247
  Baked orange and ginger cheesecake 229
  Beef and orange stew 134
  Boned duck with orange stuffing 222
  Chicken with oranges 138
  Crown of pork with orange rice 203
  Liver with parsley and orange 58
  Orange Conde 80
  Orange princess pudding 171
  Orange roll 231
  Orange terrine 178
  Orange turnabouts 163
  Orange water ice 73
  Pork with orange sauce 121
  Raised pork and orange pie 205
Osso buco 135
Oven-fried chicken 137
Ox liver stew 146
Oxtail, Braised 131
Oxtail casserole 215

Paella 221
Palmiers, Apple 238
Pancakes:
  Apricot and orange 247
  French 164
  Pineapple 157
  Savoury 175
  Wholewheat cider 123
Paprika fish turbans 114
Paprika pork 203
Paprika pork casserole 125
Pasta brunch 34
Pasta salad, Mediterranean 151
Pasties, Pork and onion 200
Pasties, Vegetable 179
Pastry, iced layer 244
Pastries, pear 245

Pâté:
F